W9-CCO-653

SB
Shojo Beat

Stepping on Roses

Vol. 9

Story & Art by
Rinko Ueda

Stepping on Roses

Volume 9
CONTENTS

Story Thus Far

During the Meiji Era, Sumi Kitamura was living a life of poverty and taking care of young orphans that her elder brother Eisuke brought home from the streets. Then, in order to pay off Eisuke's debts, she marries Soichiro Ashida. Eventually, the two grow to truly love each other.

However, Nozomu Ijuin, who is in love with Sumi, takes over Soichiro's company. When Soichiro falls ill, Sumi is unable to pay for his medical expenses. Nozomu steps in to help but only on the condition that Sumi leave Soichiro and become his wife instead. Sumi agrees, but she convinces Nozomu not to touch her until he and Miu officially divorce. Meanwhile, Sumi asks Soichiro's former employees for their help to get Ashida Products back in Soichiro's hands. Will Sumi's feelings for Soichiro reach him...?!

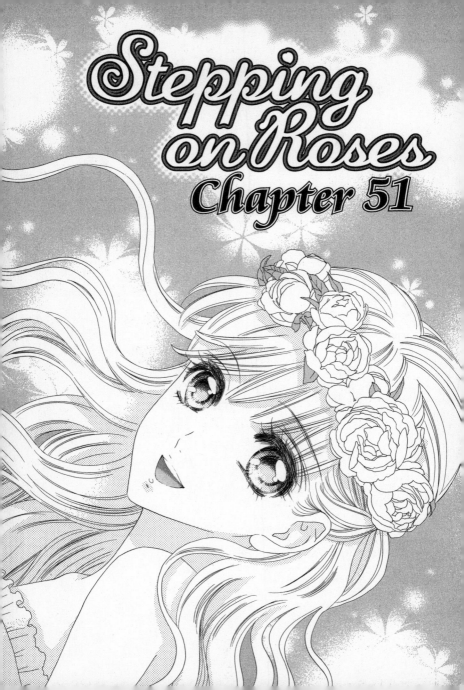

Stepping on Roses
Chapter 51

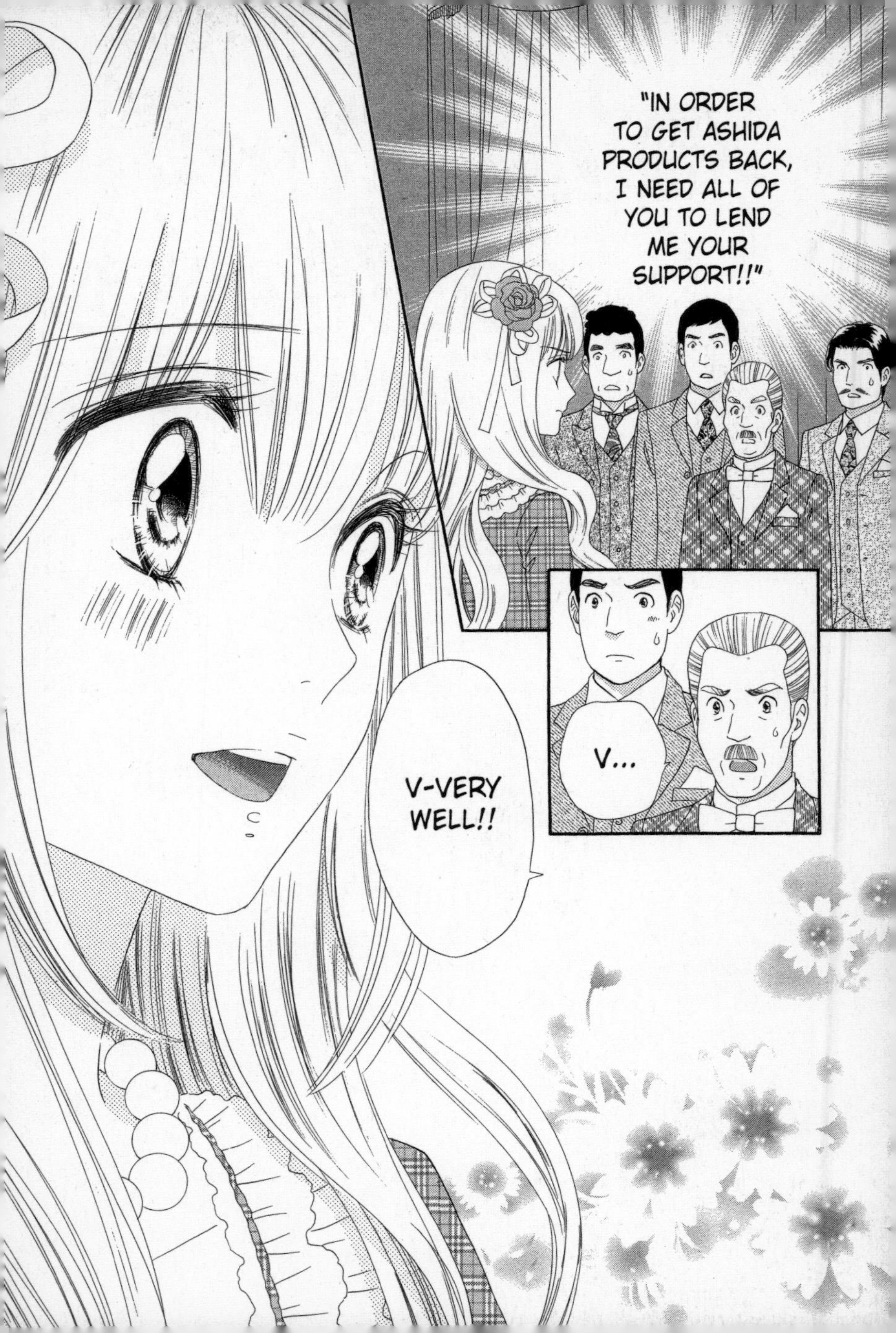
"IN ORDER TO GET ASHIDA PRODUCTS BACK, I NEED ALL OF YOU TO LEND ME YOUR SUPPORT!!"
V...
V-VERY WELL!!

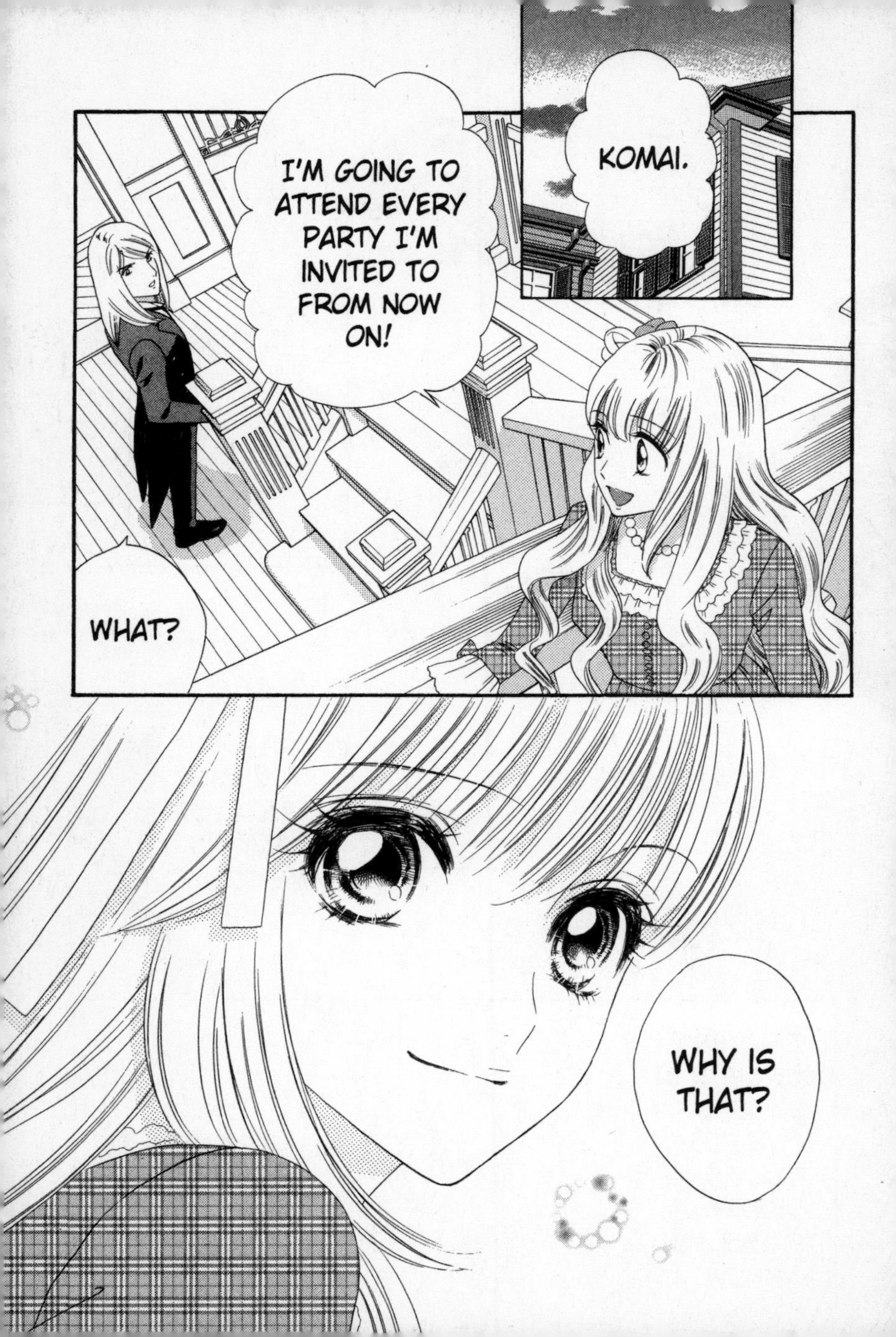
KOMAI.
I'M GOING TO ATTEND EVERY PARTY I'M INVITED TO FROM NOW ON!
WHAT?
WHY IS THAT?

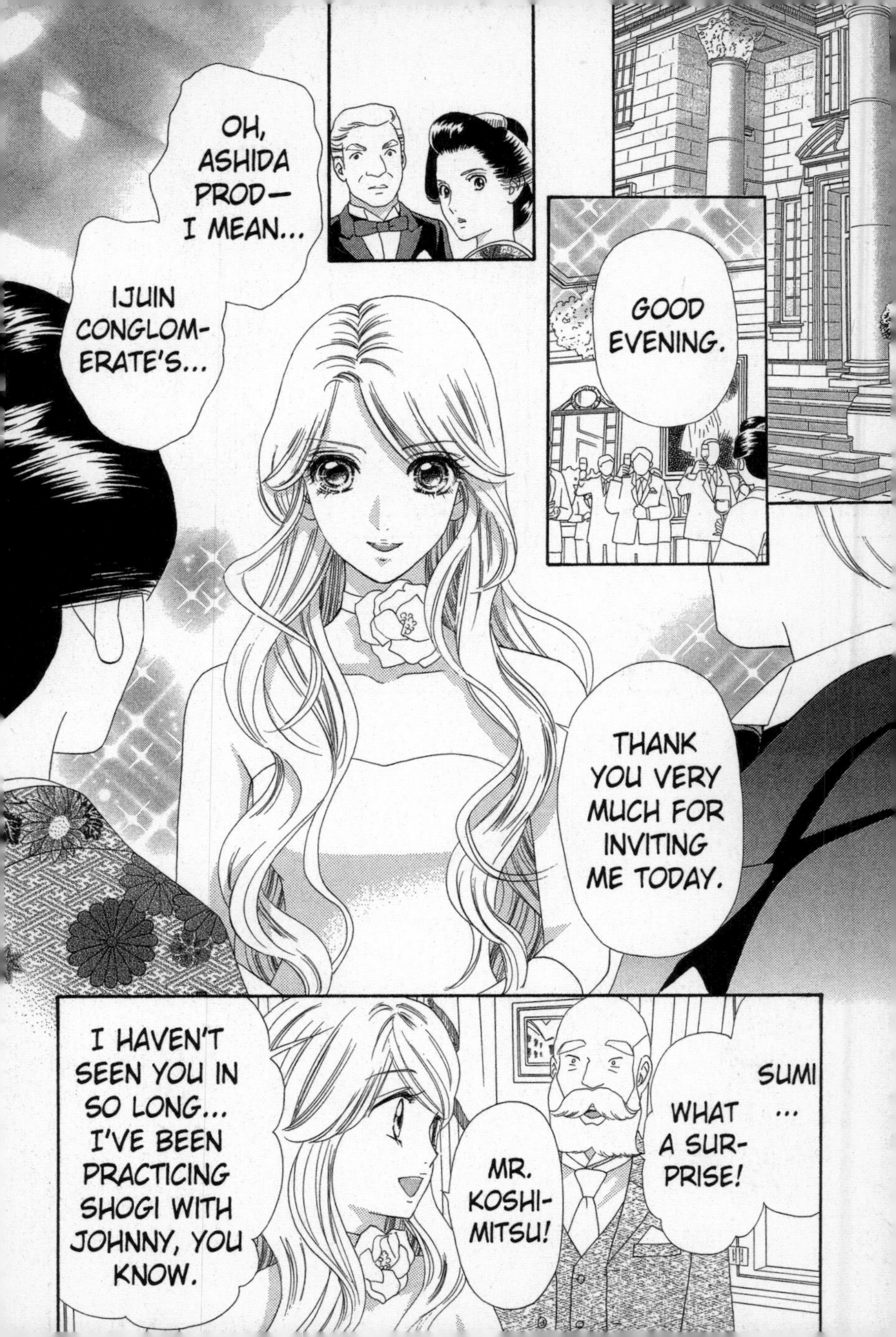
GOOD EVENING.
OH, ASHIDA PROD— I MEAN...
IJUIN CONGLOM-ERATE'S...
THANK YOU VERY MUCH FOR INVITING ME TODAY.
SUMI ...
WHAT A SUR-PRISE!
MR. KOSHI-MITSU!
I HAVEN'T SEEN YOU IN SO LONG... I'VE BEEN PRACTICING SHOGI WITH JOHNNY, YOU KNOW.

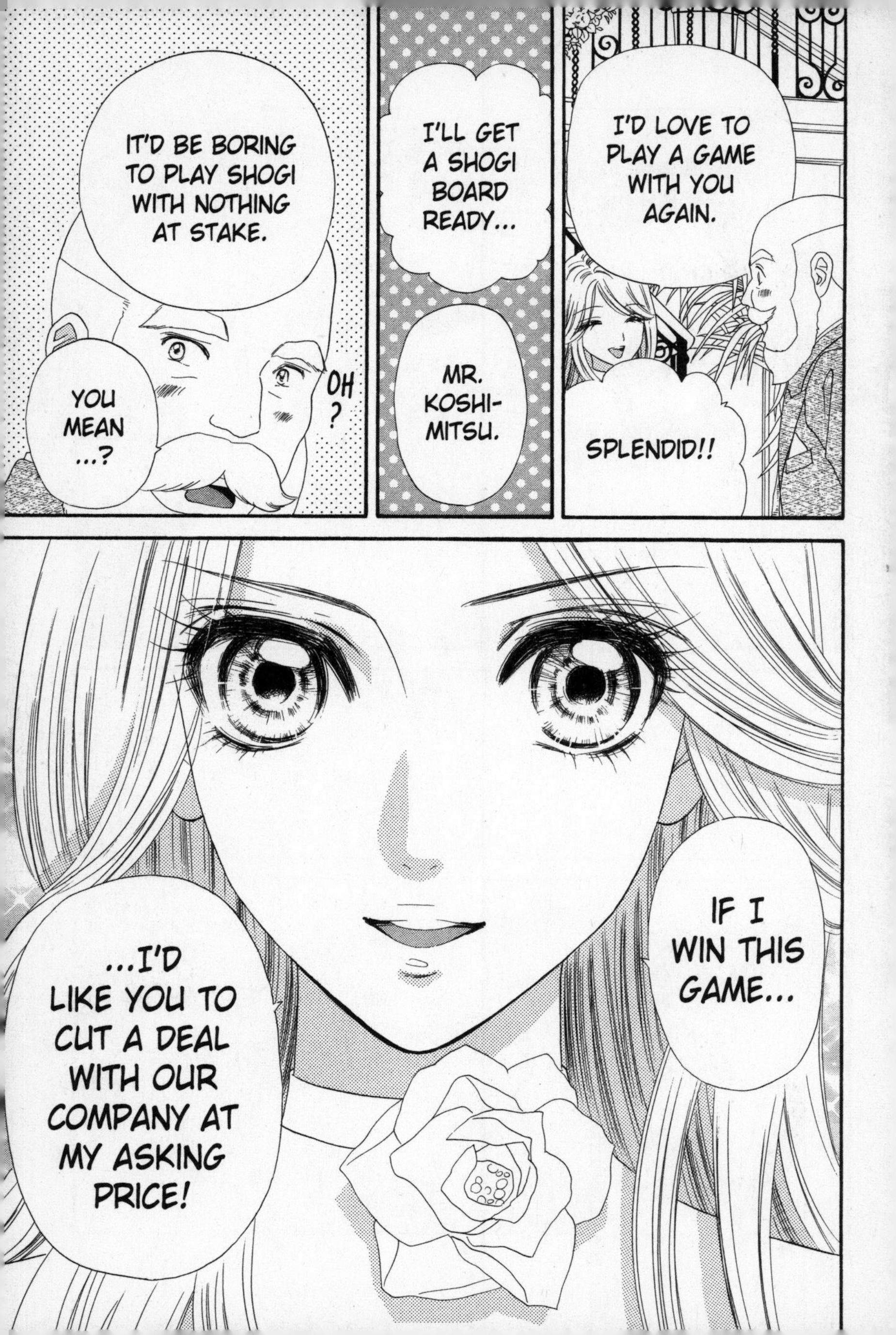
I'D LOVE TO PLAY A GAME WITH YOU AGAIN.
SPLENDID!!
I'LL GET A SHOGI BOARD READY...
MR. KOSHI-MITSU.
IT'D BE BORING TO PLAY SHOGI WITH NOTHING AT STAKE.
OH?
YOU MEAN...?
IF I WIN THIS GAME...
...I'D LIKE YOU TO CUT A DEAL WITH OUR COMPANY AT MY ASKING PRICE!

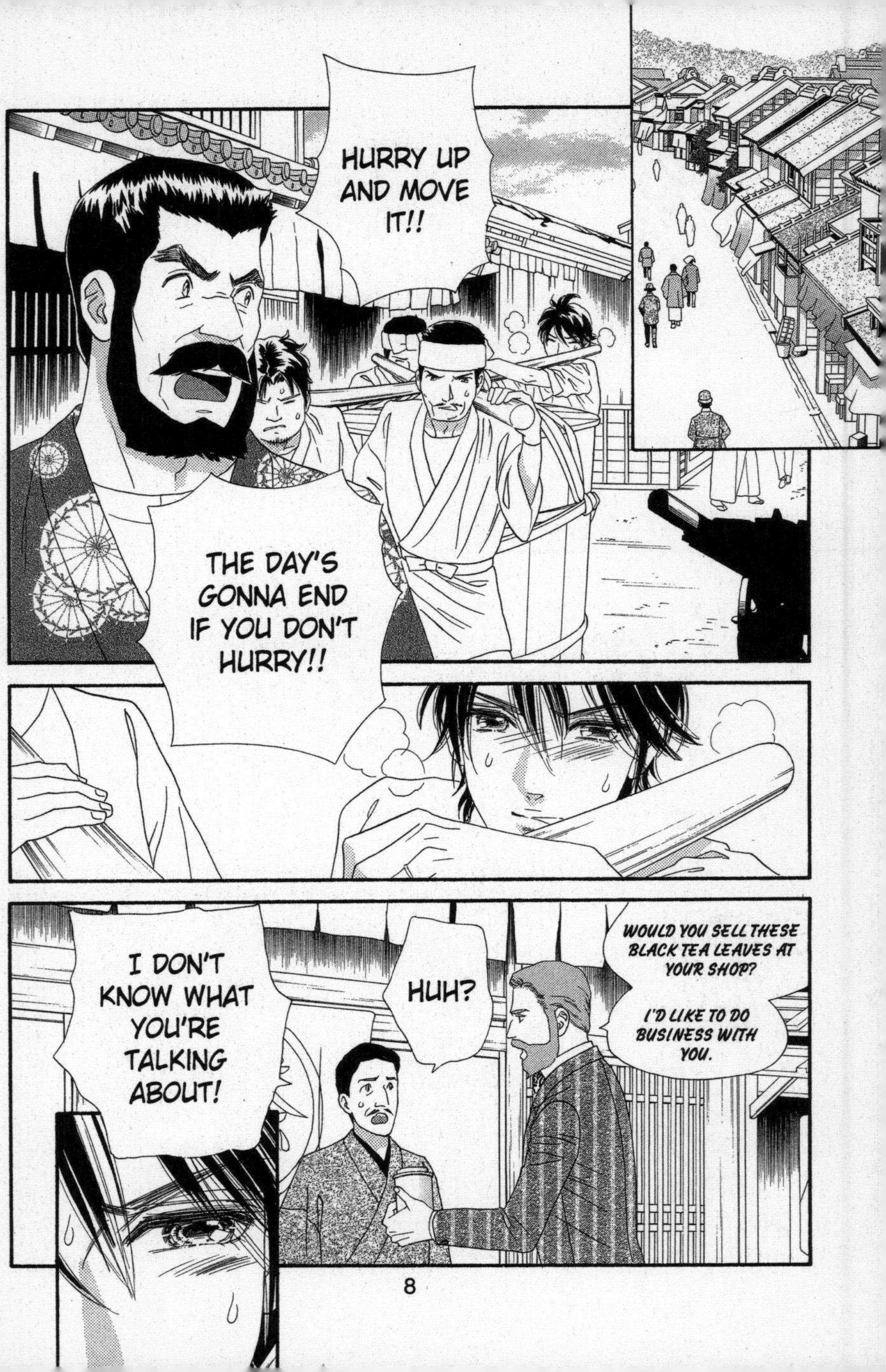
HURRY UP AND MOVE IT!!
THE DAY'S GONNA END IF YOU DON'T HURRY!!
WOULD YOU SELL THESE BLACK TEA LEAVES AT YOUR SHOP?
I'D LIKE TO DO BUSINESS WITH YOU.
HUH?
I DON'T KNOW WHAT YOU'RE TALKING ABOUT!

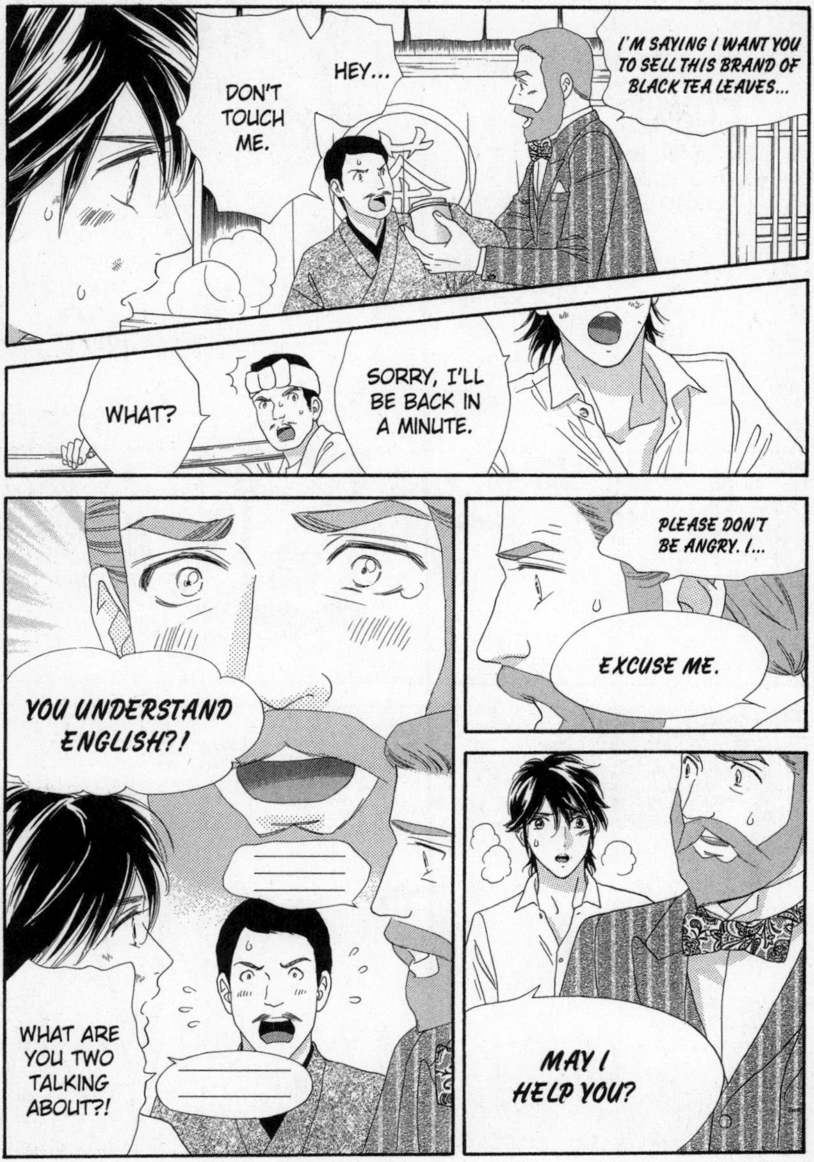

I'M SAYING I WANT YOU TO SELL THIS BRAND OF BLACK TEA LEAVES...
HEY...
DON'T TOUCH ME.
SORRY, I'LL BE BACK IN A MINUTE.
WHAT?
PLEASE DON'T BE ANGRY. I...
EXCUSE ME.
MAY I HELP YOU?
YOU UNDERSTAND ENGLISH?!
WHAT ARE YOU TWO TALKING ABOUT?!

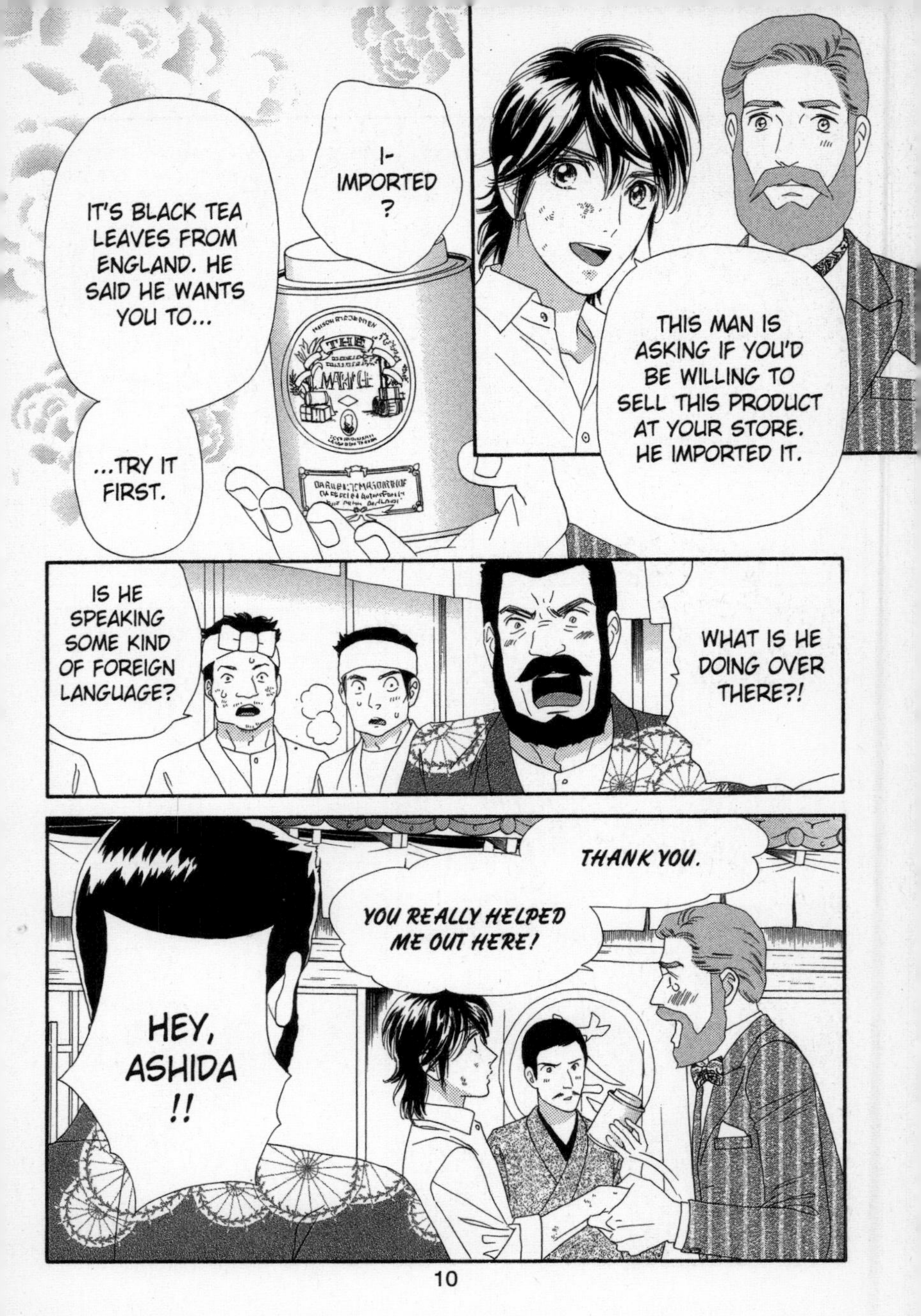
THIS MAN IS ASKING IF YOU'D BE WILLING TO SELL THIS PRODUCT AT YOUR STORE. HE IMPORTED IT.
I- IMPORTED ?
IT'S BLACK TEA LEAVES FROM ENGLAND. HE SAID HE WANTS YOU TO...
...TRY IT FIRST.
WHAT IS HE DOING OVER THERE?!
IS HE SPEAKING SOME KIND OF FOREIGN LANGUAGE?
THANK YOU.
YOU REALLY HELPED ME OUT HERE!
HEY, ASHIDA !!

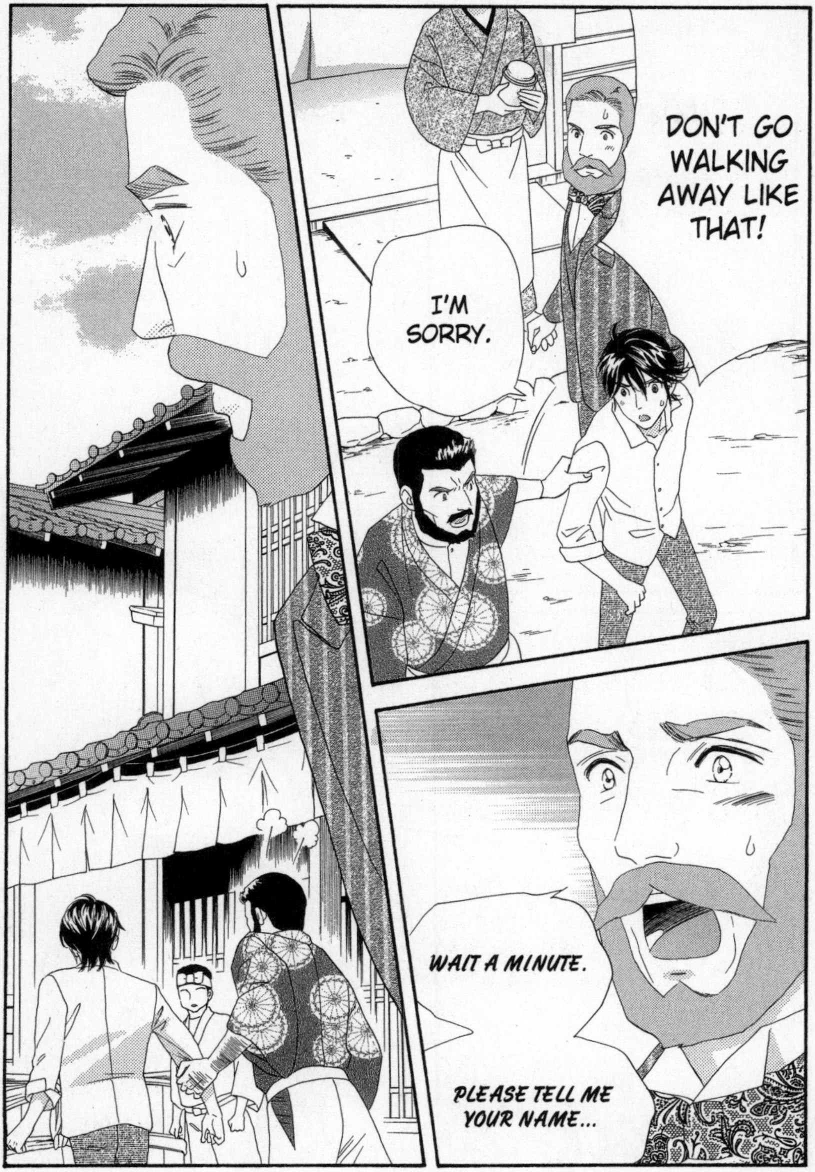
DON'T GO WALKING AWAY LIKE THAT!
I'M SORRY.
WAIT A MINUTE.
PLEASE TELL ME YOUR NAME...

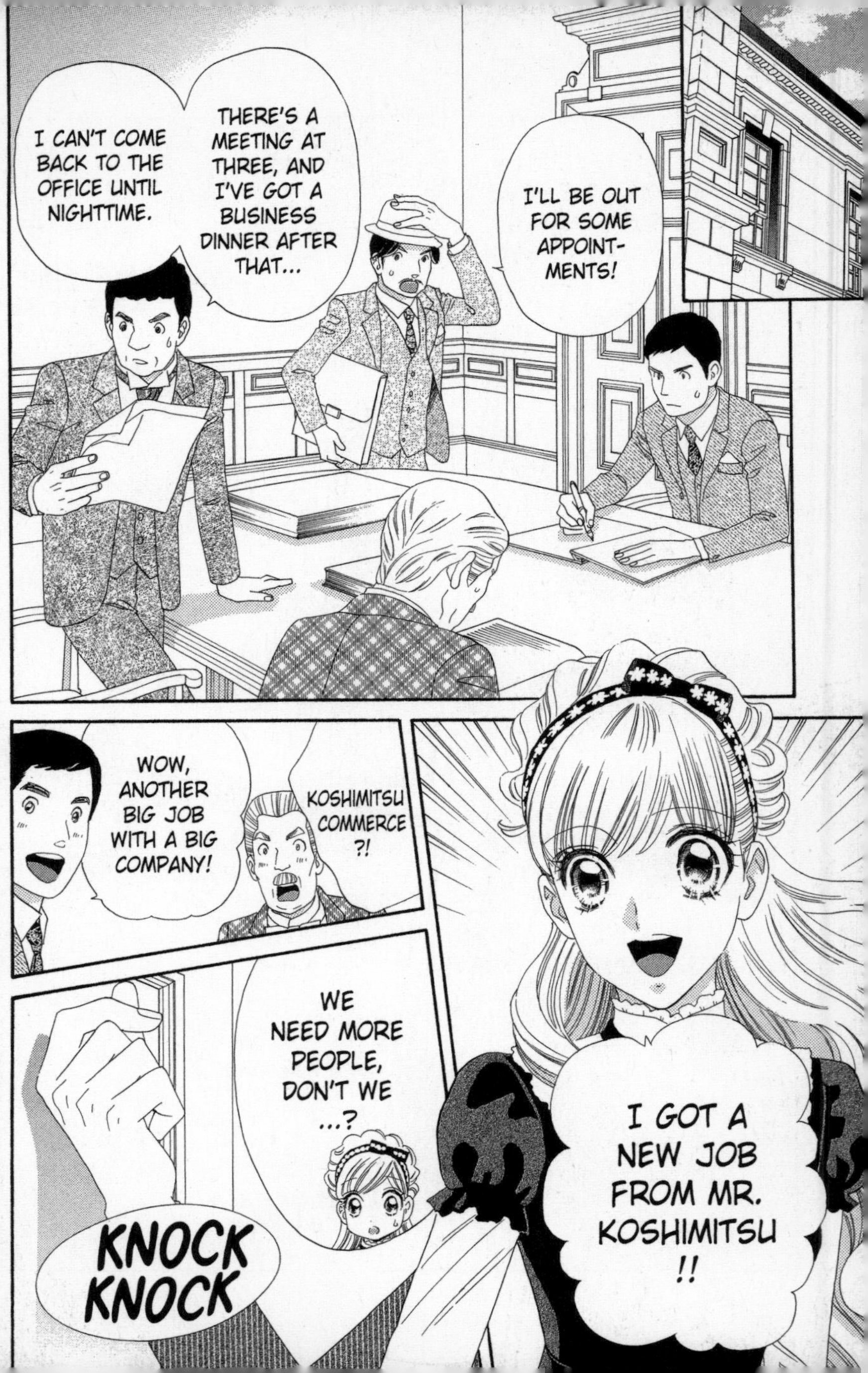
I'LL BE OUT FOR SOME APPOINT-MENTS!
THERE'S A MEETING AT THREE, AND I'VE GOT A BUSINESS DINNER AFTER THAT...
I CAN'T COME BACK TO THE OFFICE UNTIL NIGHTTIME.
I GOT A NEW JOB FROM MR. KOSHIMITSU!!
KOSHIMITSU COMMERCE?!
WOW, ANOTHER BIG JOB WITH A BIG COMPANY!
WE NEED MORE PEOPLE, DON'T WE...?
KNOCK KNOCK

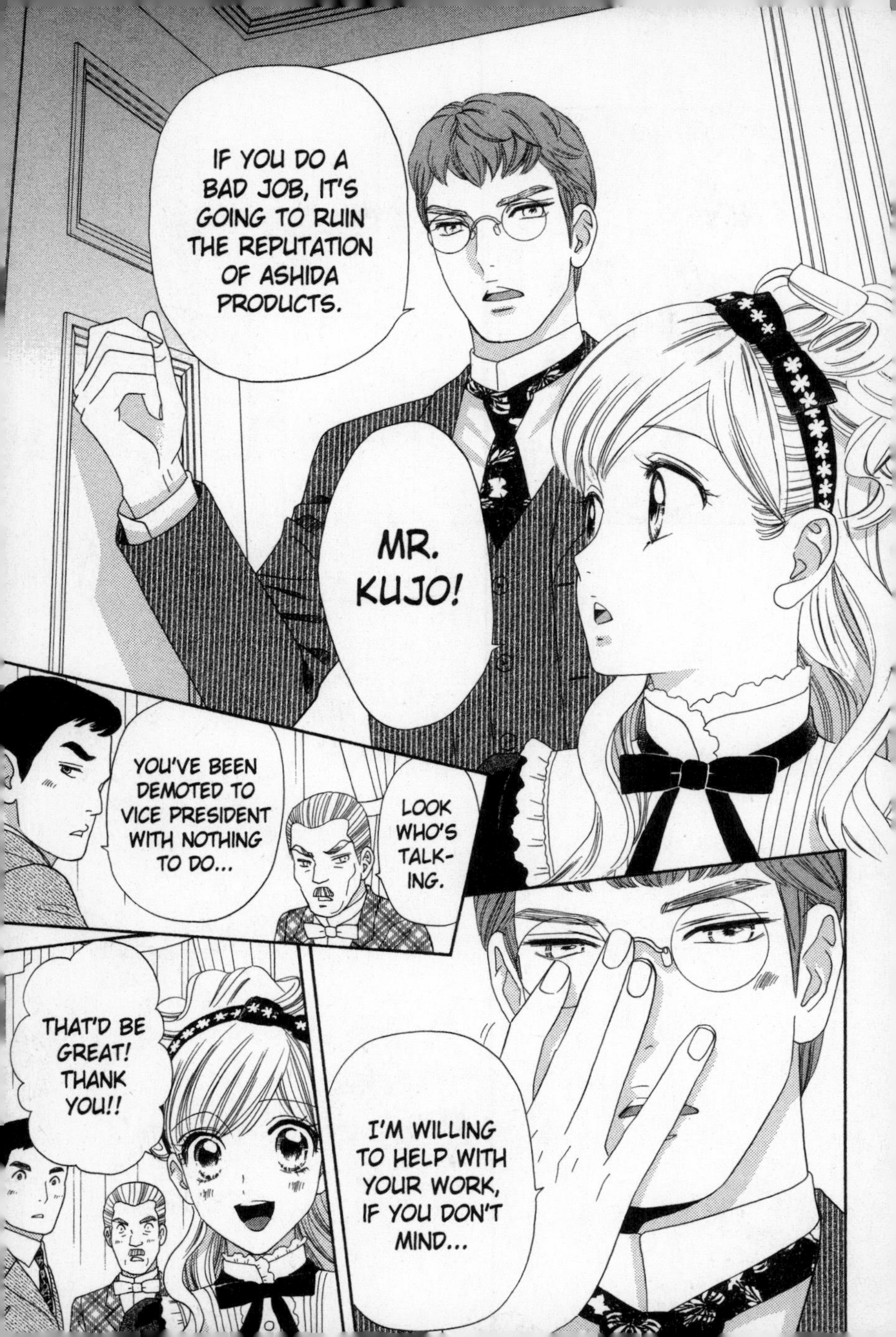
IF YOU DO A BAD JOB, IT'S GOING TO RUIN THE REPUTATION OF ASHIDA PRODUCTS.
MR. KUJO!
YOU'VE BEEN DEMOTED TO VICE PRESIDENT WITH NOTHING TO DO...
LOOK WHO'S TALK-ING.
I'M WILLING TO HELP WITH YOUR WORK, IF YOU DON'T MIND...
THAT'D BE GREAT! THANK YOU!!

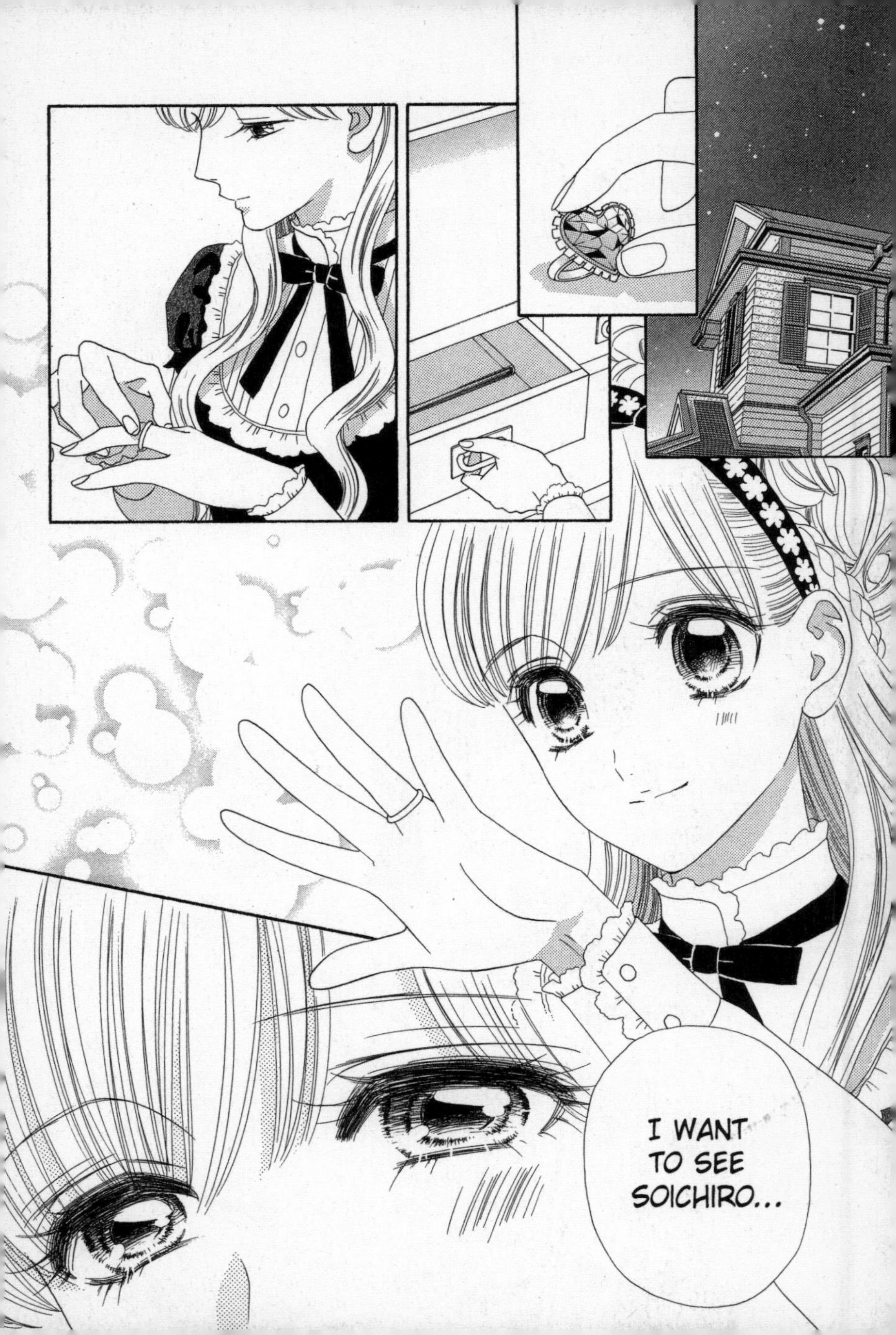
I WANT TO SEE SOICHIRO...

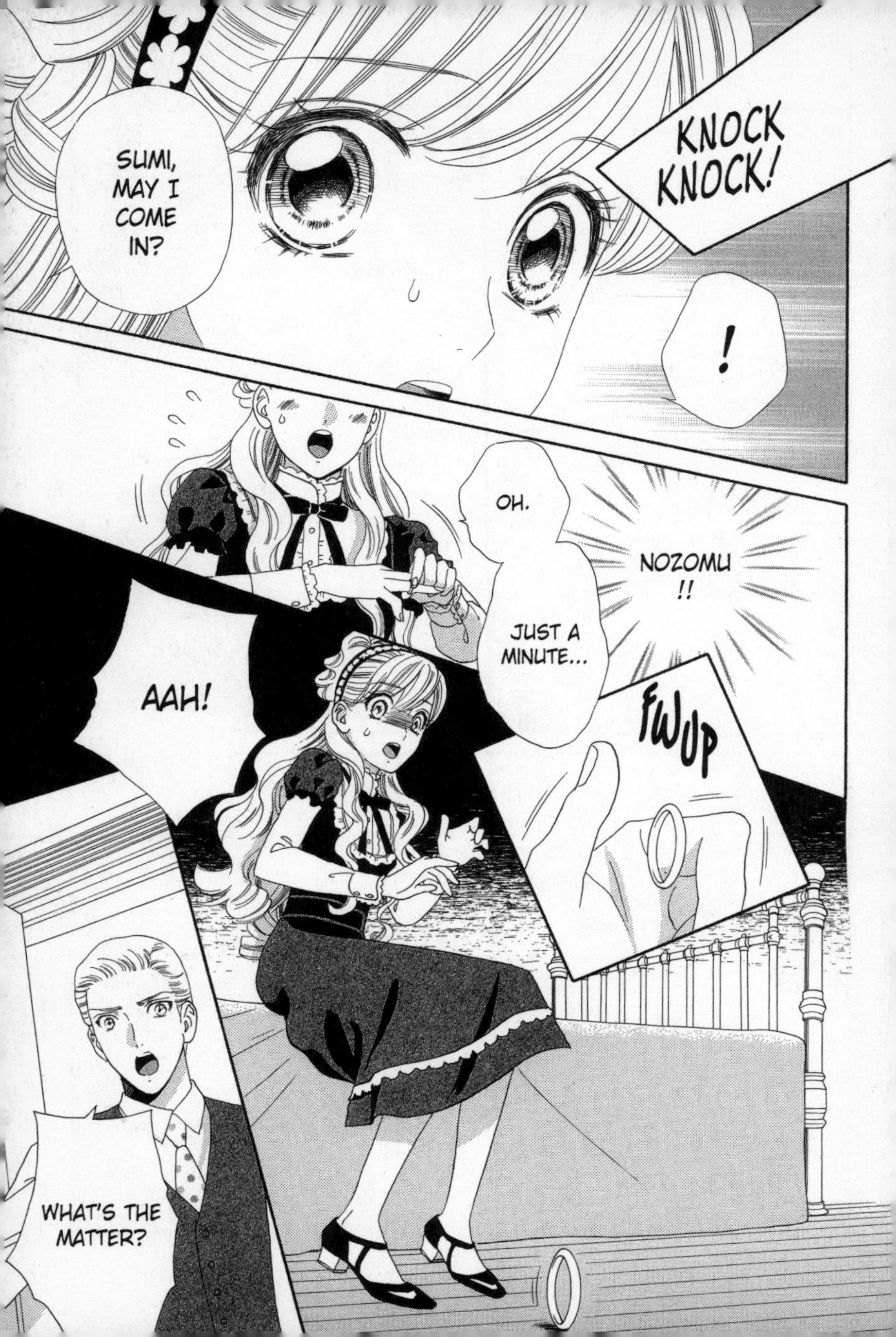
KNOCK KNOCK!
SUMI, MAY I COME IN?
!
NOZOMU !!
OH.
JUST A MINUTE...
FWUP
AAH!
WHAT'S THE MATTER?

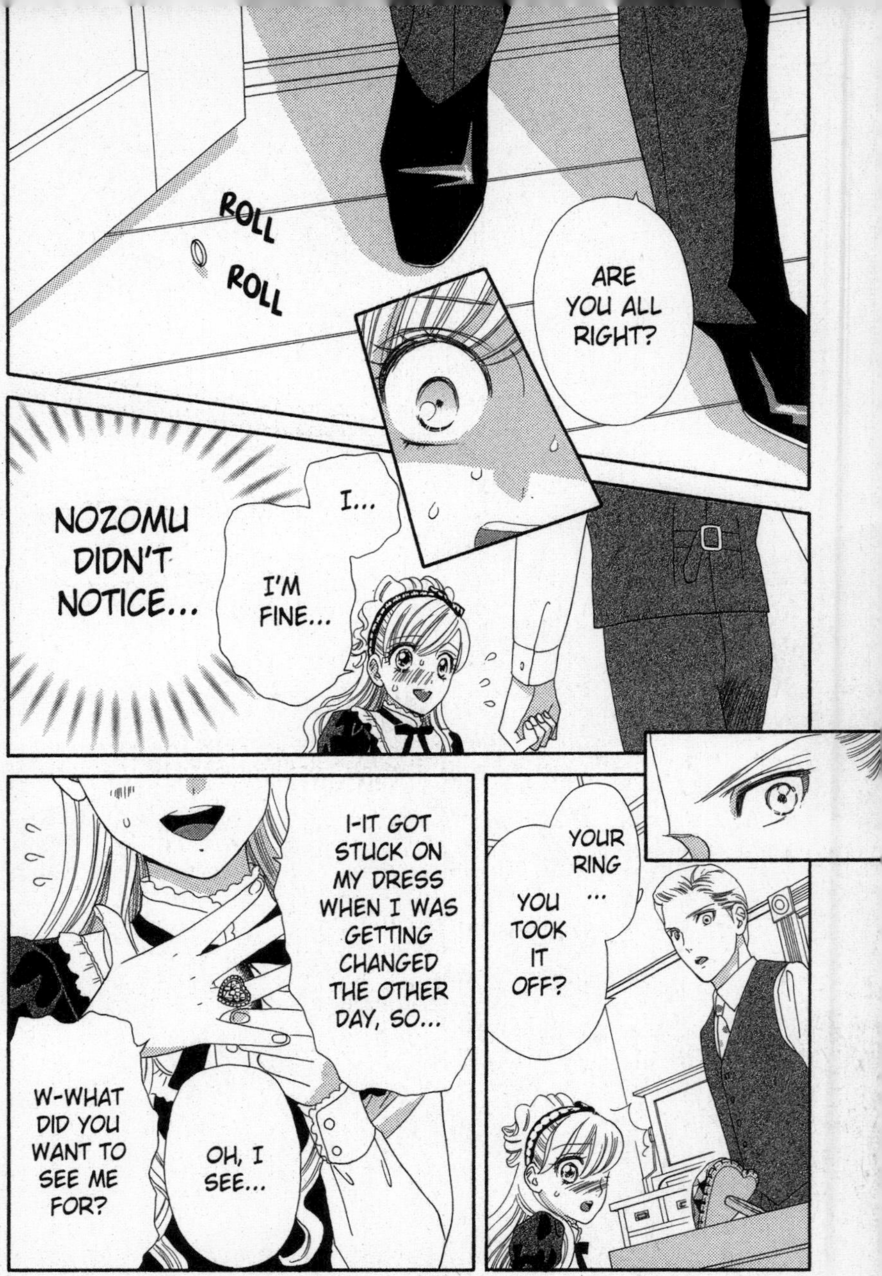
ARE YOU ALL RIGHT?
ROLL
ROLL
I...
I'M FINE...
NOZOMU DIDN'T NOTICE...
YOUR RING ...
YOU TOOK IT OFF?
I-IT GOT STUCK ON MY DRESS WHEN I WAS GETTING CHANGED THE OTHER DAY, SO...
OH, I SEE...
W-WHAT DID YOU WANT TO SEE ME FOR?

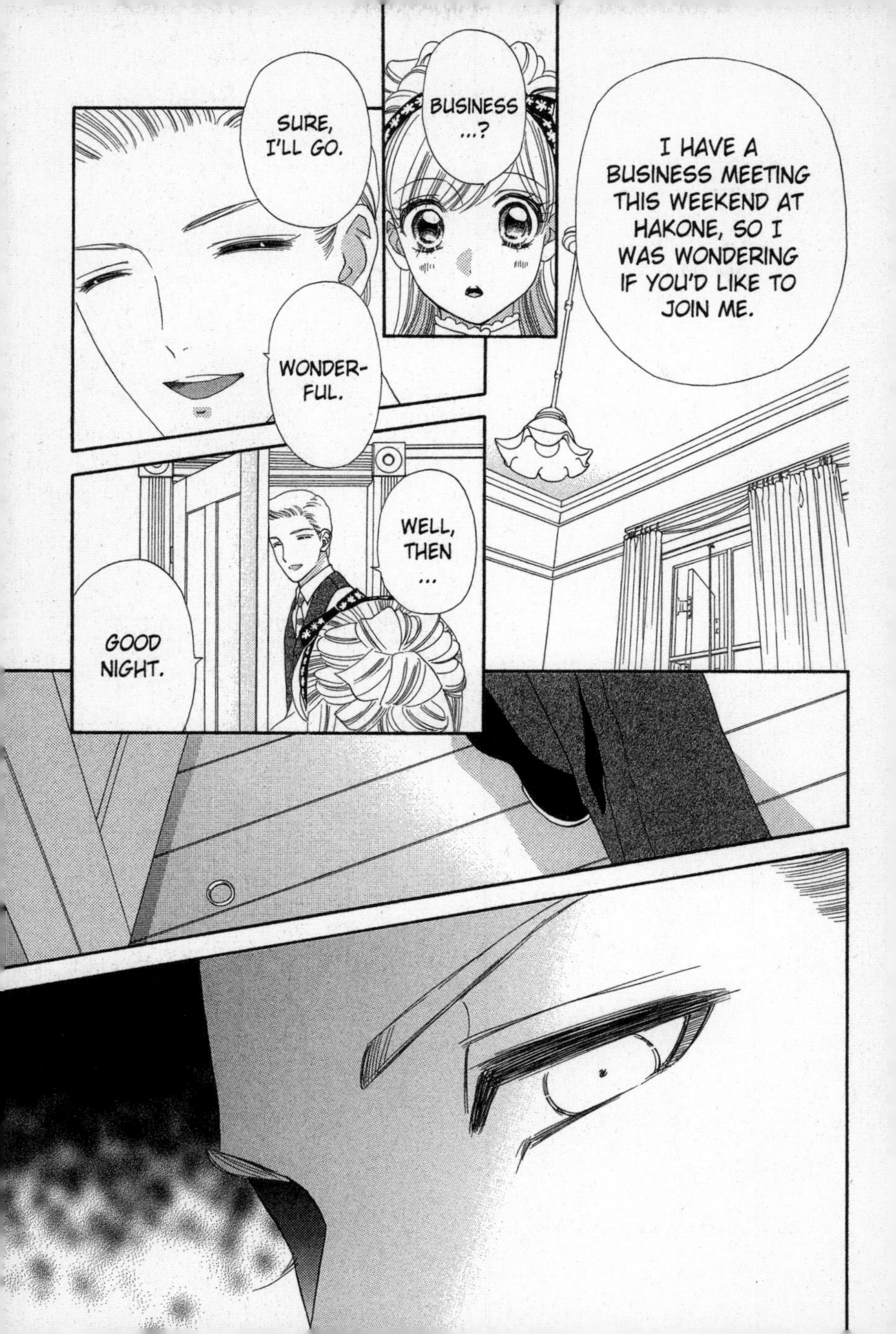
I HAVE A BUSINESS MEETING THIS WEEKEND AT HAKONE, SO I WAS WONDERING IF YOU'D LIKE TO JOIN ME.
BUSINESS ...?
SURE, I'LL GO.
WONDER-FUL.
WELL, THEN ...
GOOD NIGHT.

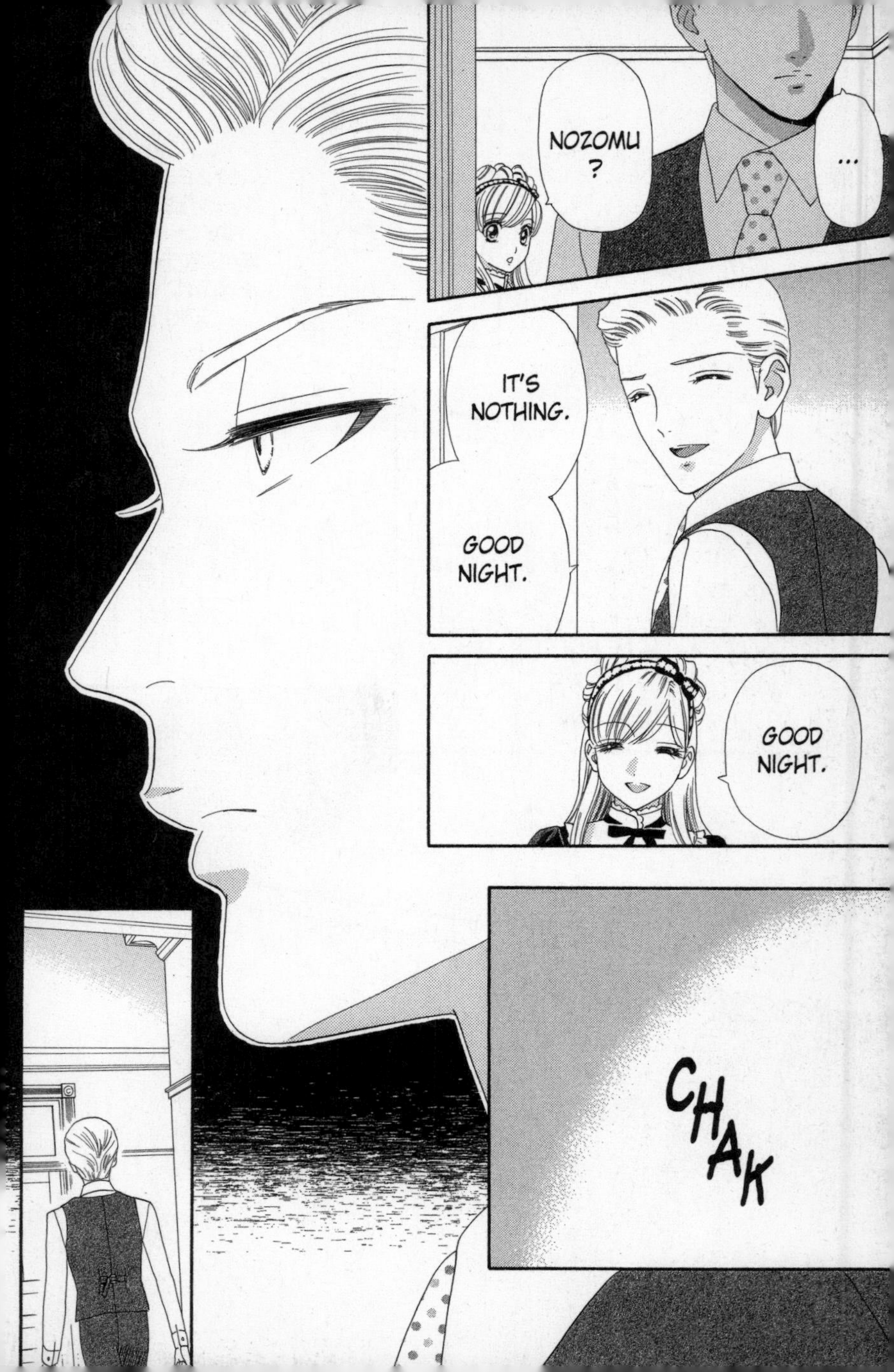
...
NOZOMU ?
IT'S NOTHING.
GOOD NIGHT.
GOOD NIGHT.
CHAK

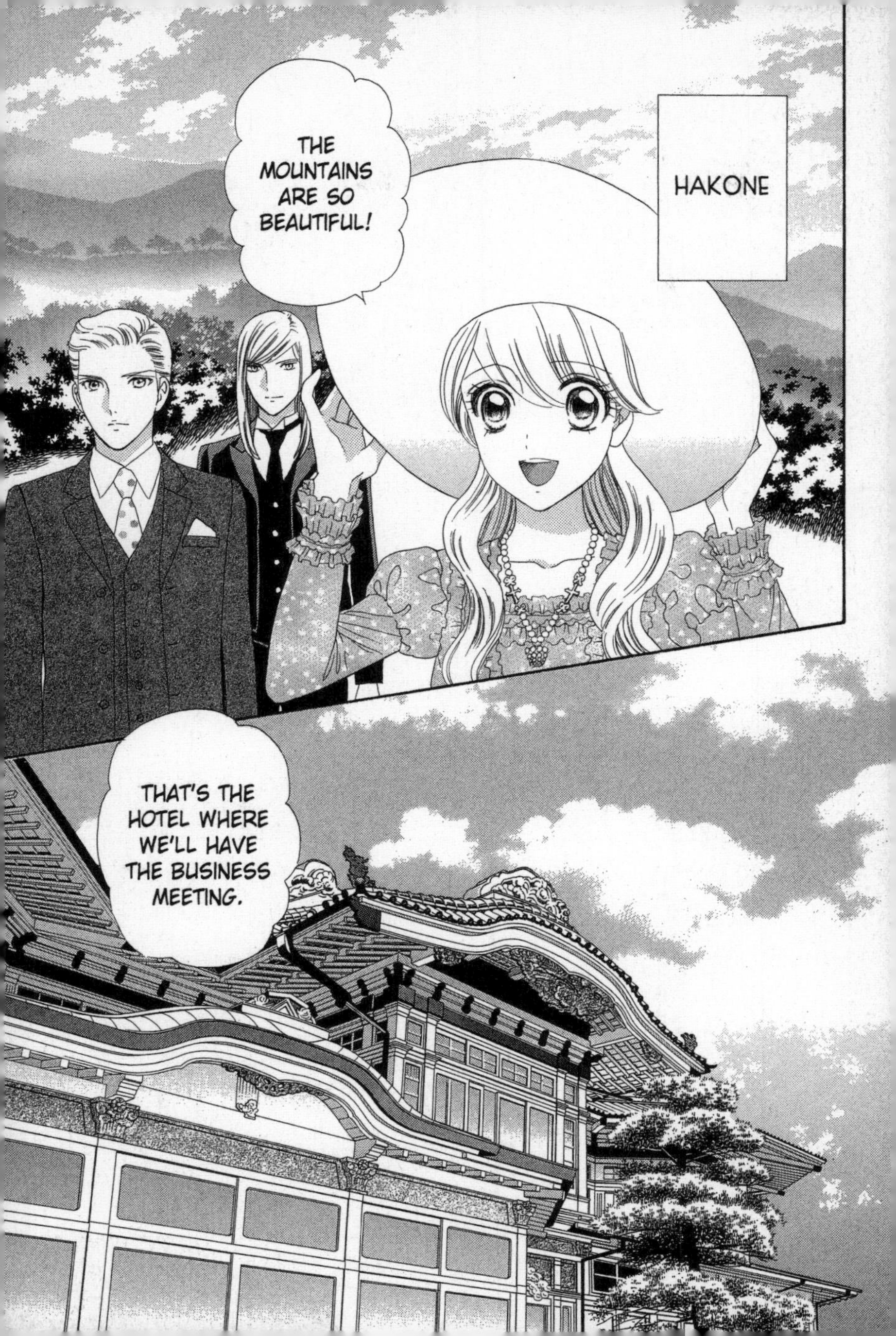
HAKONE
THE MOUNTAINS ARE SO BEAUTIFUL!
THAT'S THE HOTEL WHERE WE'LL HAVE THE BUSINESS MEETING.

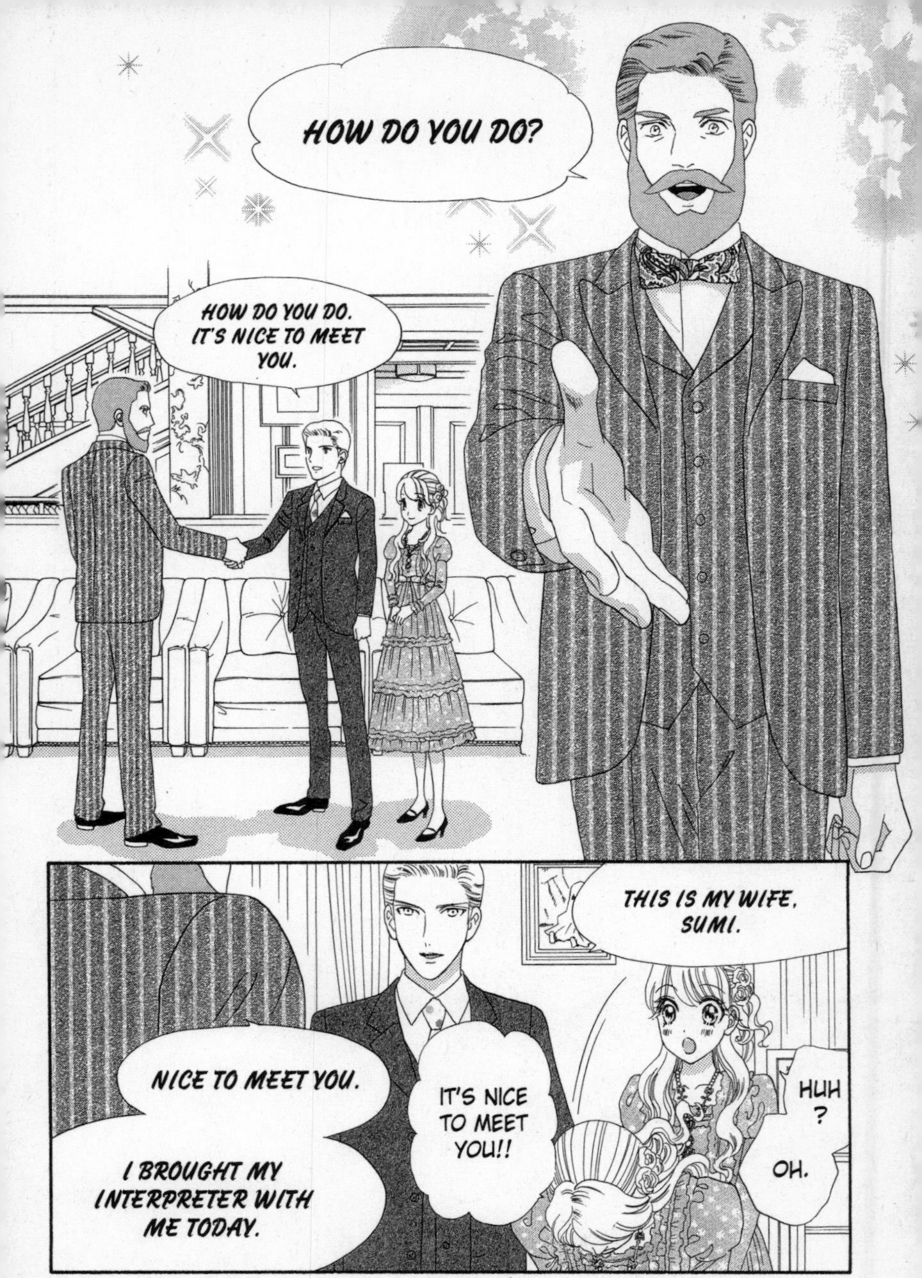
HOW DO YOU DO?
HOW DO YOU DO. IT'S NICE TO MEET YOU.
THIS IS MY WIFE, SUMI.
HUH ?
OH.
IT'S NICE TO MEET YOU!!
NICE TO MEET YOU.
I BROUGHT MY INTERPRETER WITH ME TODAY.

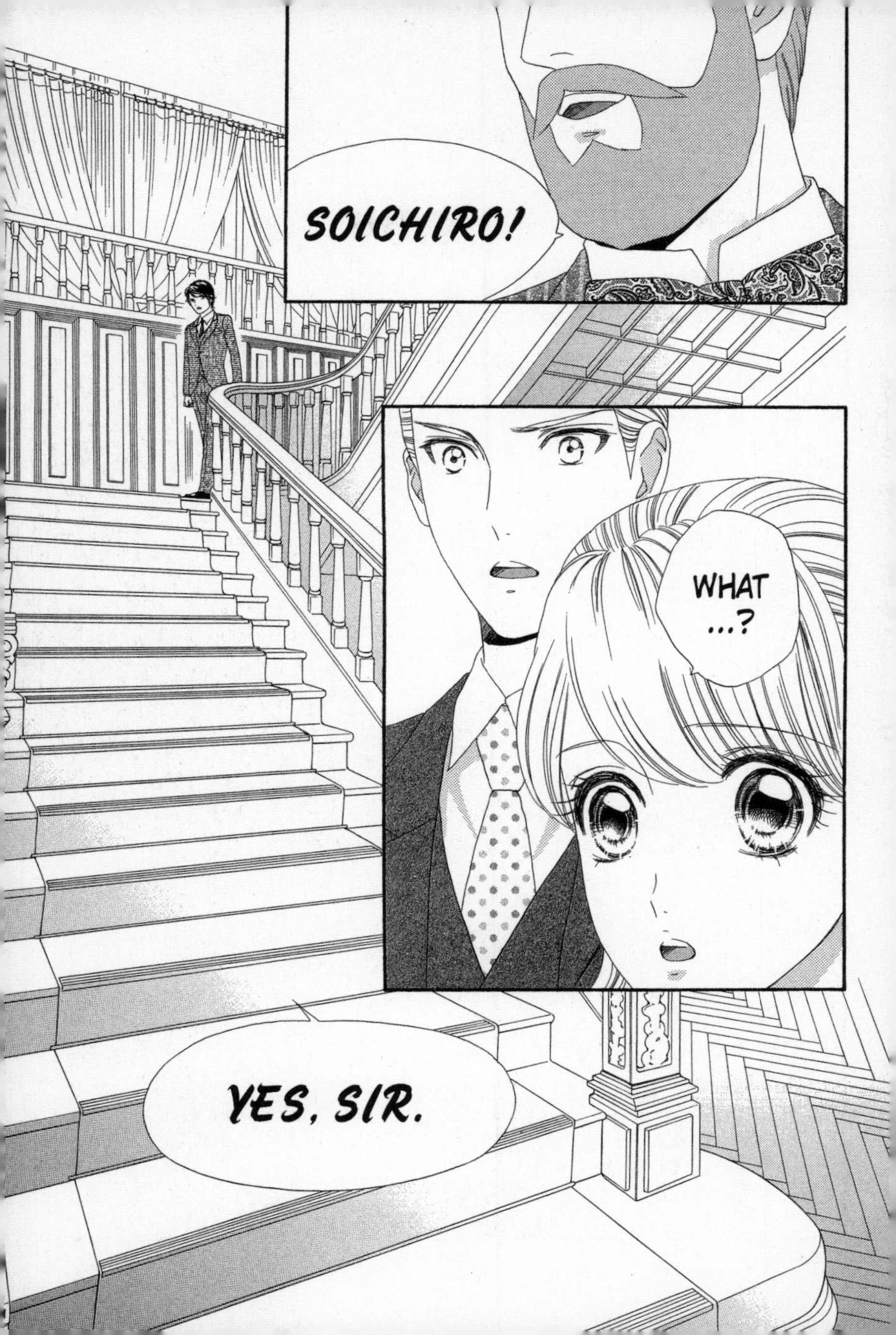
SOICHIRO!
WHAT ...?
YES, SIR.

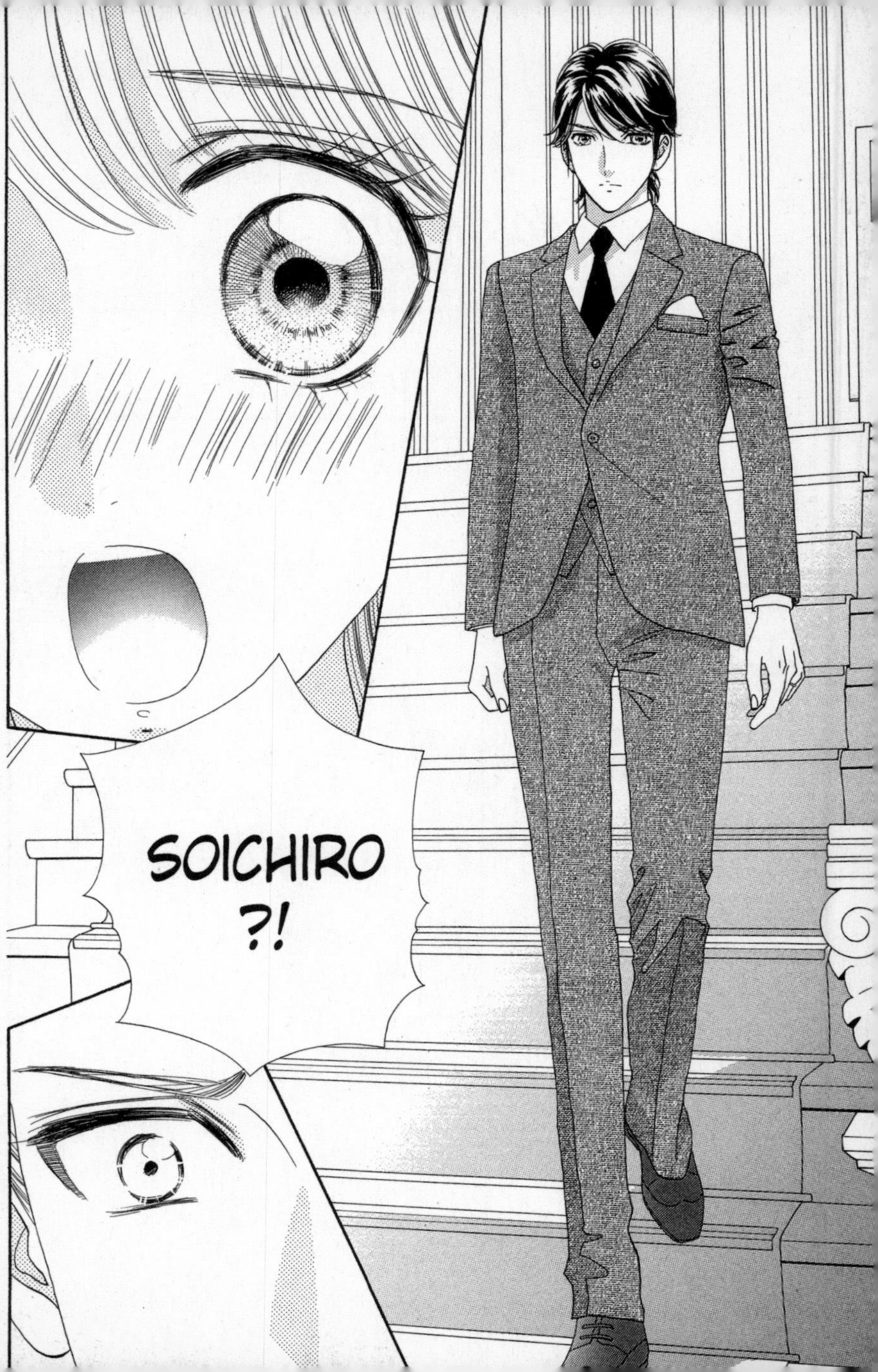
SOICHIRO ?!

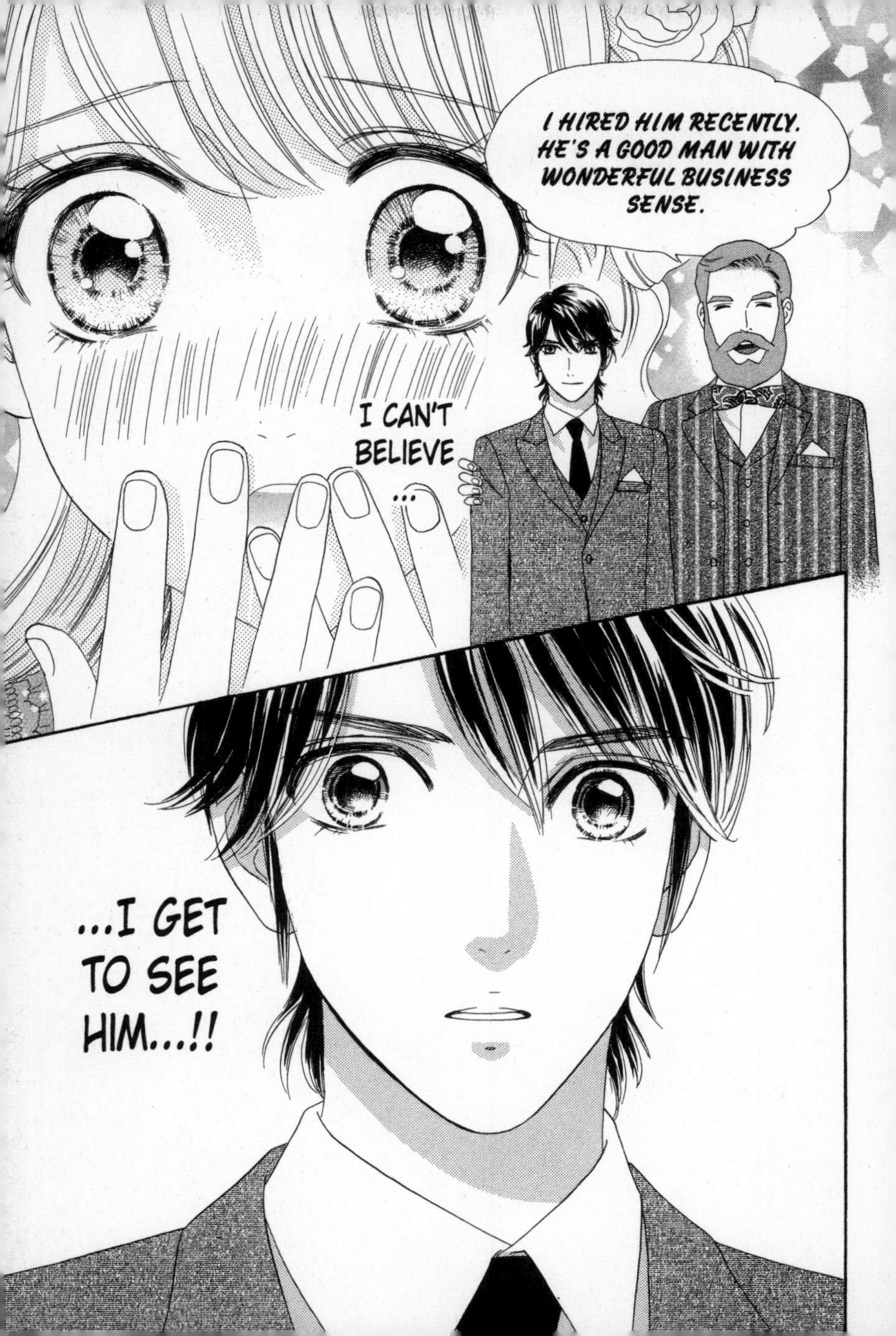
I HIRED HIM RECENTLY. HE'S A GOOD MAN WITH WONDERFUL BUSINESS SENSE.
I CAN'T BELIEVE ...
...I GET TO SEE HIM...!!

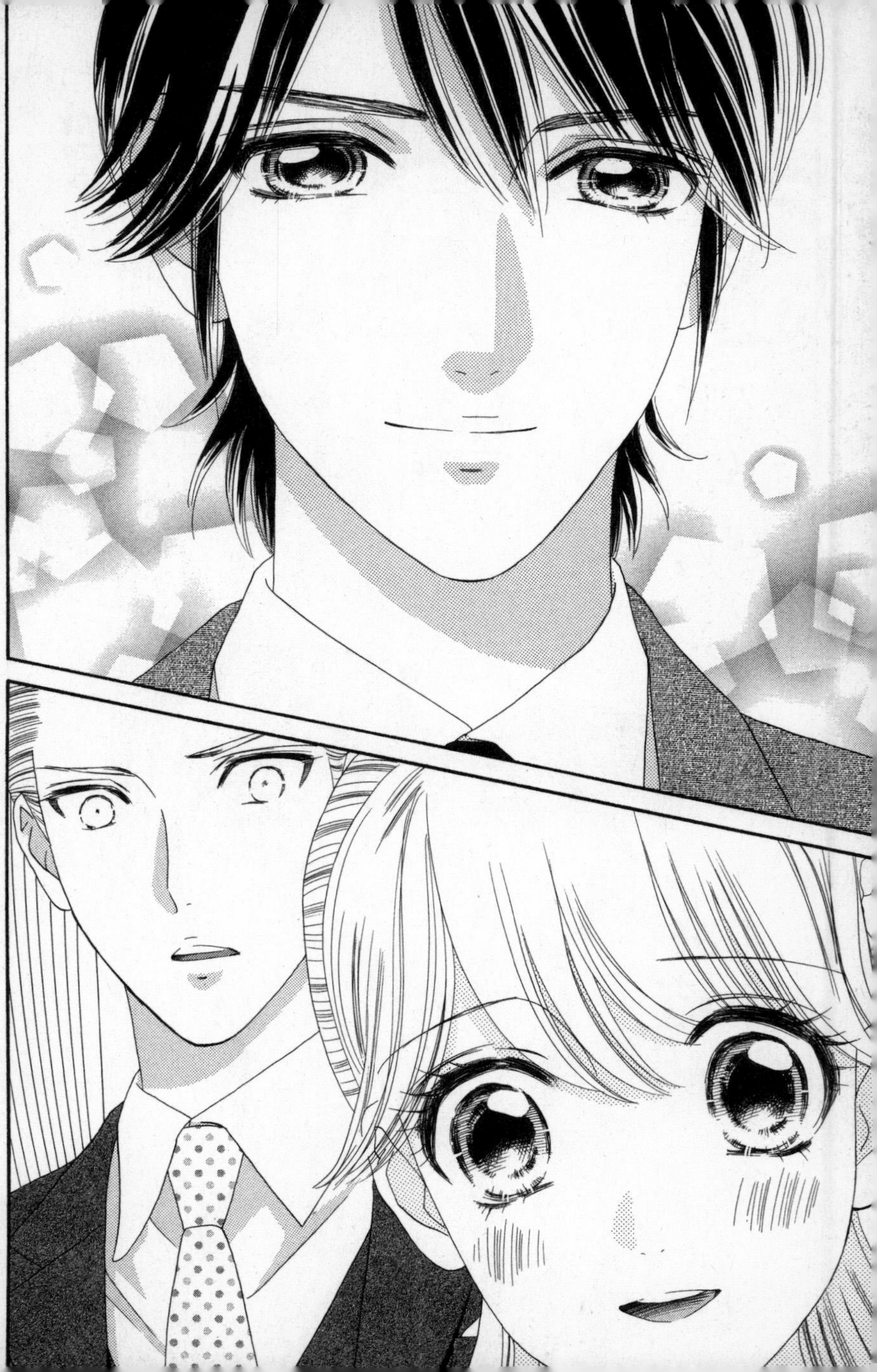

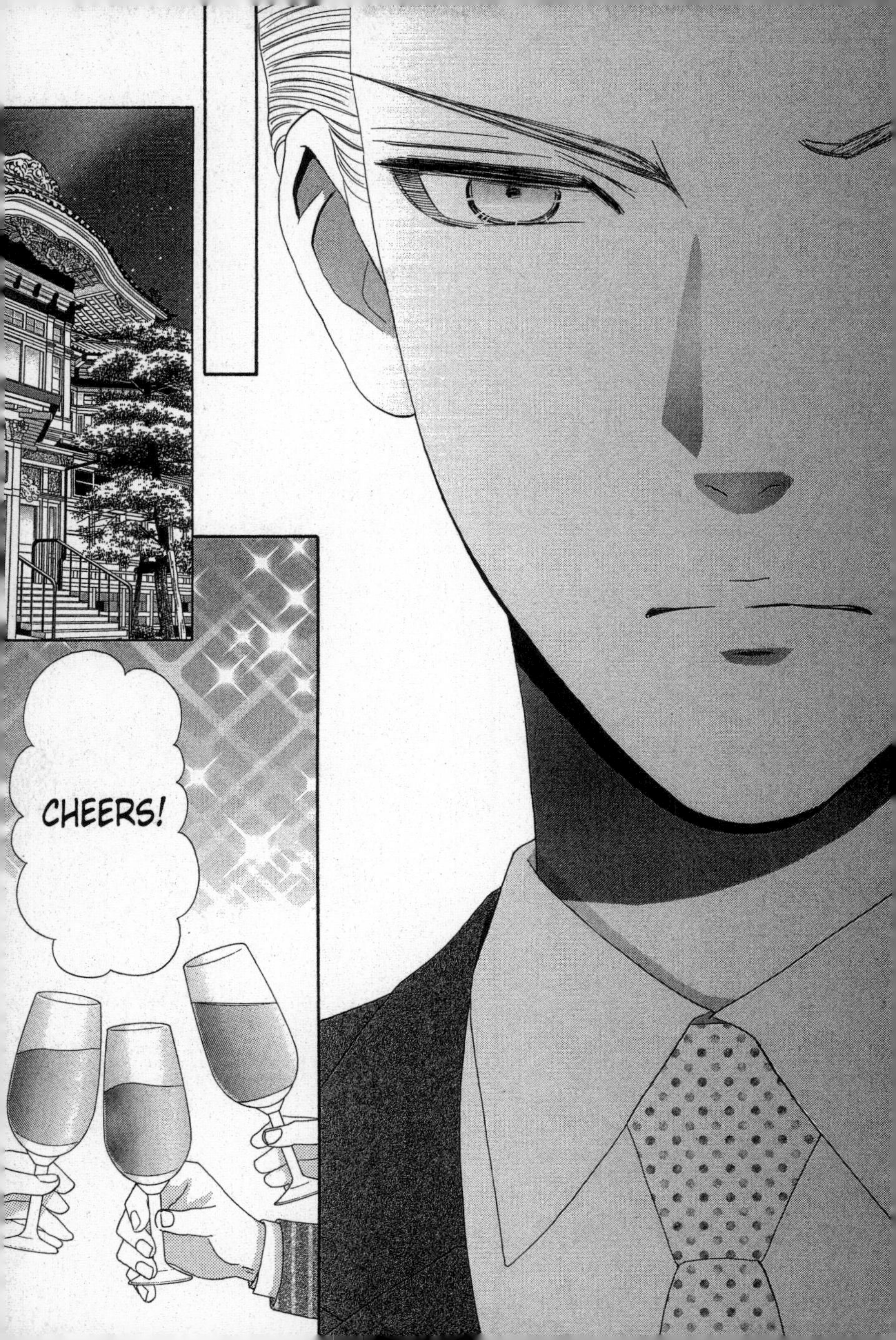
CHEERS!

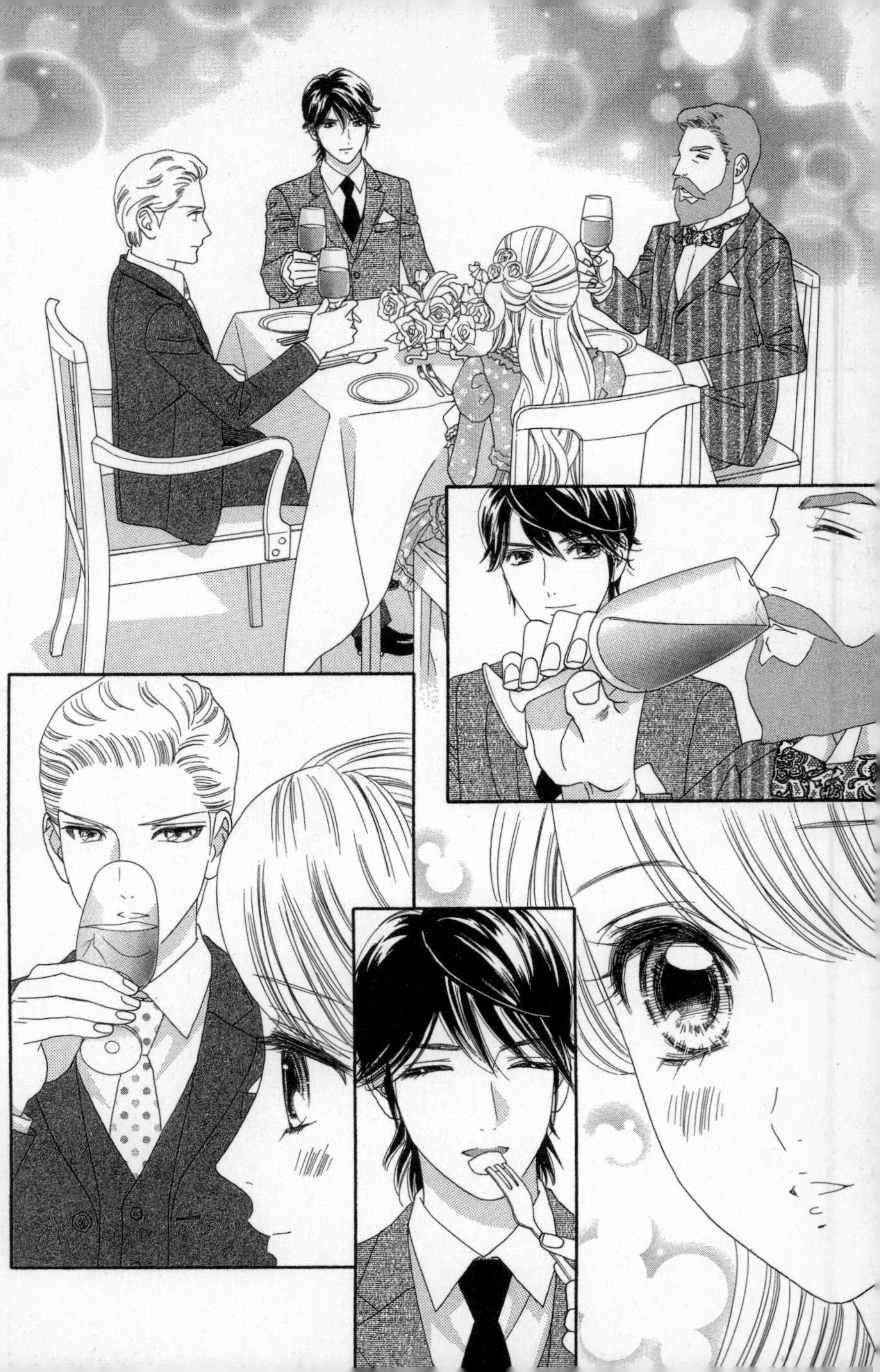

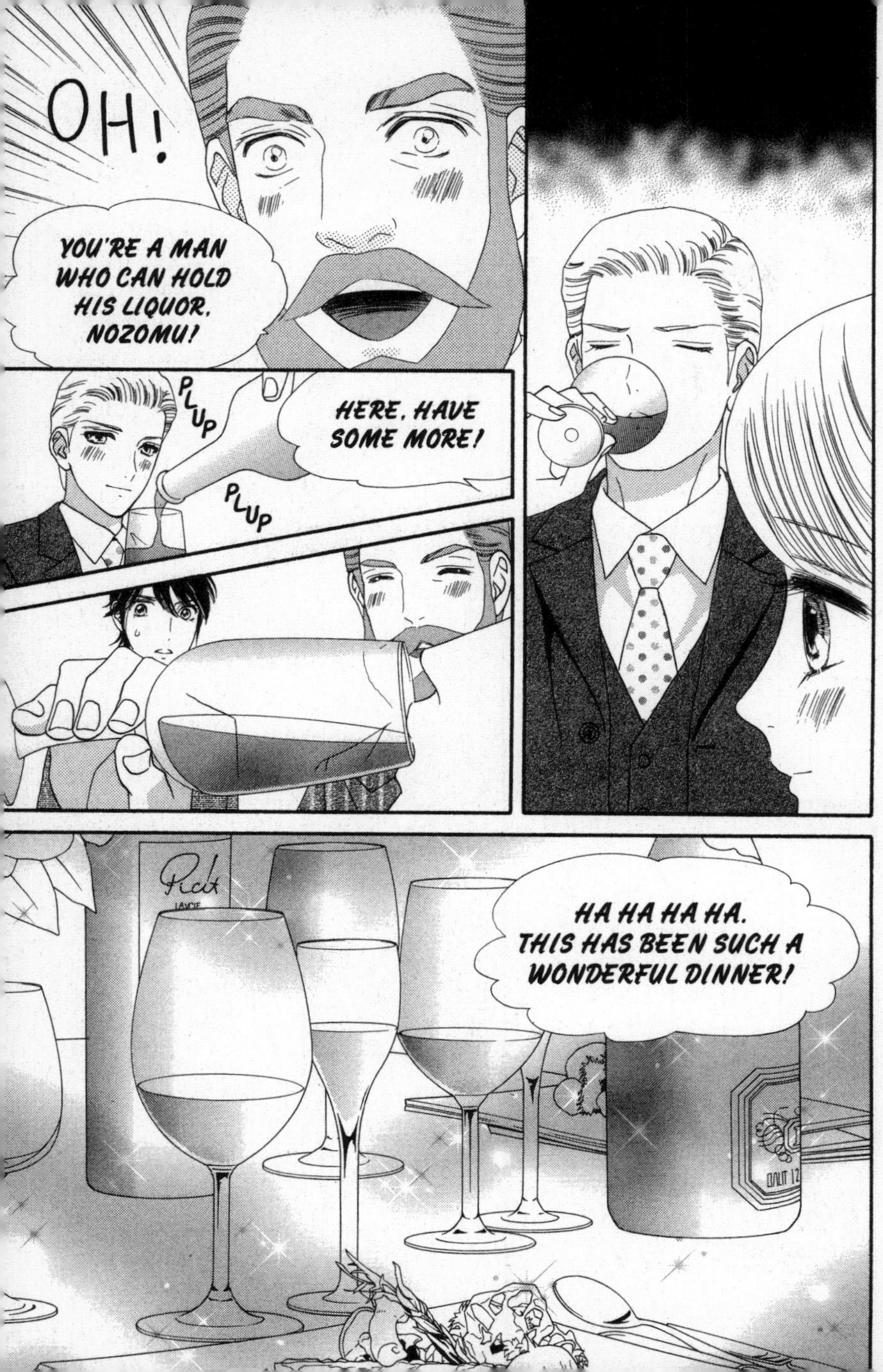
OH!
YOU'RE A MAN WHO CAN HOLD HIS LIQUOR, NOZOMU!
HERE, HAVE SOME MORE!
PLUP
PLUP
HA HA HA HA. THIS HAS BEEN SUCH A WONDERFUL DINNER!

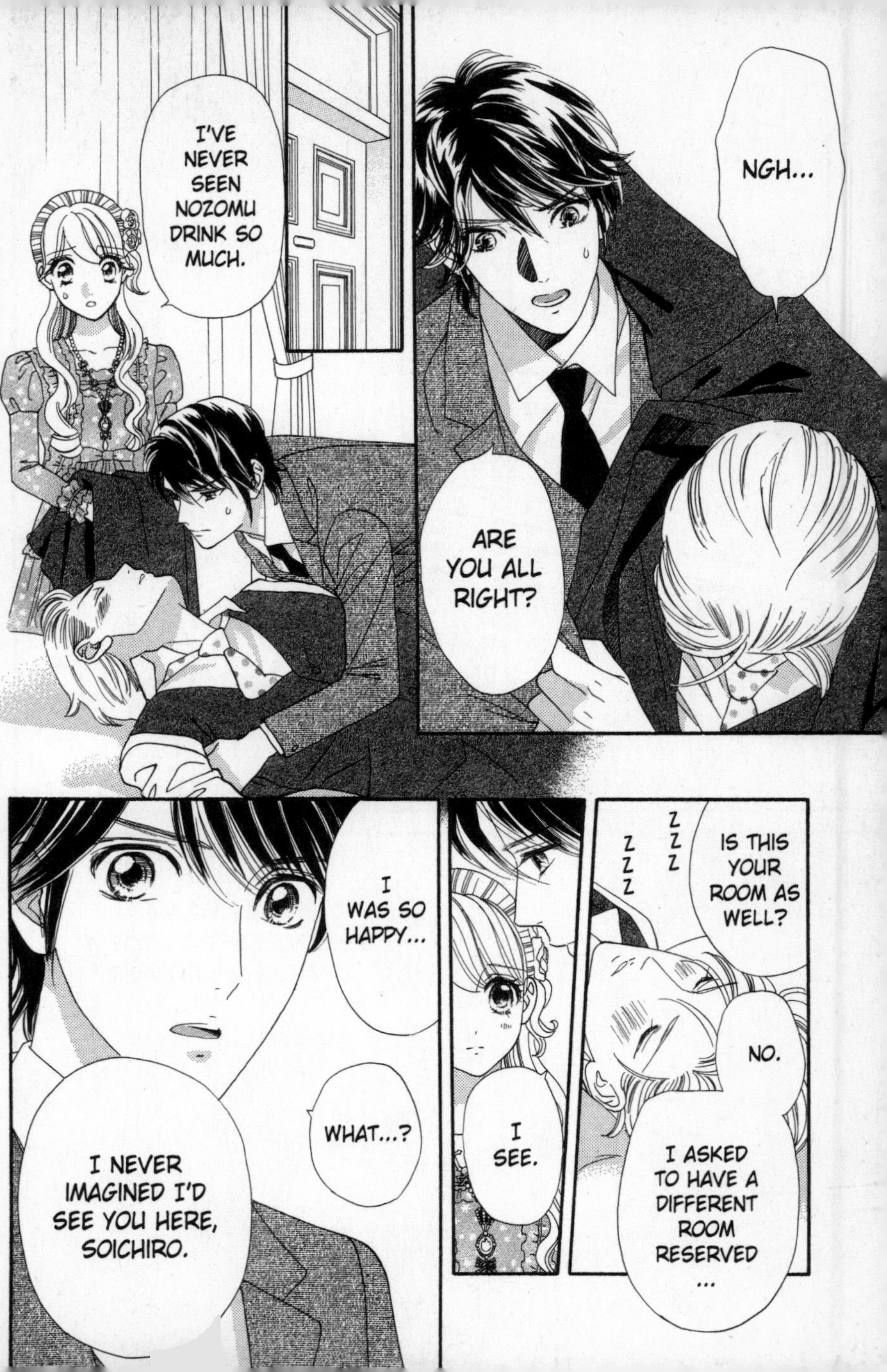
NGH...
ARE YOU ALL RIGHT?
I'VE NEVER SEEN NOZOMU DRINK SO MUCH.
Z Z Z
Z Z Z
IS THIS YOUR ROOM AS WELL?
NO.
I ASKED TO HAVE A DIFFERENT ROOM RESERVED ...
I SEE.
I WAS SO HAPPY...
WHAT...?
I NEVER IMAGINED I'D SEE YOU HERE, SOICHIRO.

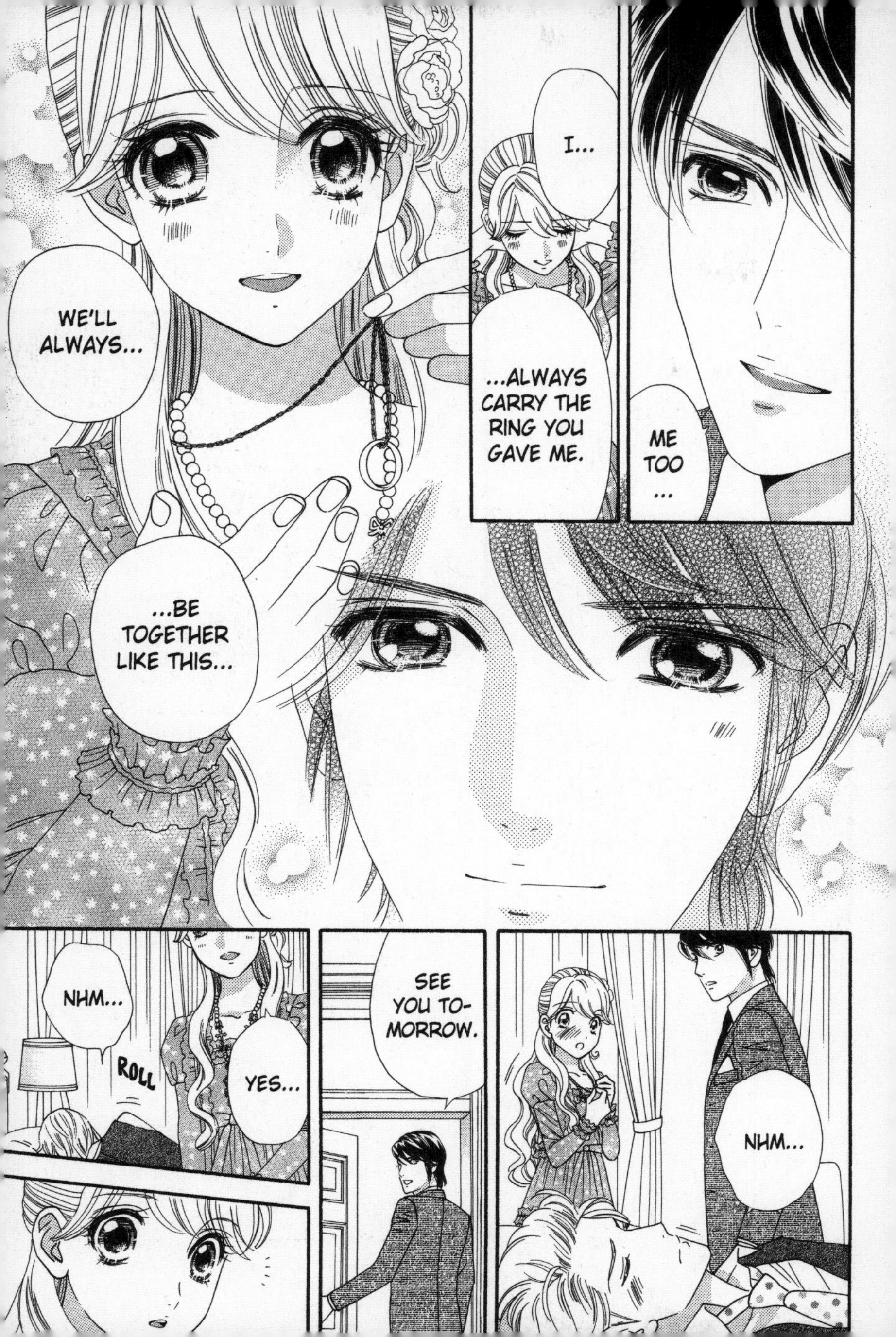
WE'LL ALWAYS...
...BE TOGETHER LIKE THIS...
I...
...ALWAYS CARRY THE RING YOU GAVE ME.
ME TOO ...
NHM...
SEE YOU TO-MORROW.
NHM...
ROLL
YES...

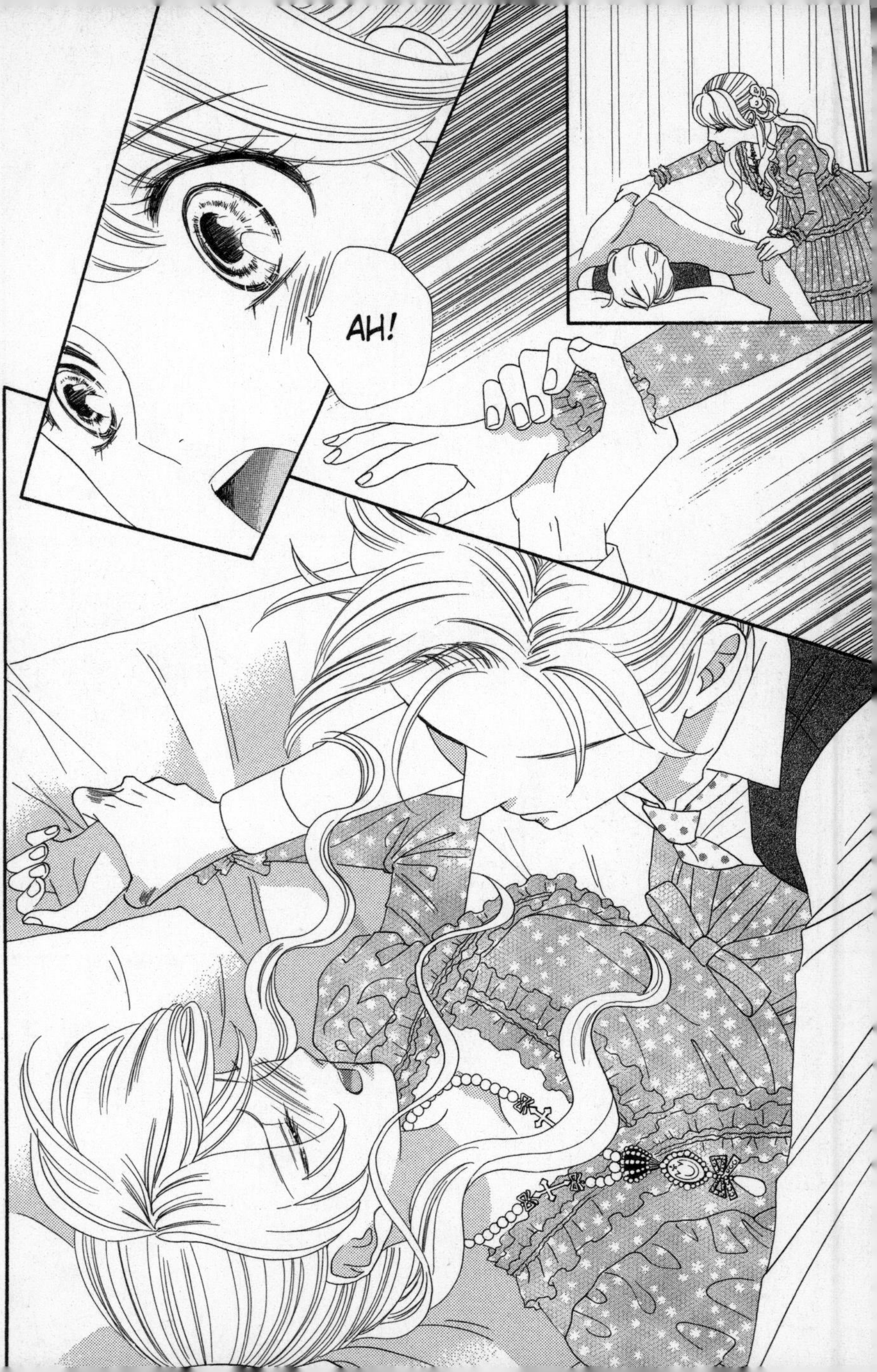
AH!

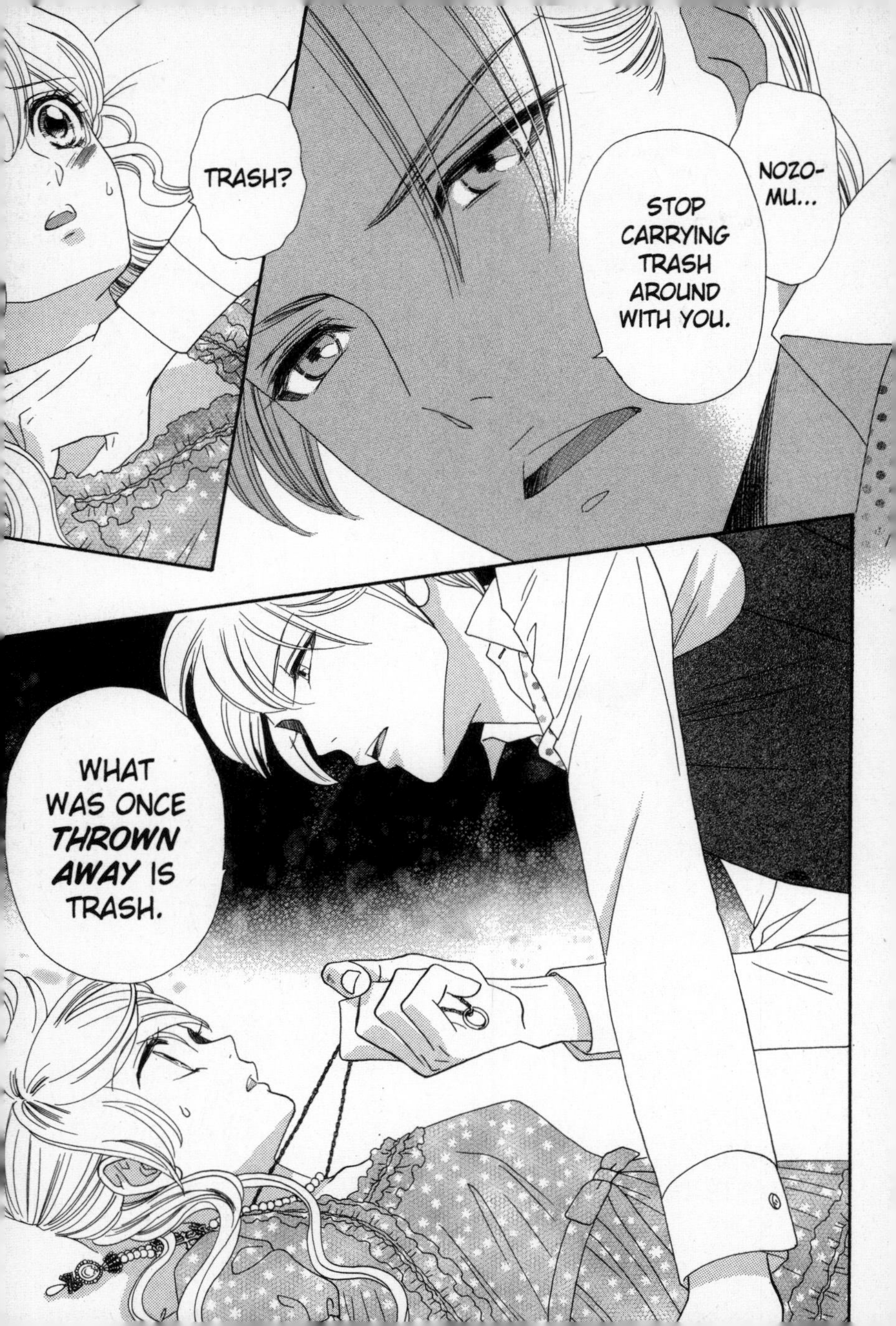
NOZOMU...
STOP CARRYING TRASH AROUND WITH YOU.
TRASH?
WHAT WAS ONCE *THROWN AWAY* IS TRASH.

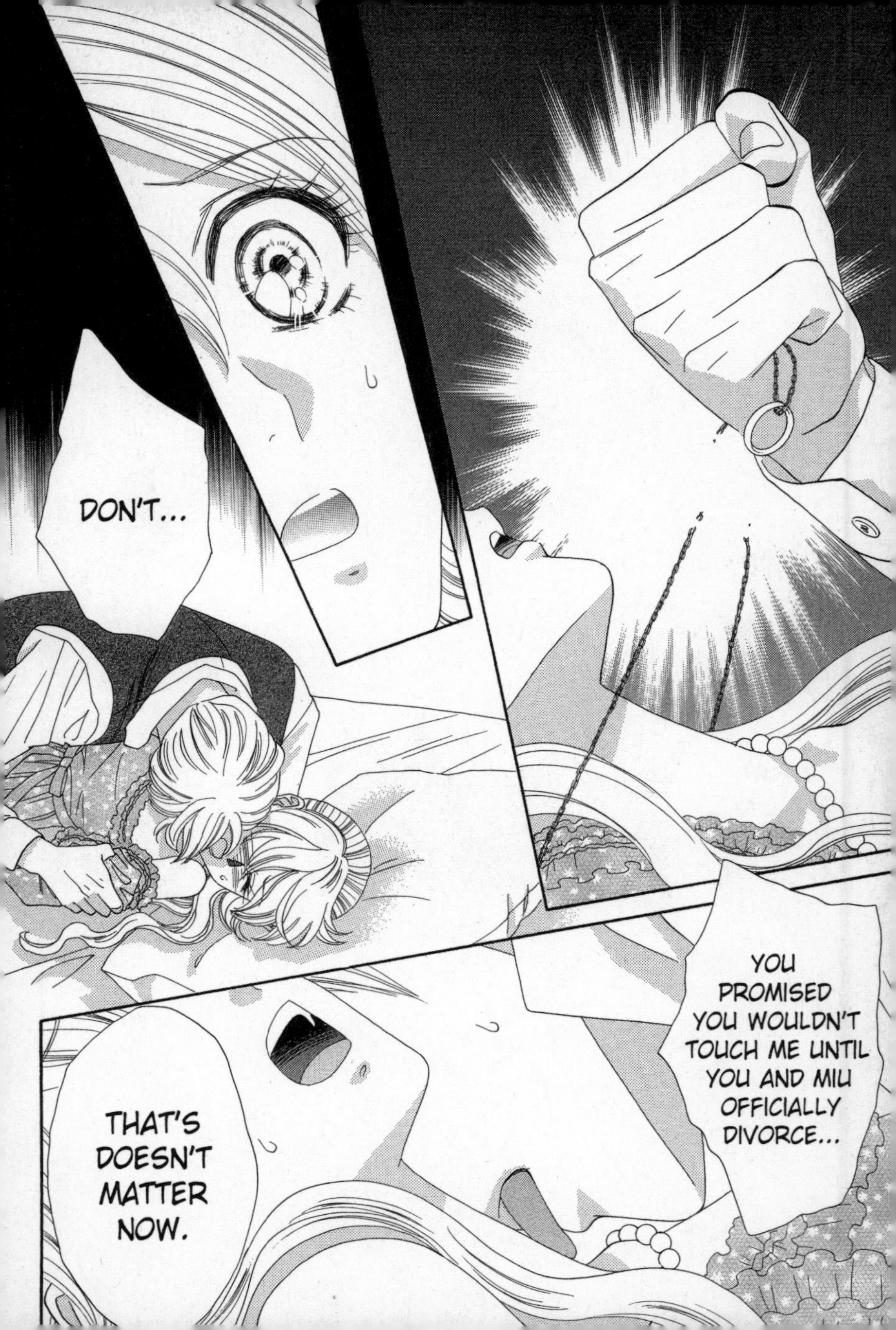
DON'T...
YOU PROMISED YOU WOULDN'T TOUCH ME UNTIL YOU AND MIU OFFICIALLY DIVORCE...
THAT'S DOESN'T MATTER NOW.

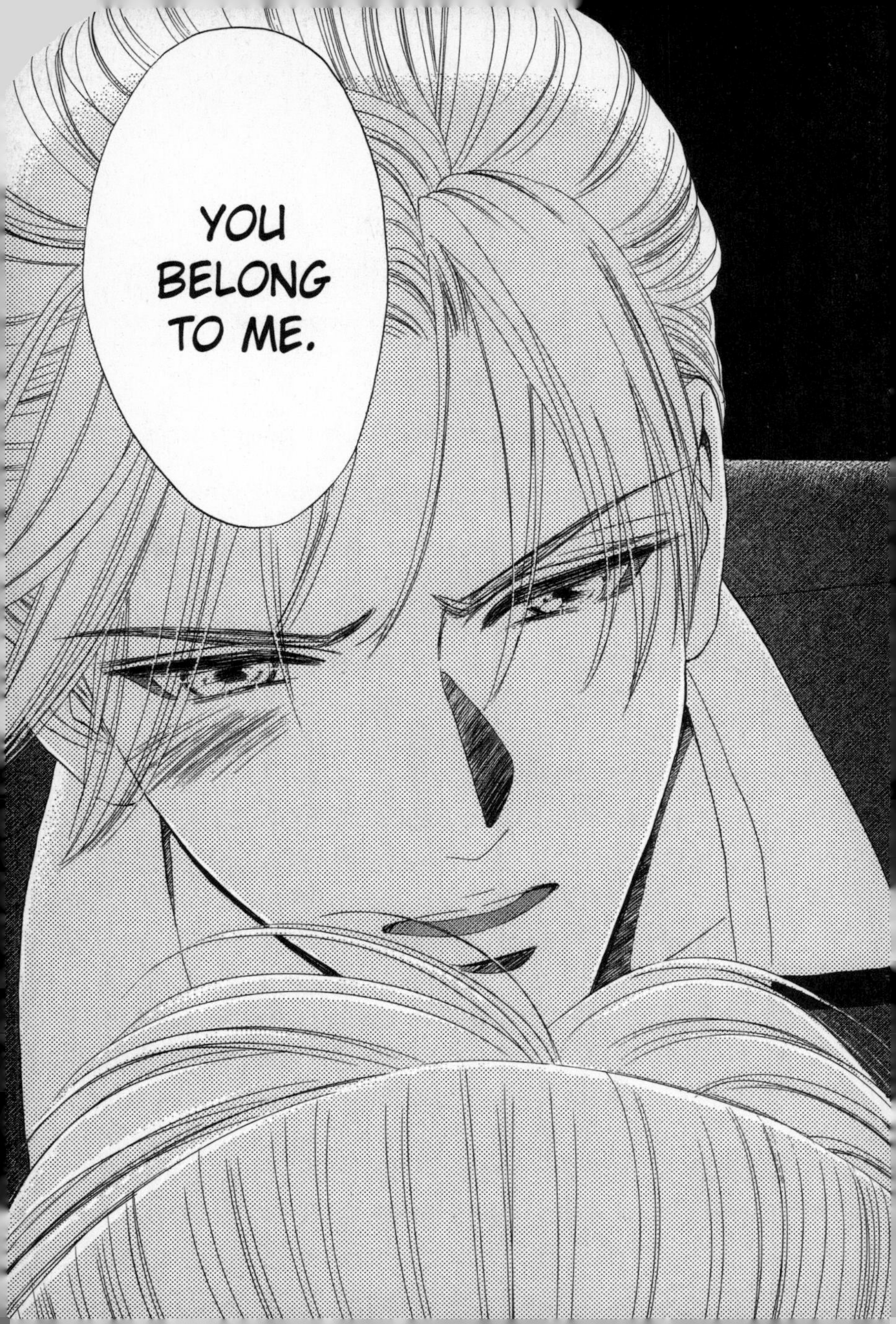
YOU BELONG TO ME.

GREETINGS —

HELLO, IT'S UE-RIN!! GUESS WHAT? THIS IS THE FINAL VOLUME!!

I WAS CREATING ALL THE CHAPTERS IN THIS VOLUME AS IF THEY WERE

THE CLIMAX OF THE STORY, SO YOU'LL FINALLY GET TO SEE *THAT

SPOILER* IN CHAPTER 55. I'M SURE YOU'VE ALL HAD A HUNCH ABOUT IT,

BUT I DECIDED ON THE RELATIONSHIP OF THOSE TWO FROM THE VERY

BEGINNING WHEN I STARTED THIS MANGA... (OH! YOU SHOULD READ THIS

NOTE AFTER YOU FINISH READING THE WHOLE VOLUME...BUT MAYBE IT'S

TOO LATE?! I'M SORRY...!!) A LOT HAS HAPPENED DURING THIS SERIES... I

GOT MARRIED, GAVE BIRTH AND MY LIFESTYLE CHANGED, BUT I'M GLAD I

WAS ABLE TO FINISH THINGS.

MY DAUGHTER THESE DAYS

I LOOK LIKE A PRINCESS, DON'T I?

APPARENTLY, SHE TURNS INTO A PRINCESS THE MOMENT SHE WRAPS A TOWEL AROUND HER.

THIS GIRL IS GOING TO ENTER KINDERGARTEN NEXT YEAR... HOW TIME FLIES...

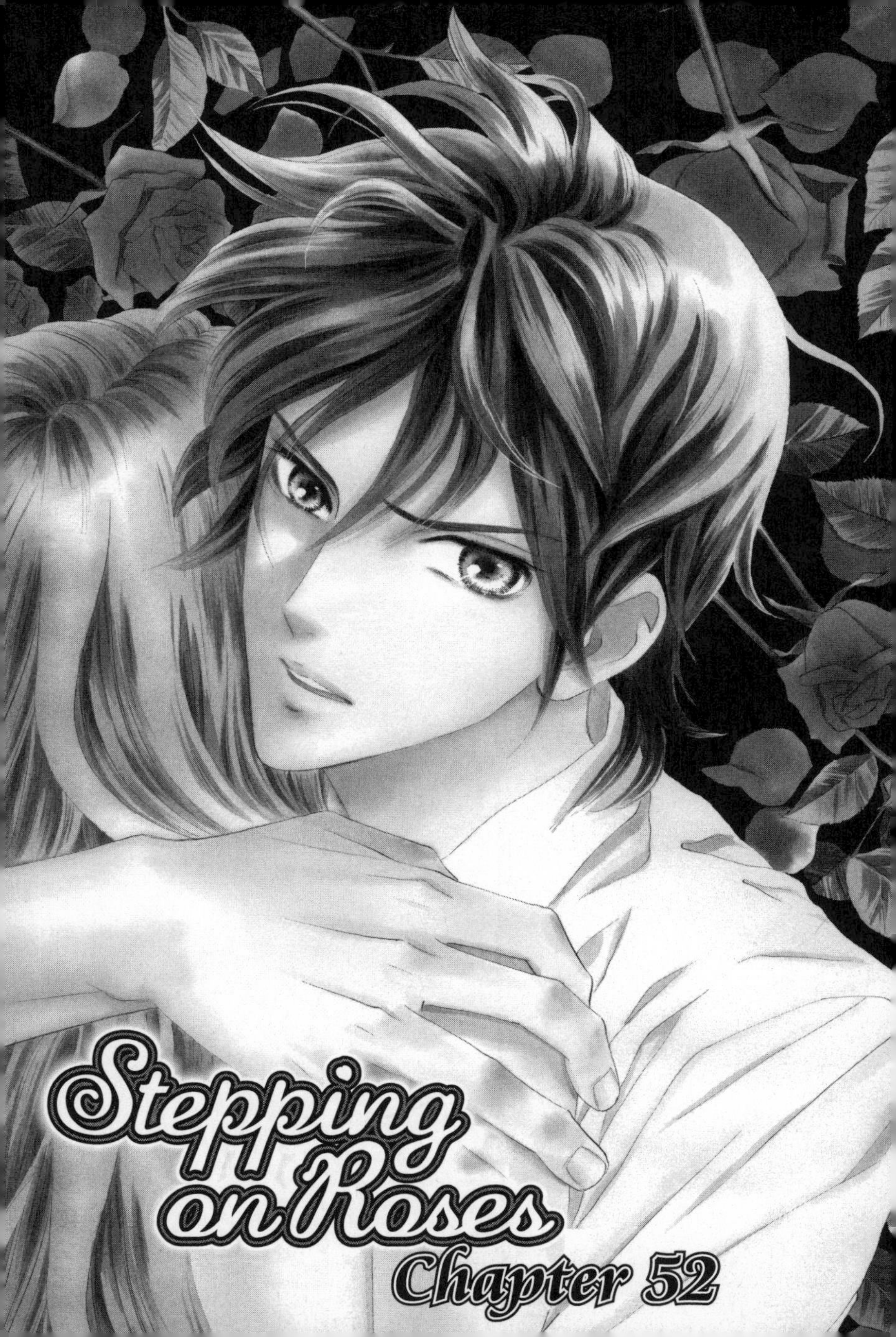
Stepping on Roses
Chapter 52

Stepping
on Roses

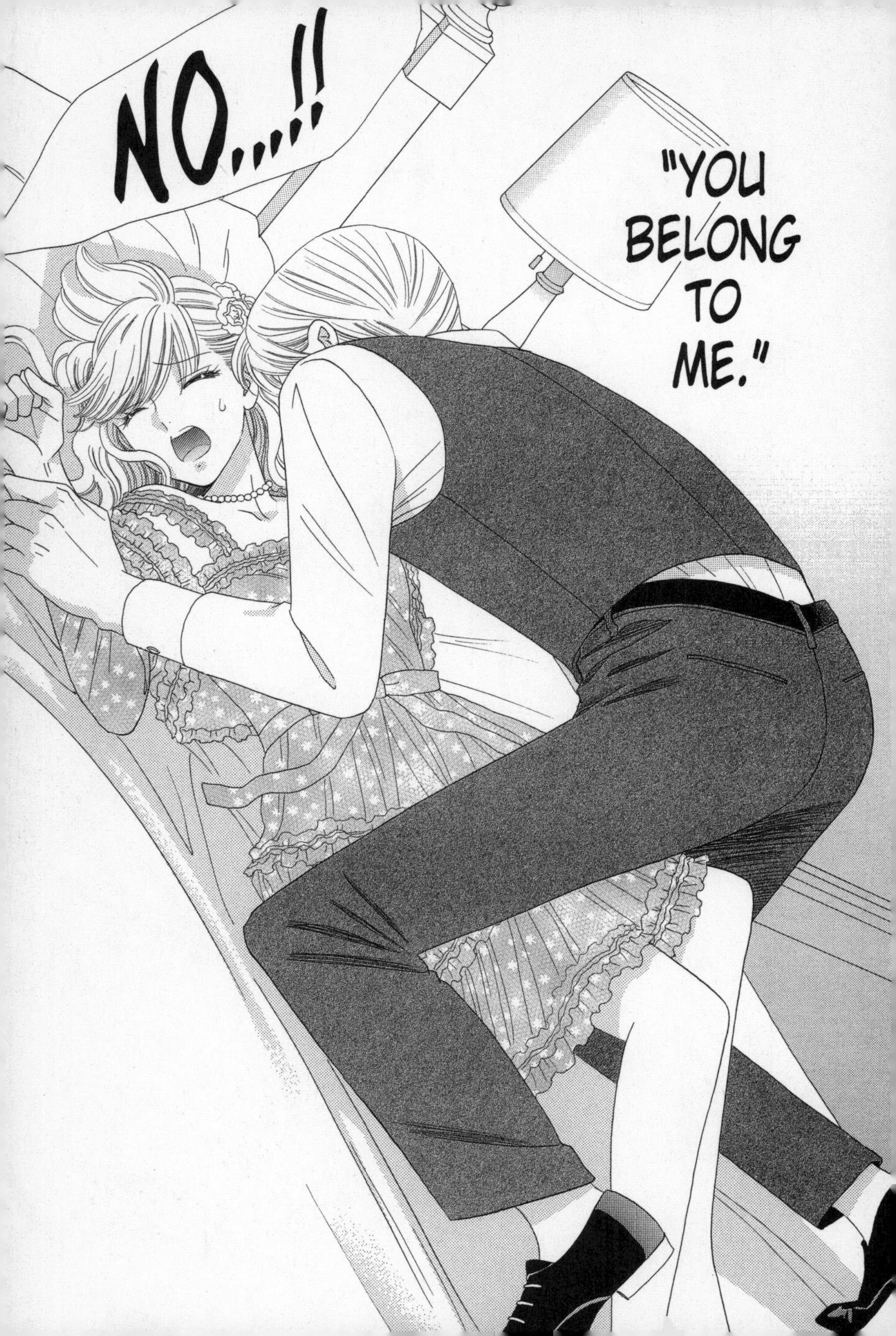
NO...!!
"YOU BELONG TO ME."

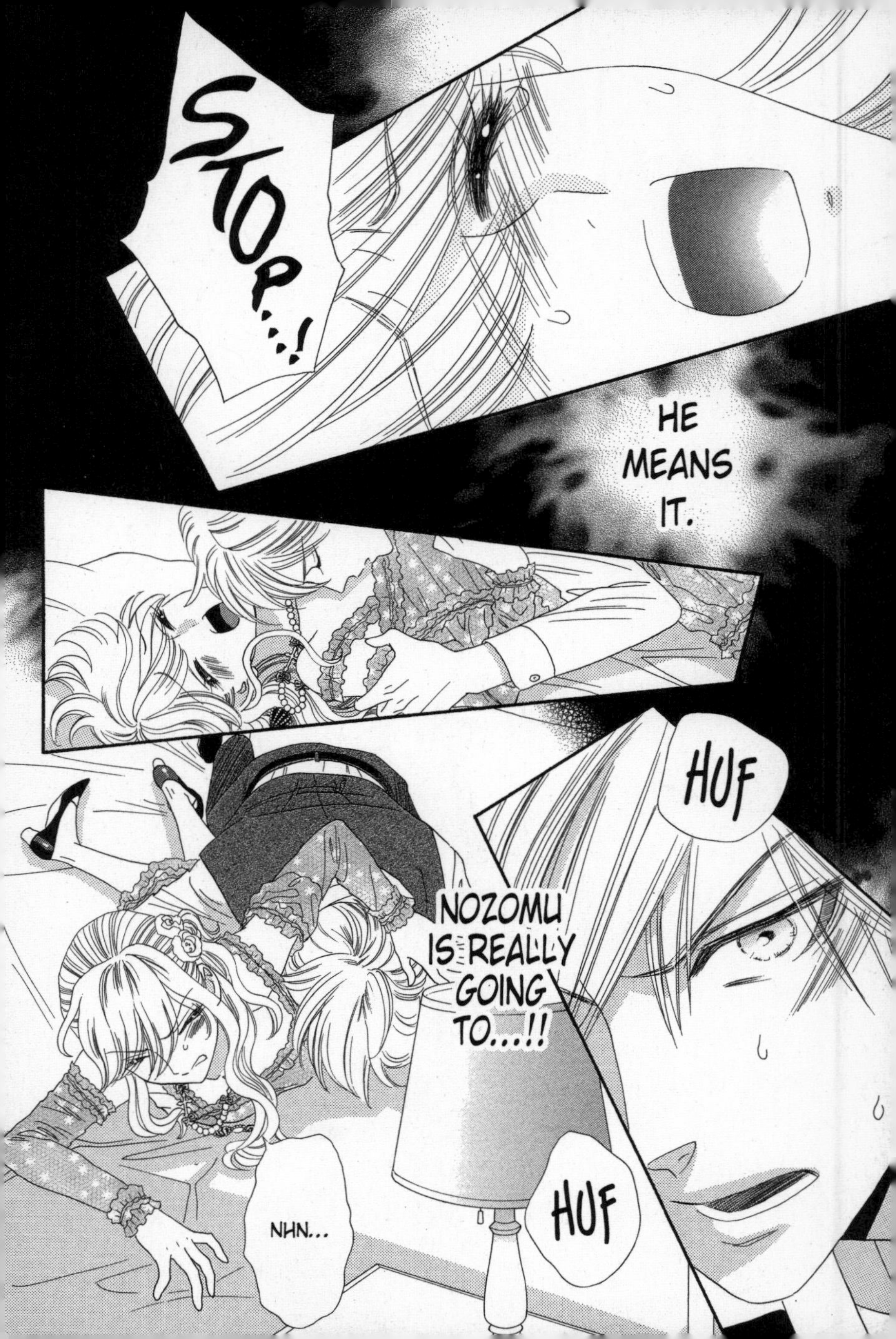
STOP...!
HE MEANS IT.
HUF
NOZOMU IS REALLY GOING TO...!!
HUF
NHN...

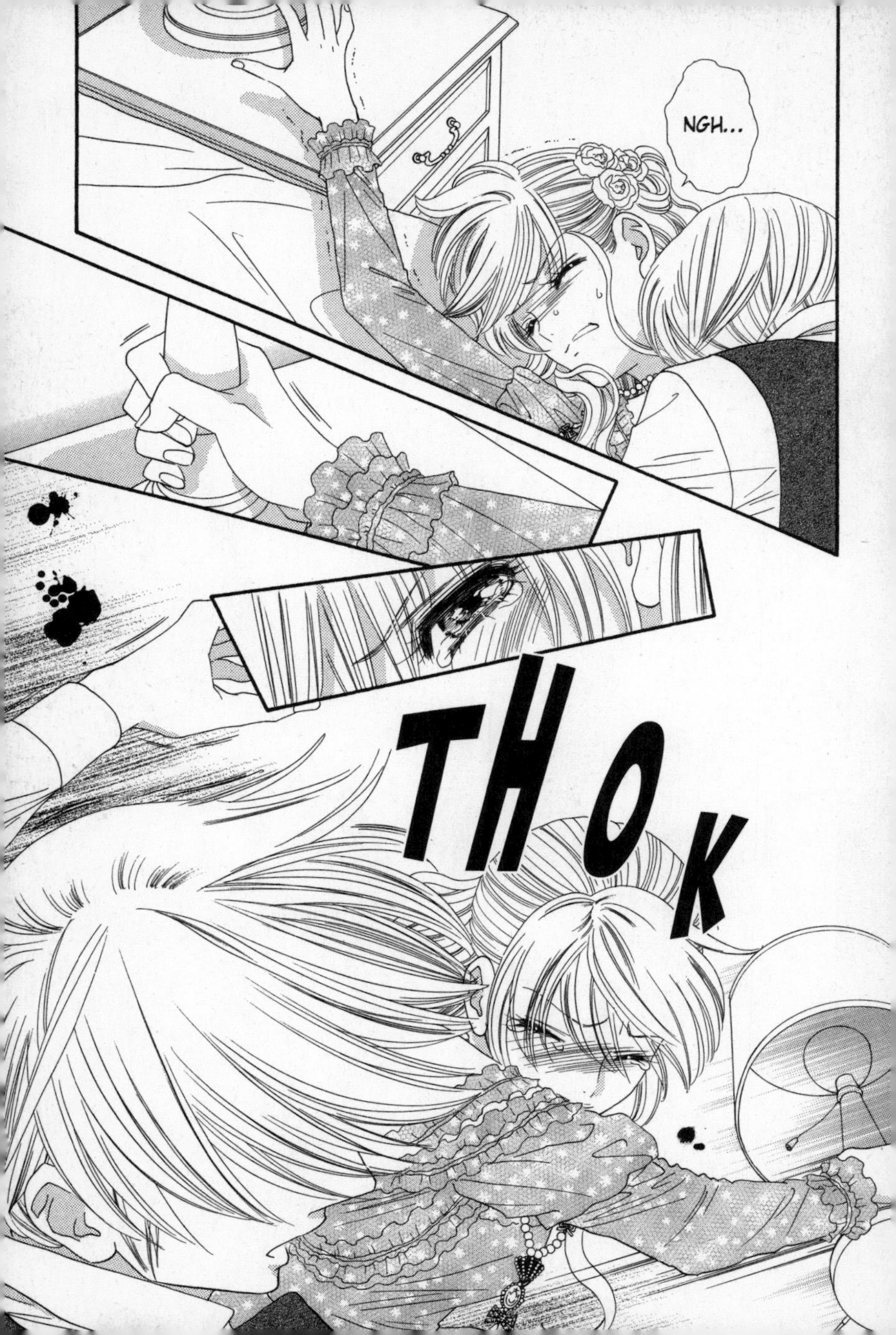
NGH...
THOK

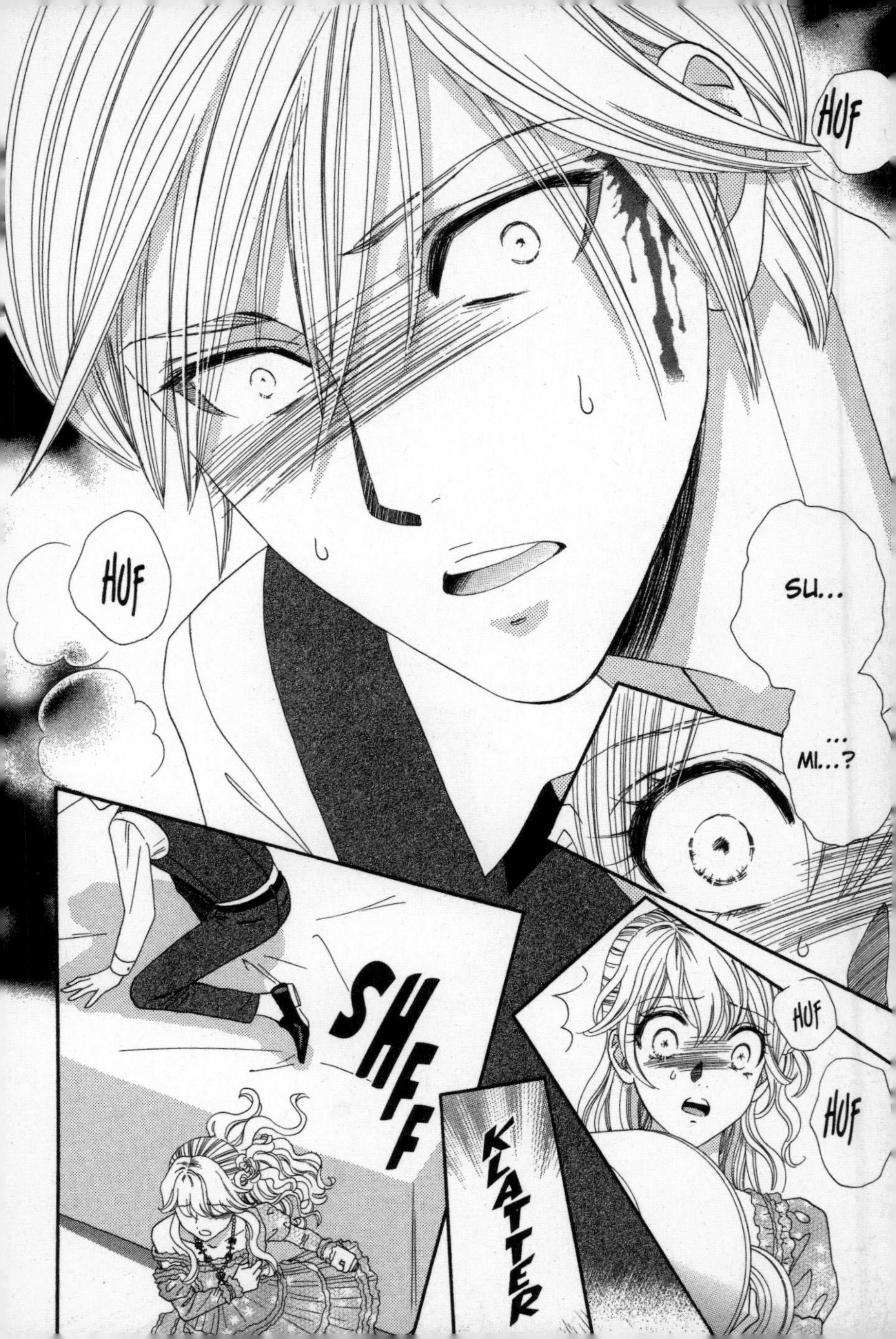
HUF
SU...
HUF
...MI...?
HUF
HUF
SHFF
KLATTER

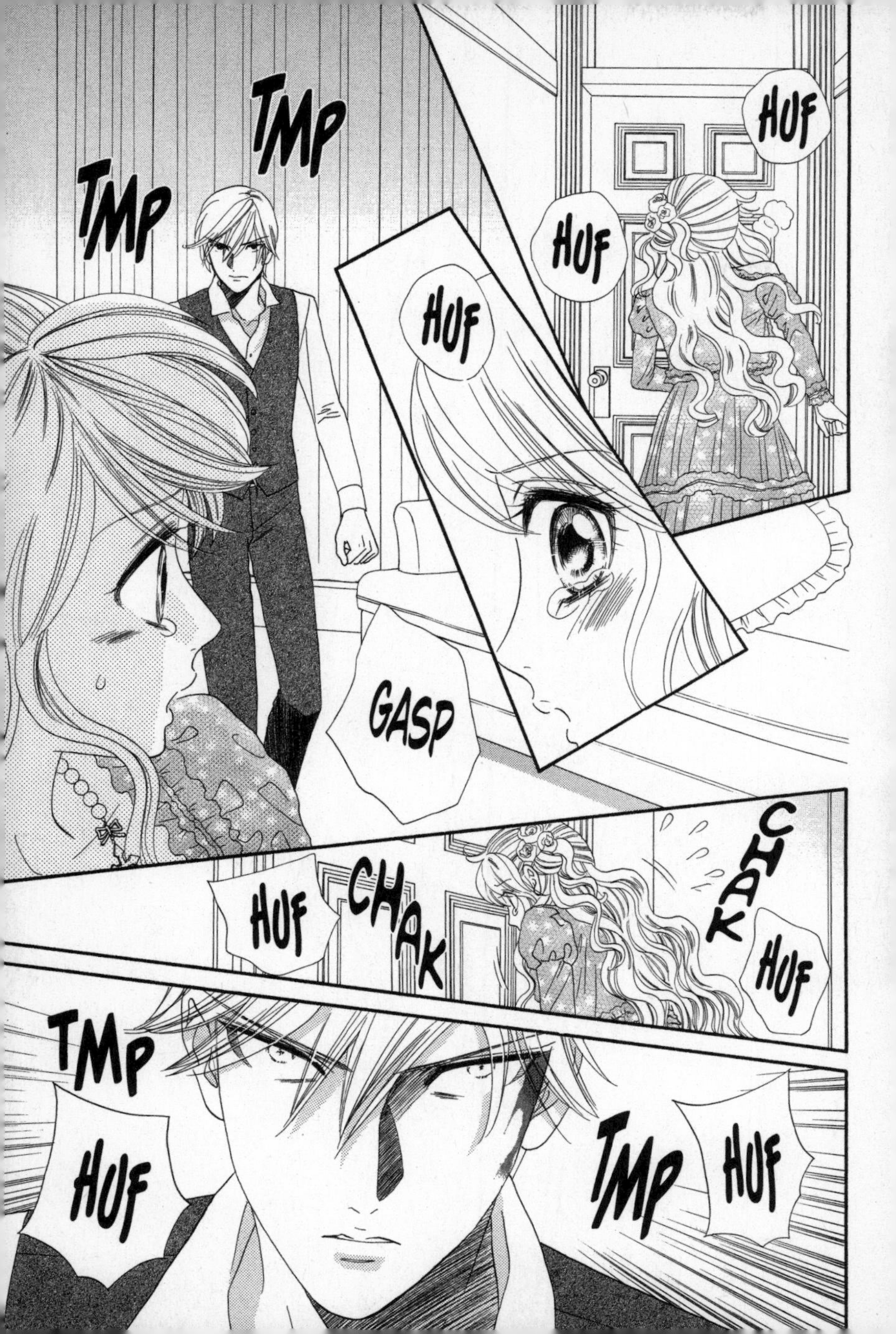
HUF
HUF
HUF
TMP
TMP
GASP
CHAK
HUF
CHAK
HUF
HUF
TMP
TMP
HUF

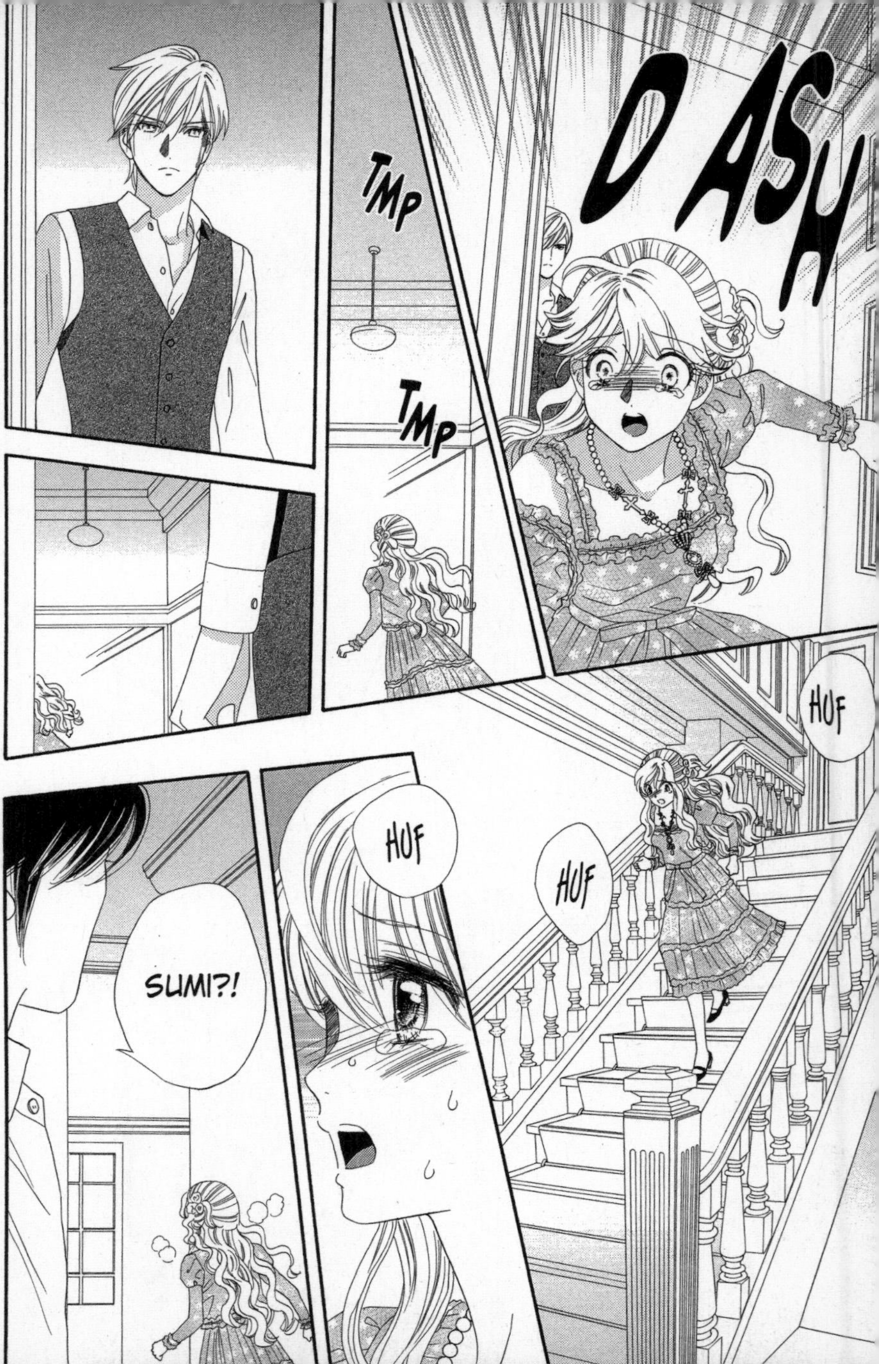
DASH
TMP
TMP
HUF
HUF
HUF
SUMI?!

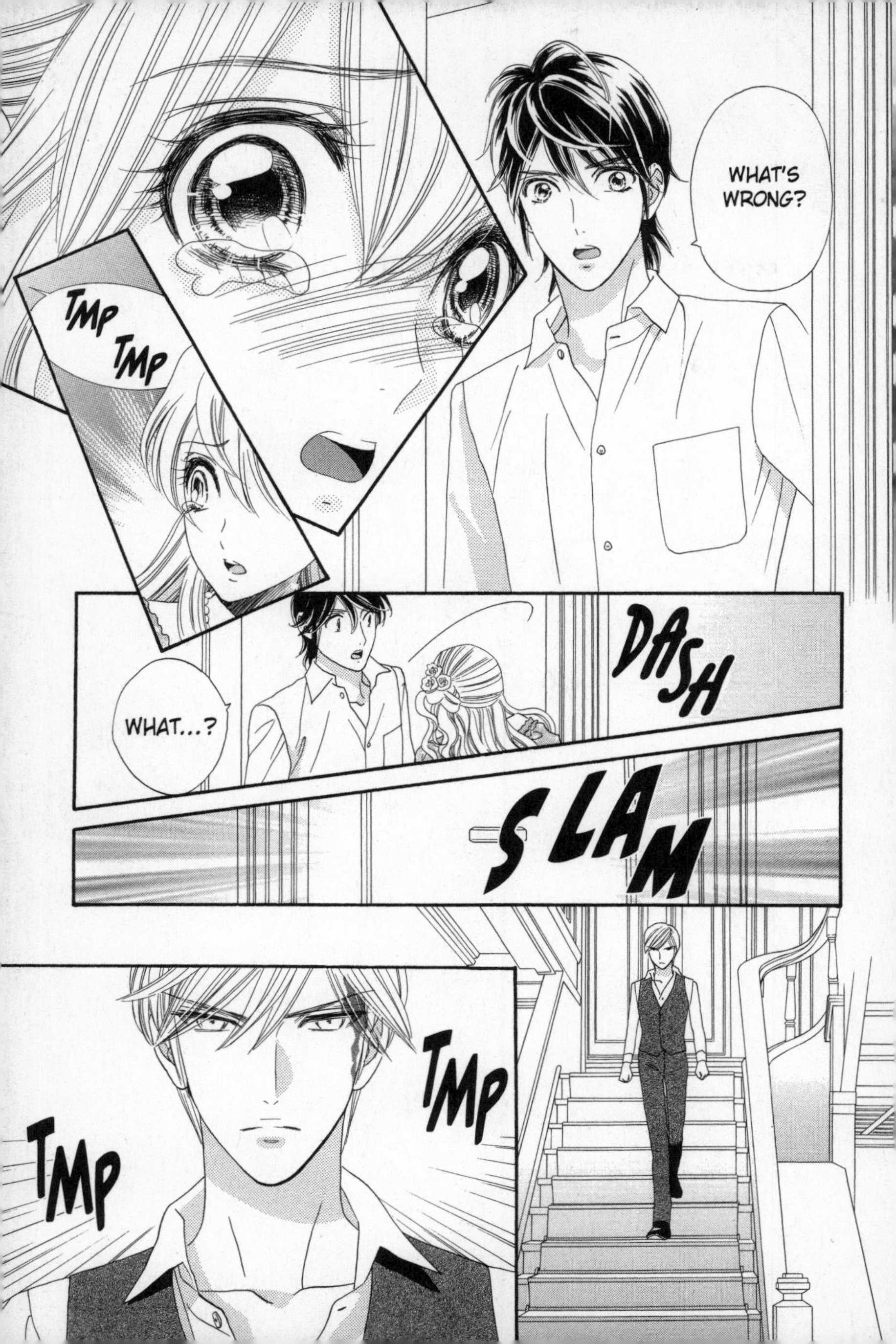
WHAT'S WRONG?
TMP TMP
DASH
WHAT...?
SLAM
TMP
TMP

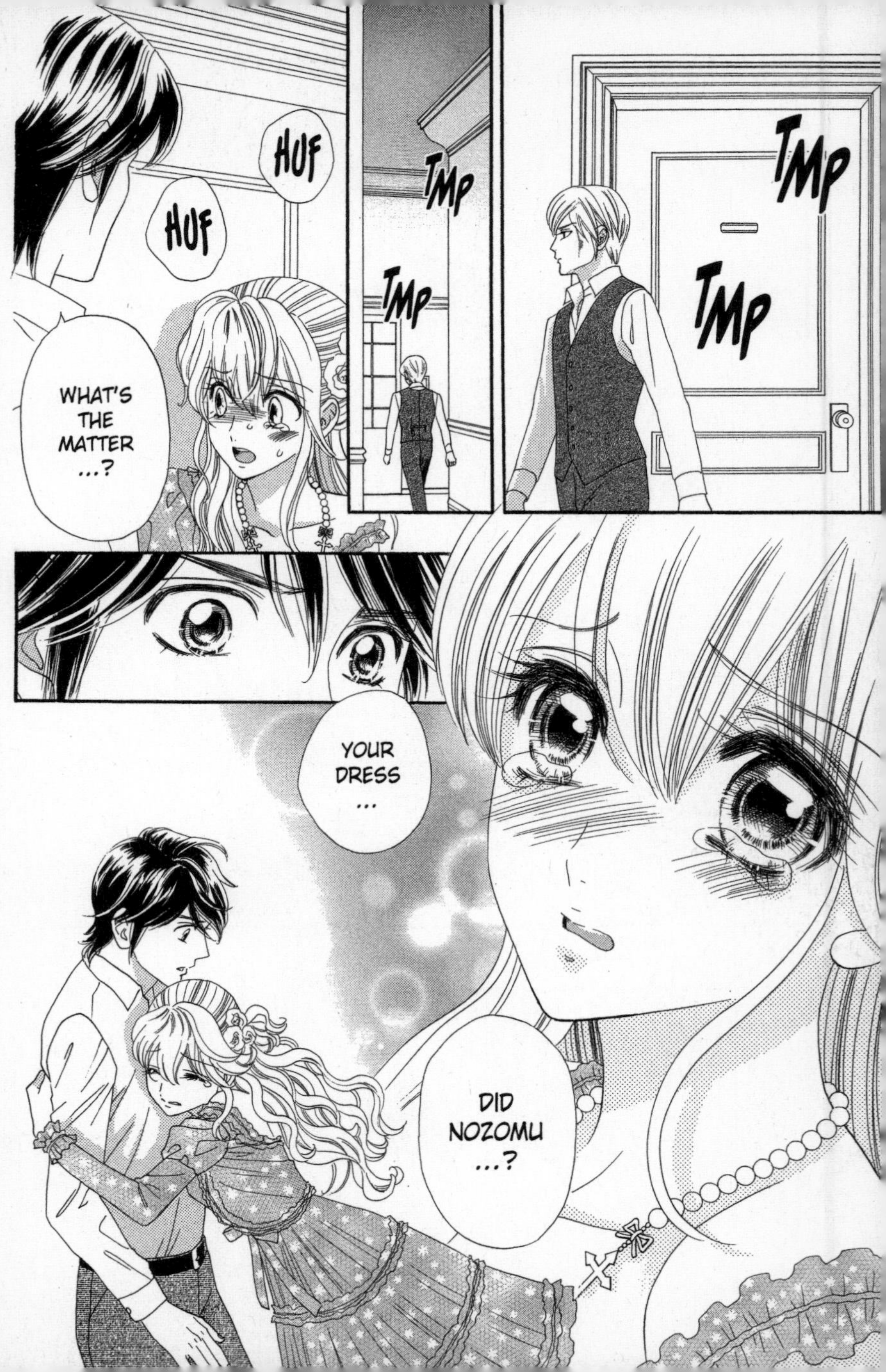
TMP
TMP
TMP
TMP
HUF
HUF
WHAT'S THE MATTER ...?
YOUR DRESS ...
DID NOZOMU ...?

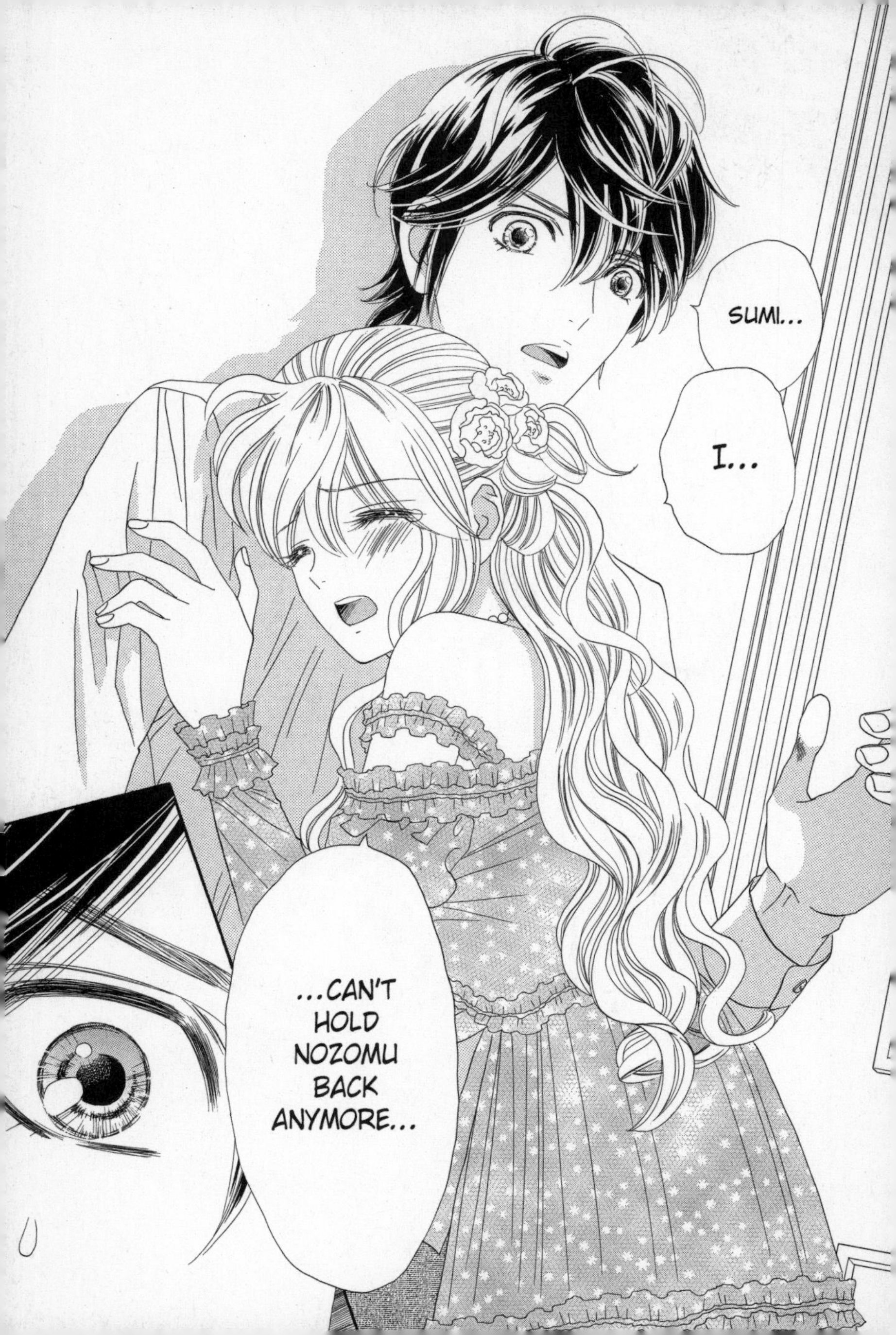
SUMI...
I...
...CAN'T HOLD NOZOMU BACK ANYMORE...

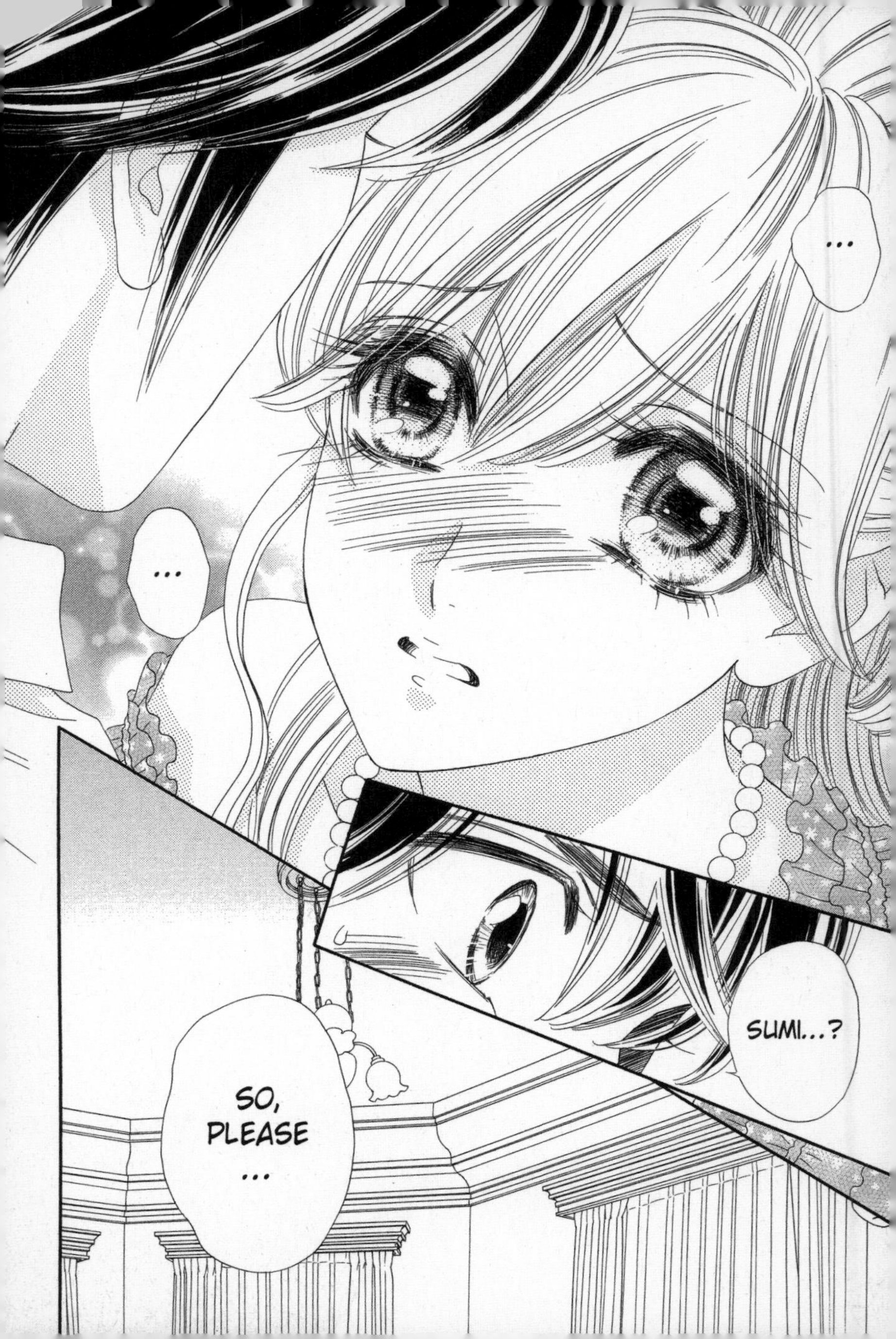
...
...
SUMI...?
SO, PLEASE ...

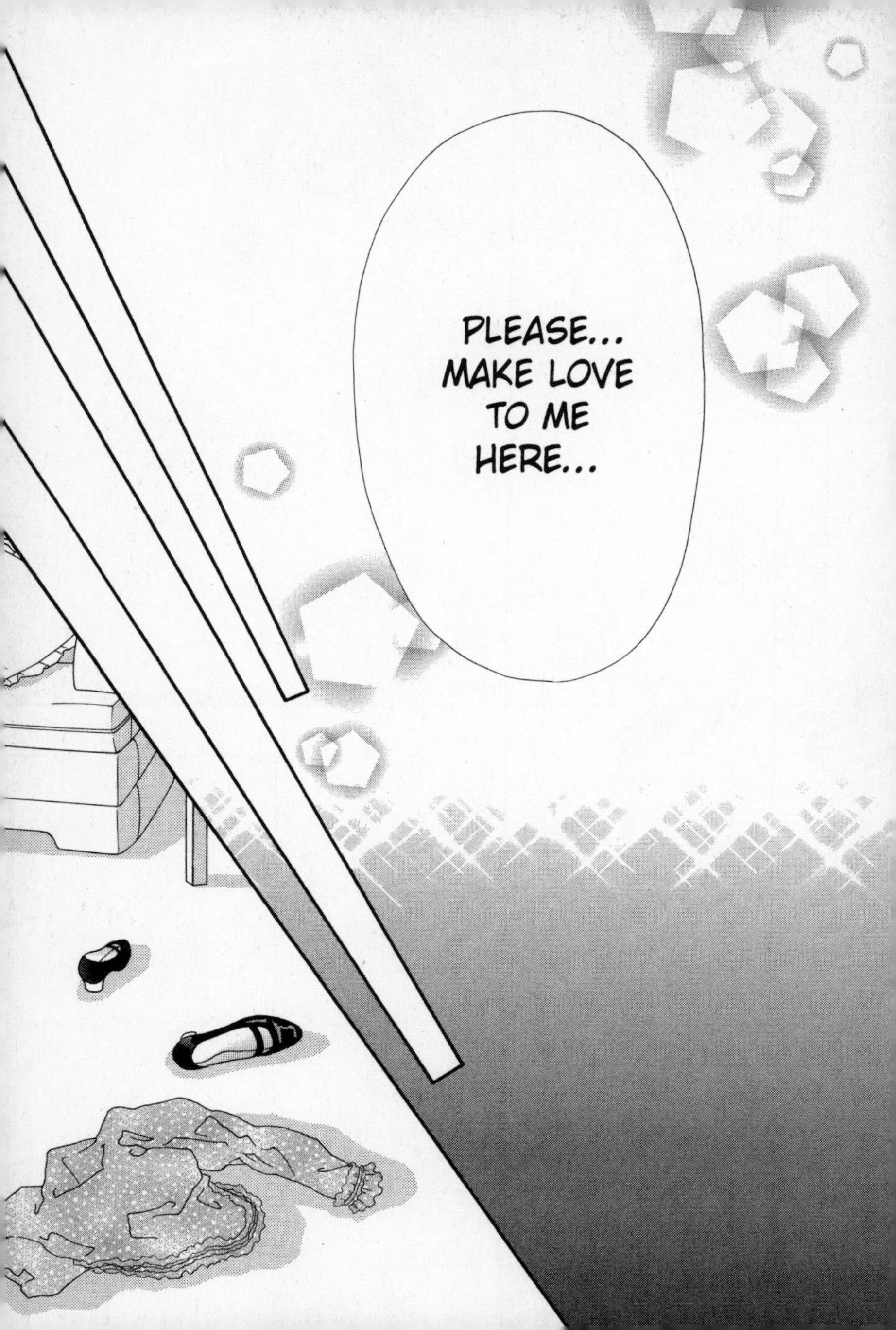
PLEASE... MAKE LOVE TO ME HERE...

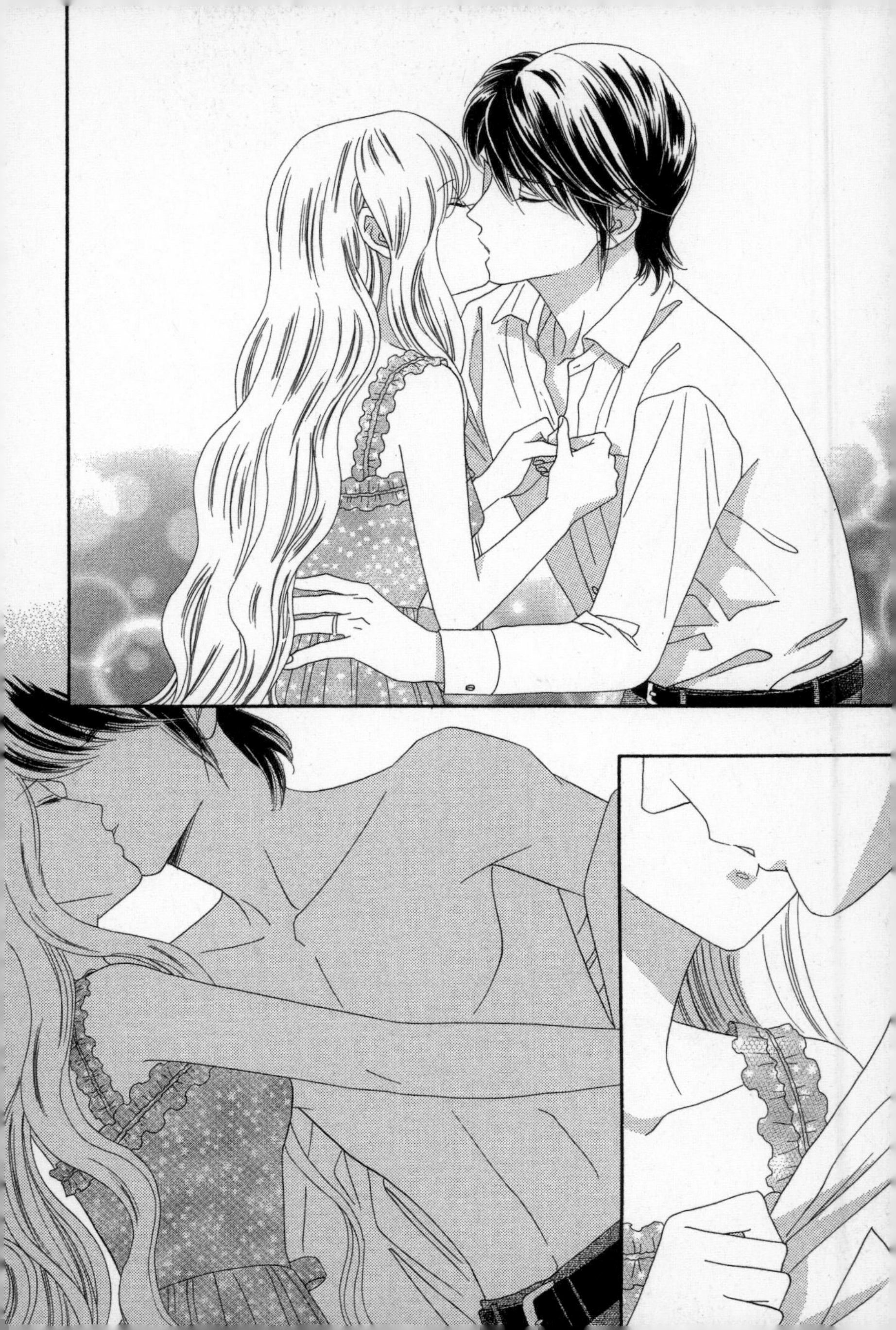

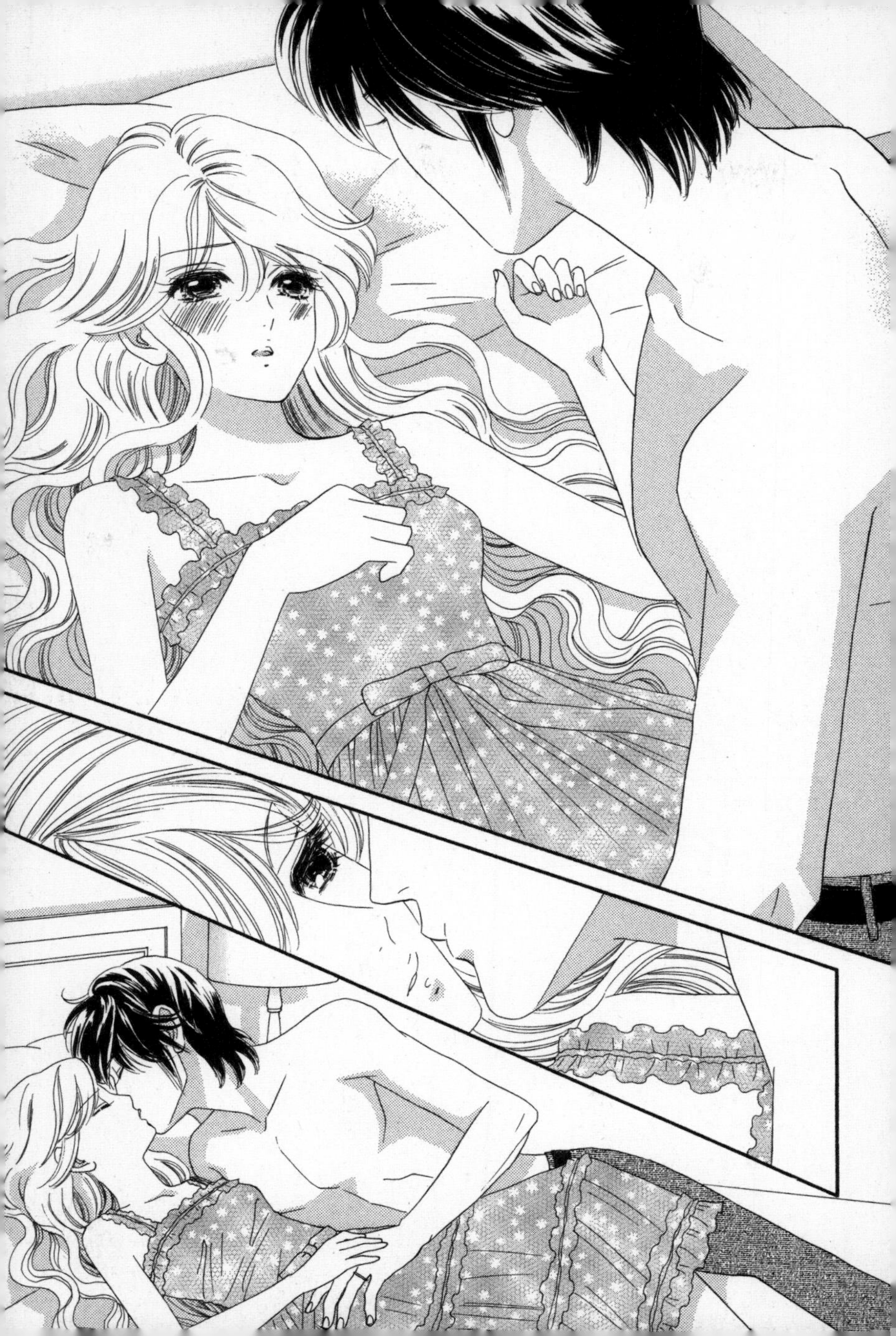

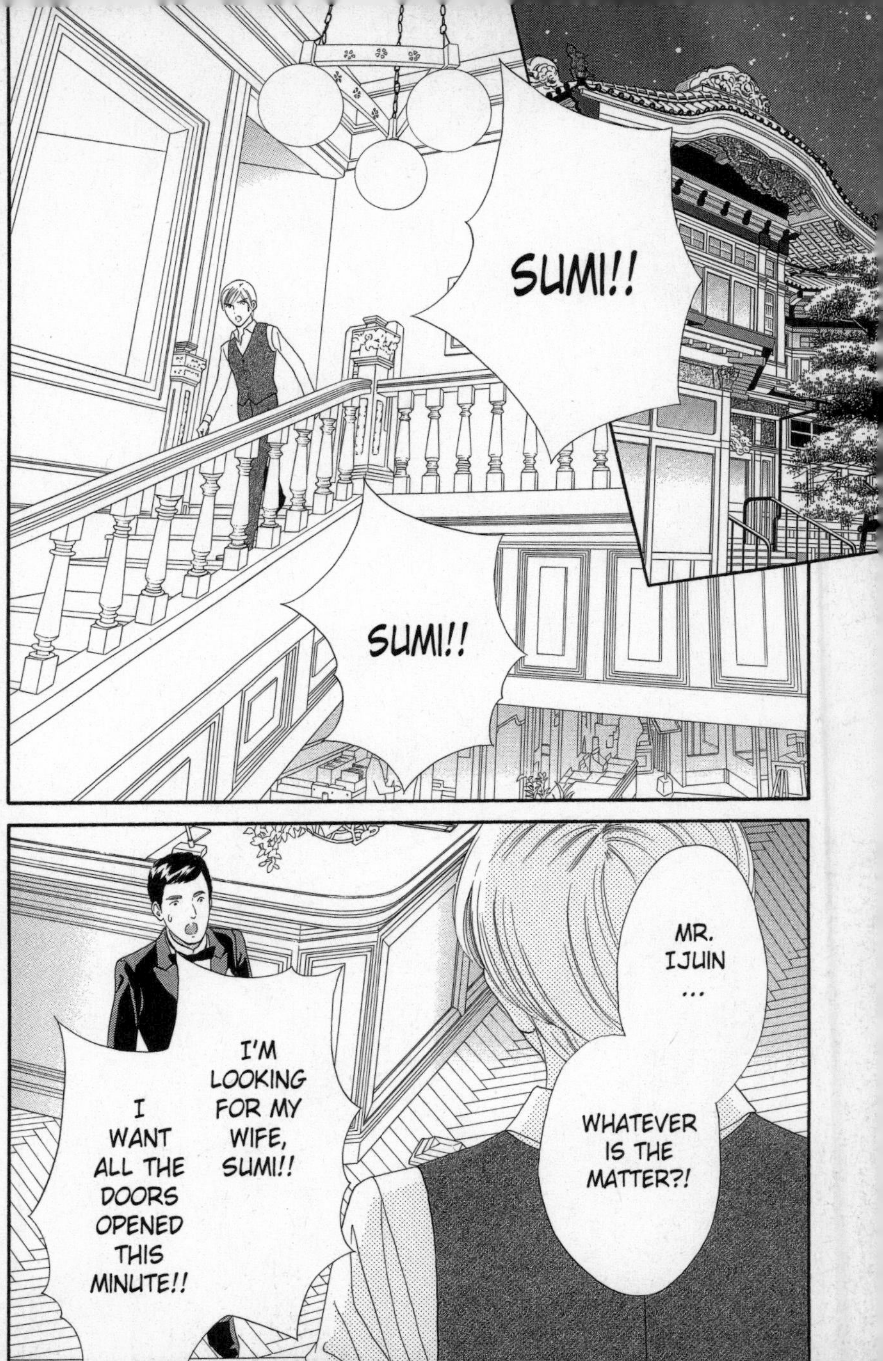
SUMI!!
SUMI!!
MR. IJUIN ...
WHATEVER IS THE MATTER?!
I'M LOOKING FOR MY WIFE, SUMI!!
I WANT ALL THE DOORS OPENED THIS MINUTE!!

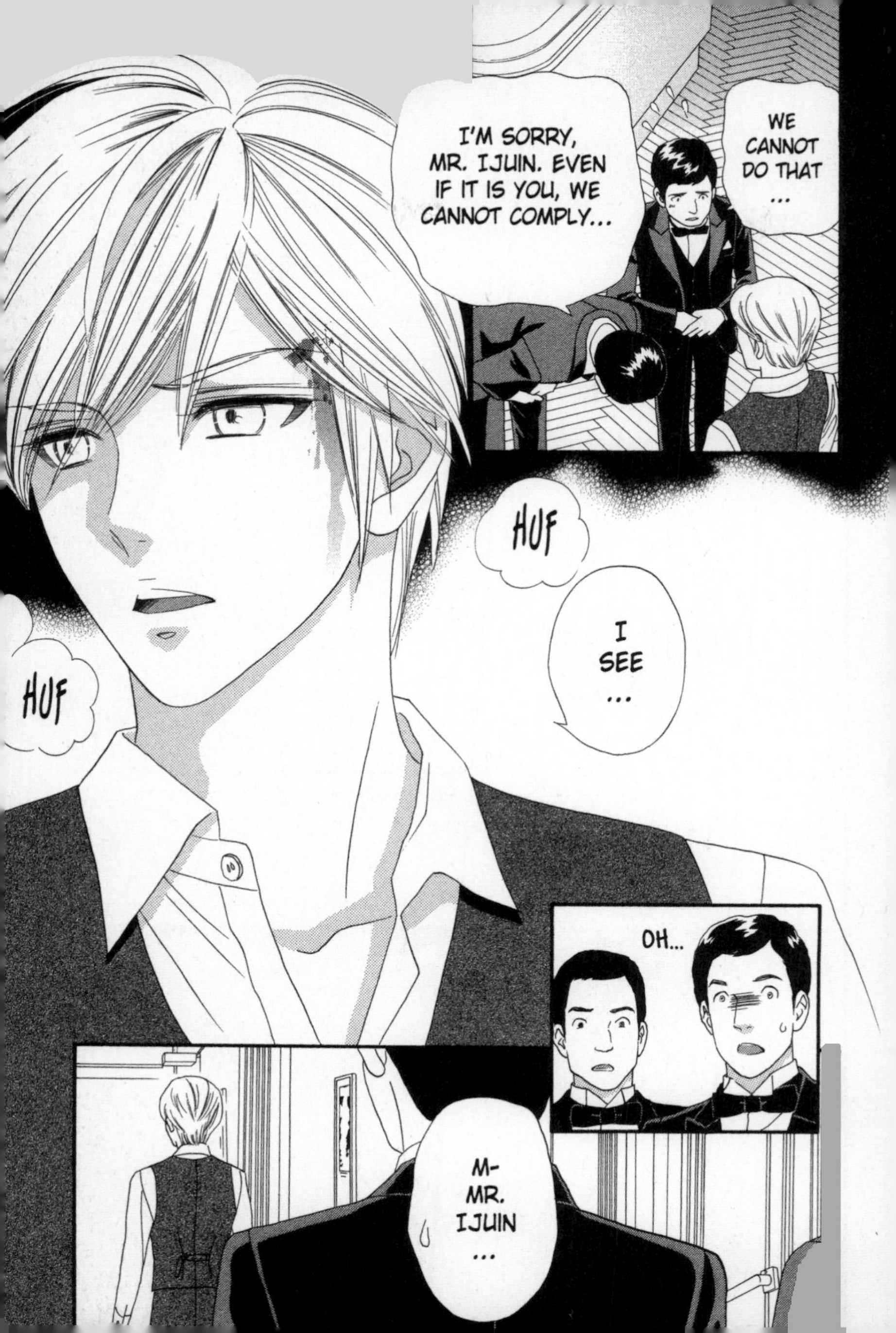
WE CANNOT DO THAT ...
I'M SORRY, MR. IJUIN. EVEN IF IT IS YOU, WE CANNOT COMPLY...
HUF
I SEE ...
HUF
OH...
M- MR. IJUIN ...

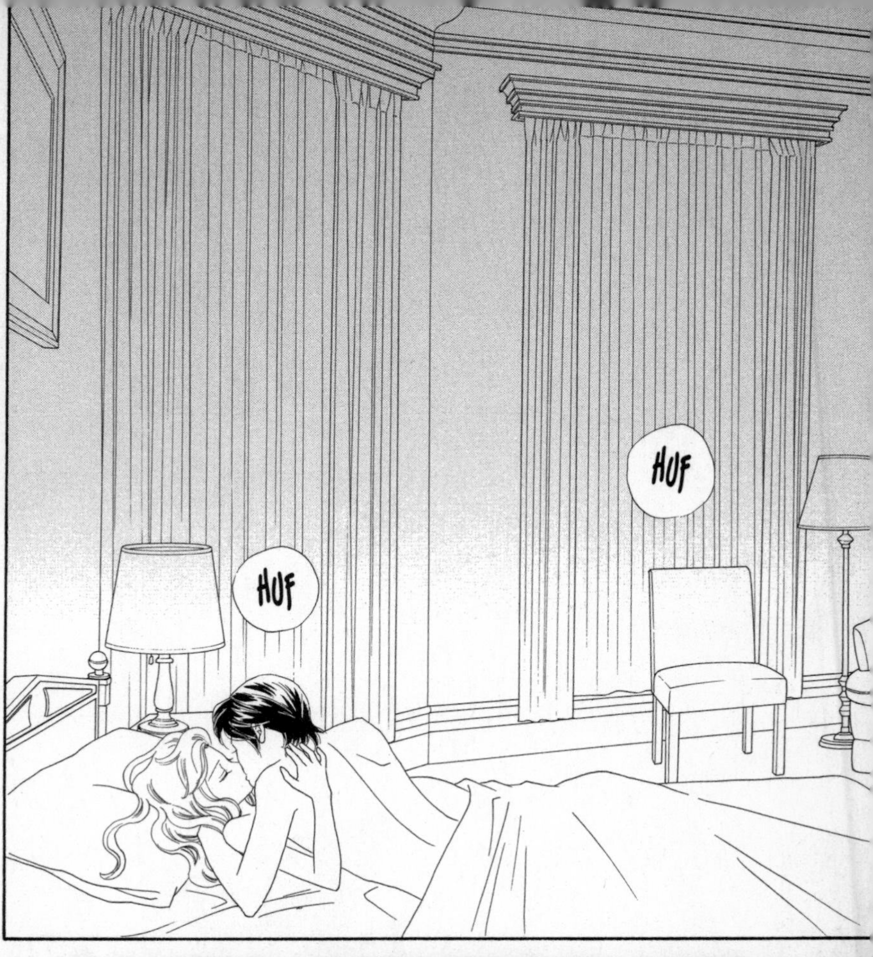
HUF
HUF
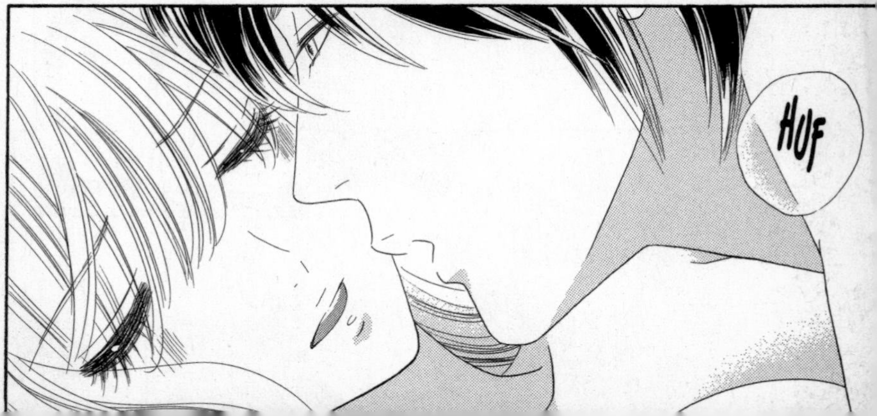
HUF

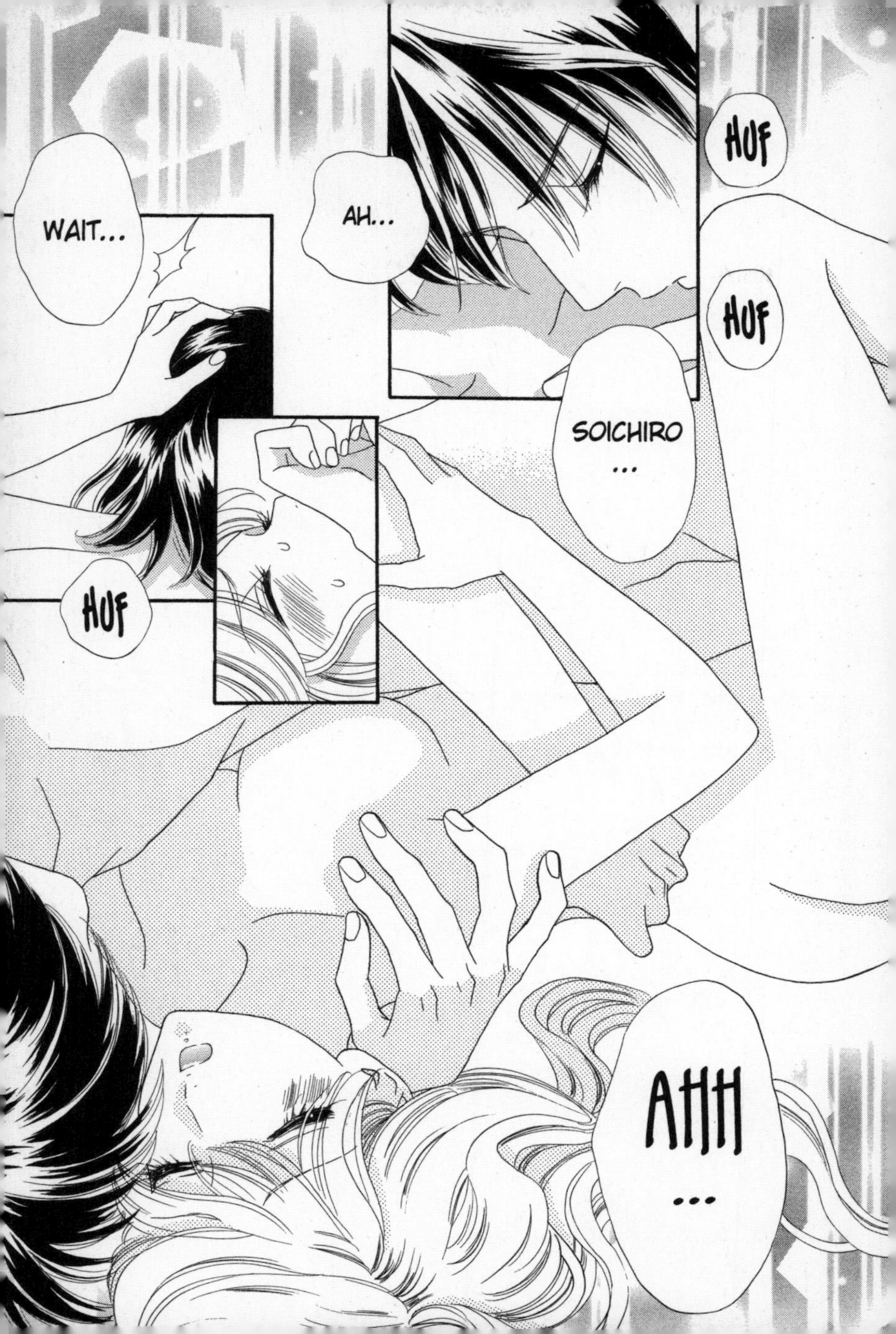
HUF
HUF
AH...
SOICHIRO ...
WAIT...
HUF
AHH ...

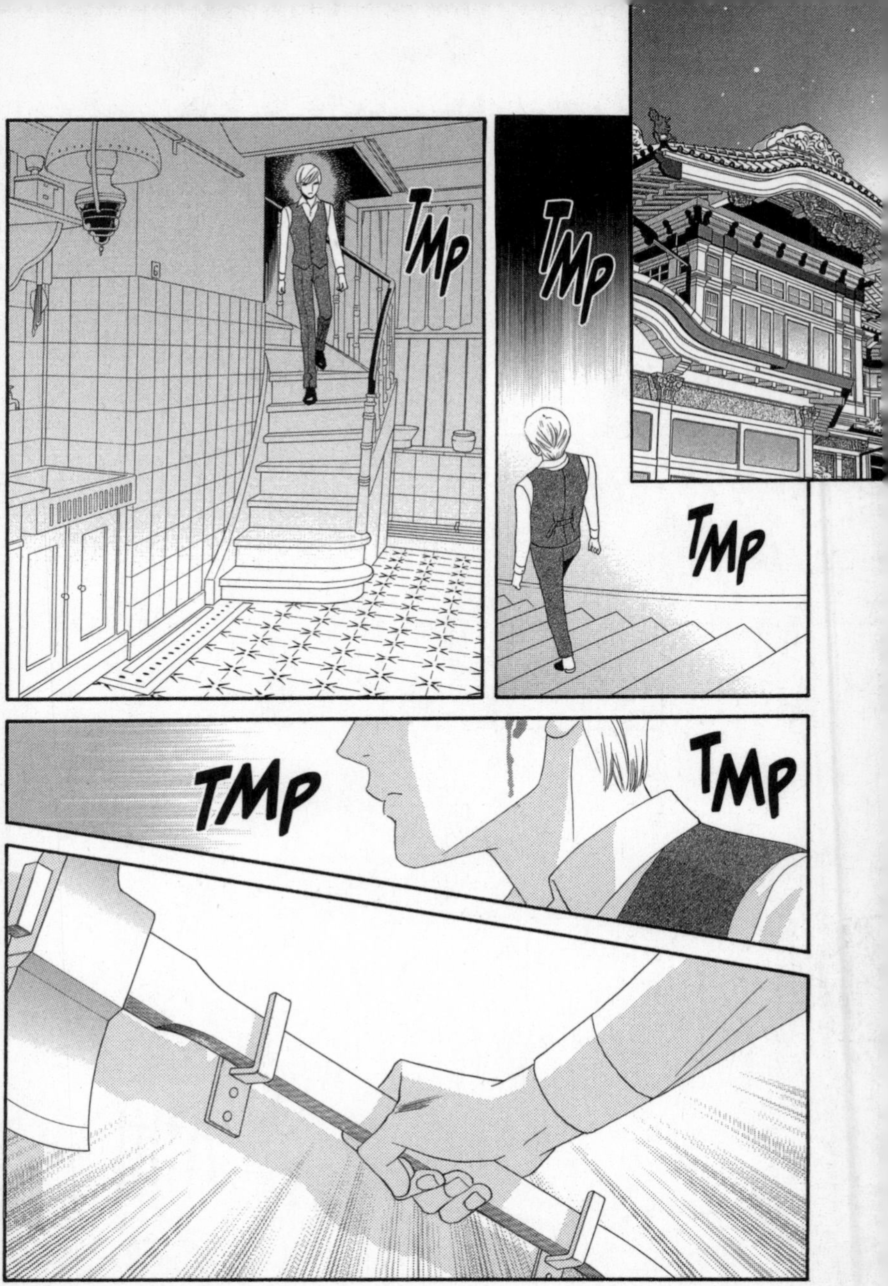
TMP
TMP
TMP
TMP
TMP

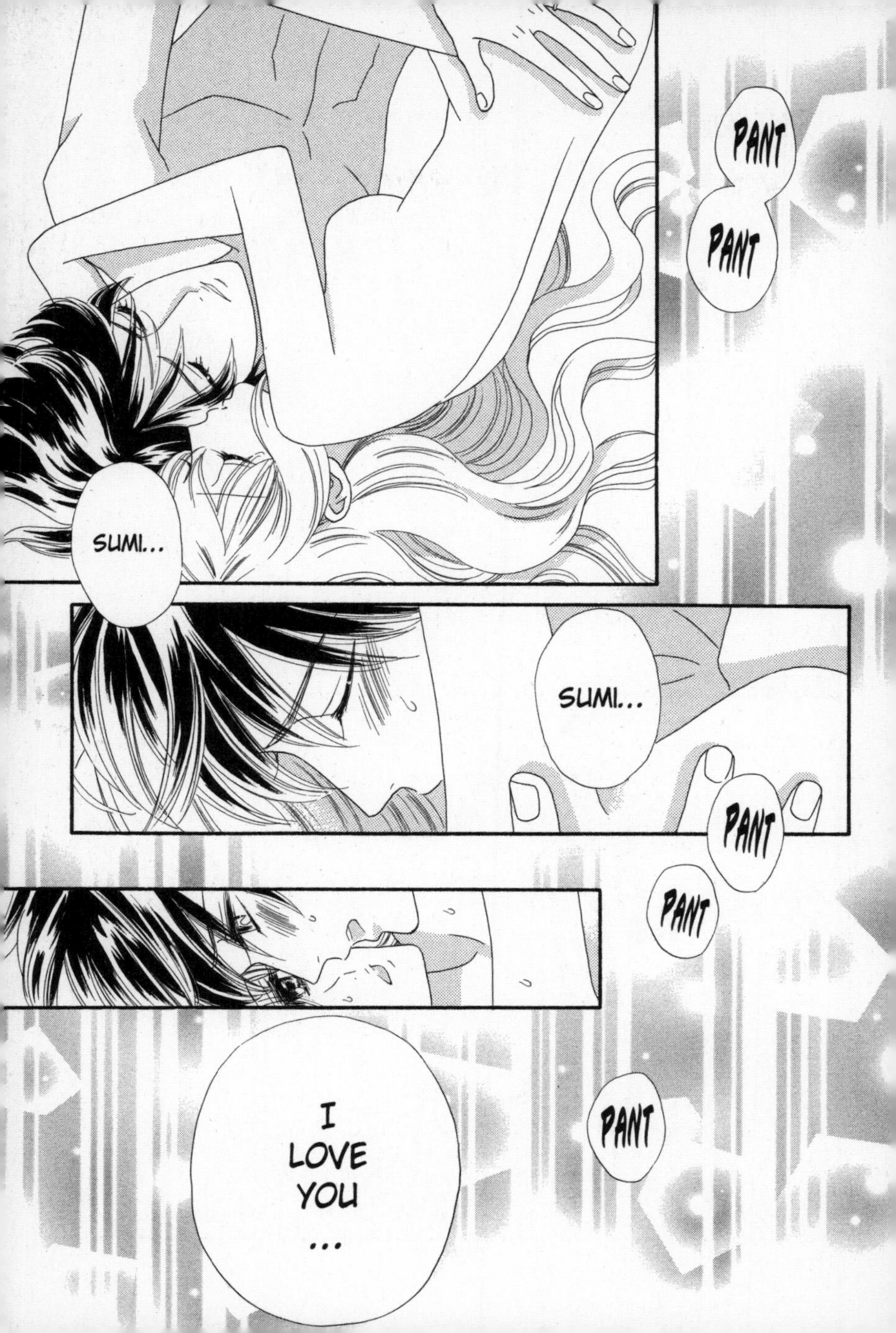
PANT
PANT
SUMI...
SUMI...
PANT
PANT
PANT
I LOVE YOU ...

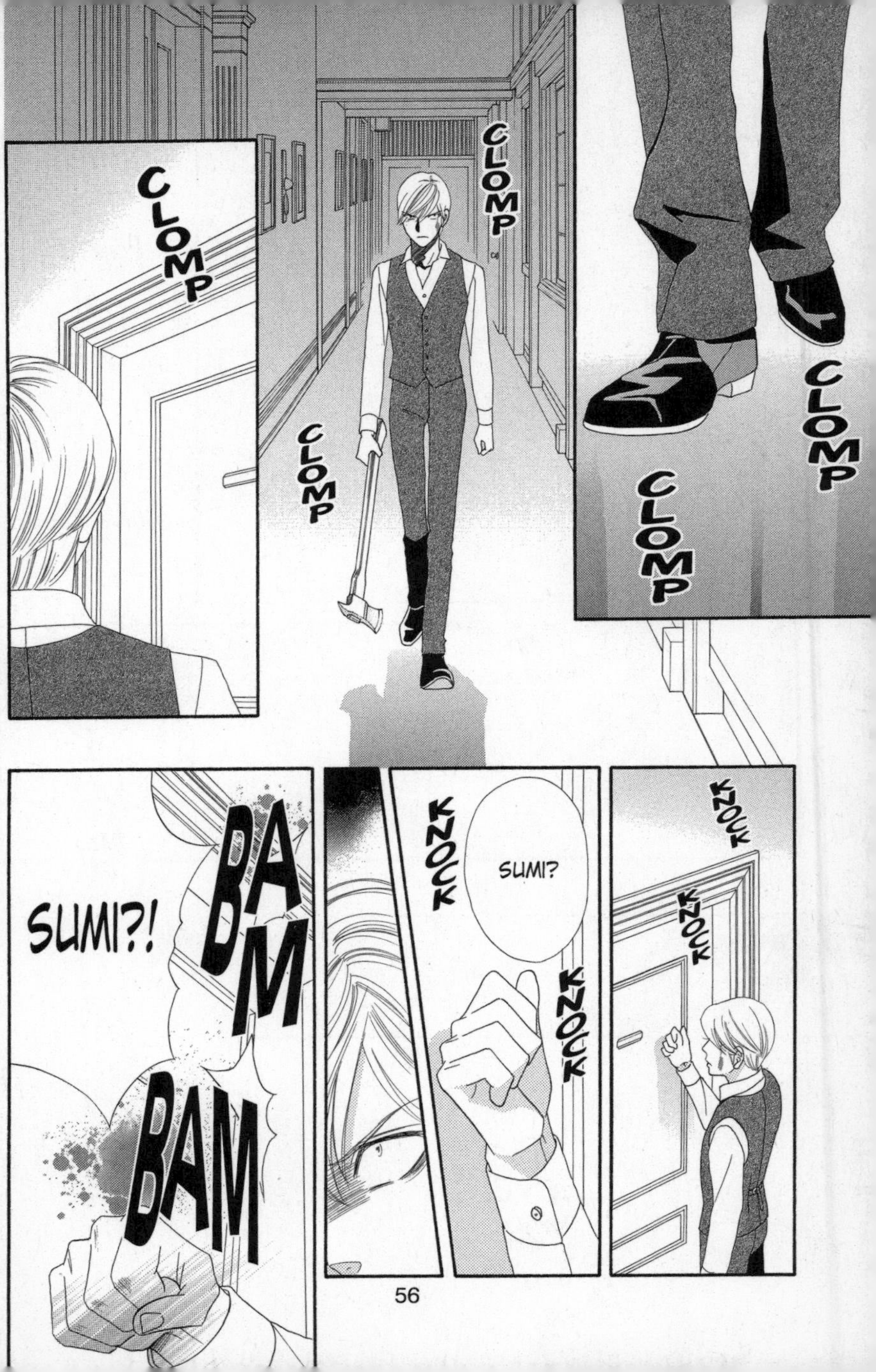
CLOMP
CLOMP
CLOMP
CLOMP
CLOMP
KNOCK
KNOCK
SUMI?
KNOCK
KNOCK
SUMI?!
BADM
BAM

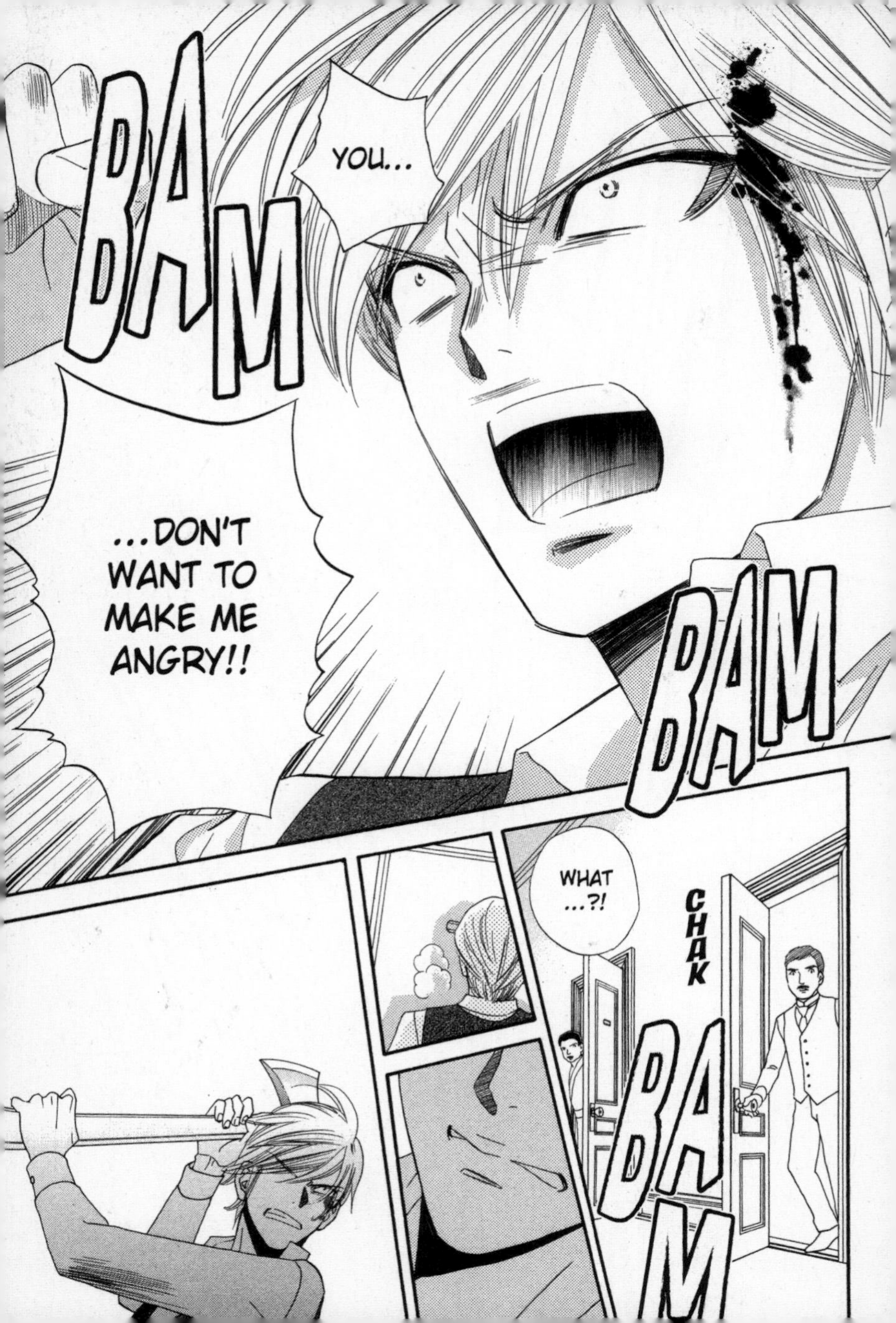
YOU...
BAM
...DON'T WANT TO MAKE ME ANGRY!!
BAM
WHAT ...?!
CHAK
BAM

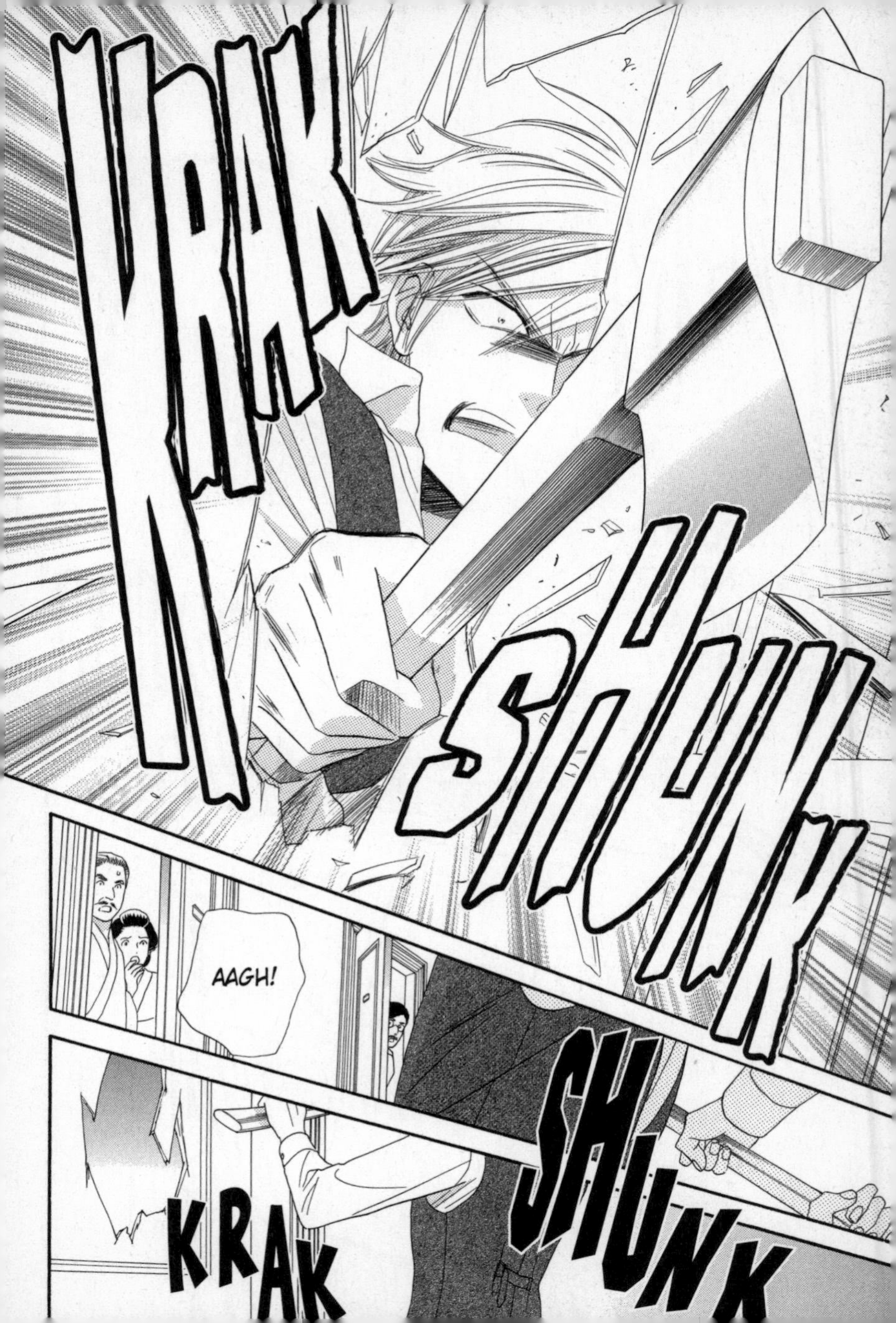
KRAK
SHUNK
AAGH!
SHUNK
KRAK

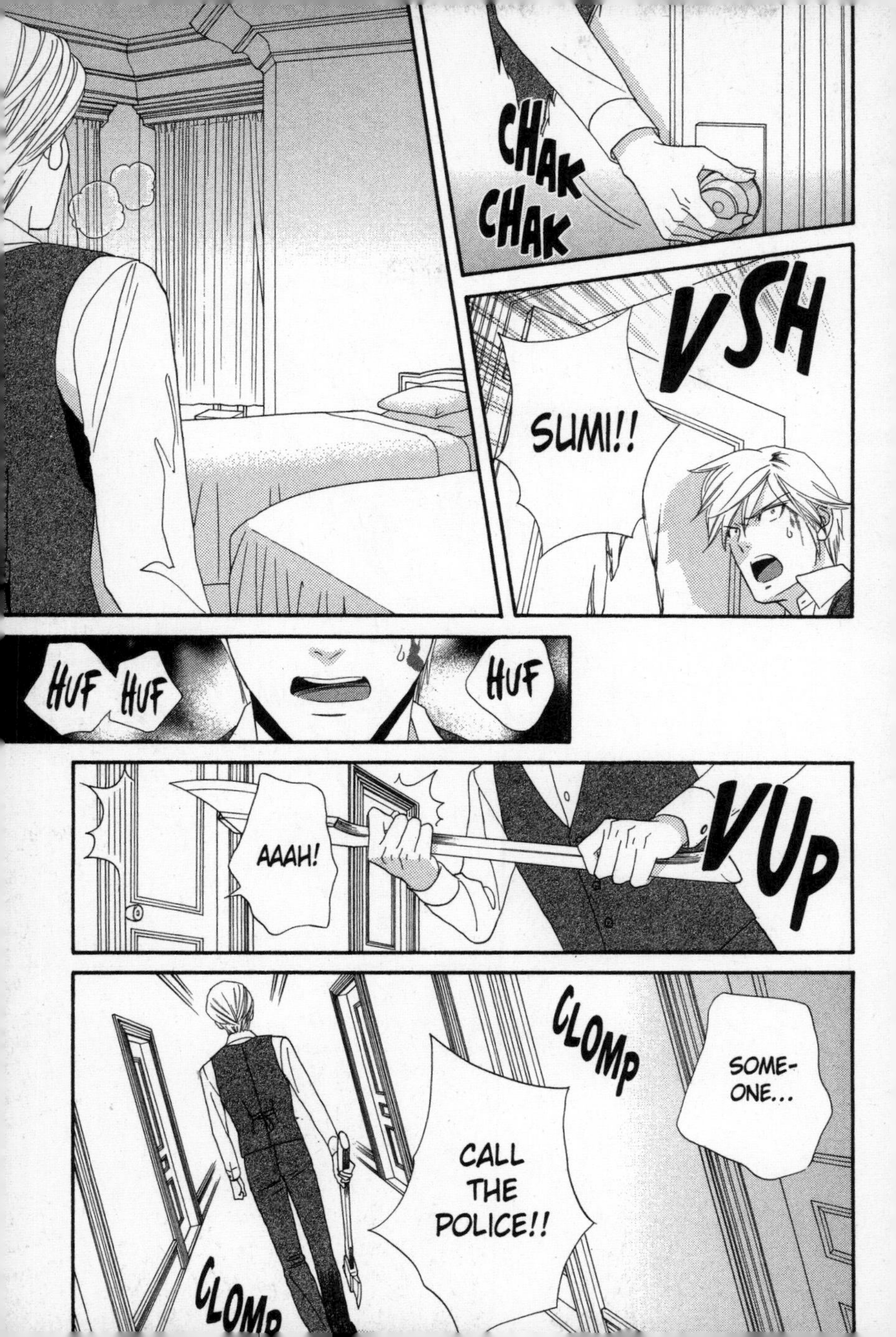
CHAK
CHAK
VSH
SUMI!!
HUF
HUF
HUF
VUP
AAAH!
SOME-ONE...
CLOMP
CALL THE POLICE!!
CLOMP

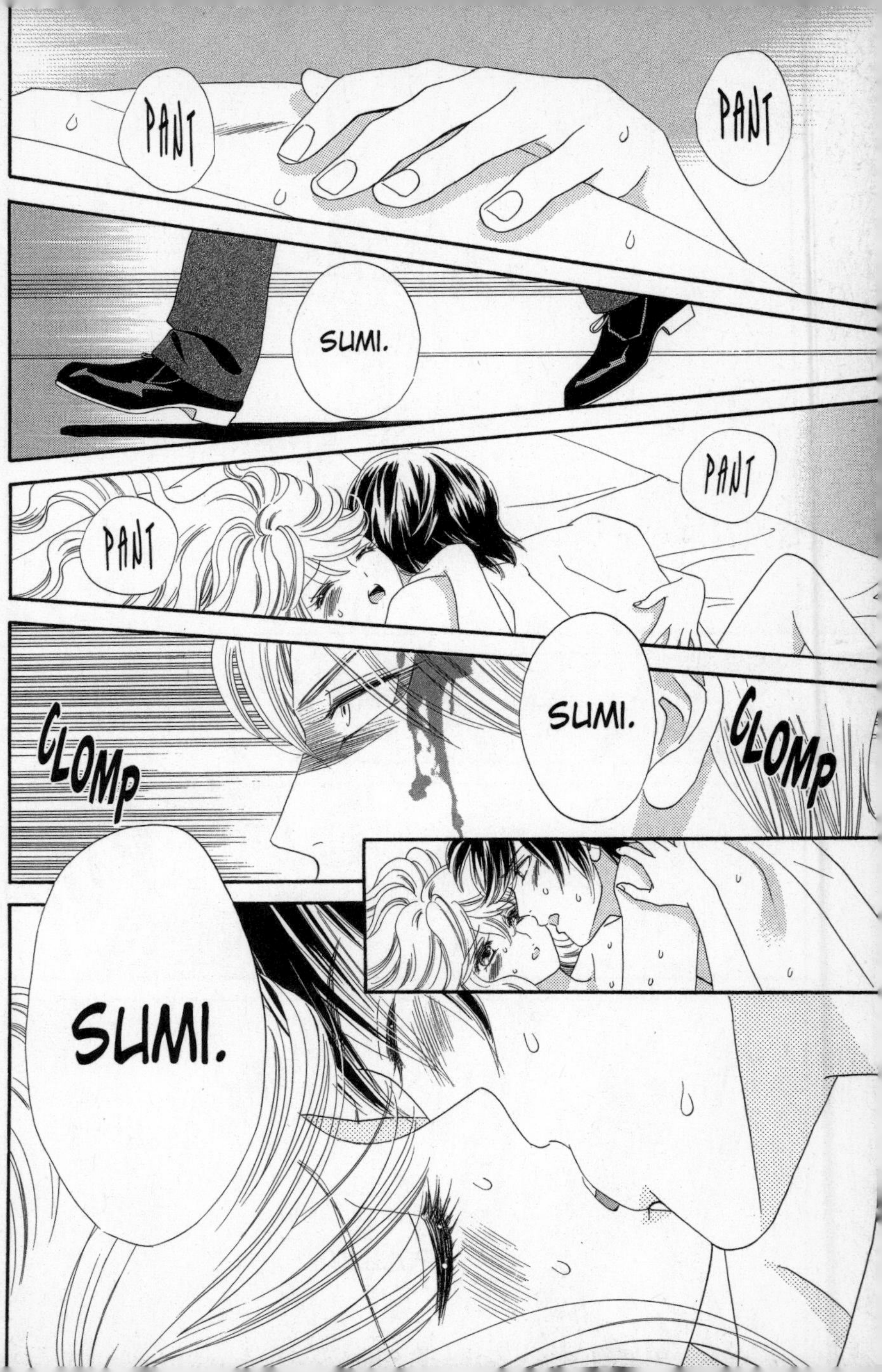
PANT
PANT
SUMI.
PANT
PANT
CLOMP
SUMI.
CLOMP
SUMI.

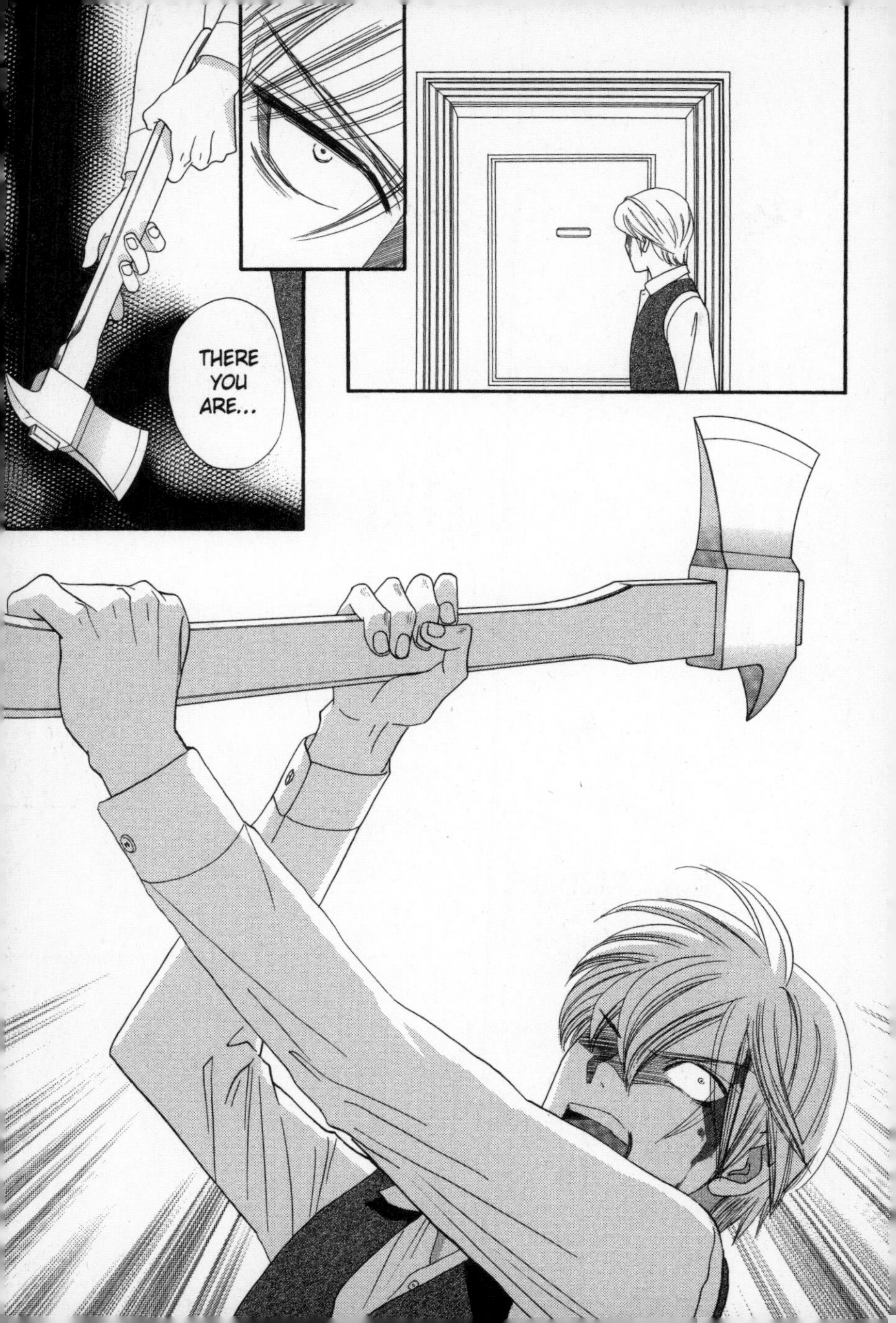
THERE YOU ARE...

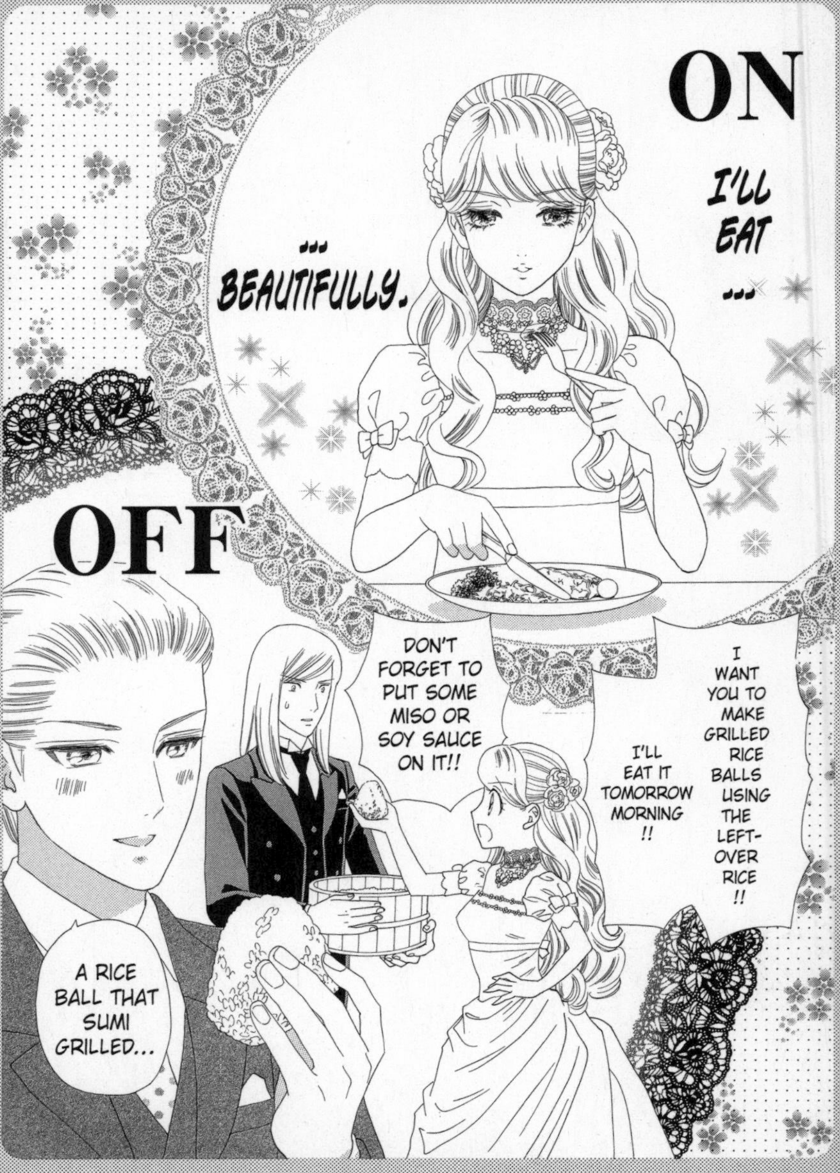
ON
I'LL EAT ...
... BEAUTIFULLY.
OFF
I WANT YOU TO MAKE GRILLED RICE BALLS USING THE LEFT-OVER RICE!!
I'LL EAT IT TOMORROW MORNING!!
DON'T FORGET TO PUT SOME MISO OR SOY SAUCE ON IT!!
A RICE BALL THAT SUMI GRILLED...

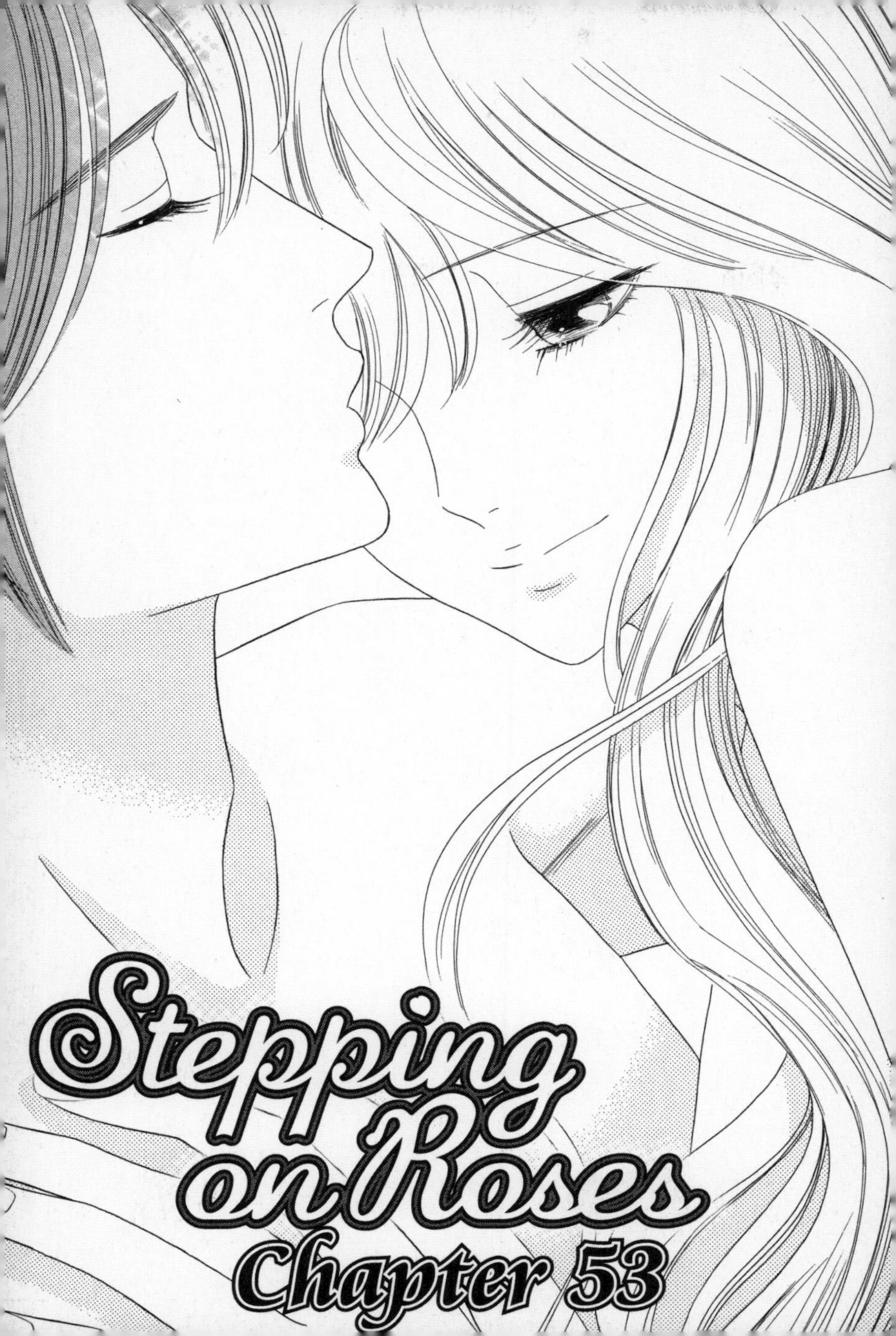
Stepping on Roses
Chapter 53

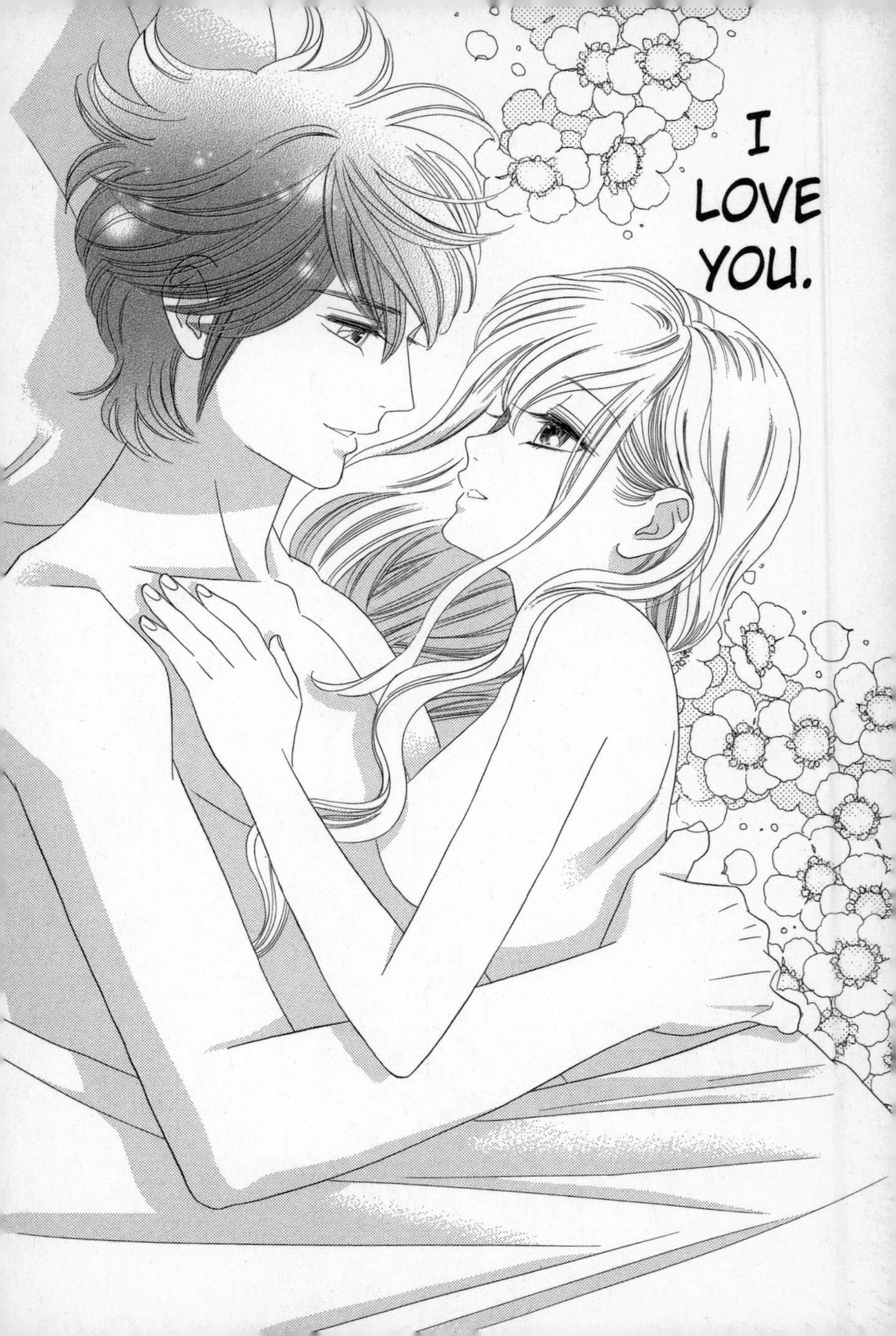
I LOVE YOU.

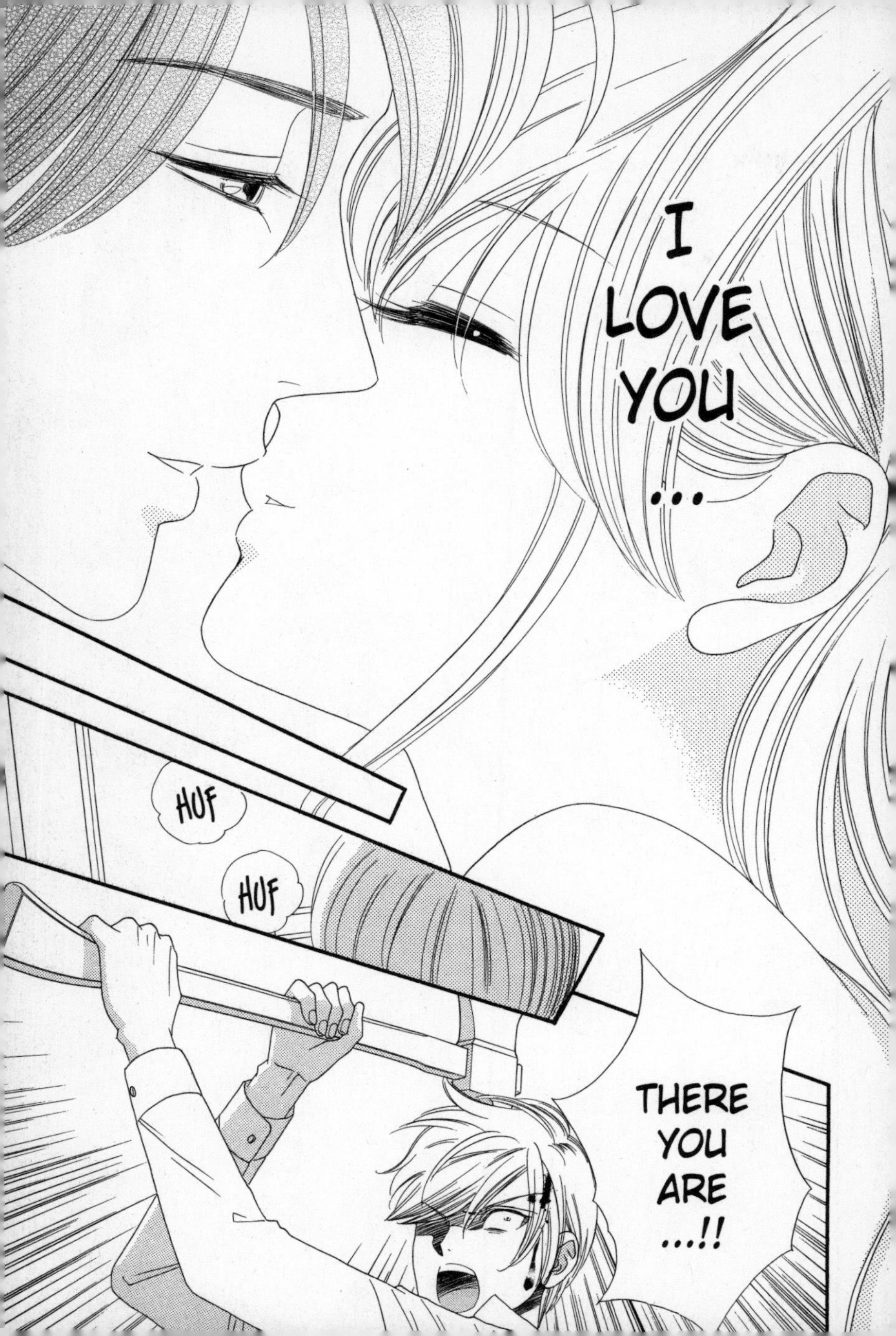
I LOVE YOU ...
HUF
HUF
THERE YOU ARE ...!!

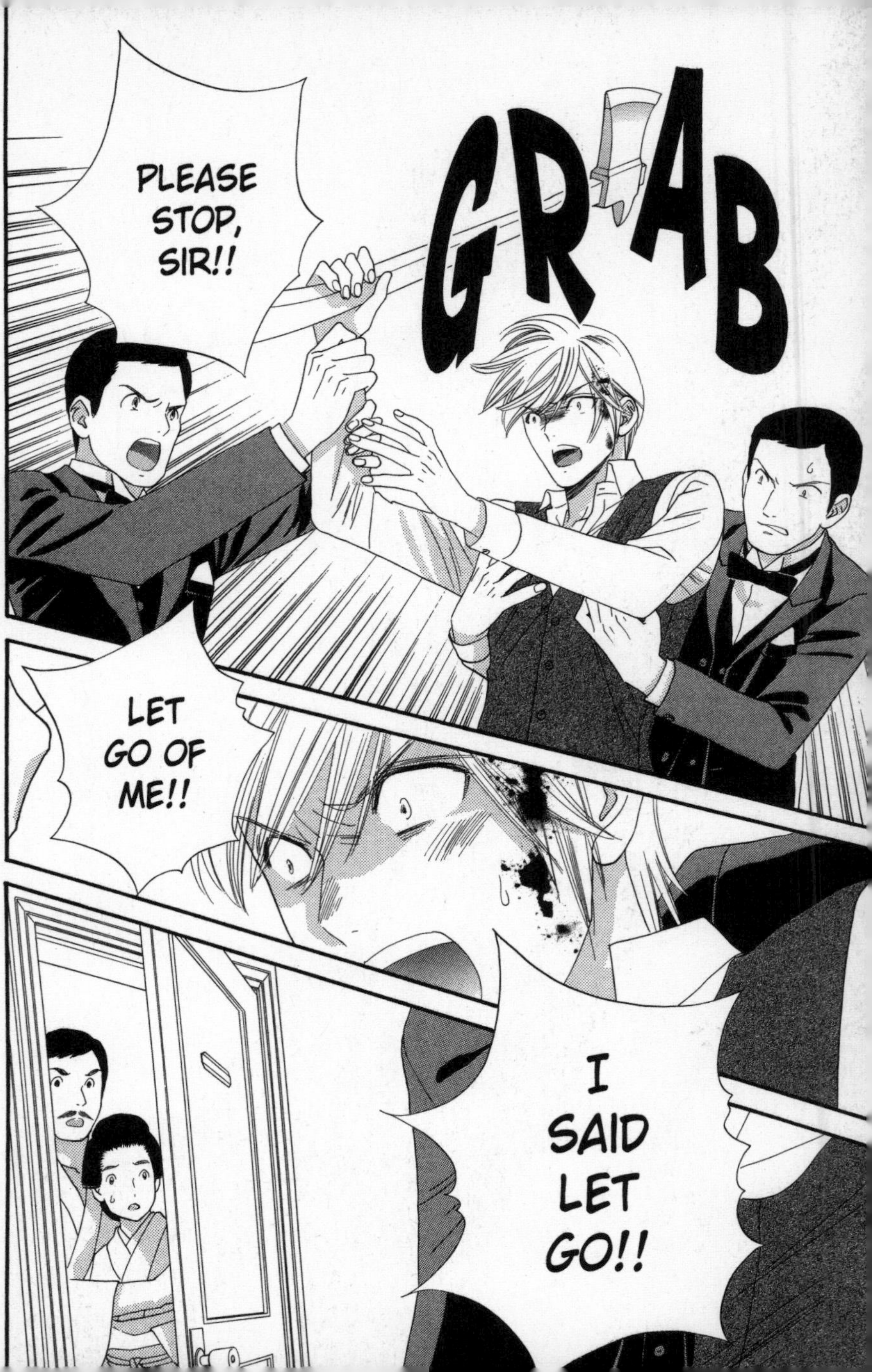
GRAB
PLEASE STOP, SIR!!
LET GO OF ME!!
I SAID LET GO!!

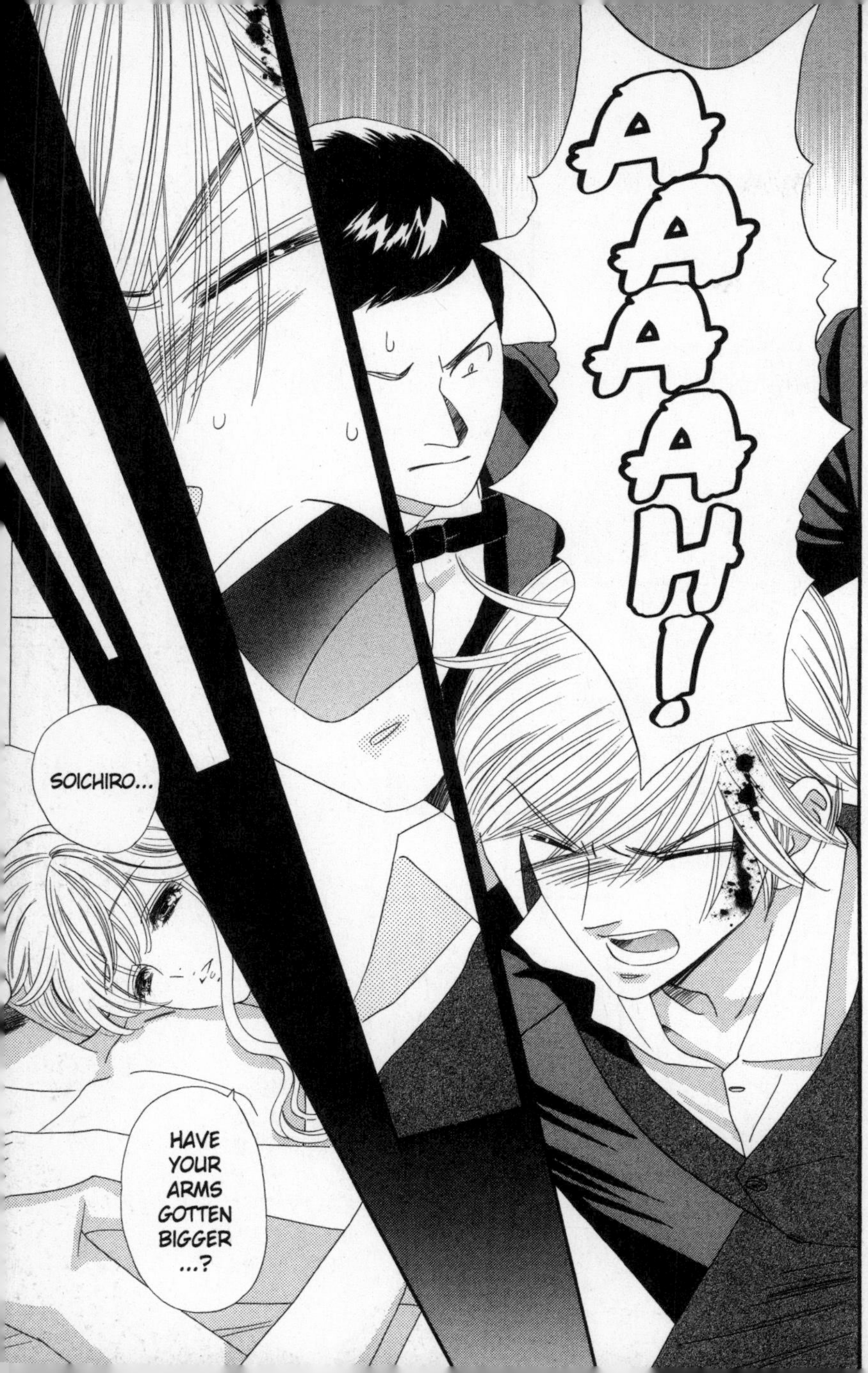
AAAAAH!
SOICHIRO...
HAVE YOUR ARMS GOTTEN BIGGER ...?

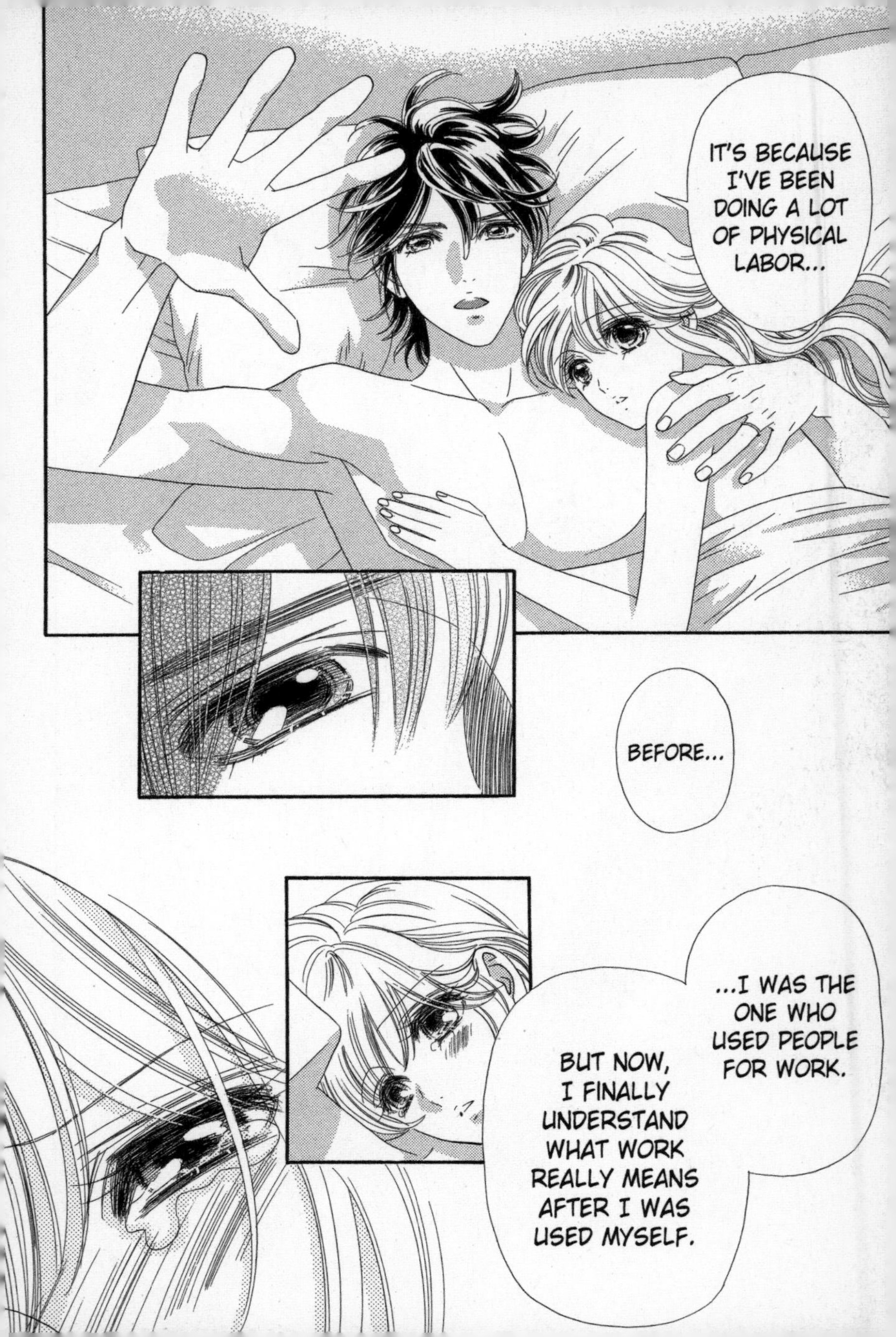
IT'S BECAUSE I'VE BEEN DOING A LOT OF PHYSICAL LABOR...
BEFORE...
...I WAS THE ONE WHO USED PEOPLE FOR WORK.
BUT NOW, I FINALLY UNDERSTAND WHAT WORK REALLY MEANS AFTER I WAS USED MYSELF.

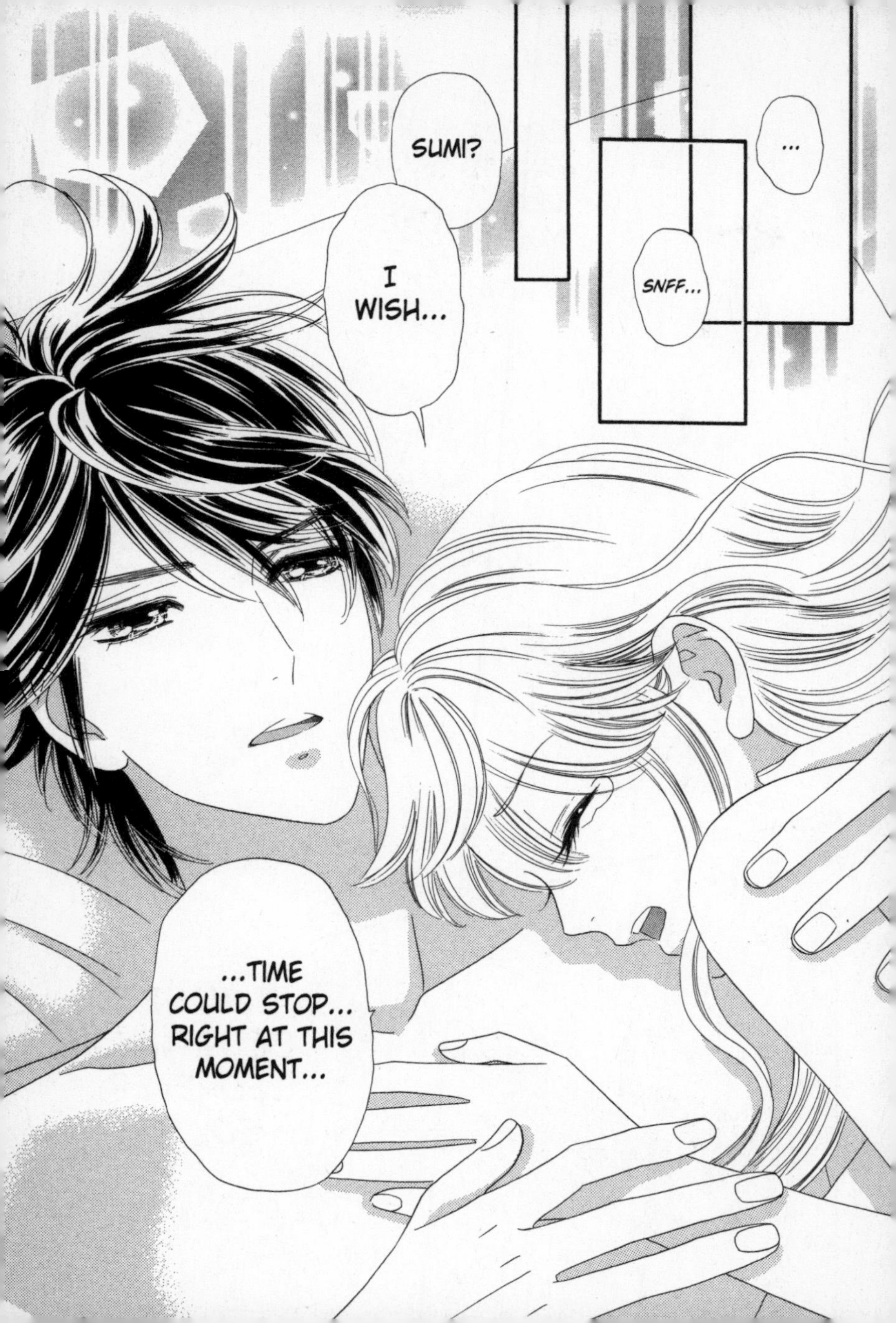
...
SNFF...
SUMI?
I WISH...
...TIME COULD STOP... RIGHT AT THIS MOMENT...

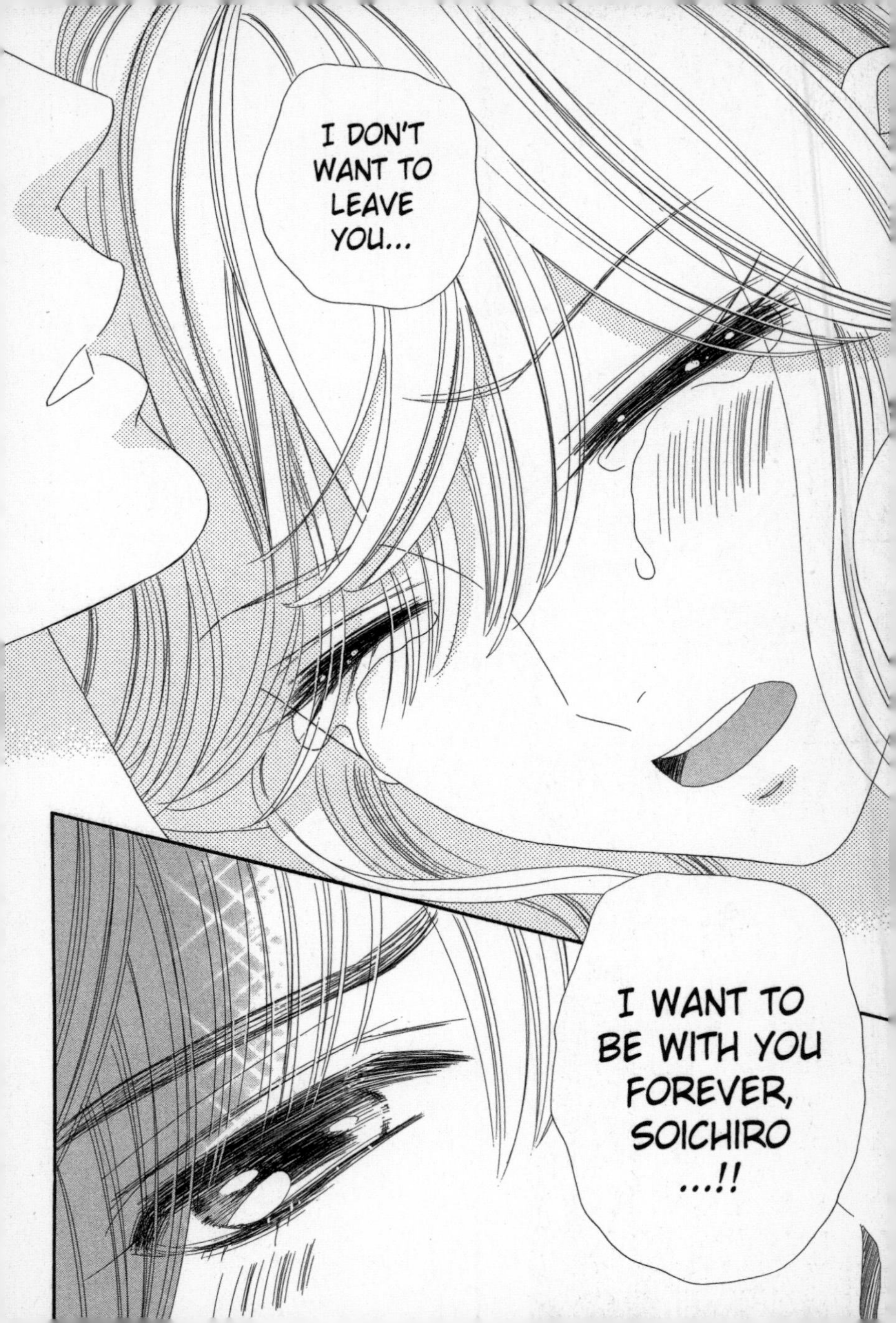
I DON'T WANT TO LEAVE YOU...
I WANT TO BE WITH YOU FOREVER, SOICHIRO ...!!

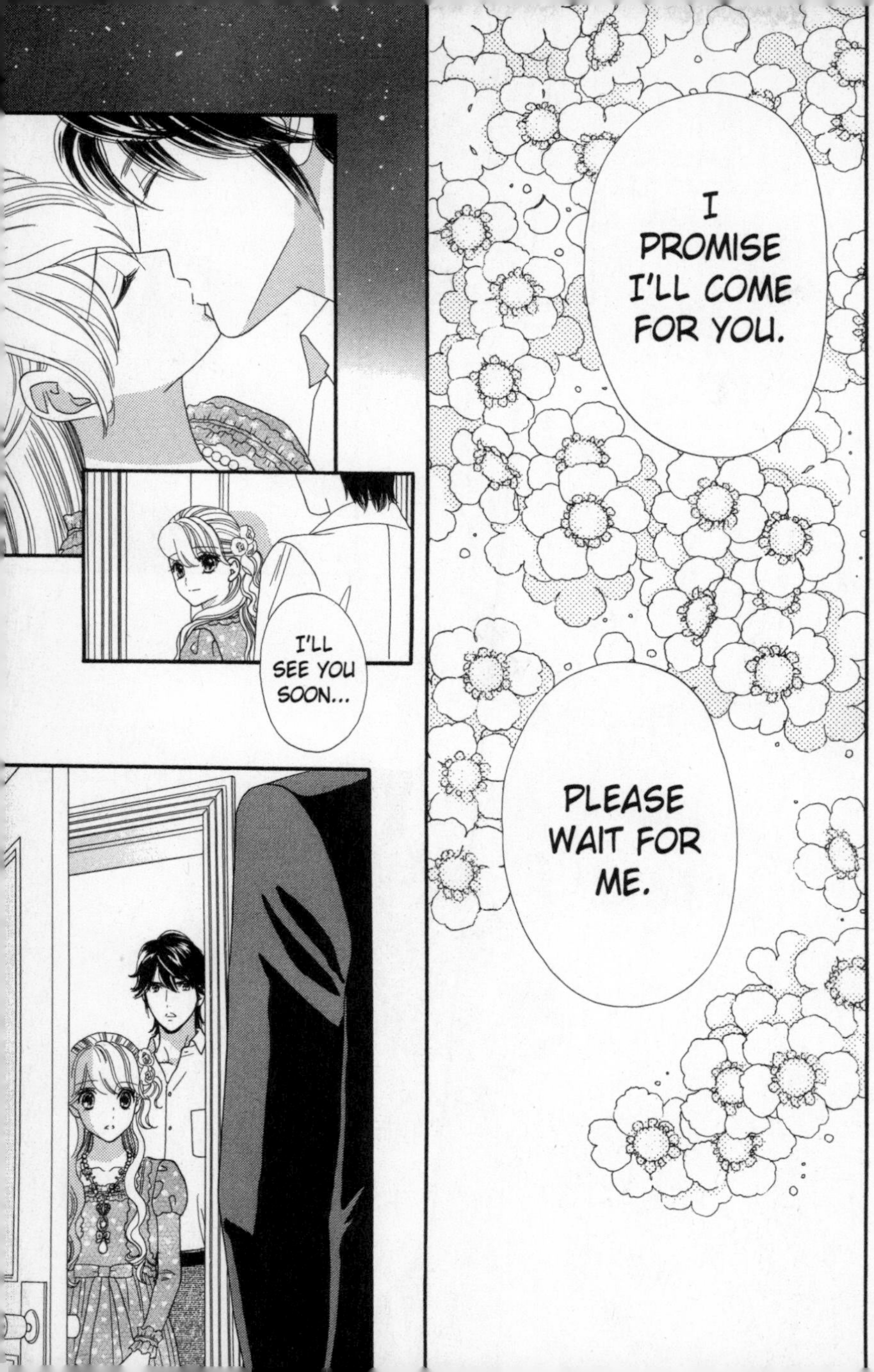
I PROMISE I'LL COME FOR YOU.
PLEASE WAIT FOR ME.
I'LL SEE YOU SOON...

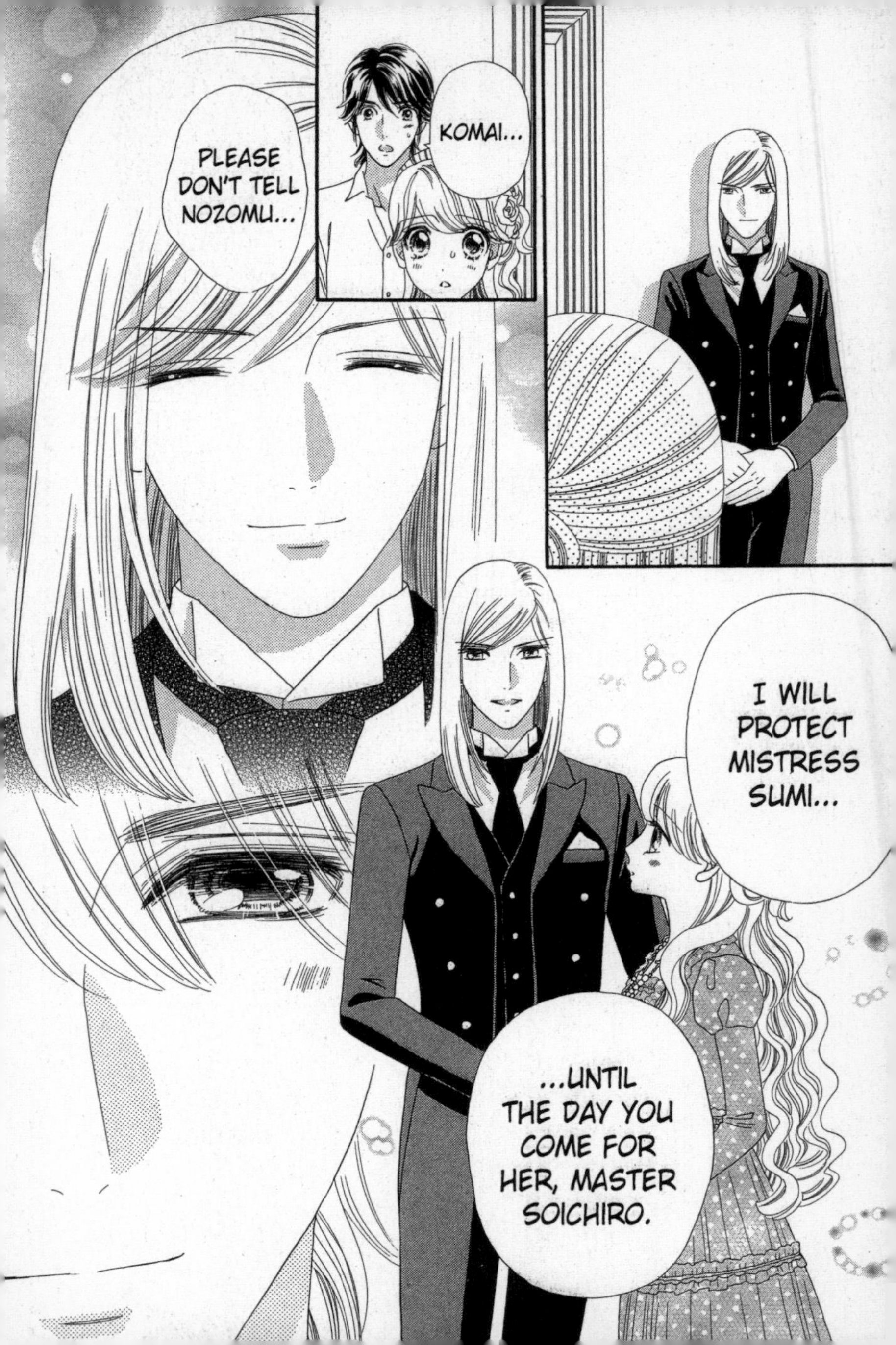
KOMAI...
I WILL PROTECT MISTRESS SUMI...
...UNTIL THE DAY YOU COME FOR HER, MASTER SOICHIRO.
PLEASE DON'T TELL NOZOMU...

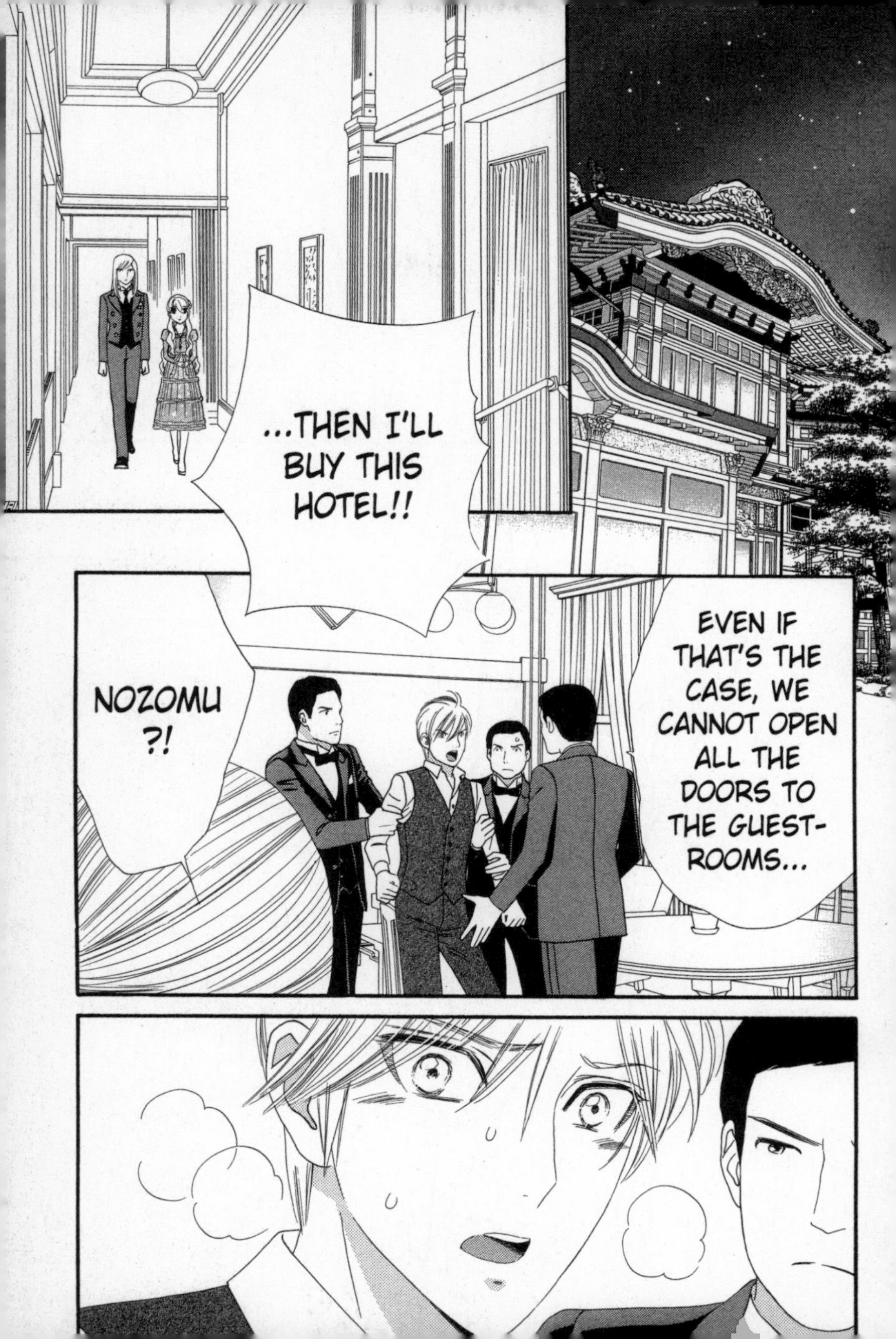
EVEN IF THAT'S THE CASE, WE CANNOT OPEN ALL THE DOORS TO THE GUEST-ROOMS...
...THEN I'LL BUY THIS HOTEL!!
NOZOMU ?!

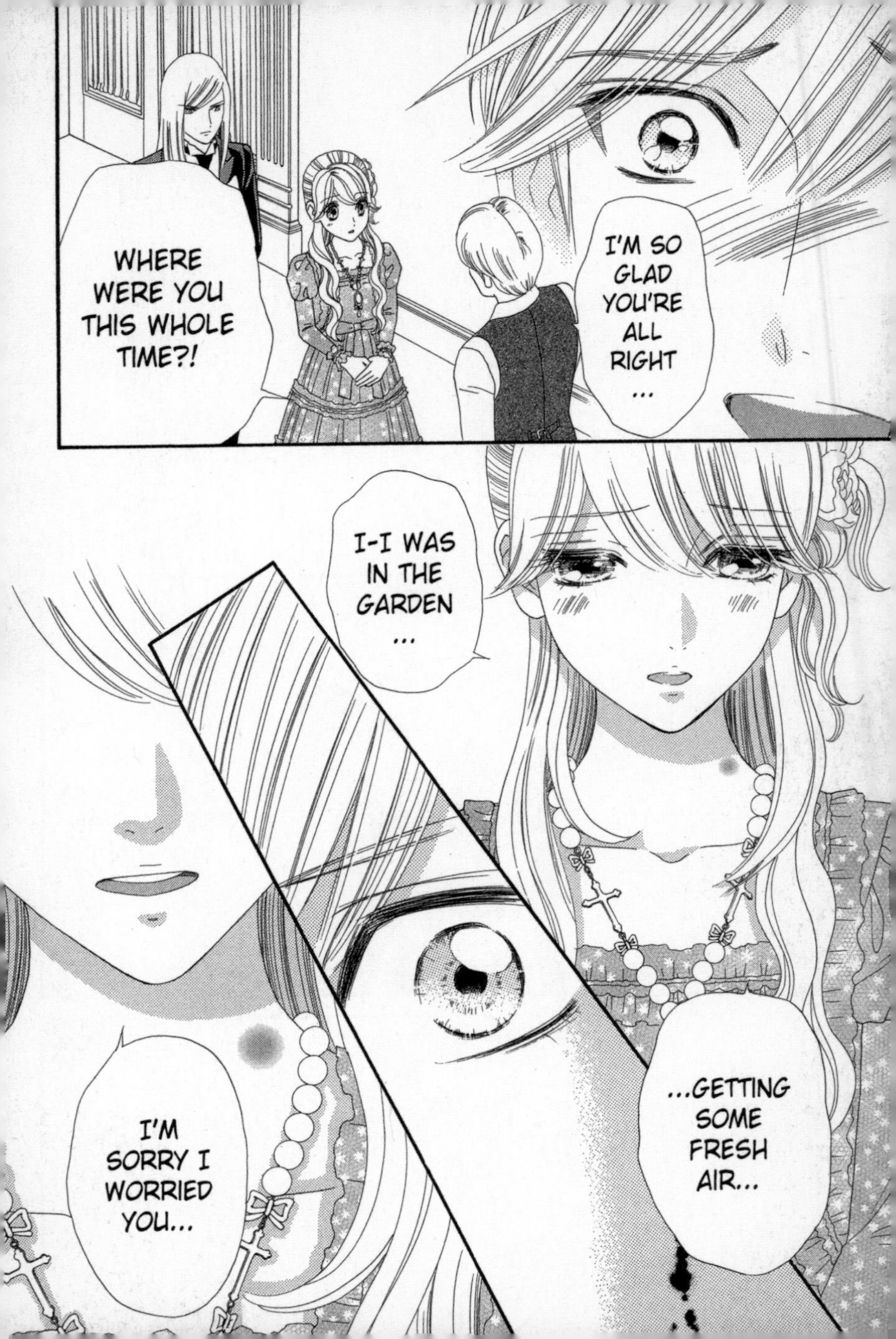
I'M SO GLAD YOU'RE ALL RIGHT...
WHERE WERE YOU THIS WHOLE TIME?!
I-I WAS IN THE GARDEN...
...GETTING SOME FRESH AIR...
I'M SORRY I WORRIED YOU...

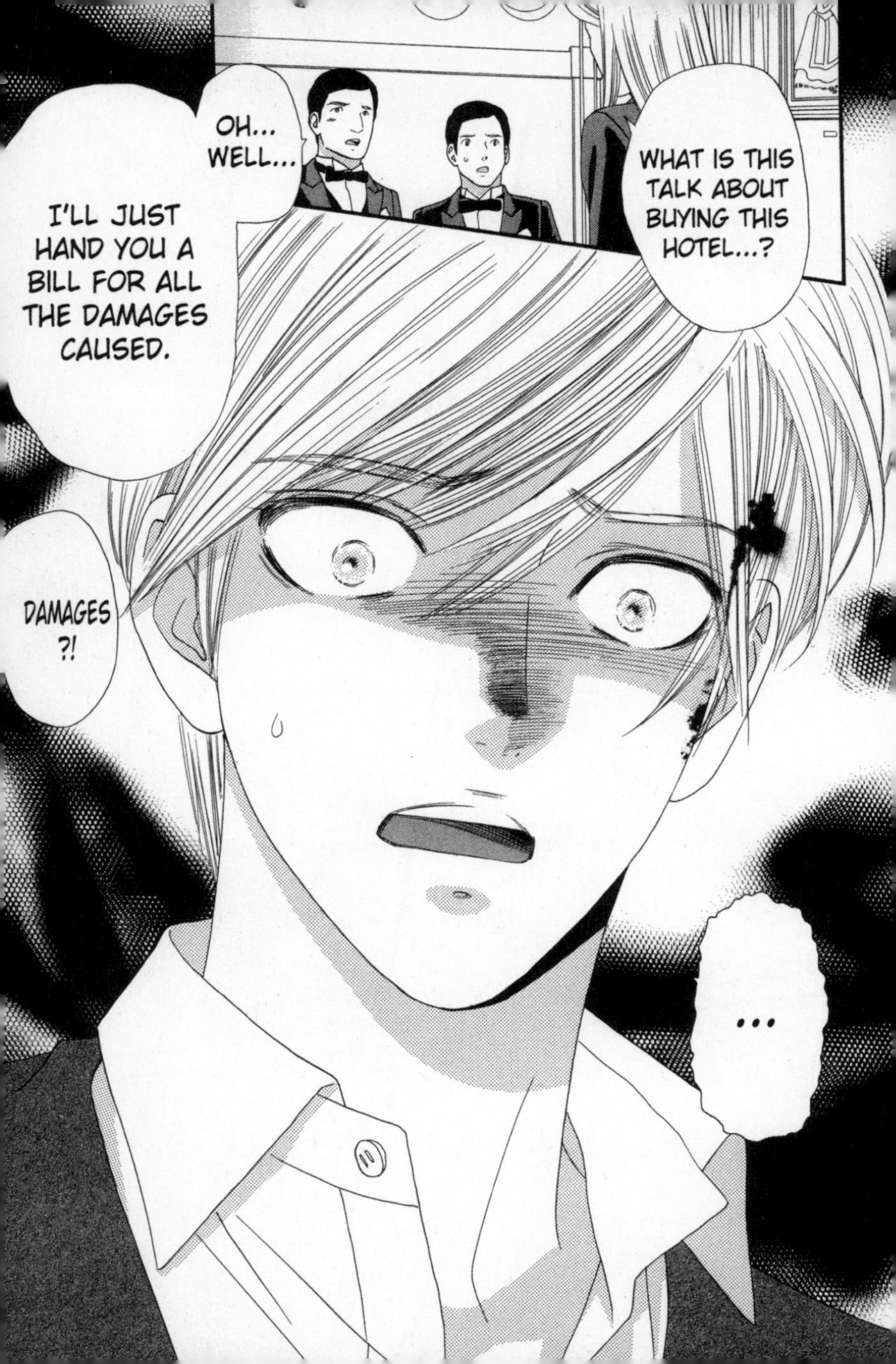

WHAT IS THIS TALK ABOUT BUYING THIS HOTEL...?
OH... WELL...
I'LL JUST HAND YOU A BILL FOR ALL THE DAMAGES CAUSED.
DAMAGES ?!
...

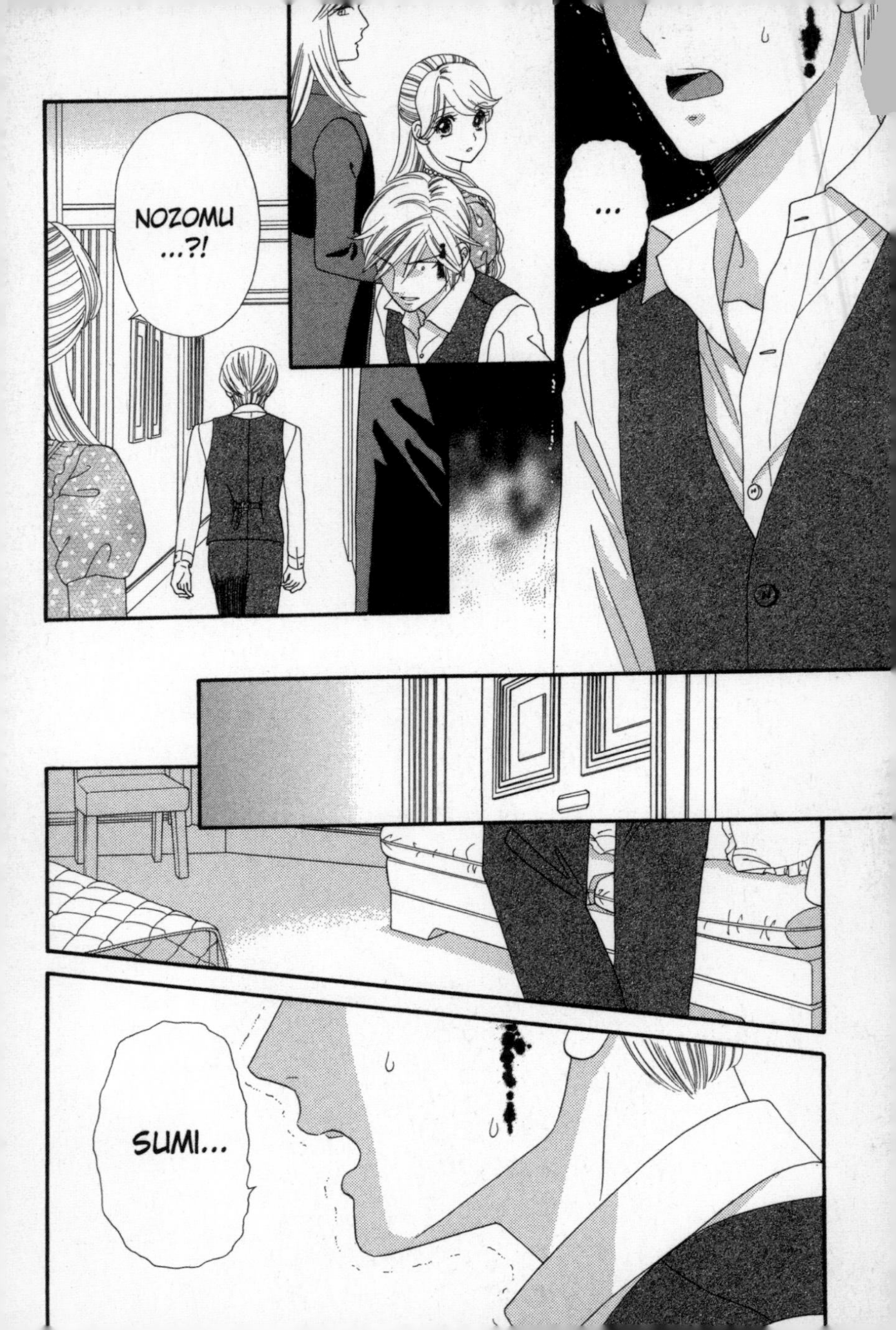
...
NOZOMU ...?!
SUMI...

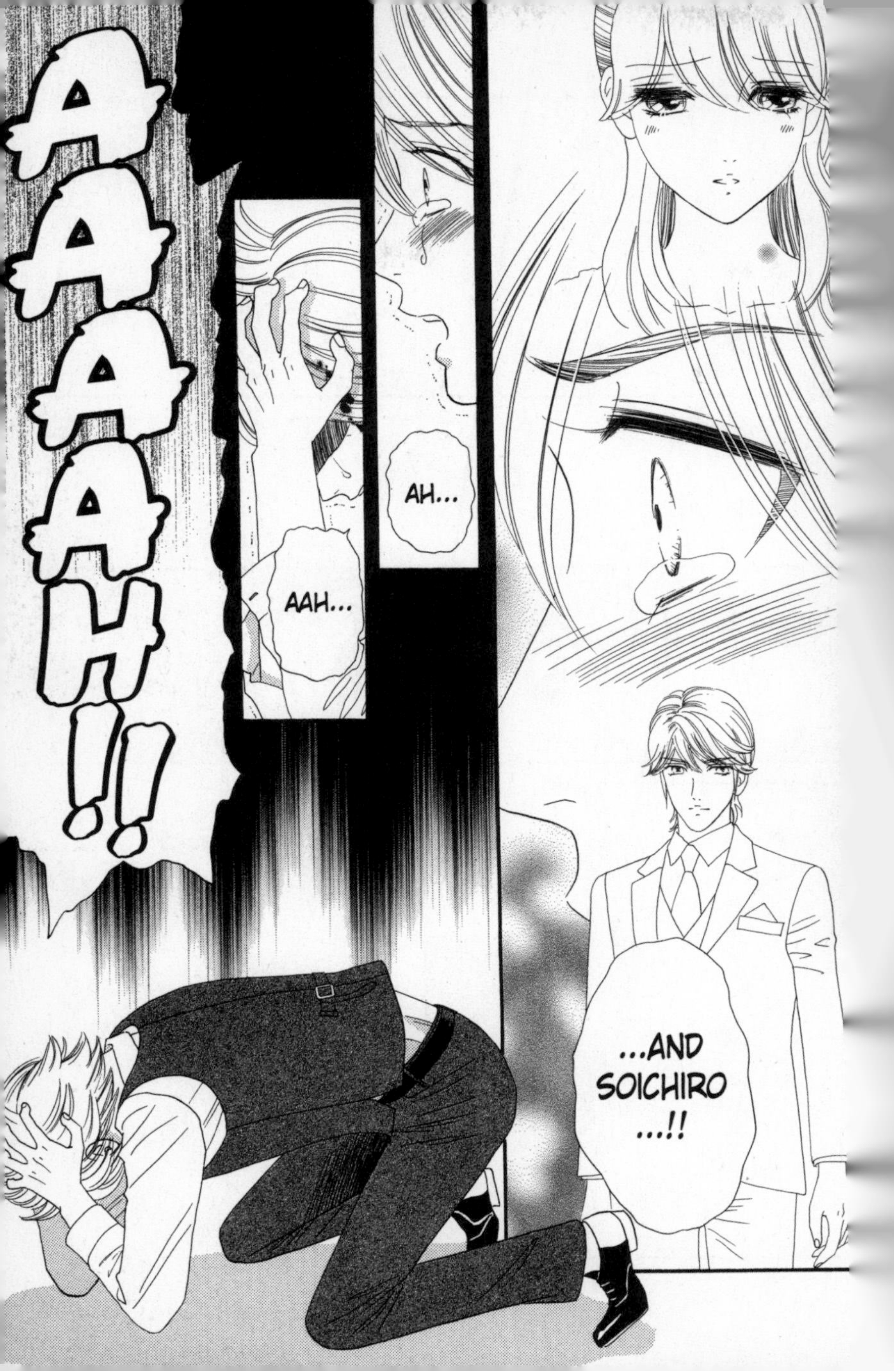
AH...
AAH...
AAAAH!!
...AND SOICHIRO ...!!

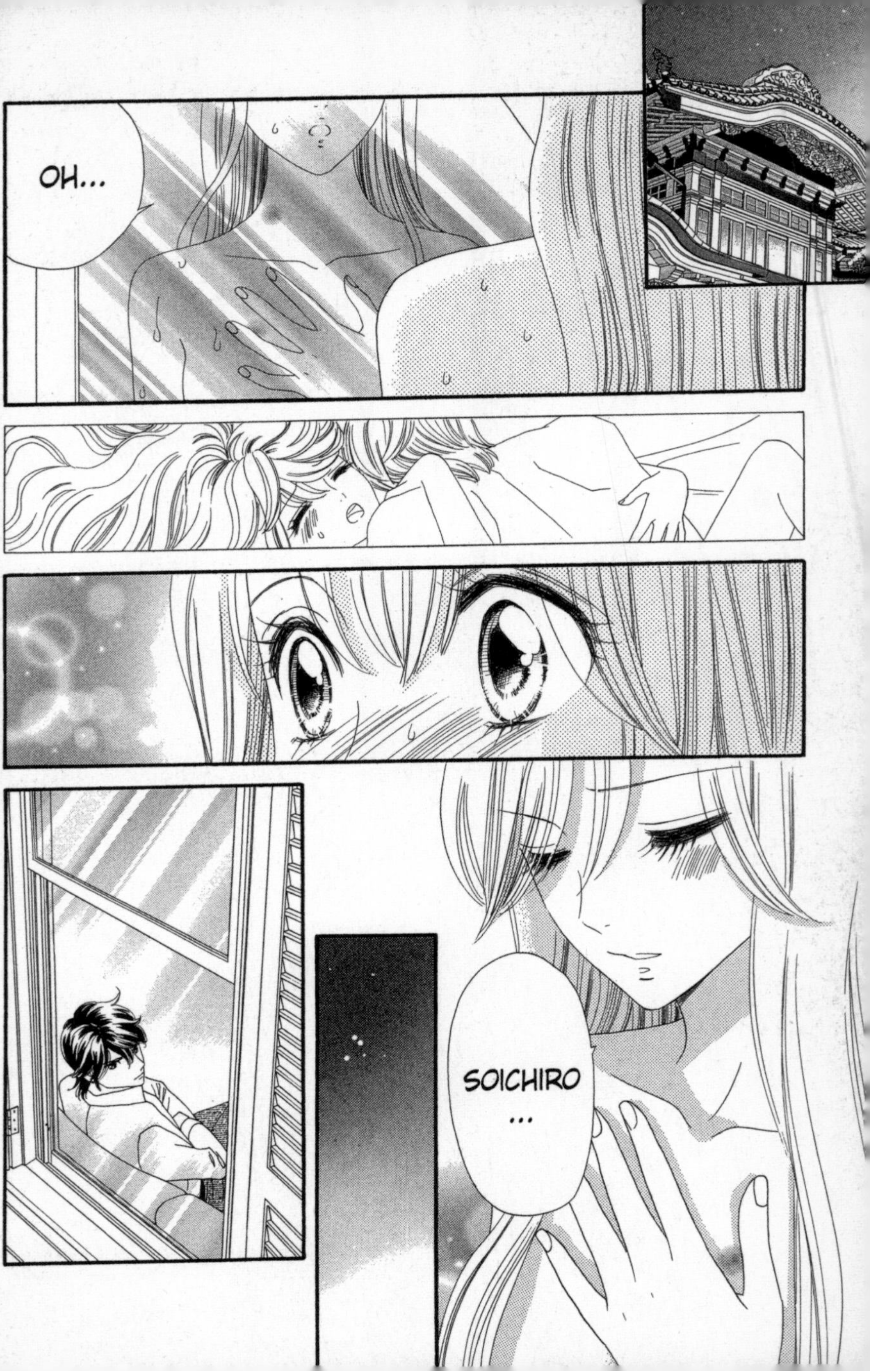
OH...
SOICHIRO
...

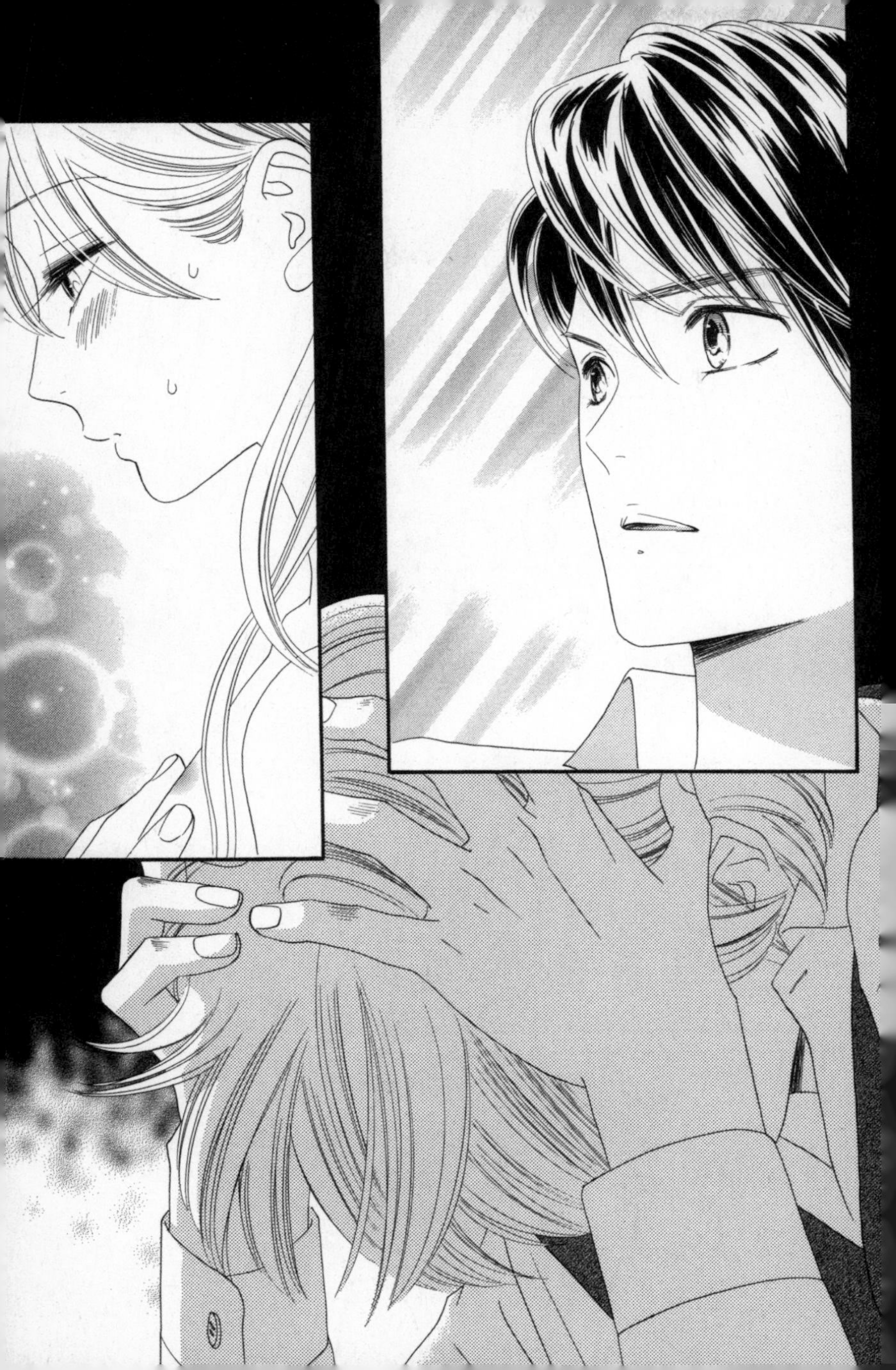

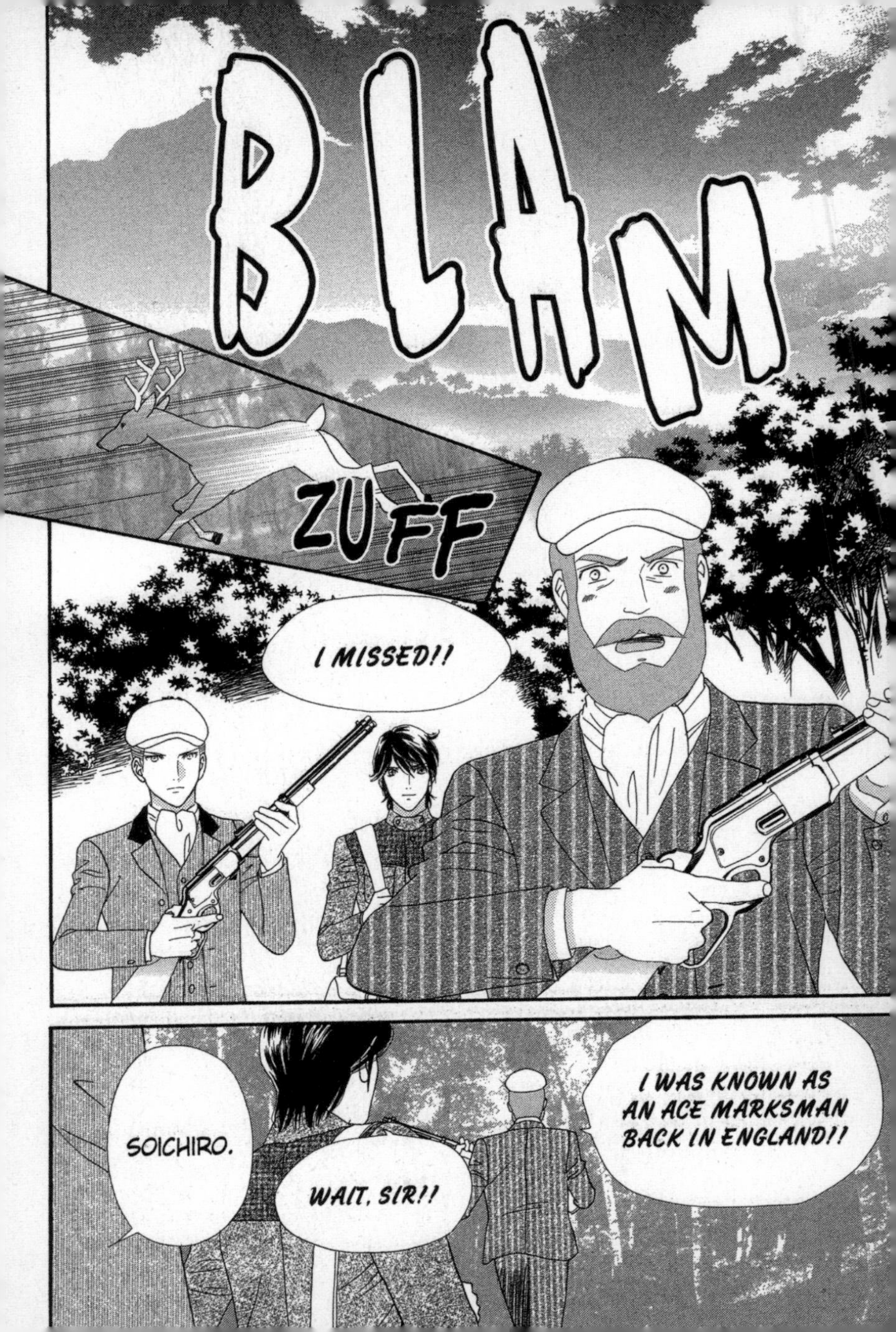
BLAM
ZUFF
I MISSED!!
I WAS KNOWN AS AN ACE MARKSMAN BACK IN ENGLAND!!
WAIT, SIR!!
SOICHIRO.

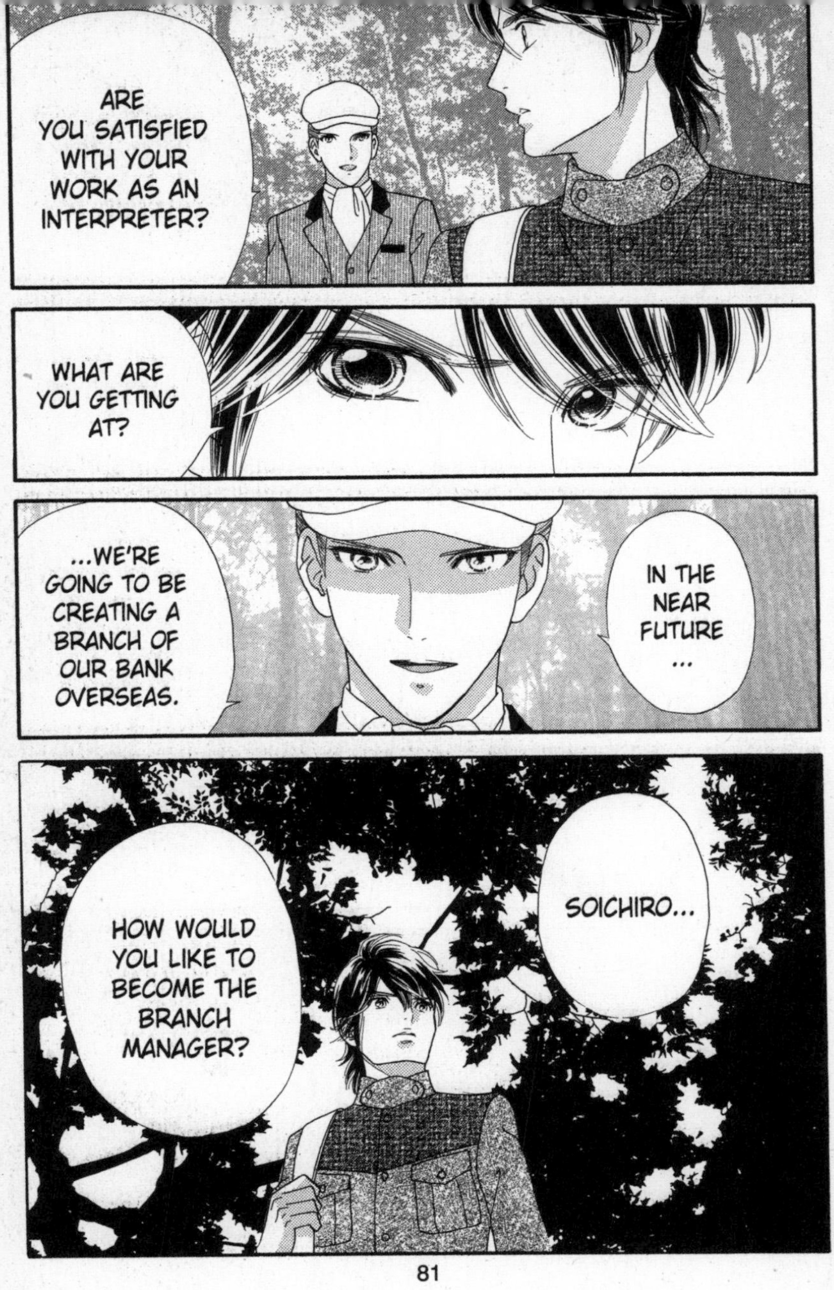
ARE YOU SATISFIED WITH YOUR WORK AS AN INTERPRETER?
WHAT ARE YOU GETTING AT?
IN THE NEAR FUTURE...
...WE'RE GOING TO BE CREATING A BRANCH OF OUR BANK OVERSEAS.
SOICHIRO...
HOW WOULD YOU LIKE TO BECOME THE BRANCH MANAGER?

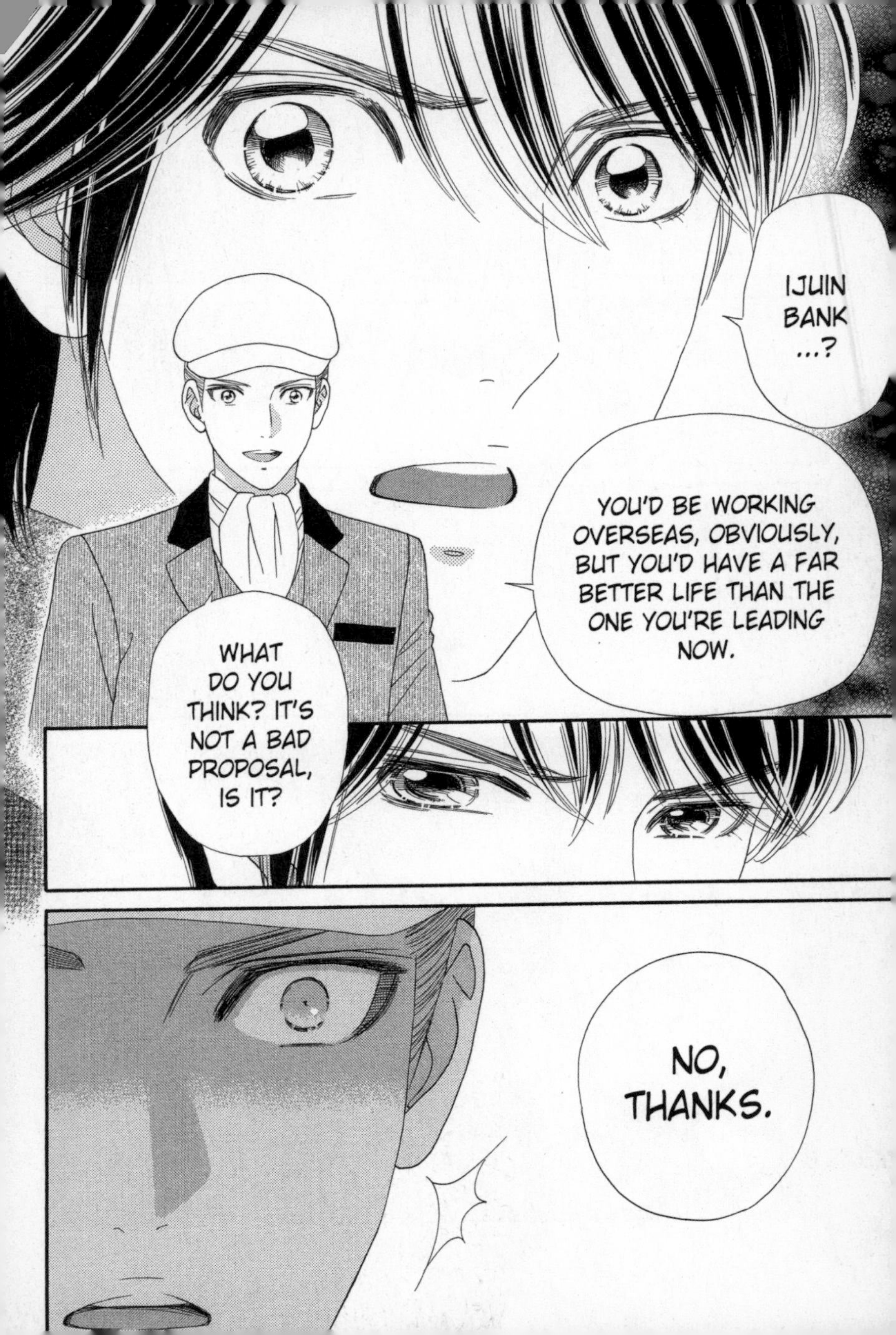
IJUIN BANK ...?
YOU'D BE WORKING OVERSEAS, OBVIOUSLY, BUT YOU'D HAVE A FAR BETTER LIFE THAN THE ONE YOU'RE LEADING NOW.
WHAT DO YOU THINK? IT'S NOT A BAD PROPOSAL, IS IT?
NO, THANKS.

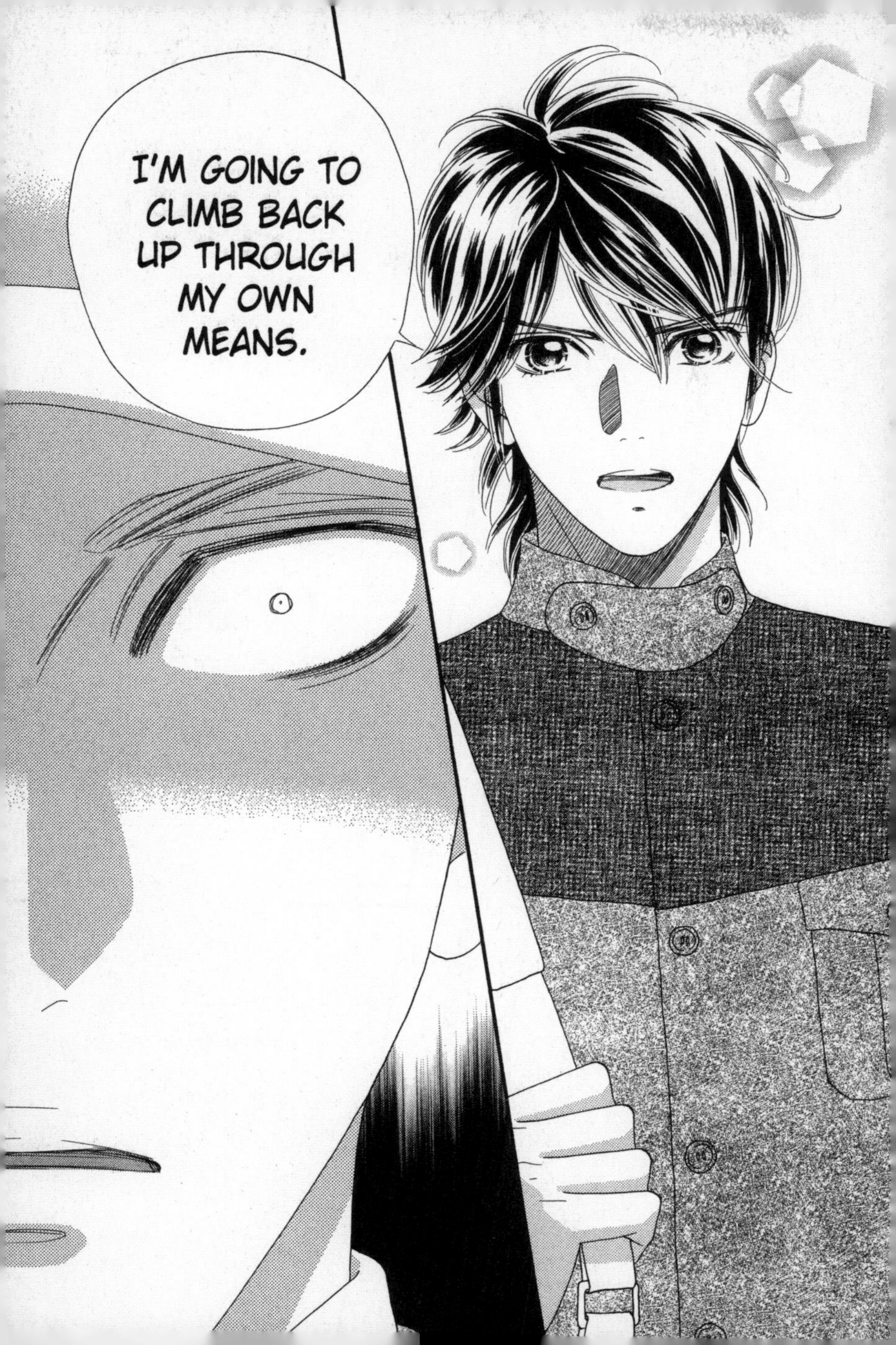
I'M GOING TO CLIMB BACK UP THROUGH MY OWN MEANS.

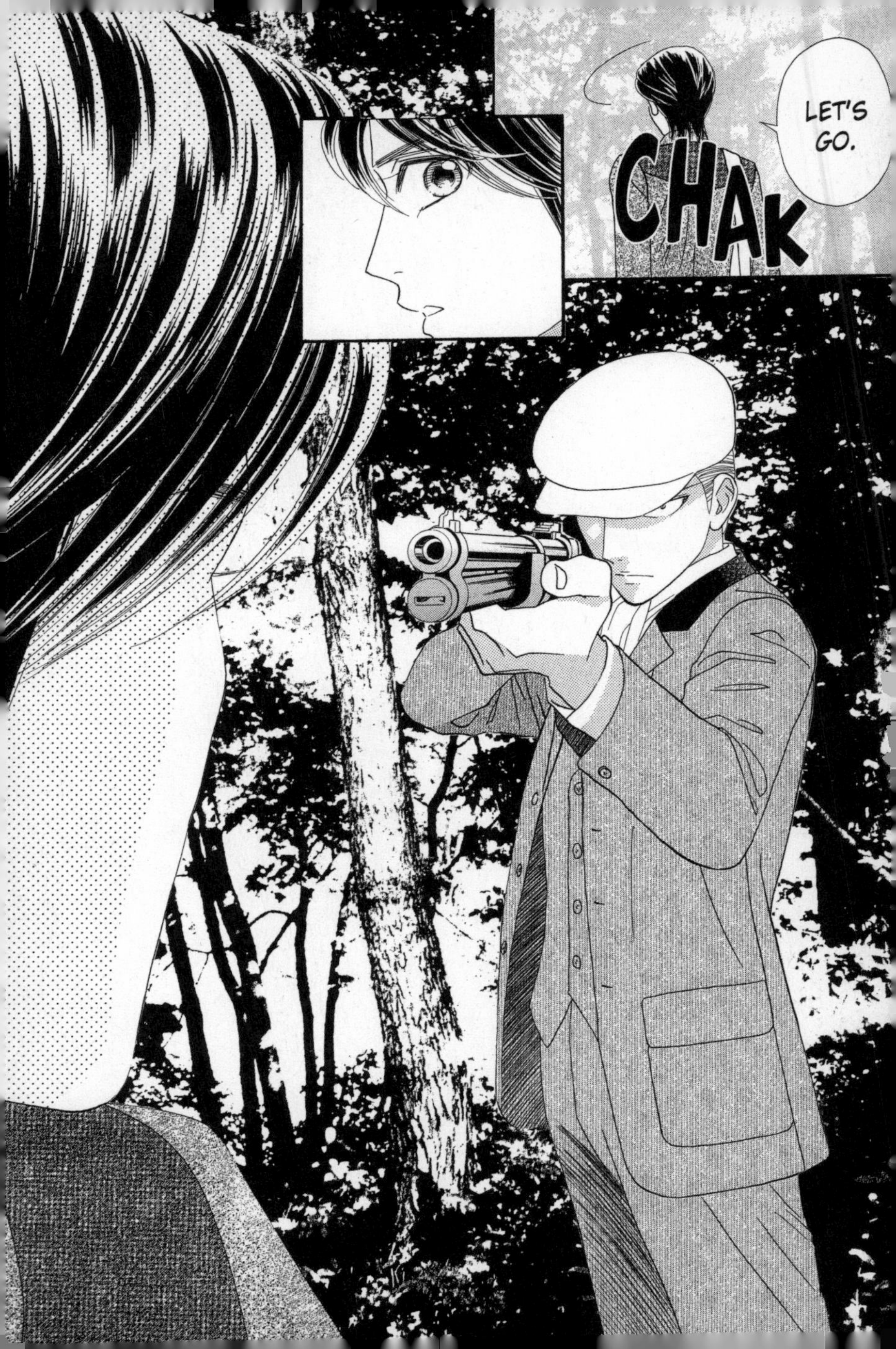
LET'S GO.
CHAK

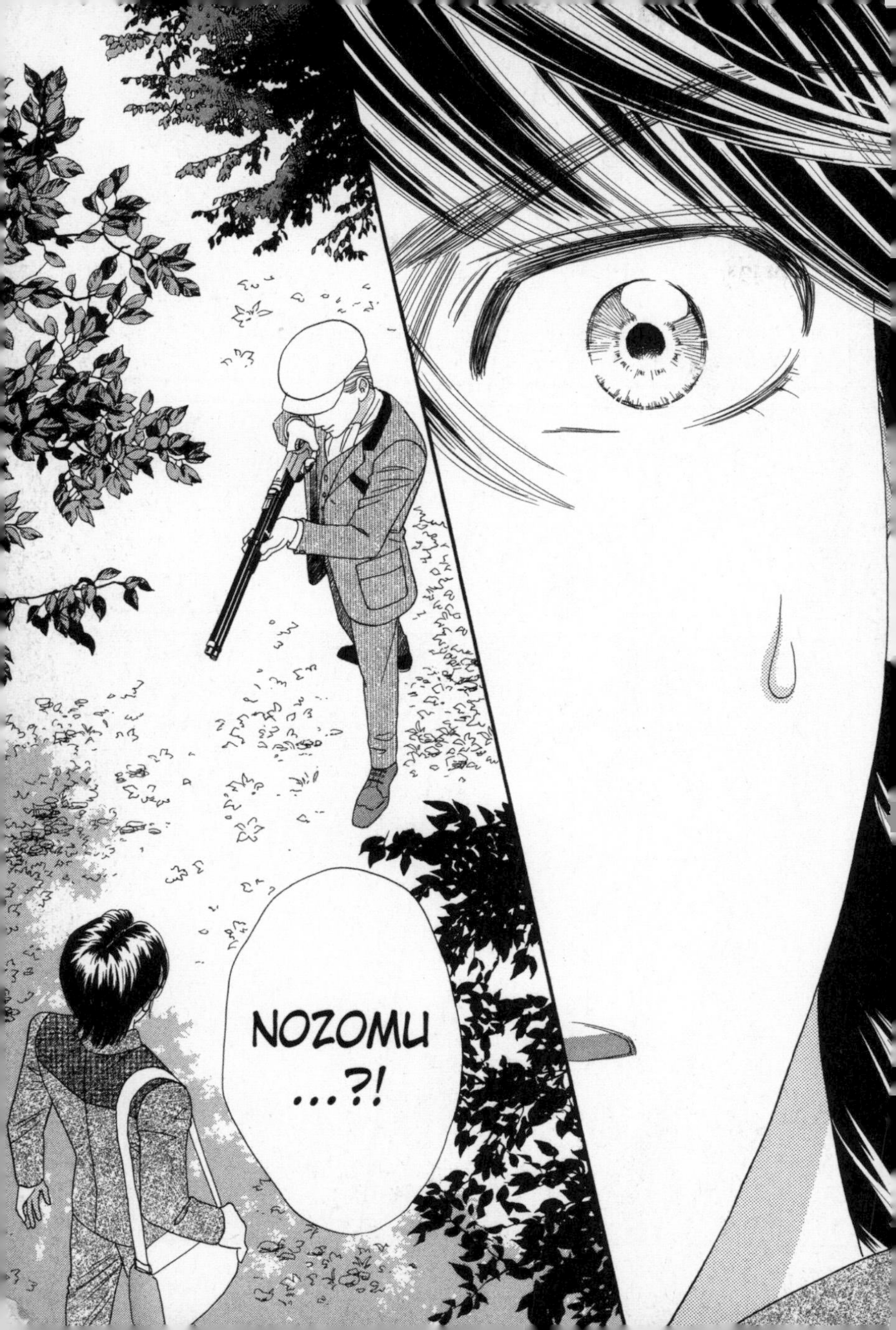
NOZOMU ...?!

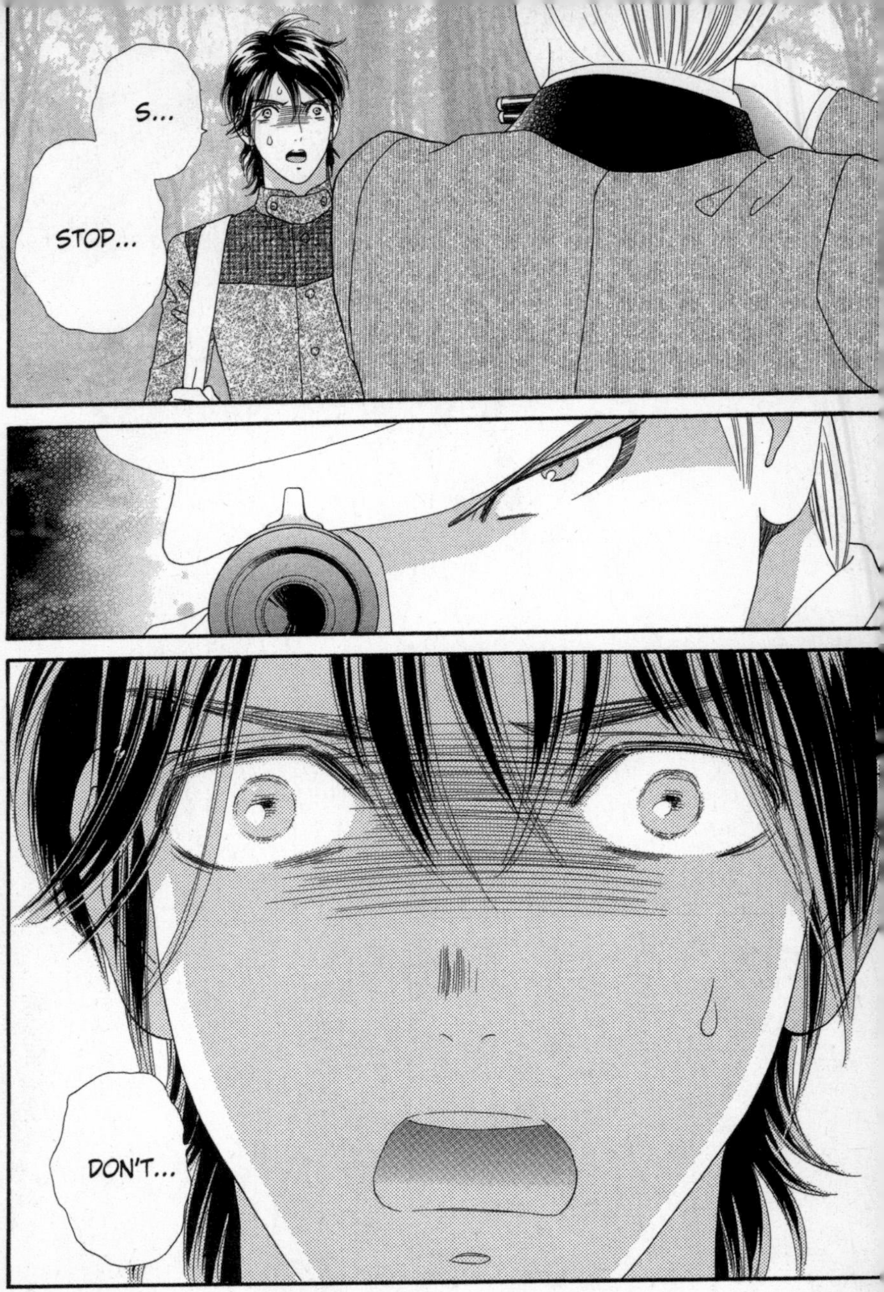
S...
STOP...
DON'T...

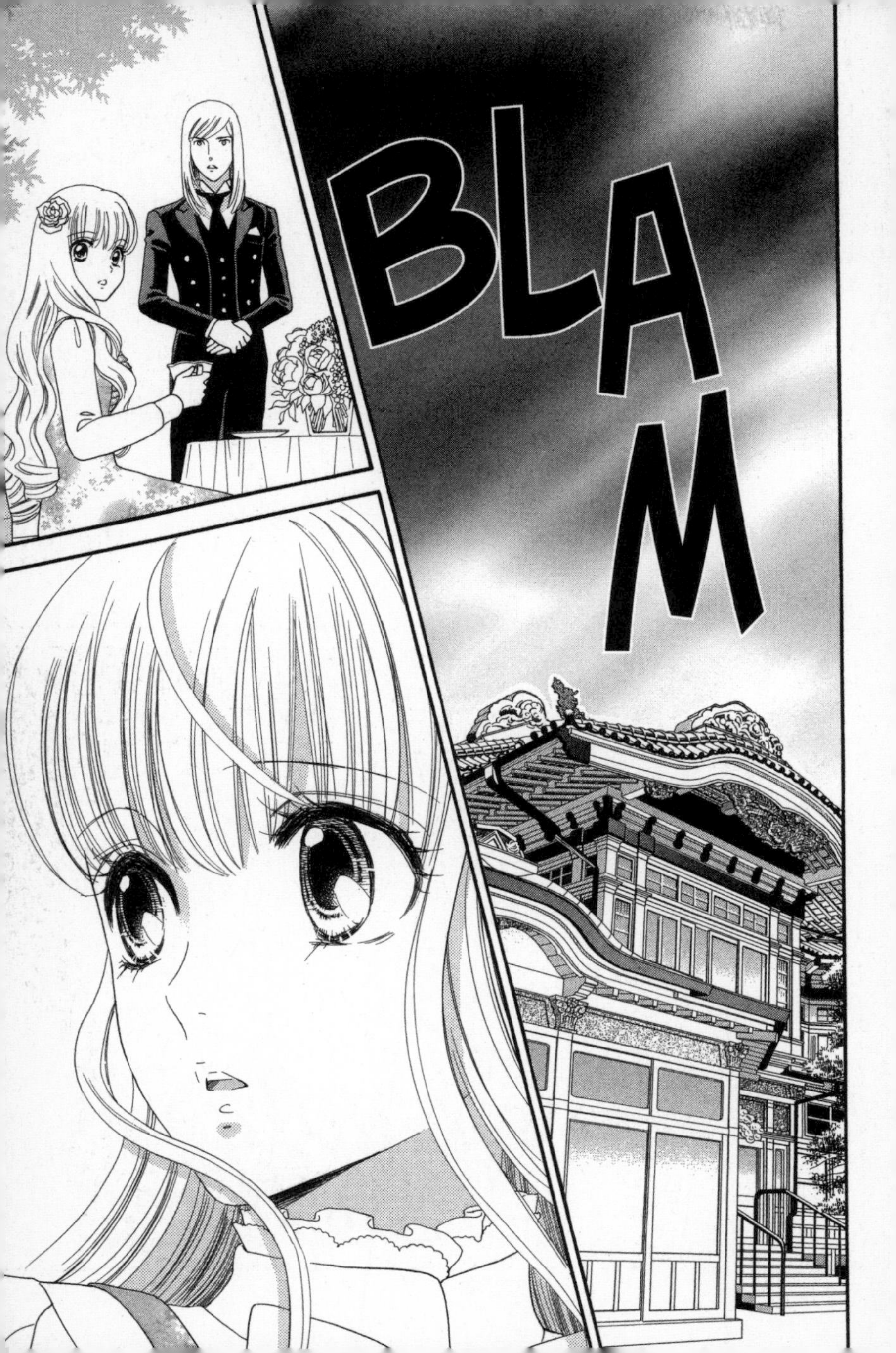
BLAM

Stepping on Roses

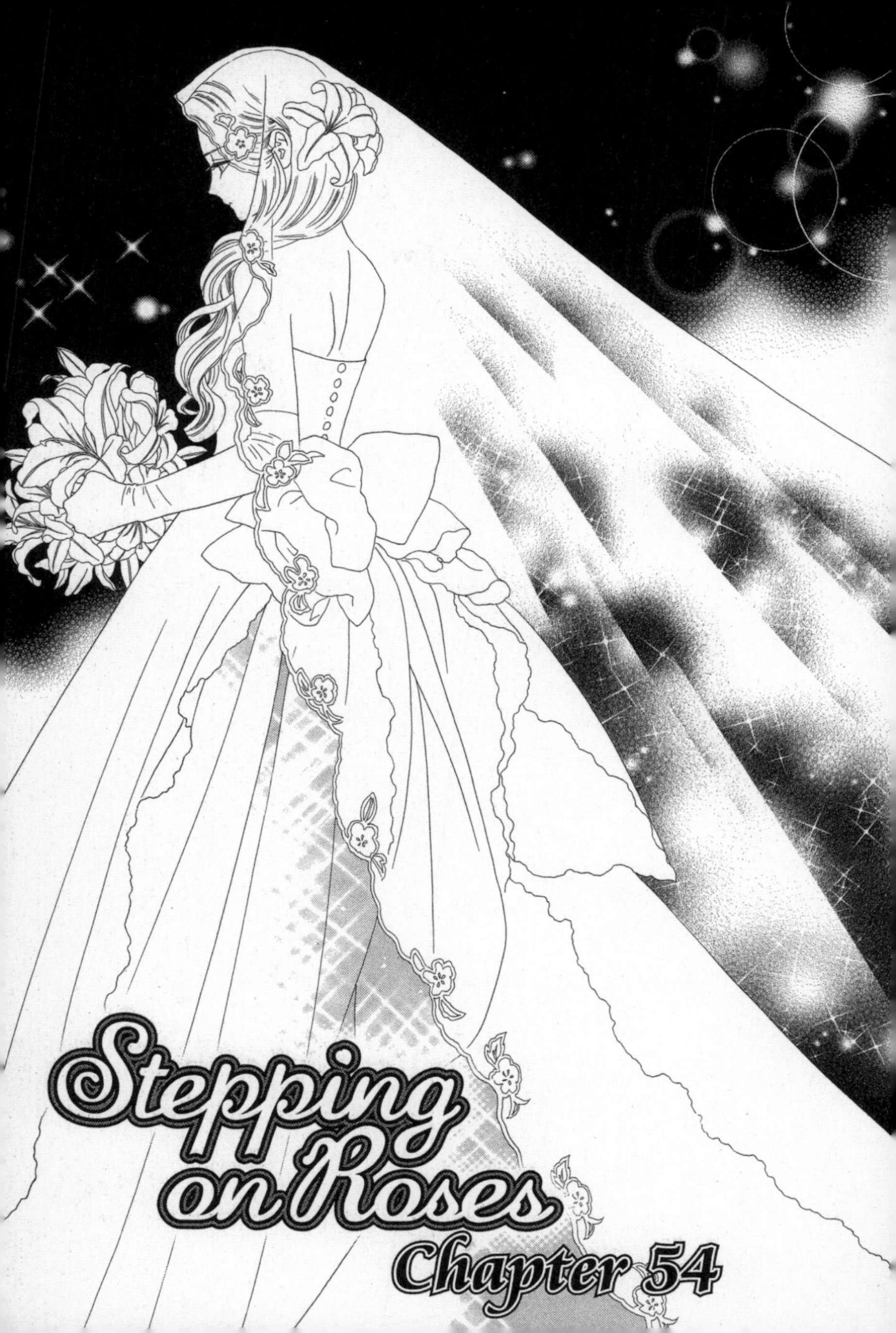
Stepping on Roses
Chapter 54

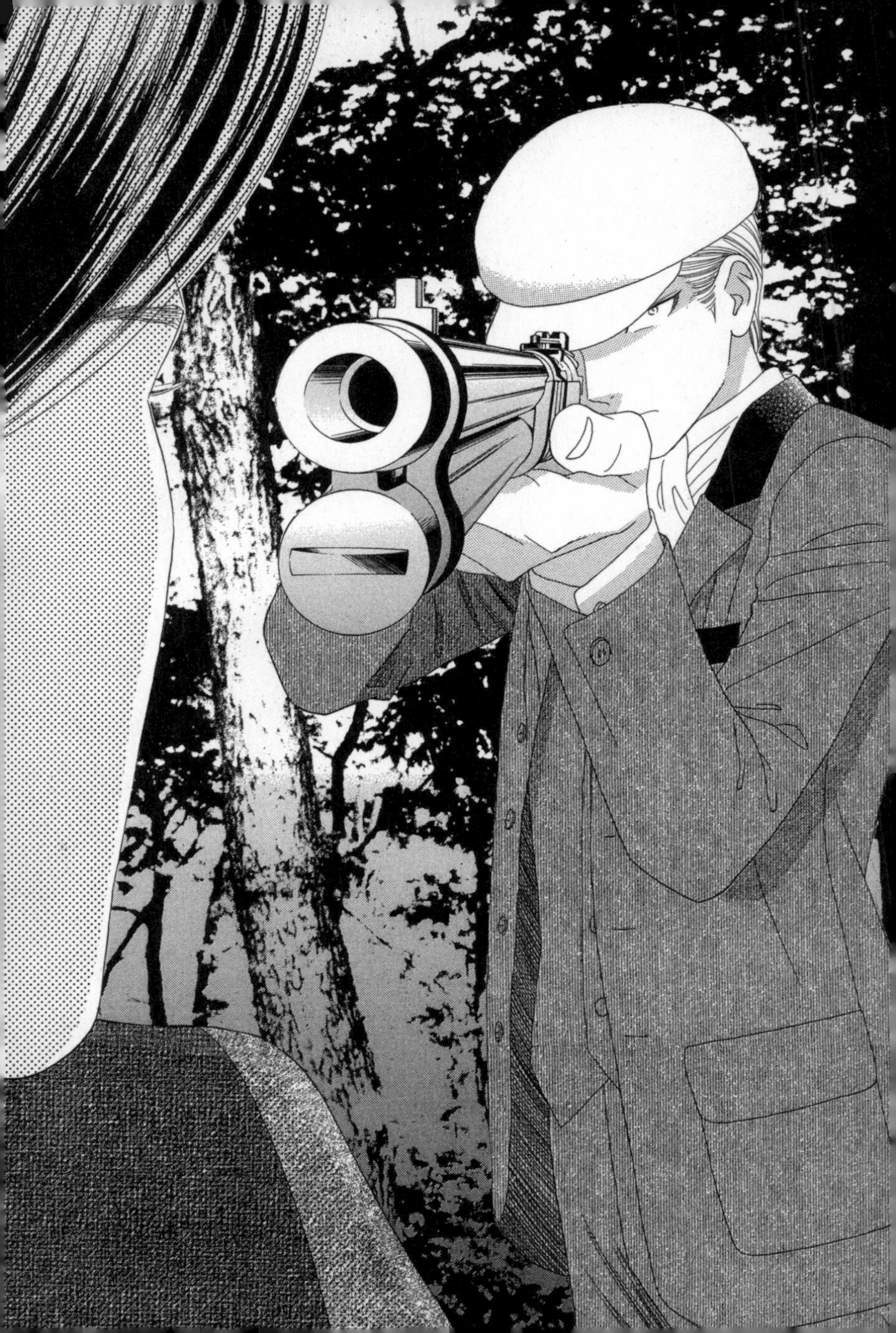

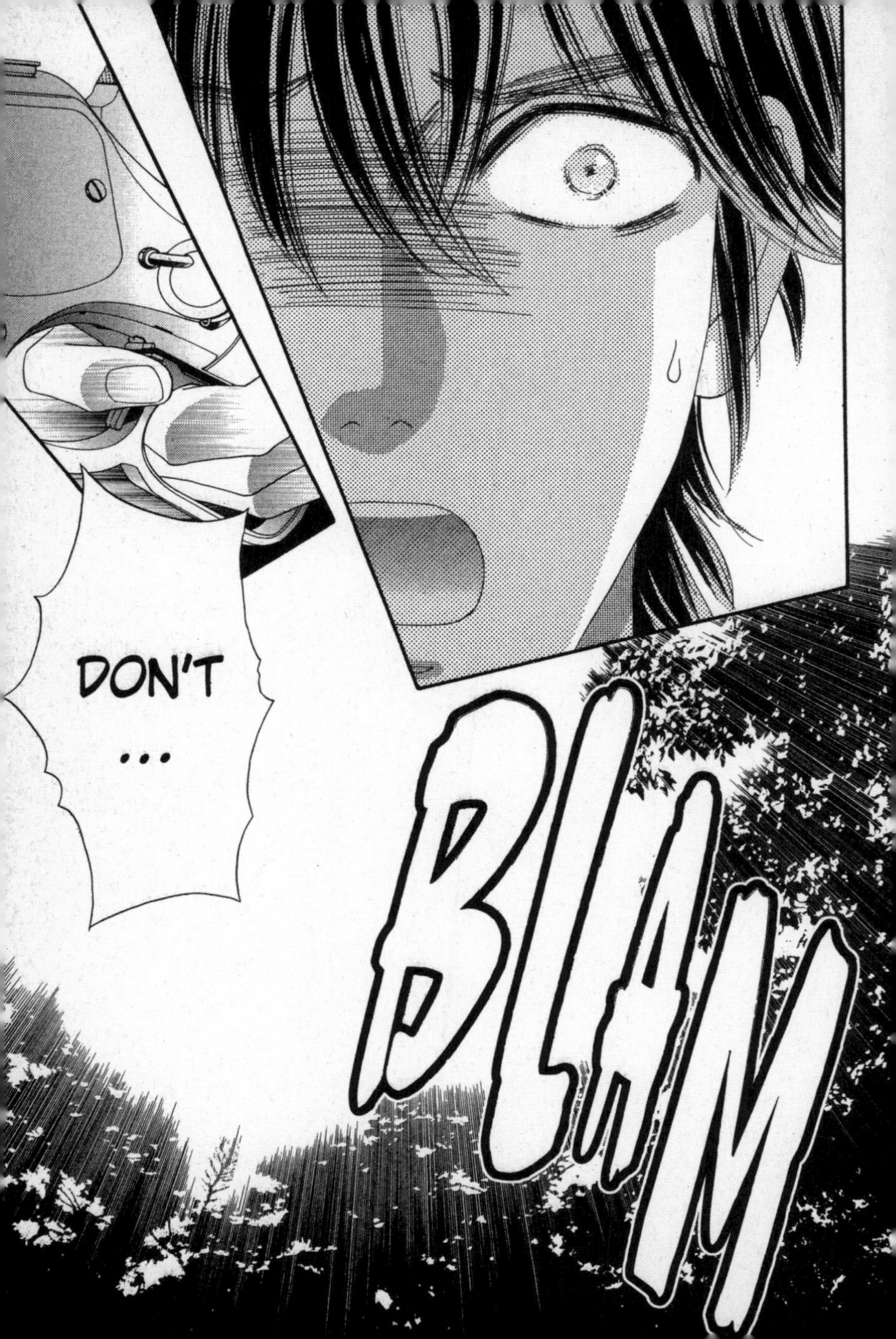
DON'T
...
BLAM

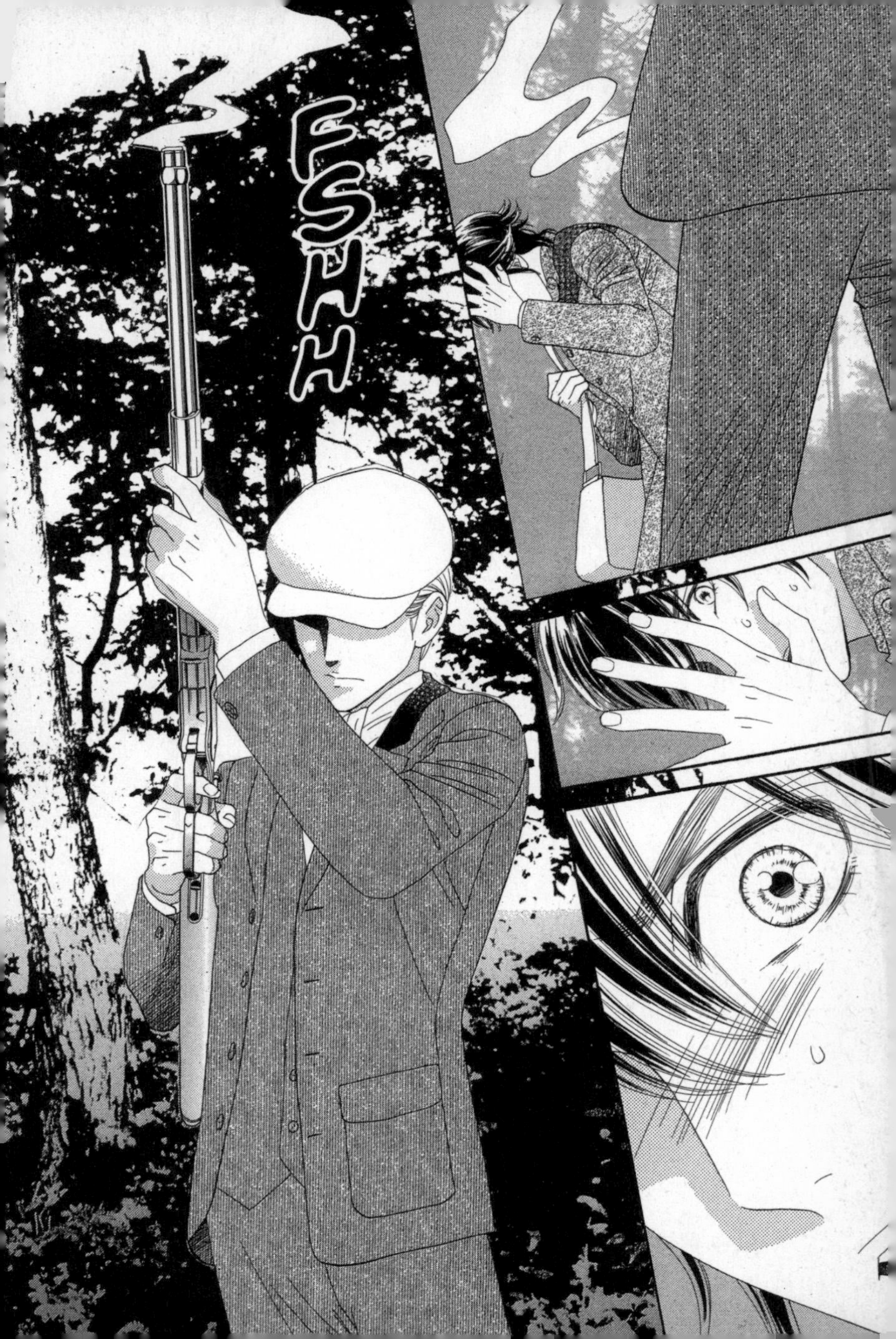
FSHHH

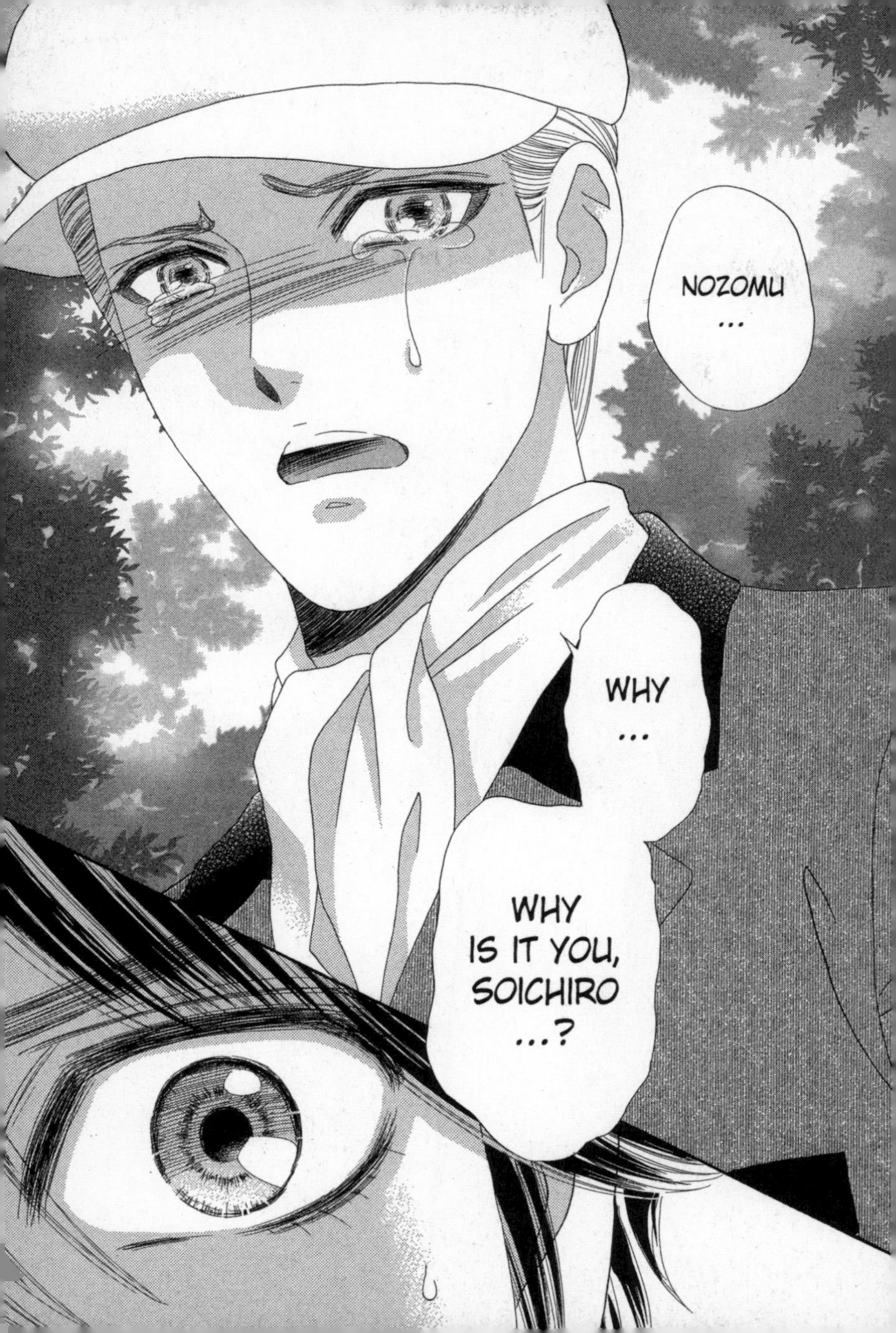
NOZOMU ...
WHY ...
WHY IS IT YOU, SOICHIRO ...?

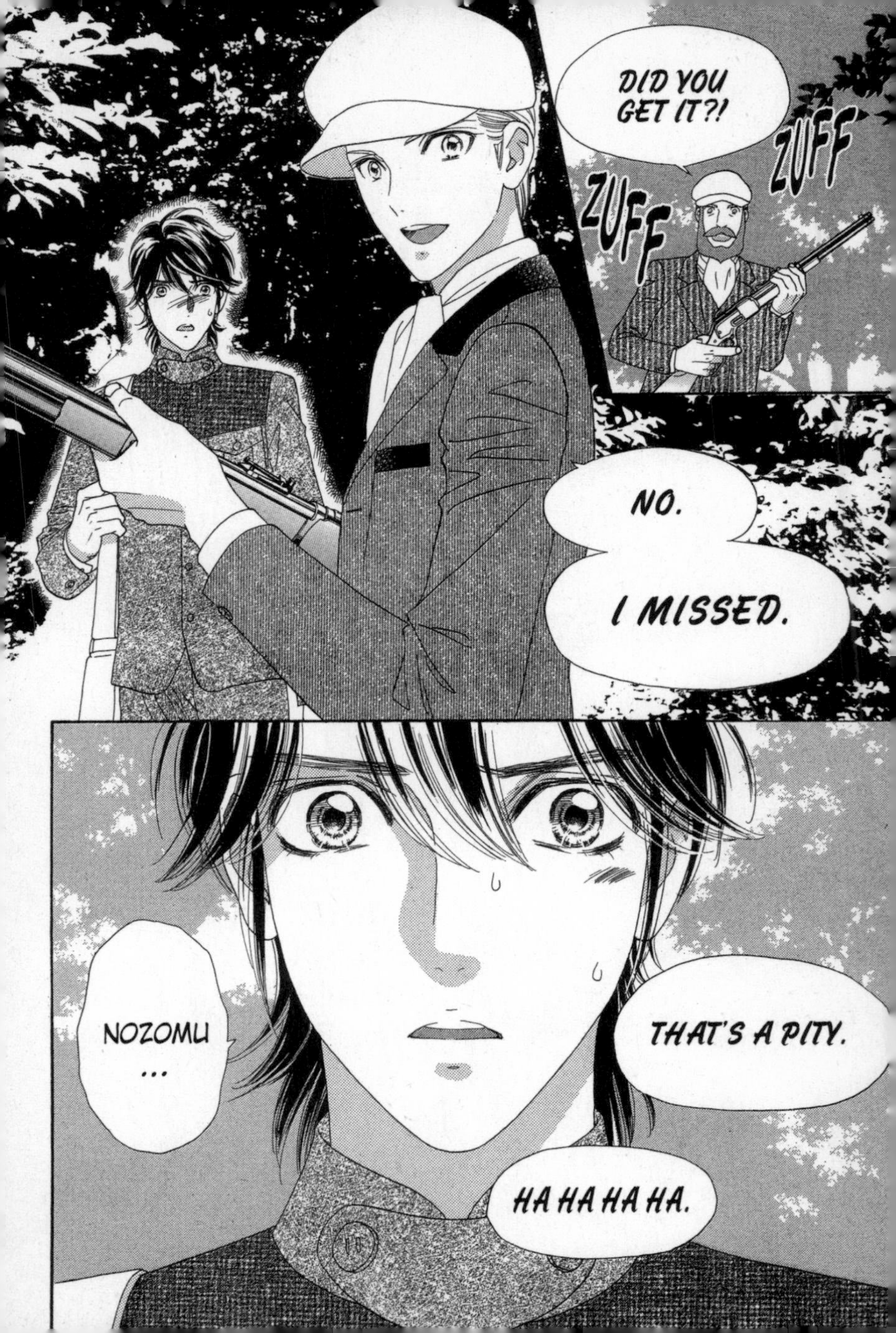
DID YOU GET IT?!
ZUFF
ZUFF
NO.
I MISSED.
THAT'S A PITY.
HA HA HA HA HA.
NOZOMU ...

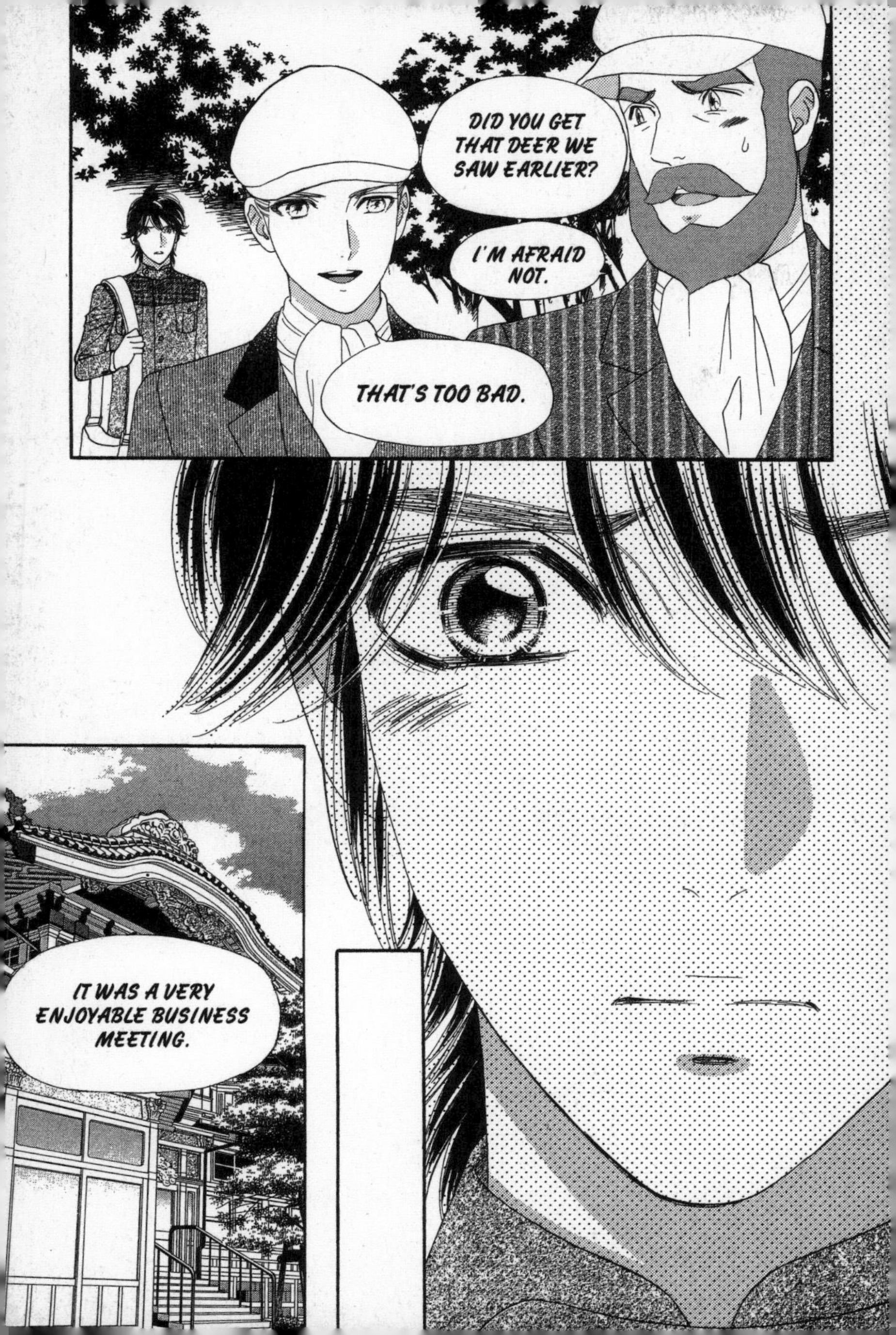
DID YOU GET THAT DEER WE SAW EARLIER?
I'M AFRAID NOT.
THAT'S TOO BAD.
IT WAS A VERY ENJOYABLE BUSINESS MEETING.

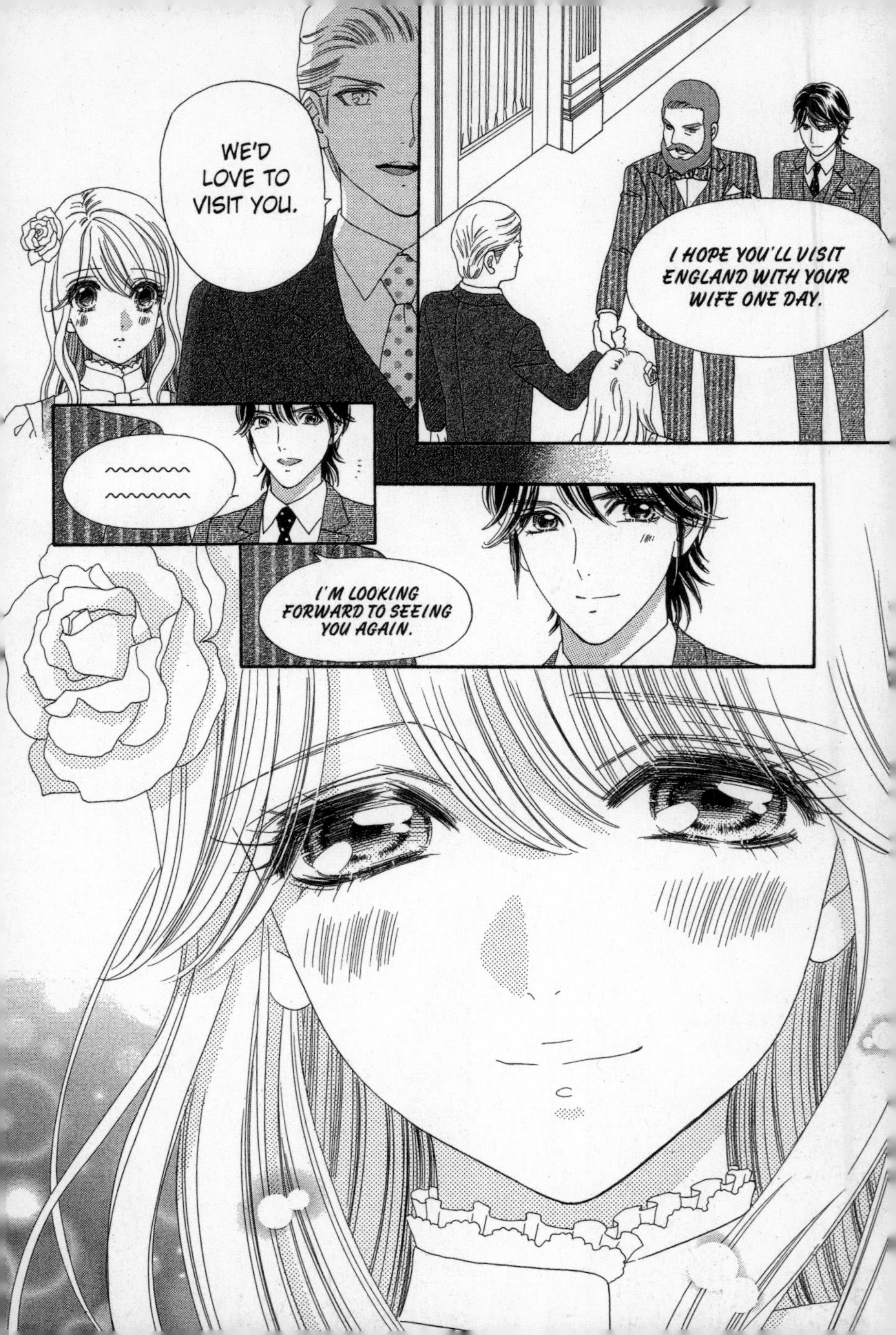
I HOPE YOU'LL VISIT ENGLAND WITH YOUR WIFE ONE DAY.
WE'D LOVE TO VISIT YOU.
I'M LOOKING FORWARD TO SEEING YOU AGAIN.

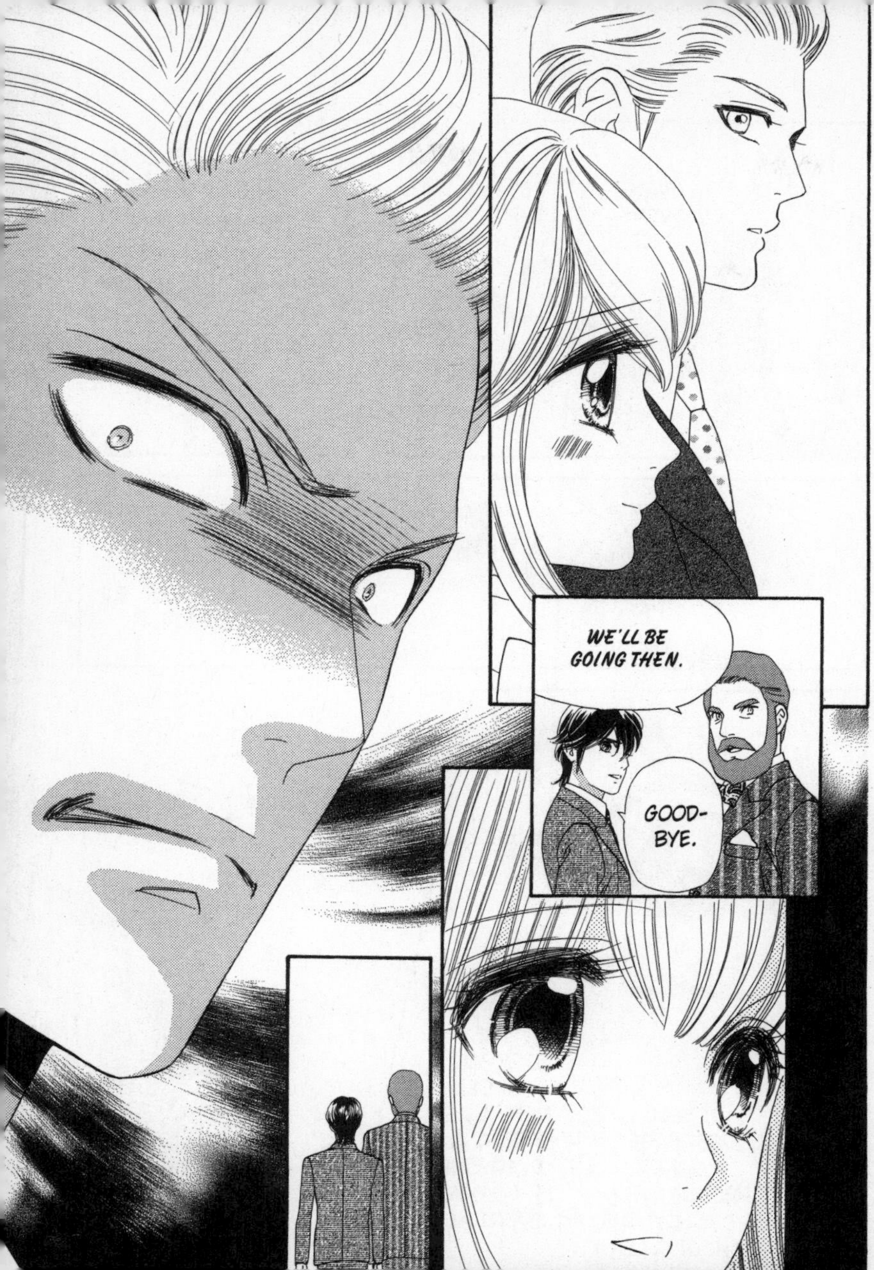
WE'LL BE GOING THEN.
GOOD-BYE.

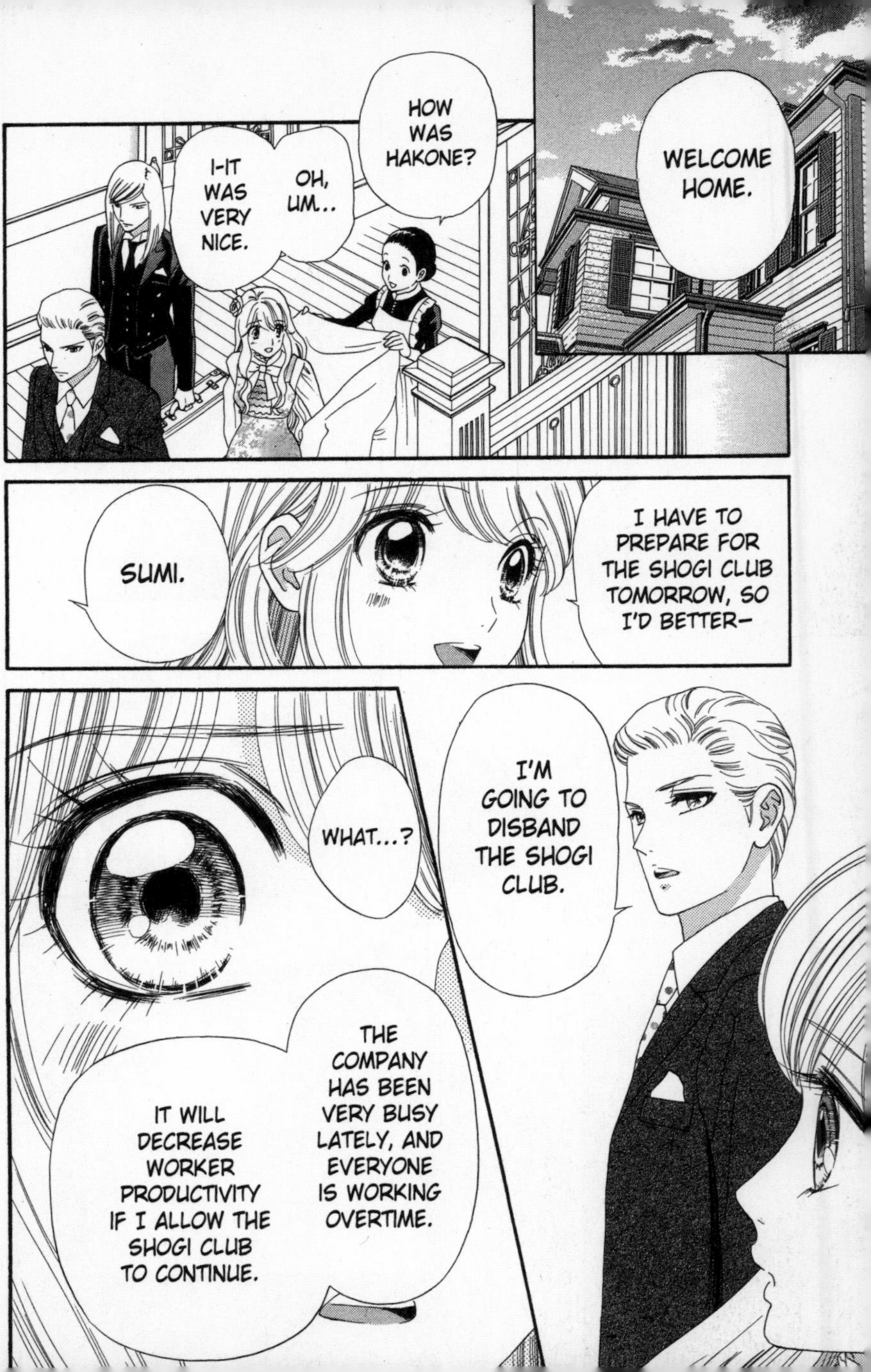
WELCOME HOME.
HOW WAS HAKONE?
OH, UM...
I-IT WAS VERY NICE.
I HAVE TO PREPARE FOR THE SHOGI CLUB TOMORROW, SO I'D BETTER—
SUMI.
I'M GOING TO DISBAND THE SHOGI CLUB.
WHAT...?
THE COMPANY HAS BEEN VERY BUSY LATELY, AND EVERYONE IS WORKING OVERTIME.
IT WILL DECREASE WORKER PRODUCTIVITY IF I ALLOW THE SHOGI CLUB TO CONTINUE.

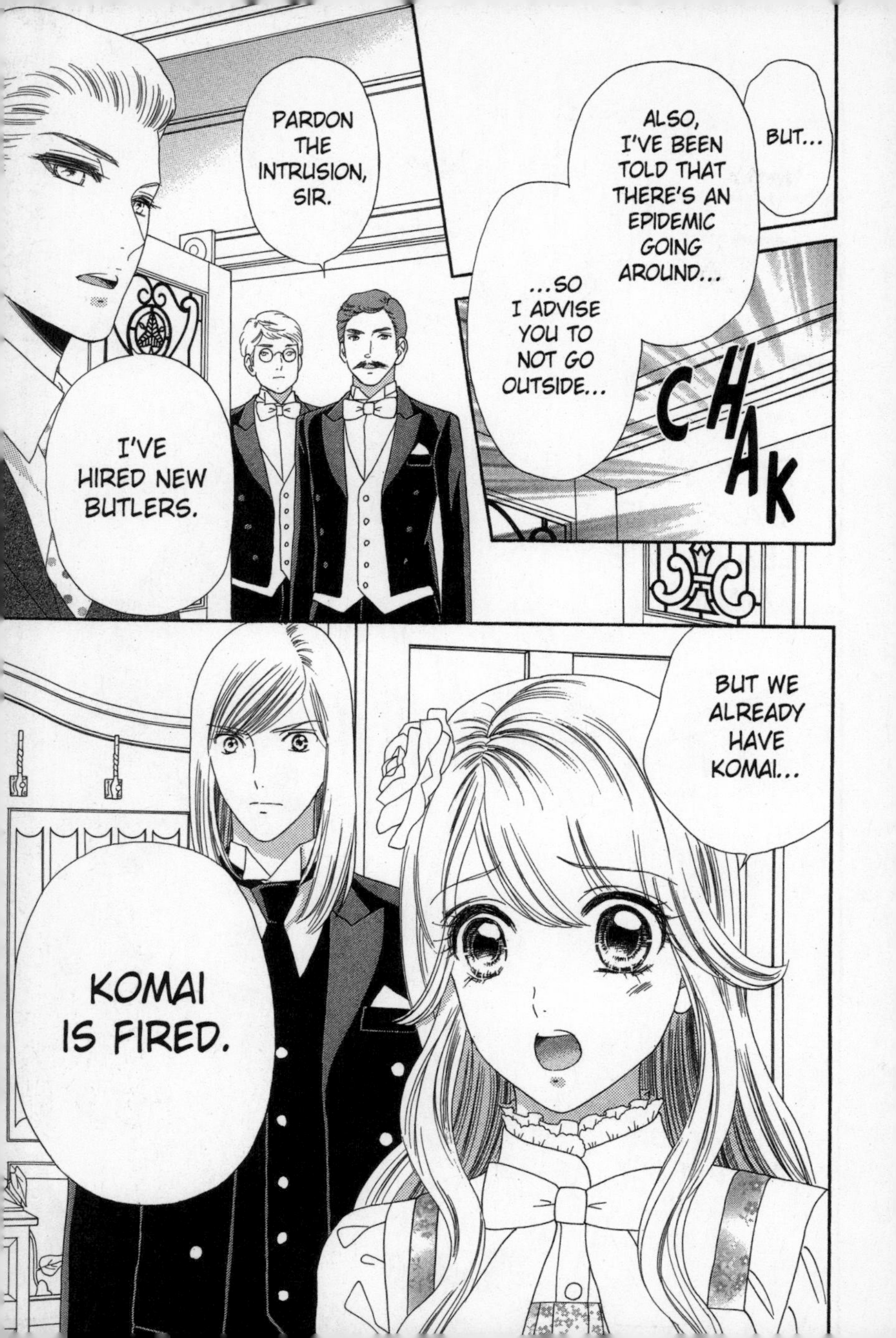
BUT...
ALSO, I'VE BEEN TOLD THAT THERE'S AN EPIDEMIC GOING AROUND...
...SO I ADVISE YOU TO NOT GO OUTSIDE...
CHAK
PARDON THE INTRUSION, SIR.
I'VE HIRED NEW BUTLERS.
BUT WE ALREADY HAVE KOMAI...
KOMAI IS FIRED.

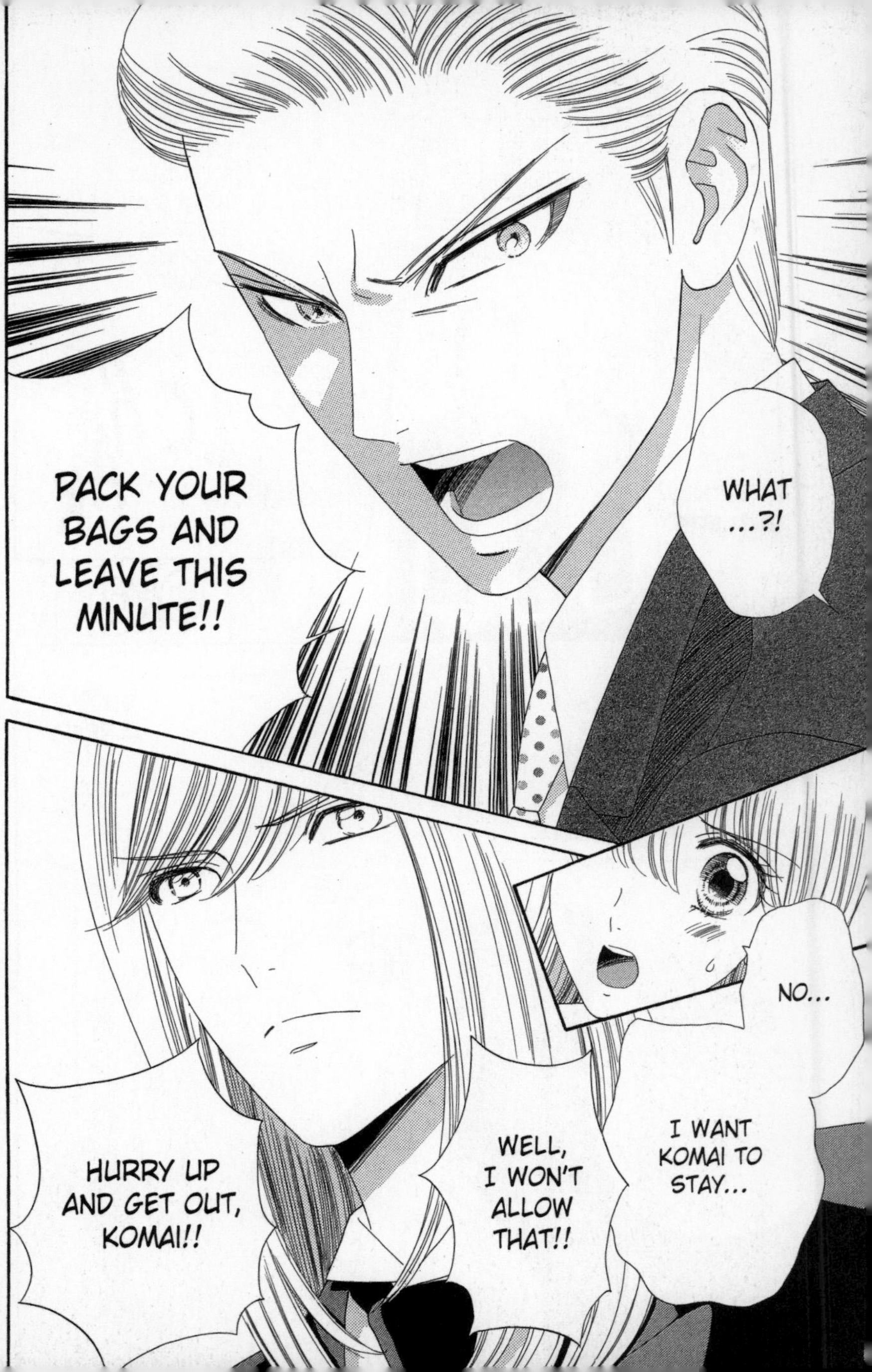
WHAT ...?!
PACK YOUR BAGS AND LEAVE THIS MINUTE!!
NO...
I WANT KOMAI TO STAY...
WELL, I WON'T ALLOW THAT!!
HURRY UP AND GET OUT, KOMAI!!

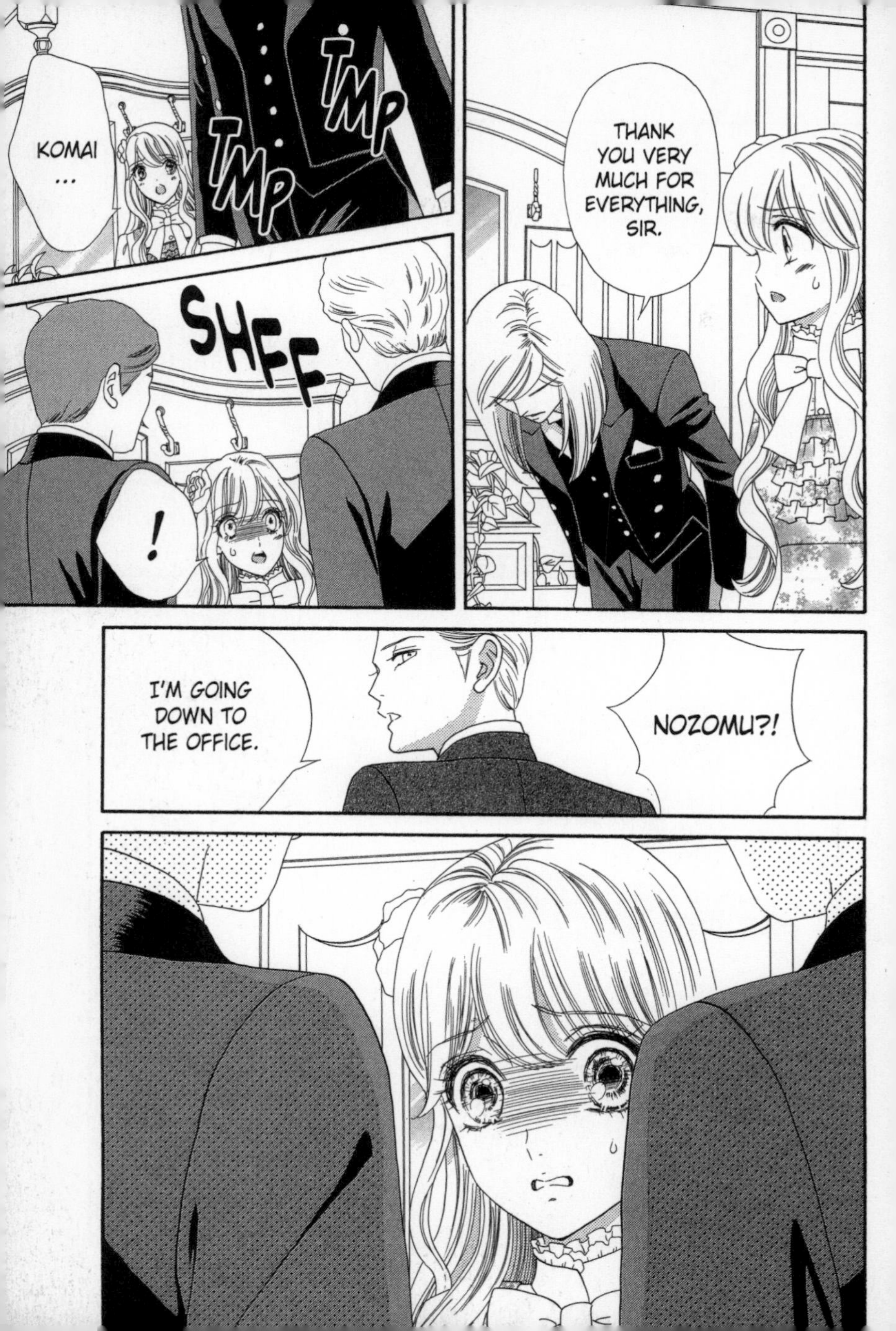
THANK YOU VERY MUCH FOR EVERYTHING, SIR.
TMP
TMP
KOMAI ...
SHFF
!
NOZOMU?!
I'M GOING DOWN TO THE OFFICE.

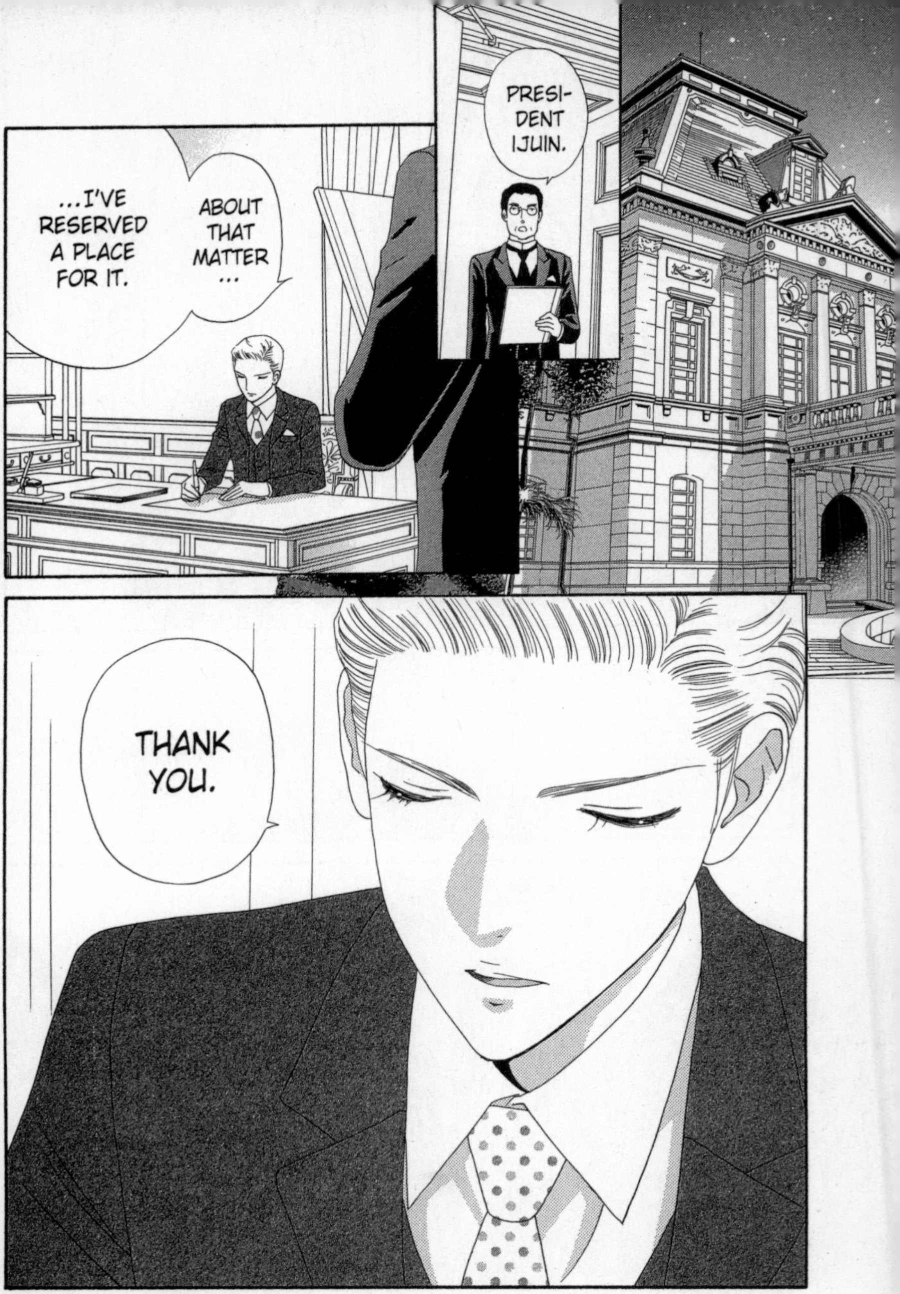
PRESIDENT IJUIN.
ABOUT THAT MATTER...
...I'VE RESERVED A PLACE FOR IT.
THANK YOU.

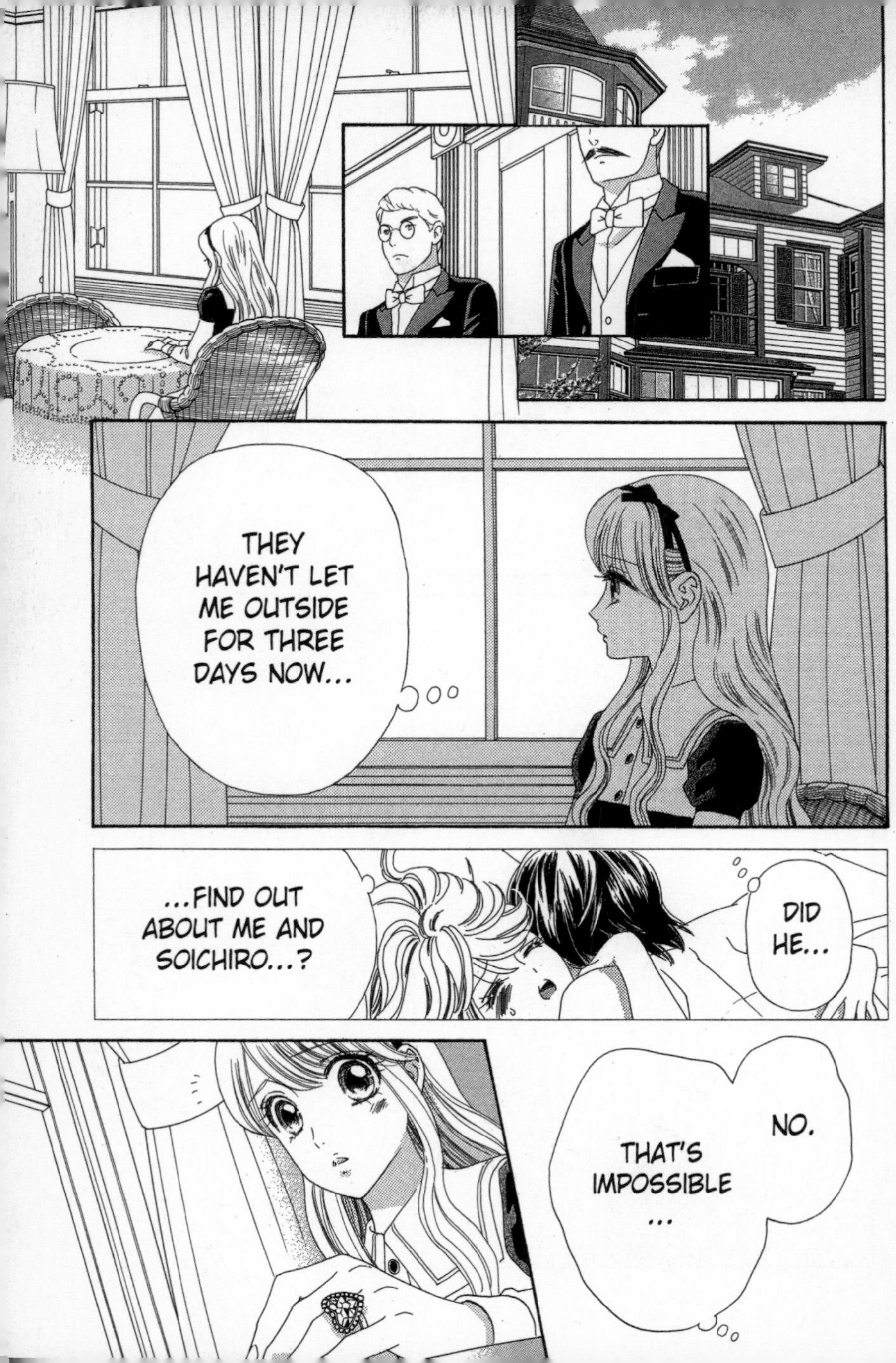
THEY HAVEN'T LET ME OUTSIDE FOR THREE DAYS NOW...
DID HE...
...FIND OUT ABOUT ME AND SOICHIRO...?
NO.
THAT'S IMPOSSIBLE ...

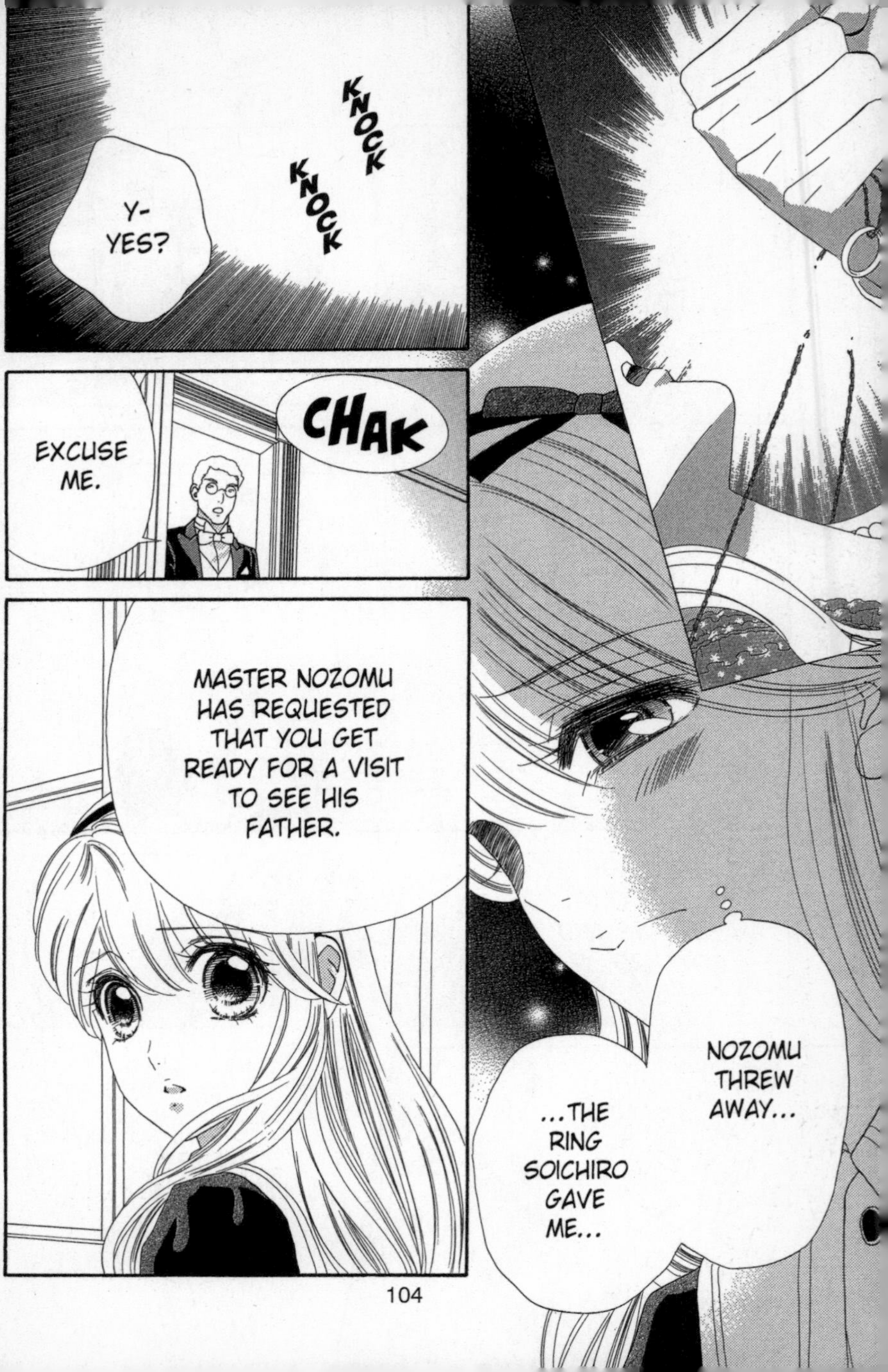
NOZOMU THREW AWAY...
...THE RING SOICHIRO GAVE ME...
KNOCK
KNOCK
Y-YES?
CHAK
EXCUSE ME.
MASTER NOZOMU HAS REQUESTED THAT YOU GET READY FOR A VISIT TO SEE HIS FATHER.

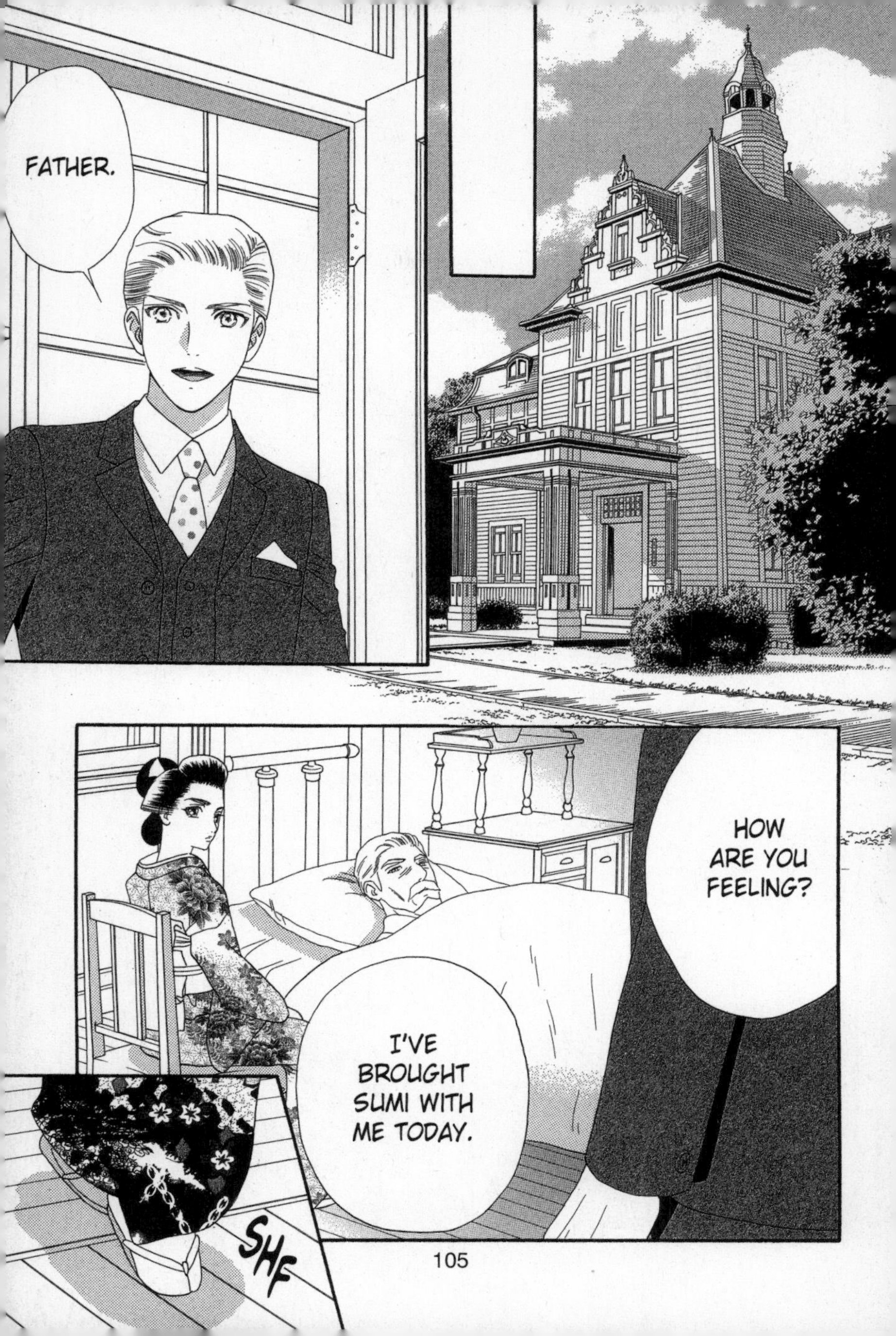
FATHER.
HOW ARE YOU FEELING?
I'VE BROUGHT SUMI WITH ME TODAY.
SHF

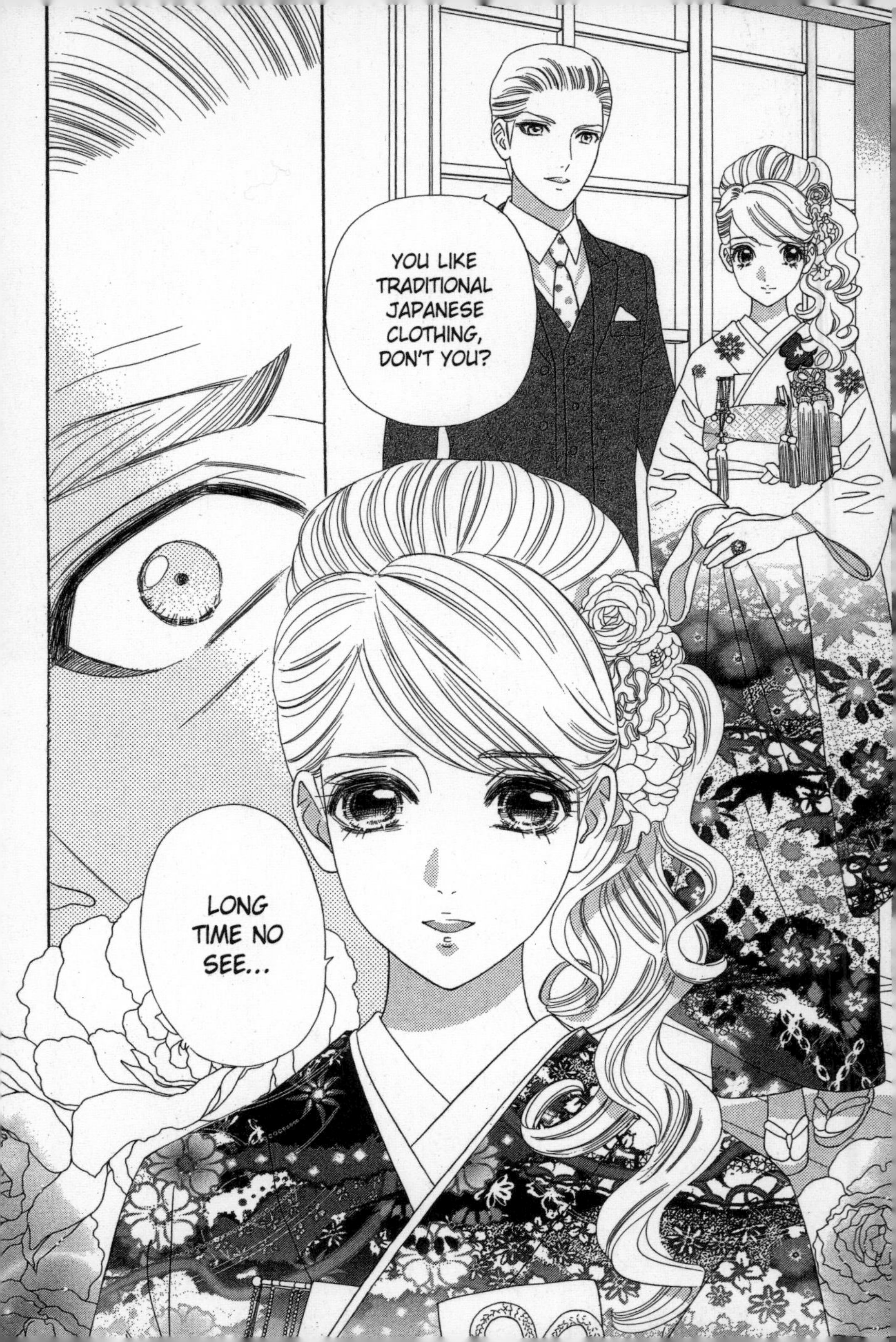
YOU LIKE TRADITIONAL JAPANESE CLOTHING, DON'T YOU?
LONG TIME NO SEE...

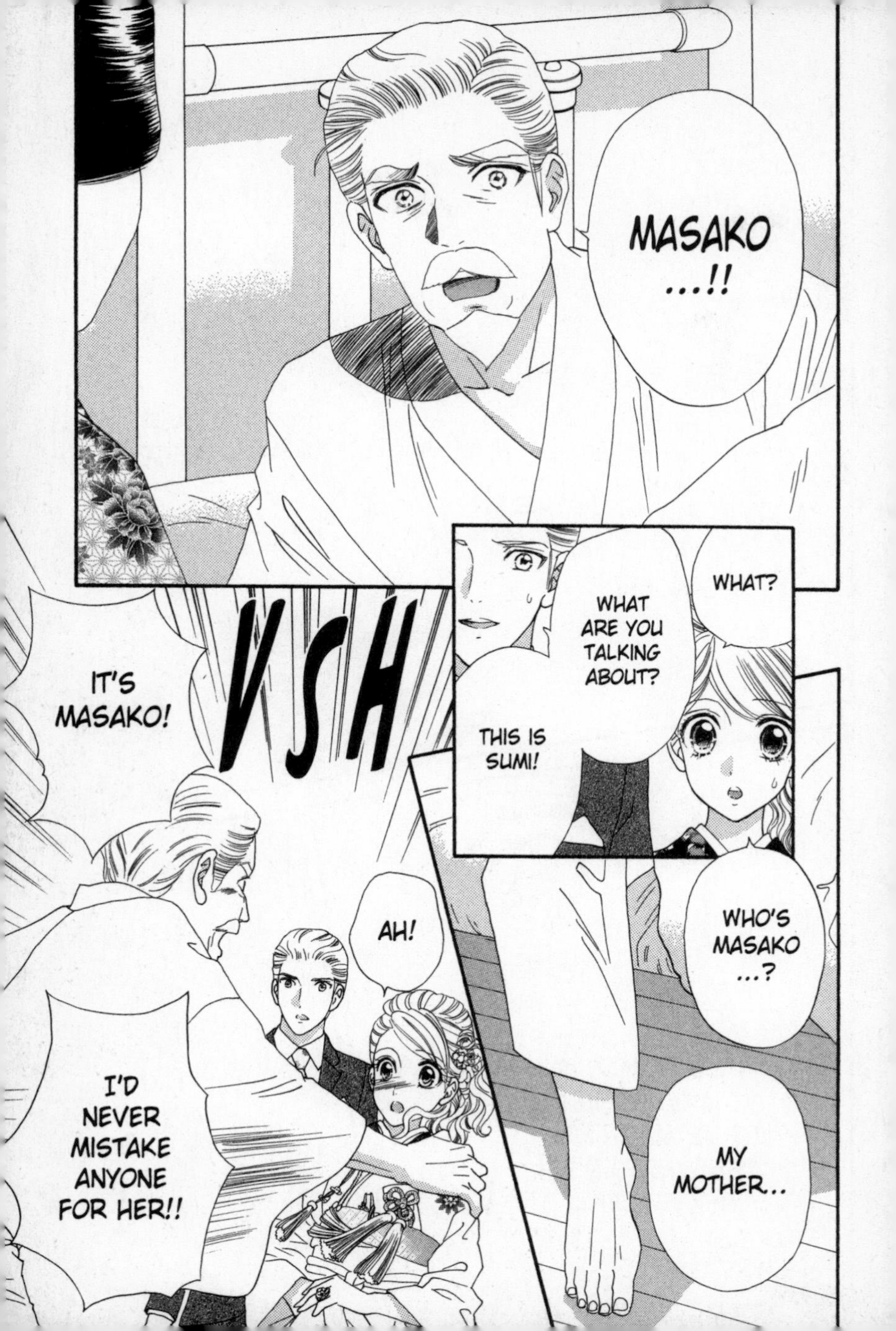

MASAKO ...!!
WHAT?
WHAT ARE YOU TALKING ABOUT?
THIS IS SUMI!
VSH
IT'S MASAKO!
AH!
I'D NEVER MISTAKE ANYONE FOR HER!!
WHO'S MASAKO ...?
MY MOTHER..

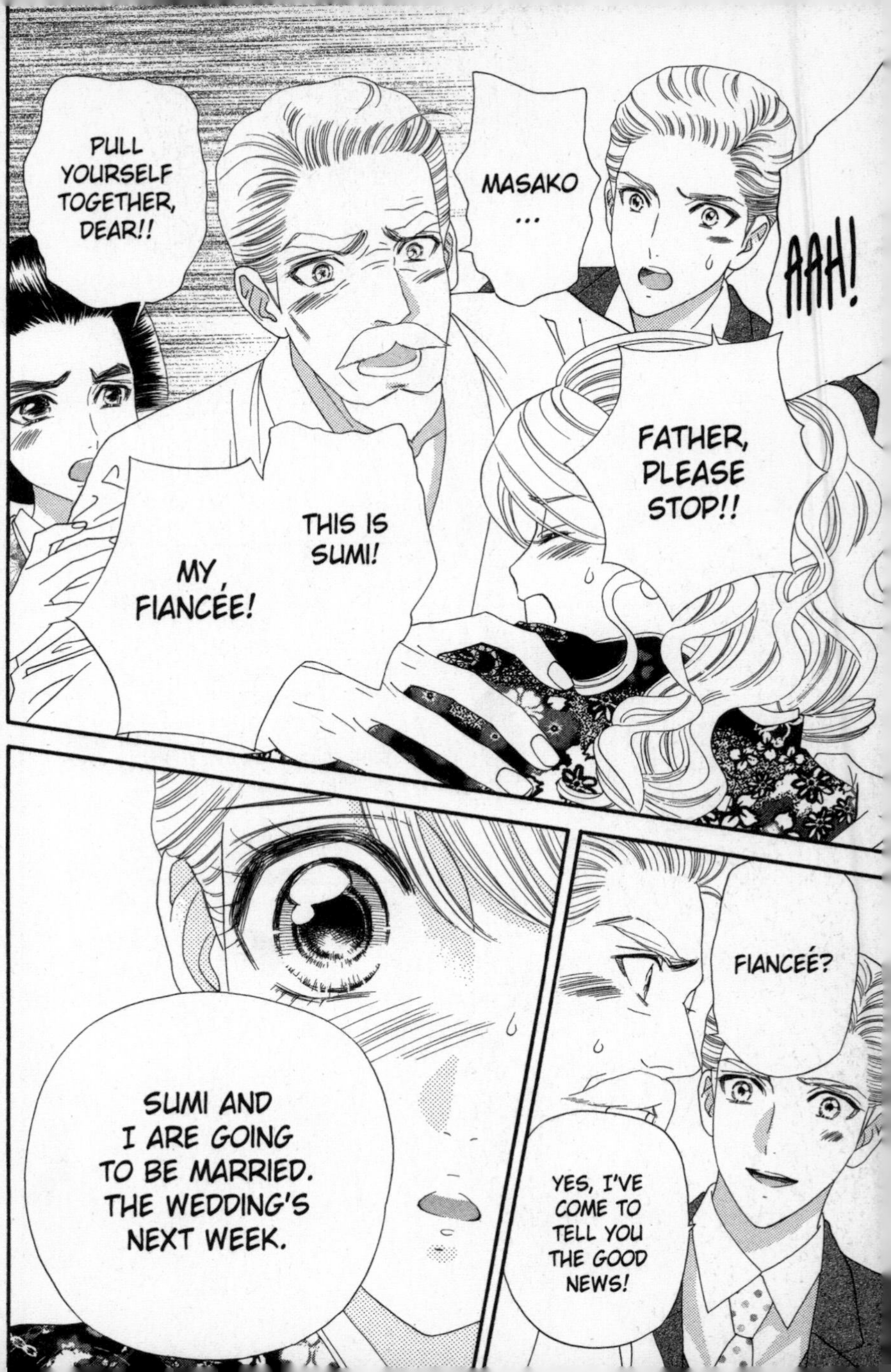
AAH!
MASAKO ...
PULL YOURSELF TOGETHER, DEAR!!
FATHER, PLEASE STOP!!
THIS IS SUMI!
MY FIANCÉE!
FIANCEÉ?
YES, I'VE COME TO TELL YOU THE GOOD NEWS!
SUMI AND I ARE GOING TO BE MARRIED. THE WEDDING'S NEXT WEEK.

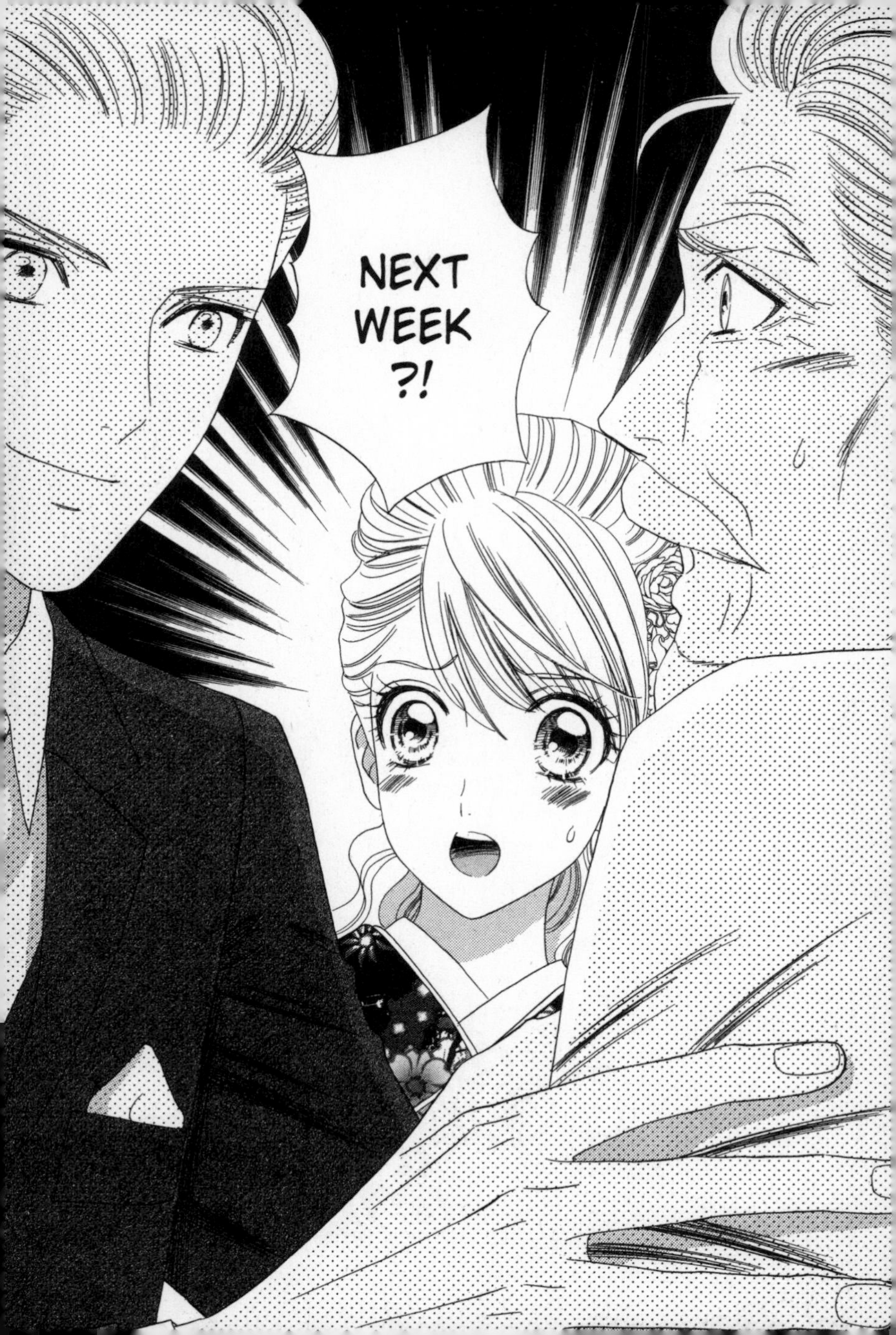
NEXT WEEK ?!

Stepping on Roses

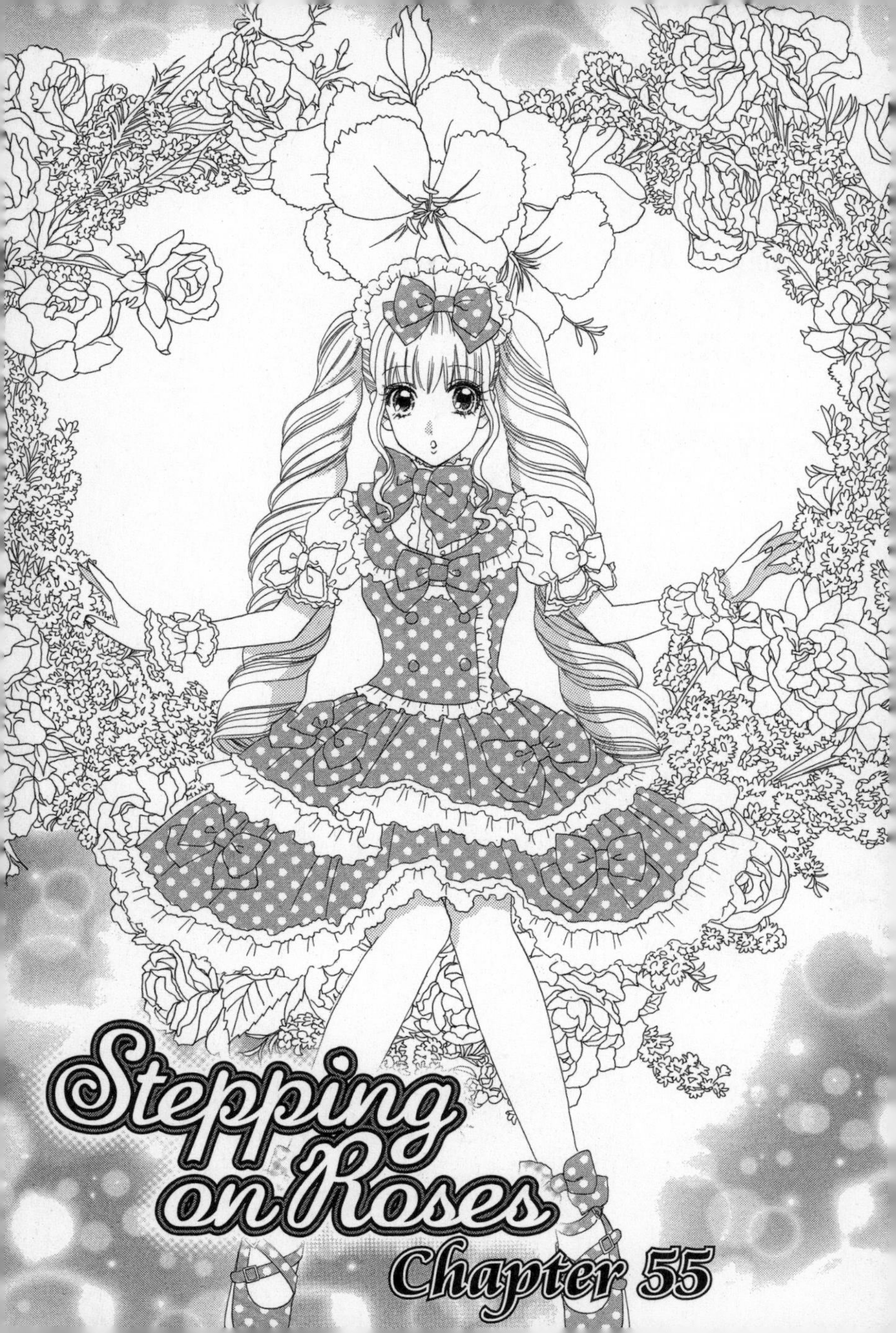
Stepping on Roses
Chapter 55

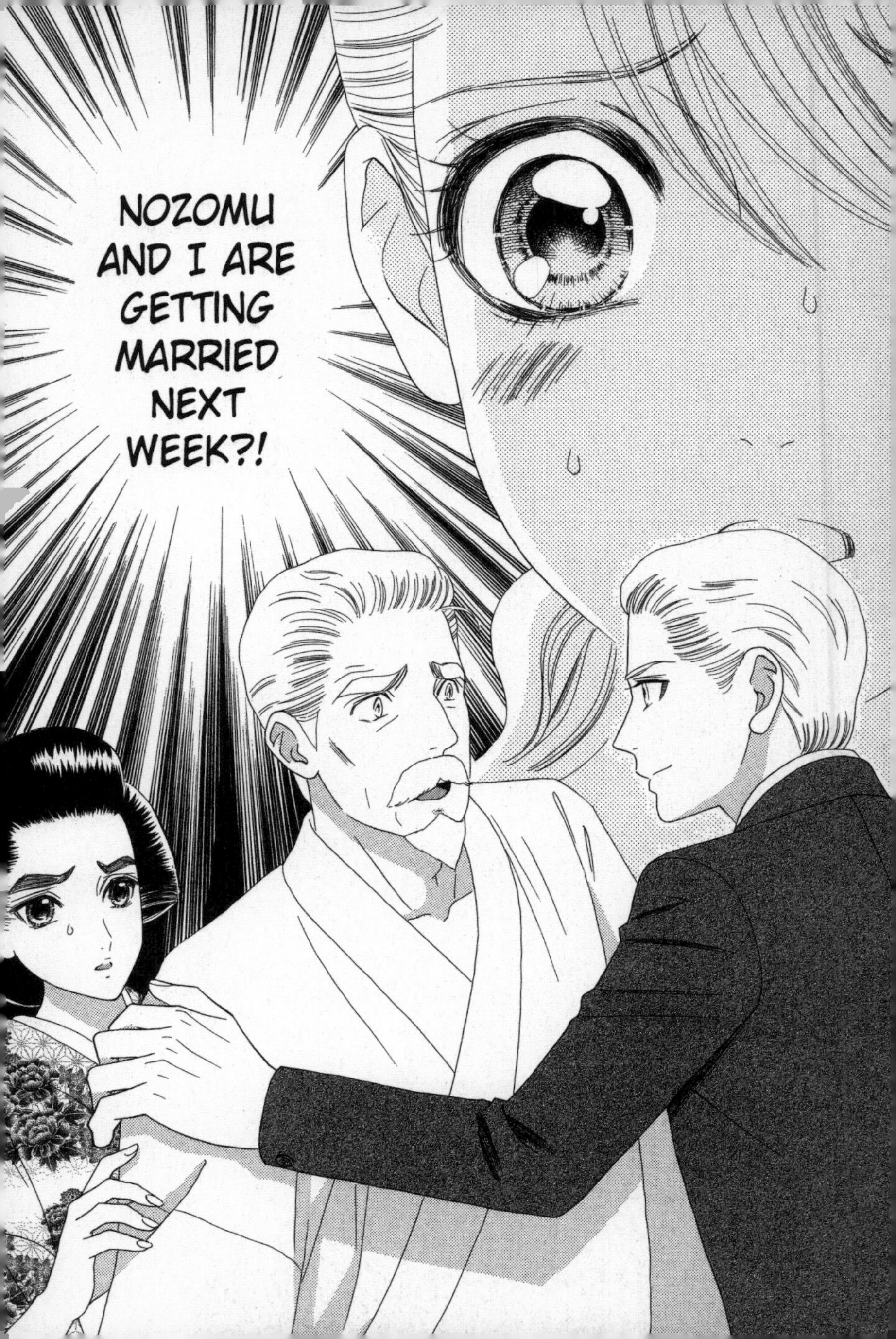
NOZOMU AND I ARE GETTING MARRIED NEXT WEEK?!

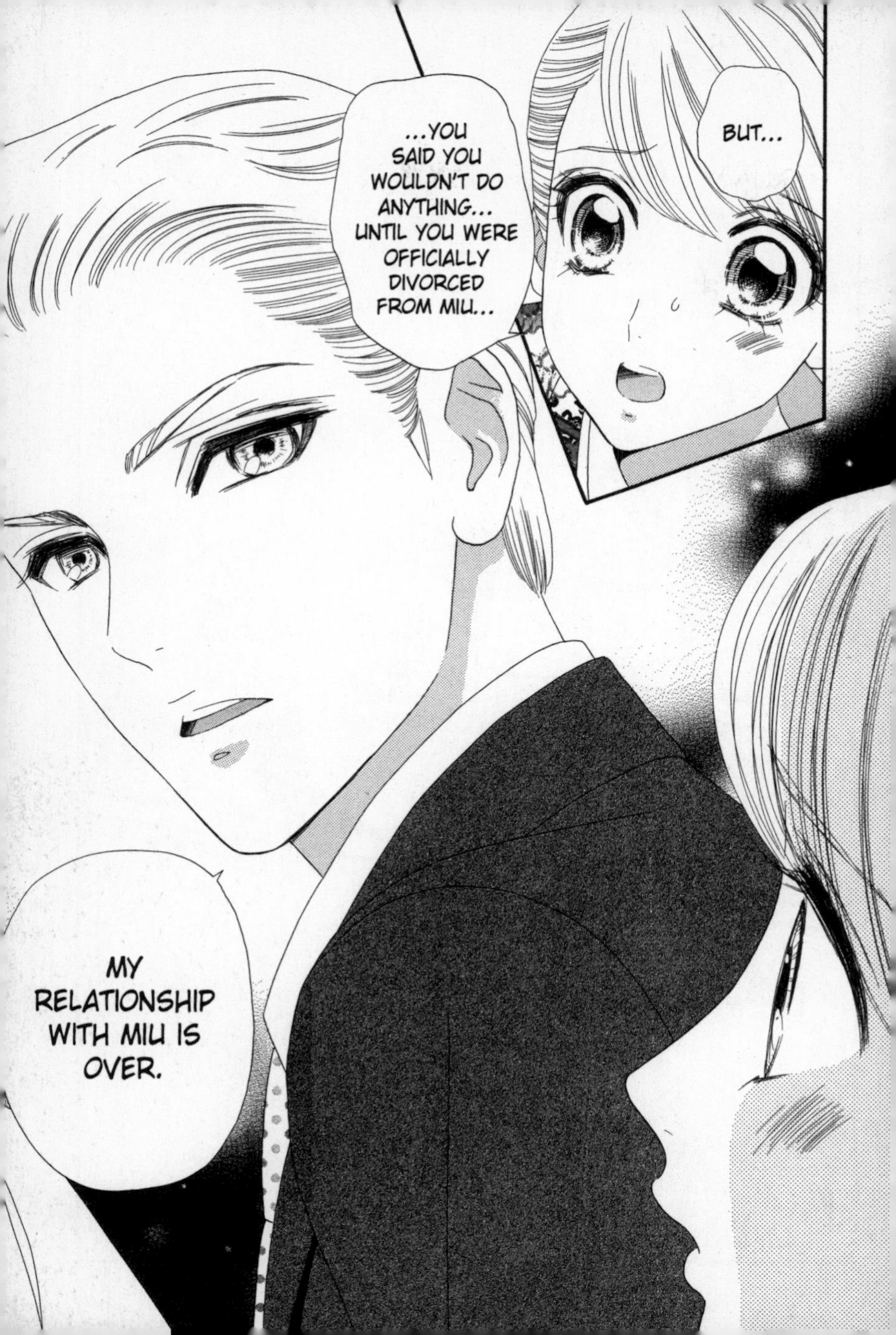
BUT...
...YOU SAID YOU WOULDN'T DO ANYTHING... UNTIL YOU WERE OFFICIALLY DIVORCED FROM MIU...
MY RELATIONSHIP WITH MIU IS OVER.

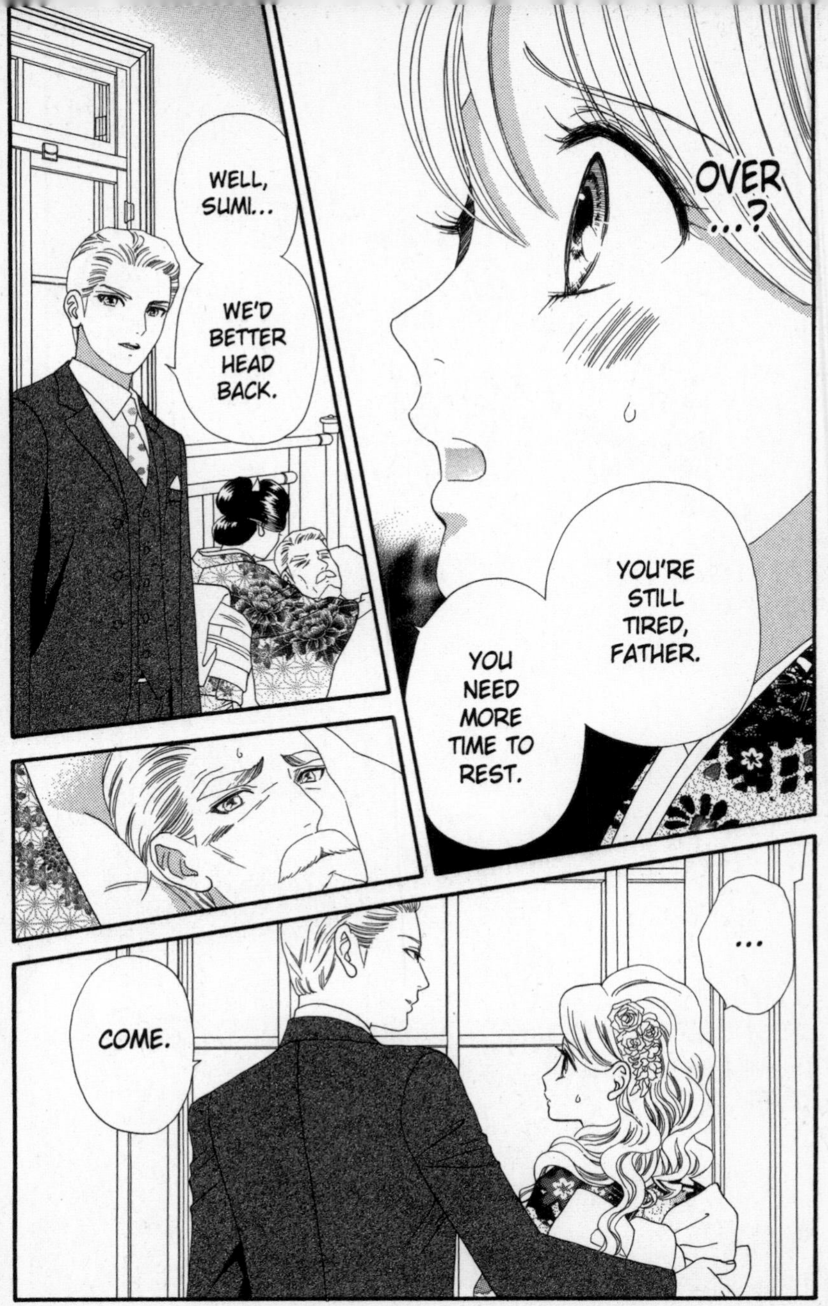
OVER ...?
YOU'RE STILL TIRED, FATHER.
YOU NEED MORE TIME TO REST.
WELL, SUMI...
WE'D BETTER HEAD BACK.
...
COME.

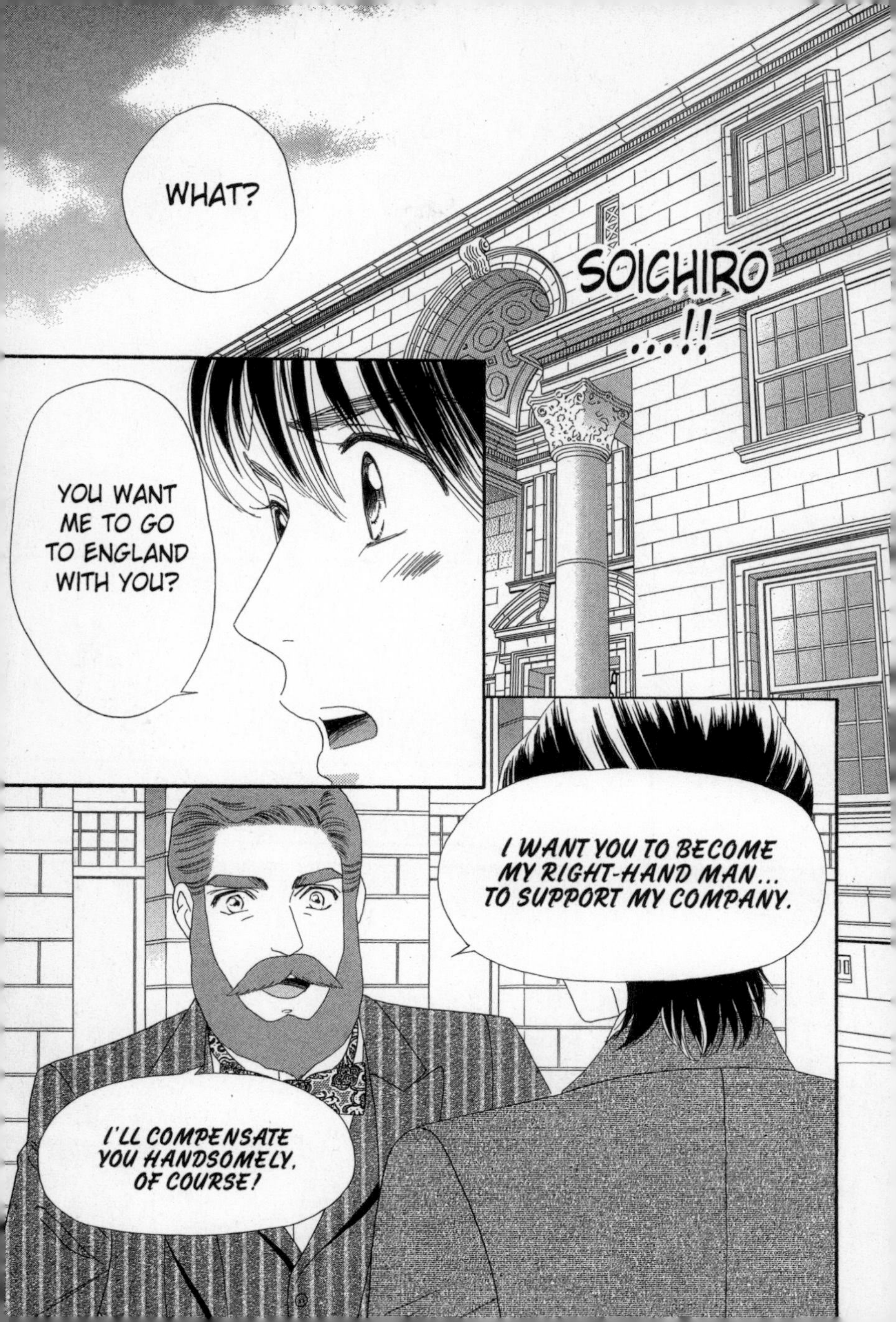
SOICHIRO ...!!
WHAT?
YOU WANT ME TO GO TO ENGLAND WITH YOU?
I WANT YOU TO BECOME MY RIGHT-HAND MAN... TO SUPPORT MY COMPANY.
I'LL COMPENSATE YOU HANDSOMELY, OF COURSE!

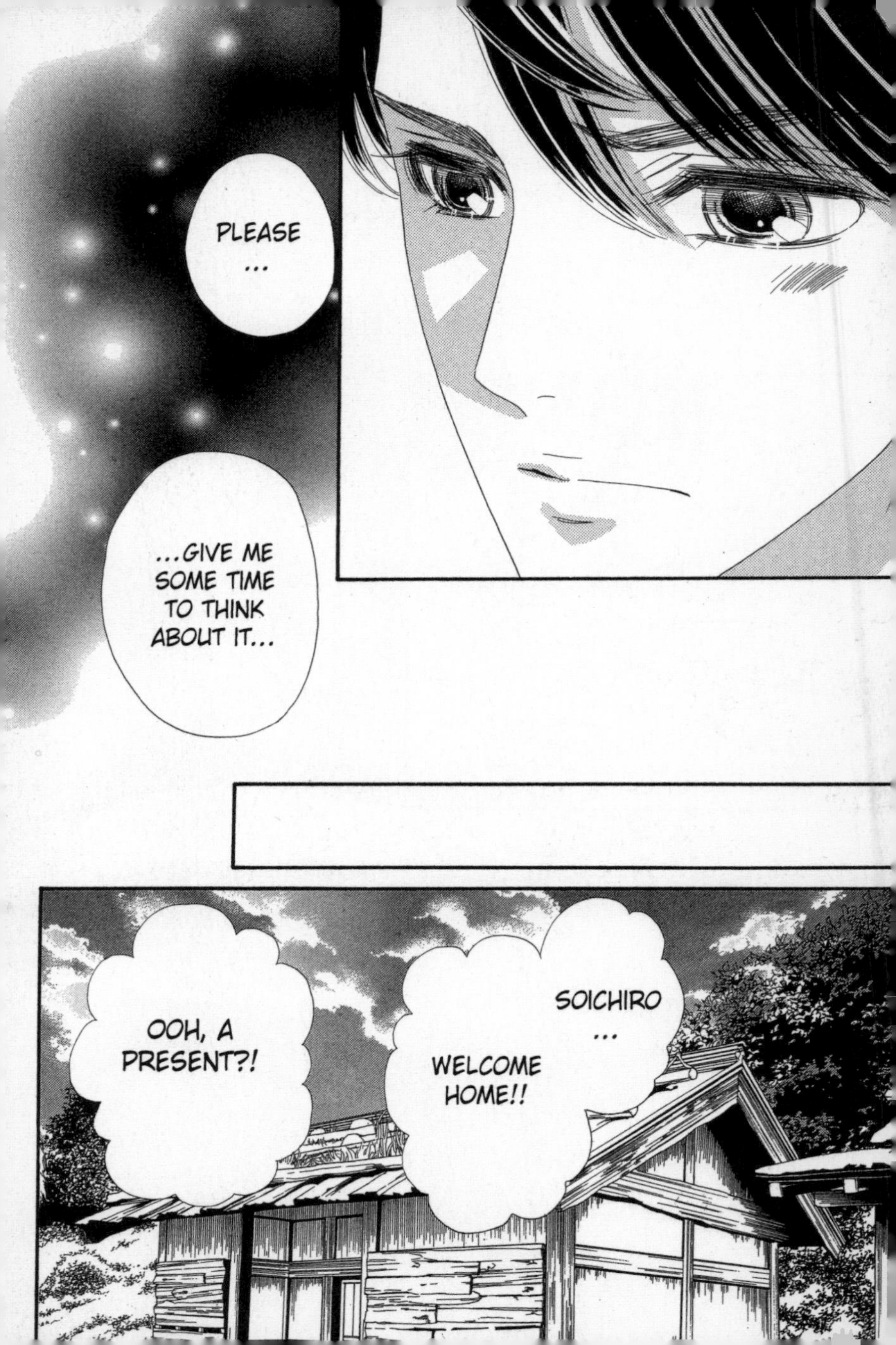
PLEASE ...
...GIVE ME SOME TIME TO THINK ABOUT IT...
SOICHIRO ... WELCOME HOME!!
OOH, A PRESENT?!

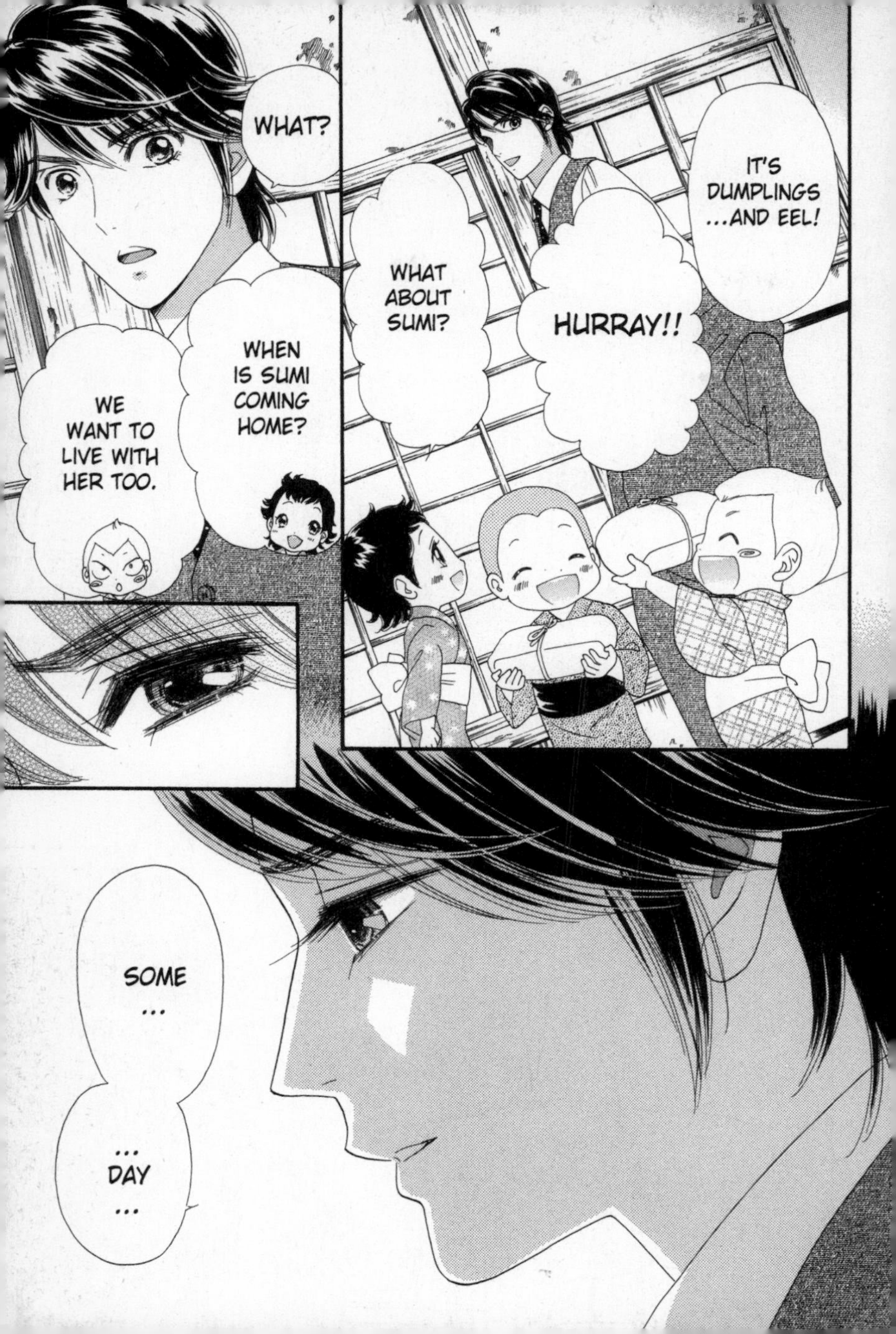
IT'S DUMPLINGS ...AND EEL!
HURRAY!!
WHAT ABOUT SUMI?
WHAT?
WHEN IS SUMI COMING HOME?
WE WANT TO LIVE WITH HER TOO.
SOME ...
... DAY ...

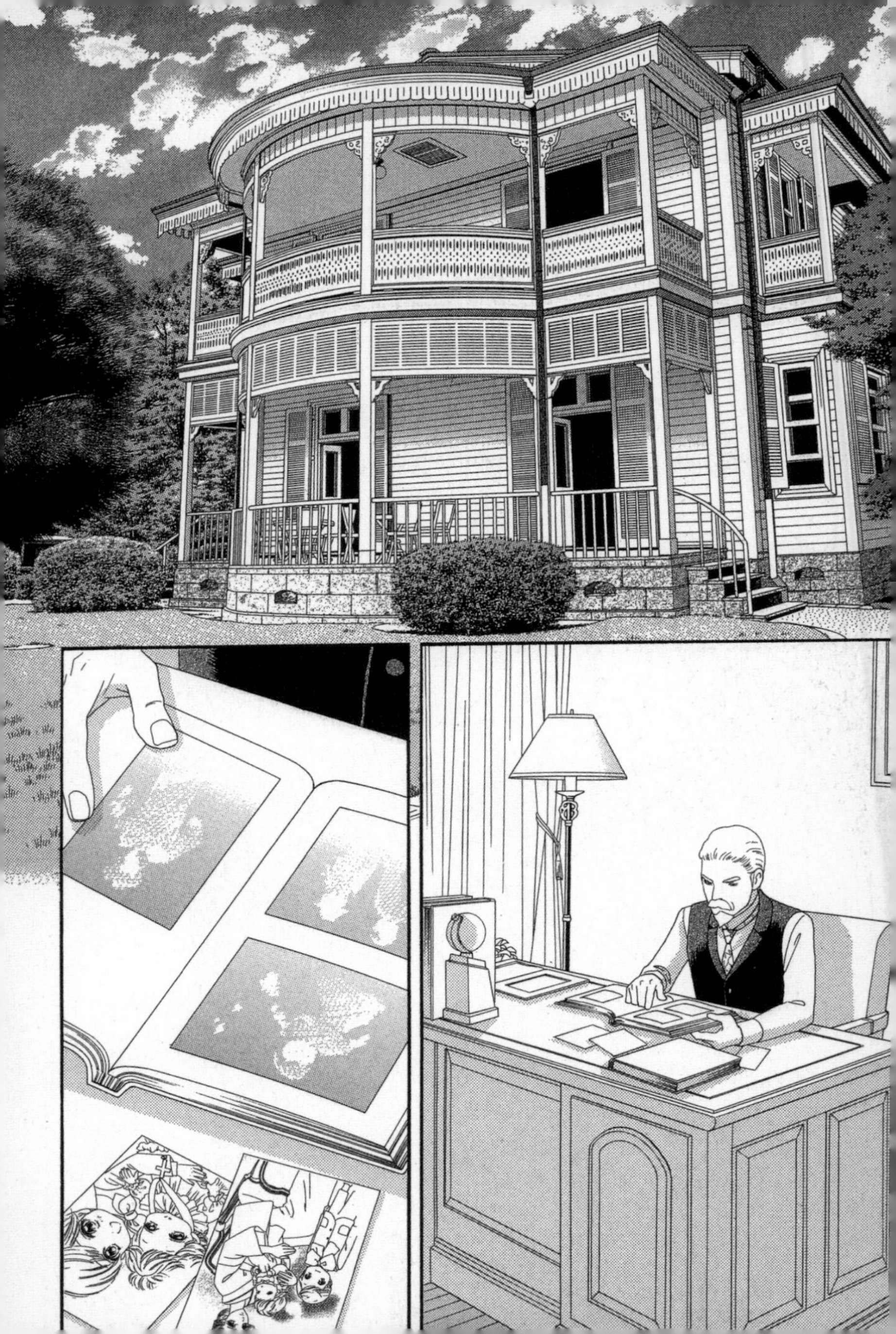

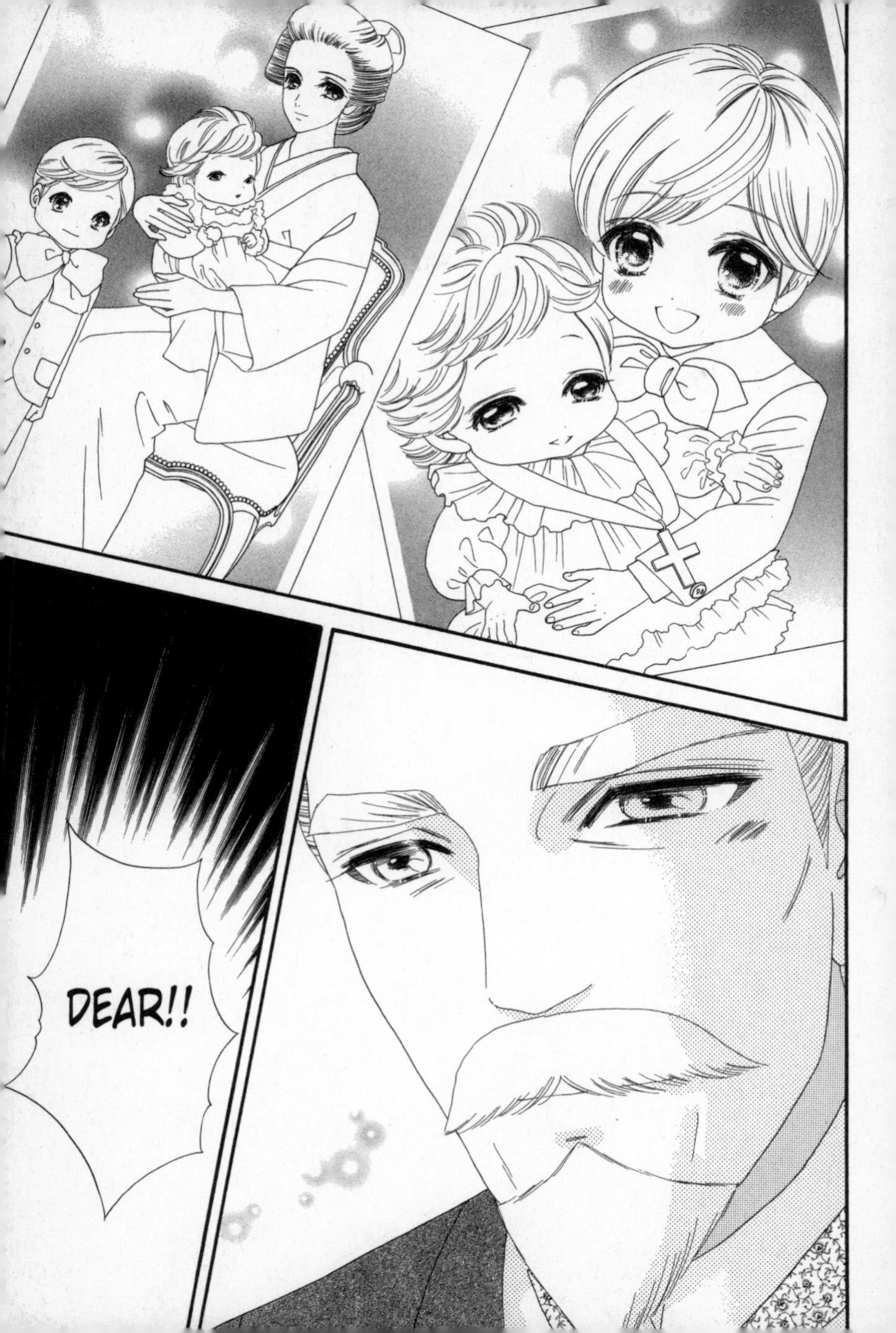
DEAR!!

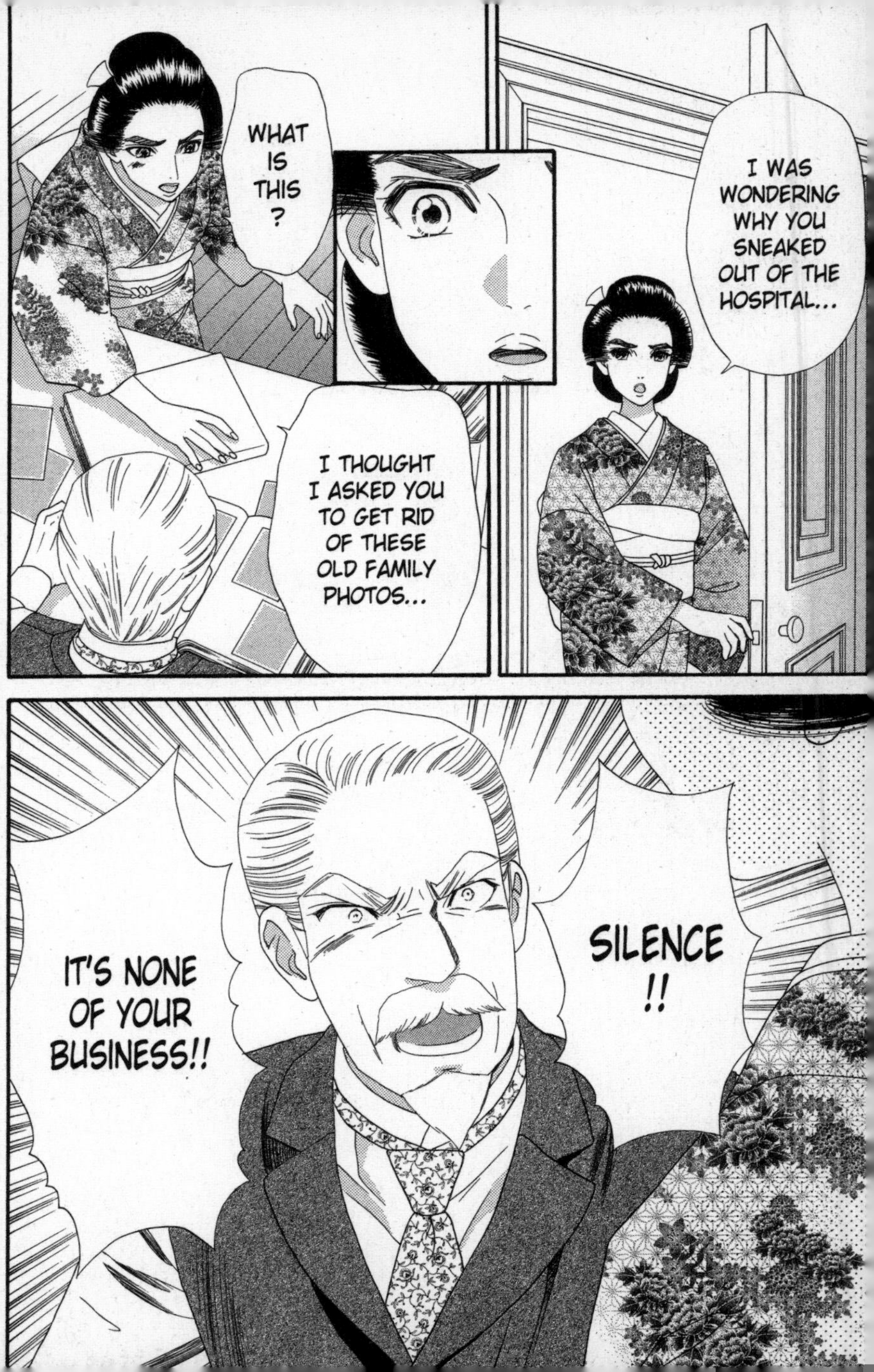
I WAS WONDERING WHY YOU SNEAKED OUT OF THE HOSPITAL...
WHAT IS THIS?
I THOUGHT I ASKED YOU TO GET RID OF THESE OLD FAMILY PHOTOS...
SILENCE!!
IT'S NONE OF YOUR BUSINESS!!

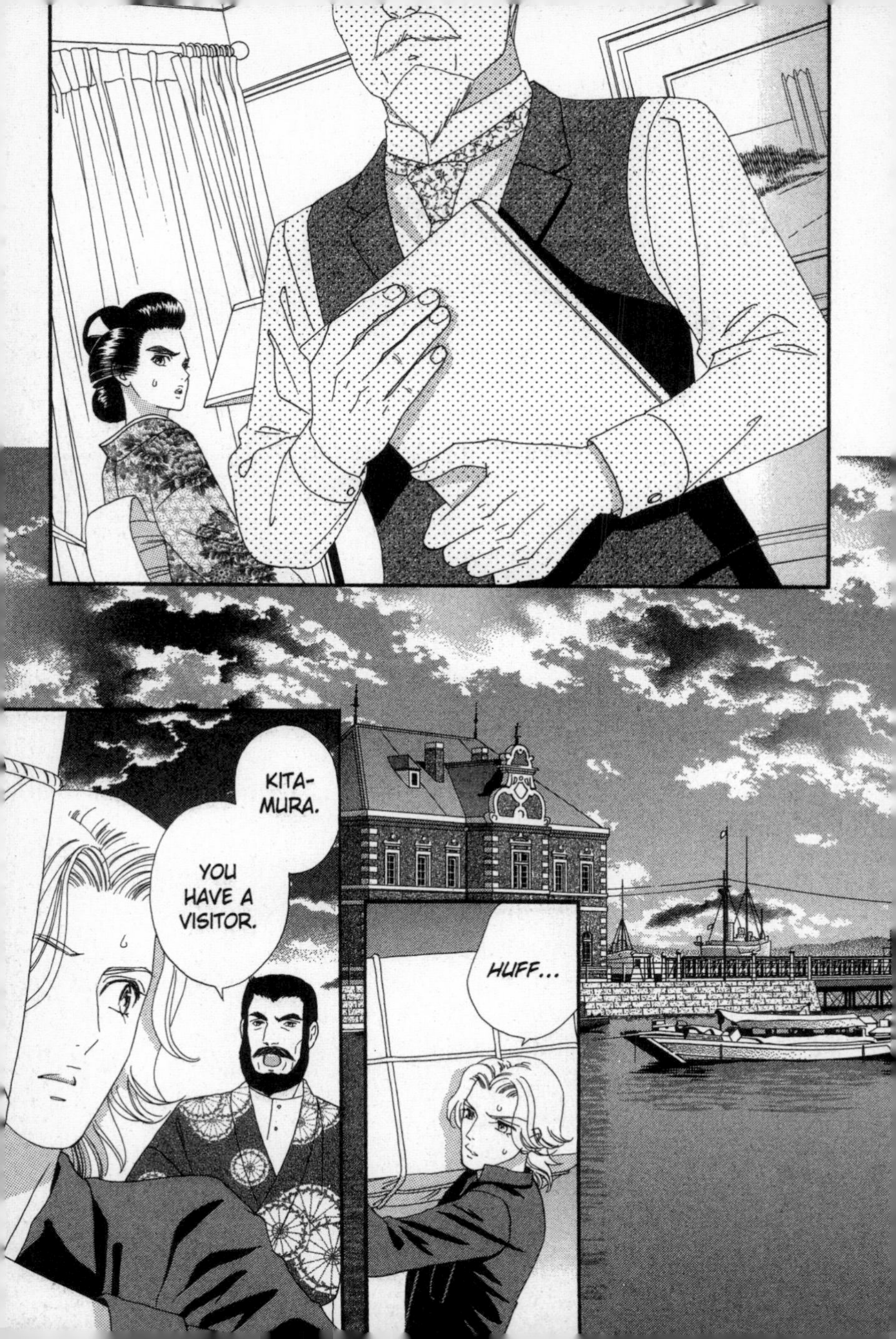
HUFF...
KITA-MURA.
YOU HAVE A VISITOR.

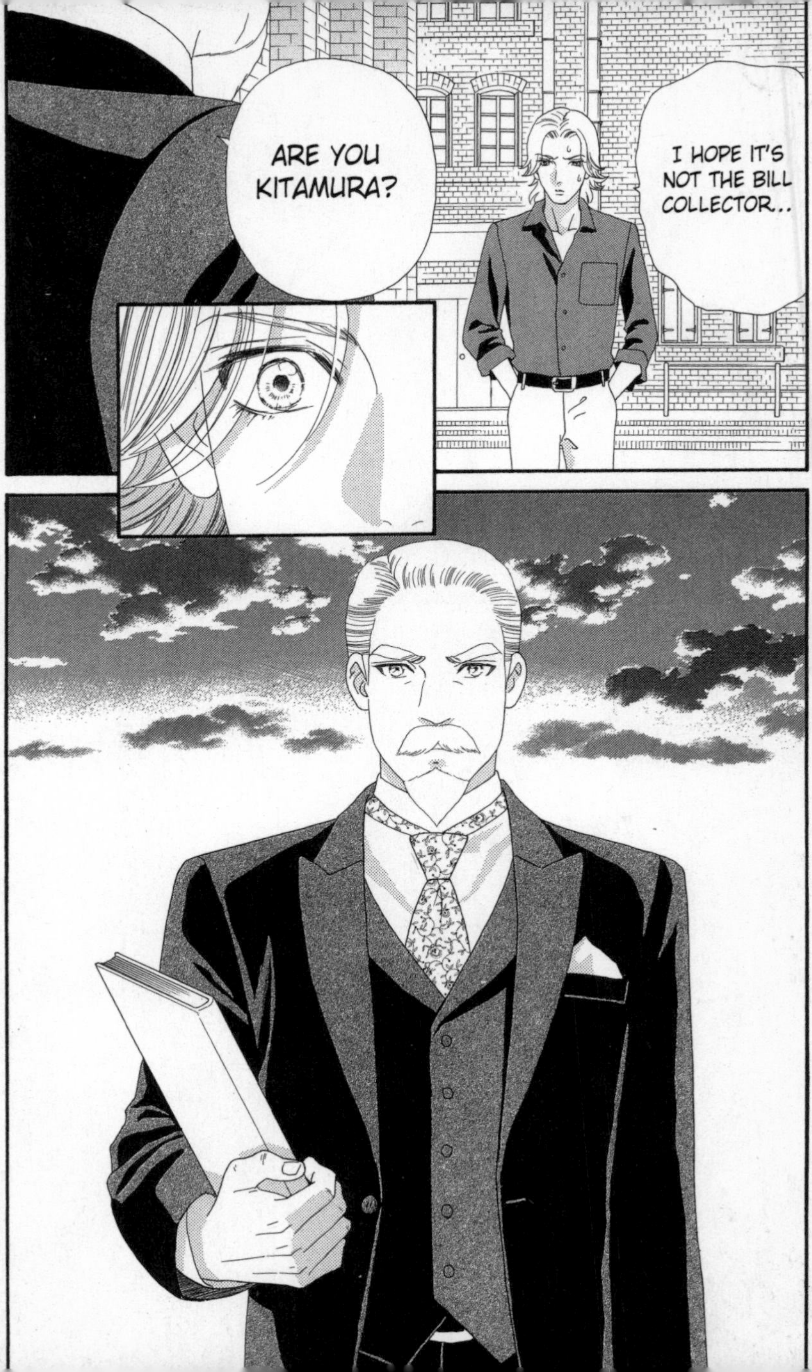
I HOPE IT'S NOT THE BILL COLLECTOR...
ARE YOU KITAMURA?

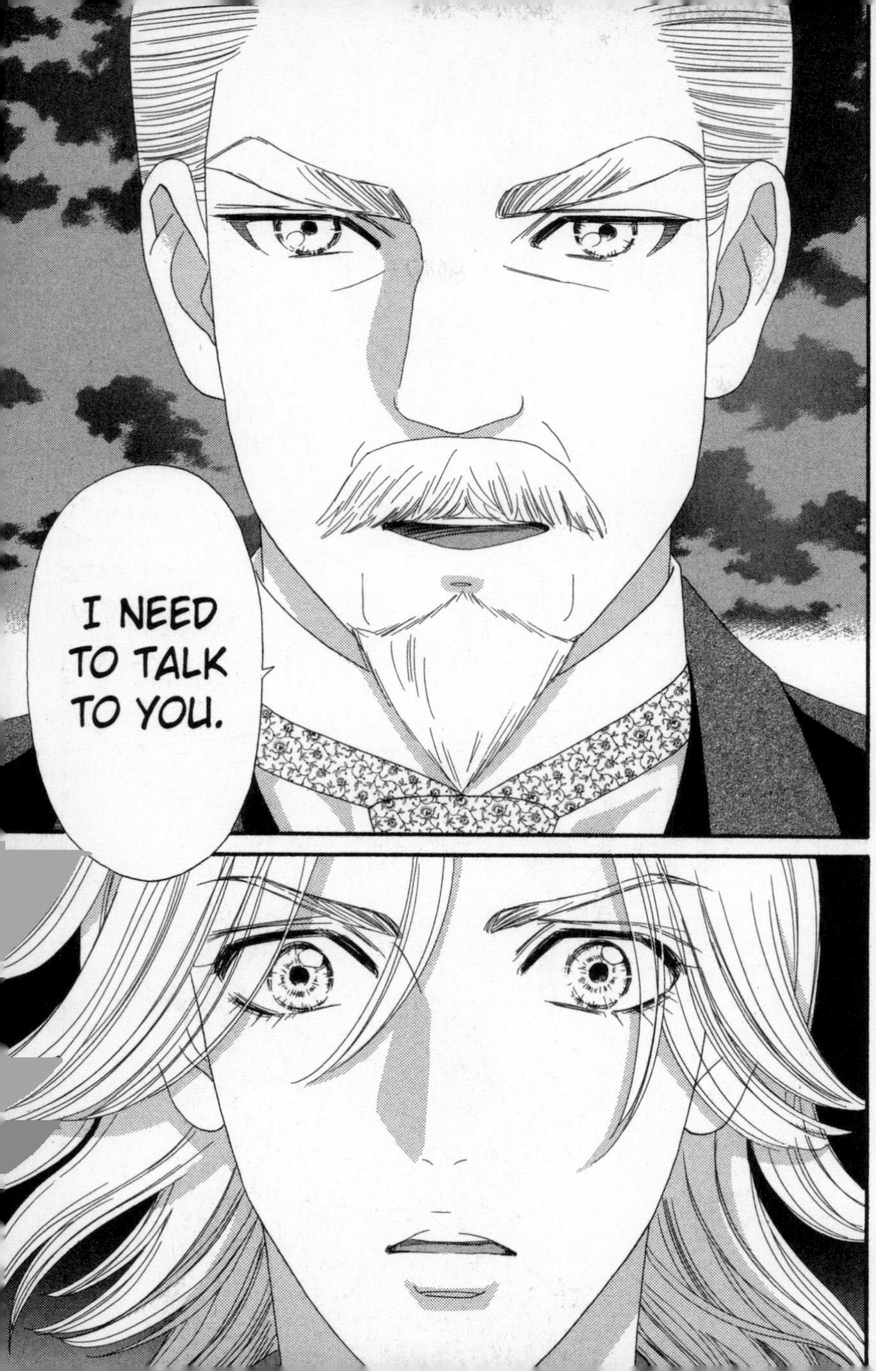
I NEED TO TALK TO YOU.

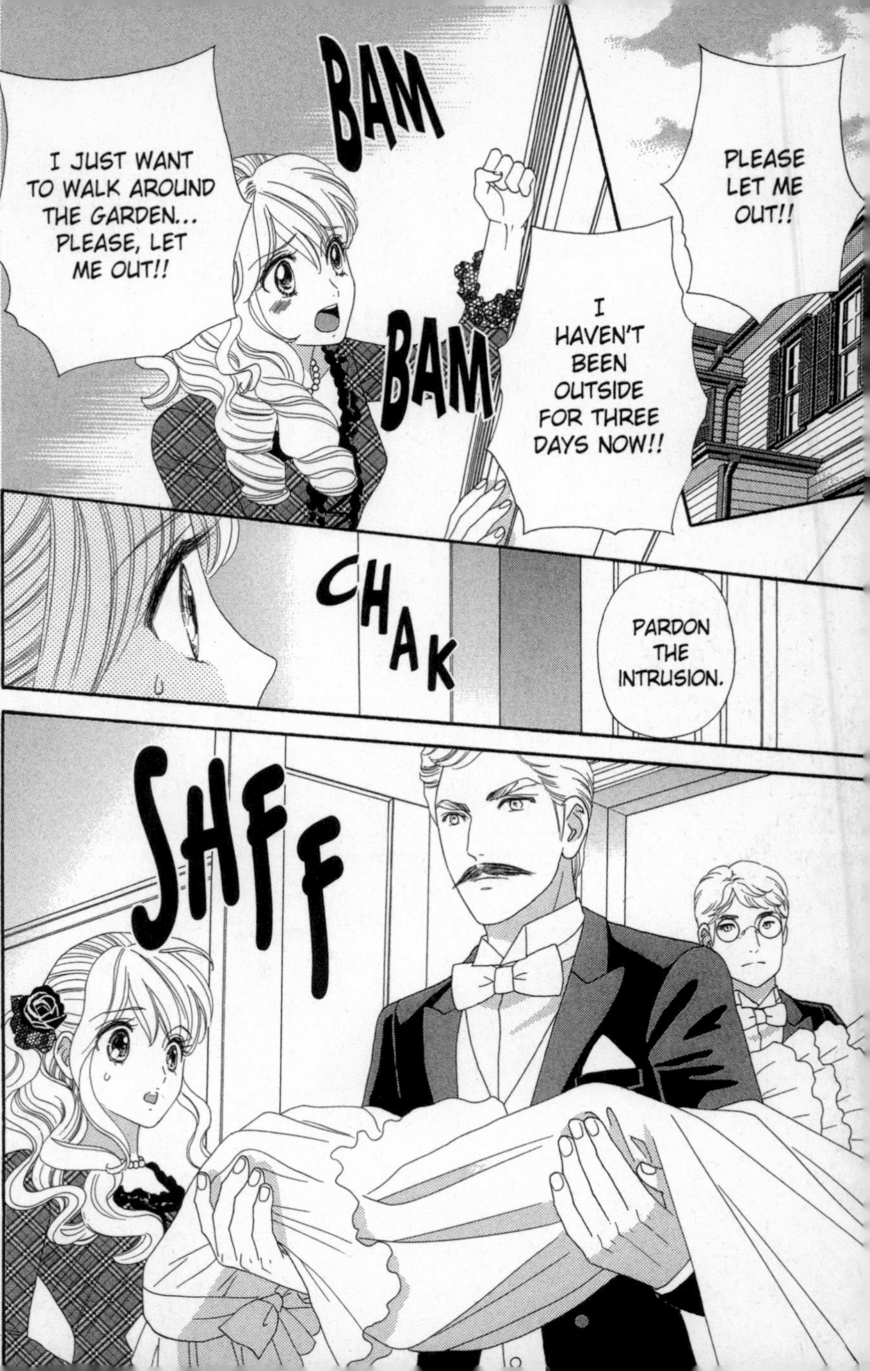
PLEASE LET ME OUT!!
BAM
I HAVEN'T BEEN OUTSIDE FOR THREE DAYS NOW!!
BAM
I JUST WANT TO WALK AROUND THE GARDEN... PLEASE, LET ME OUT!!
PARDON THE INTRUSION.
CHAK
SHFF

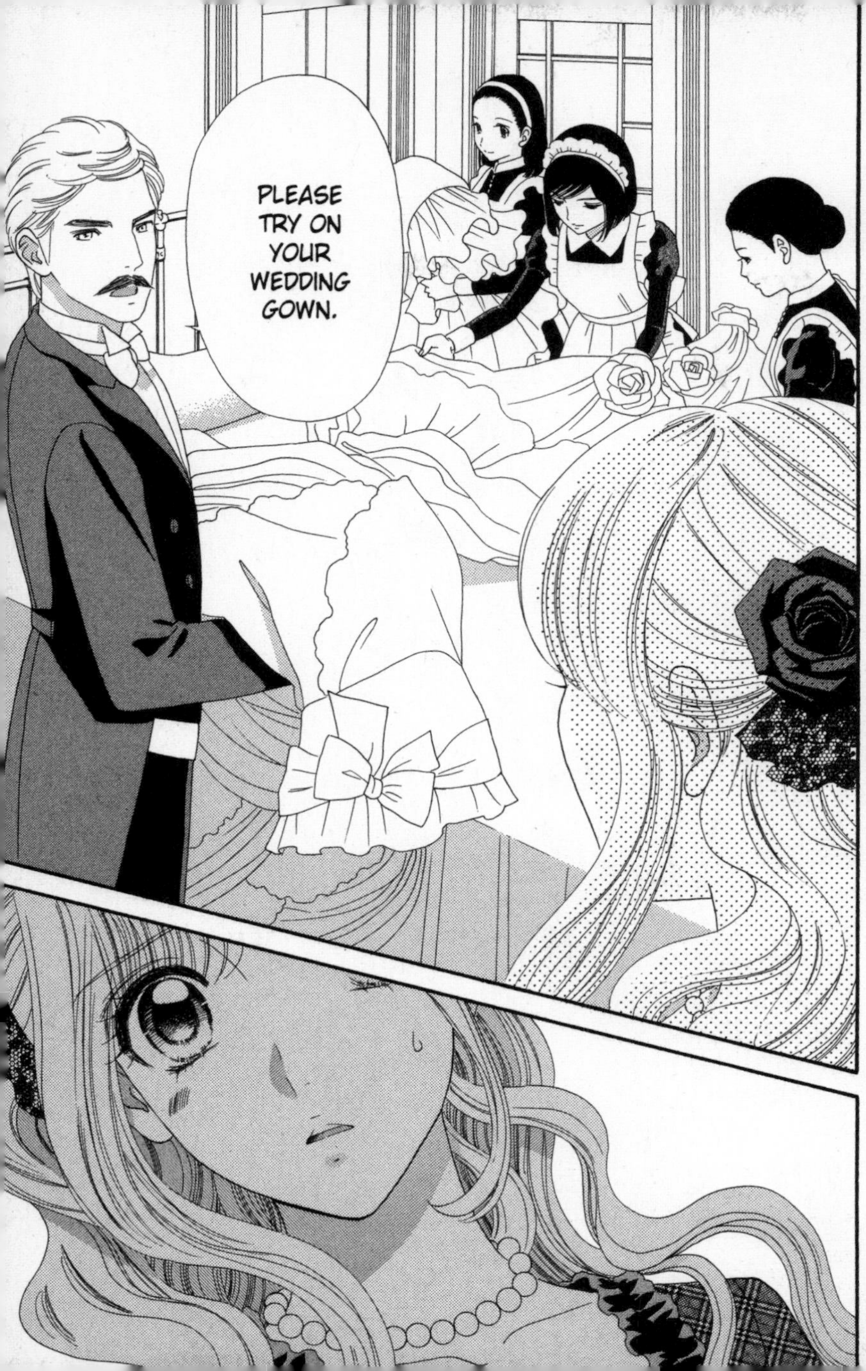
PLEASE TRY ON YOUR WEDDING GOWN.

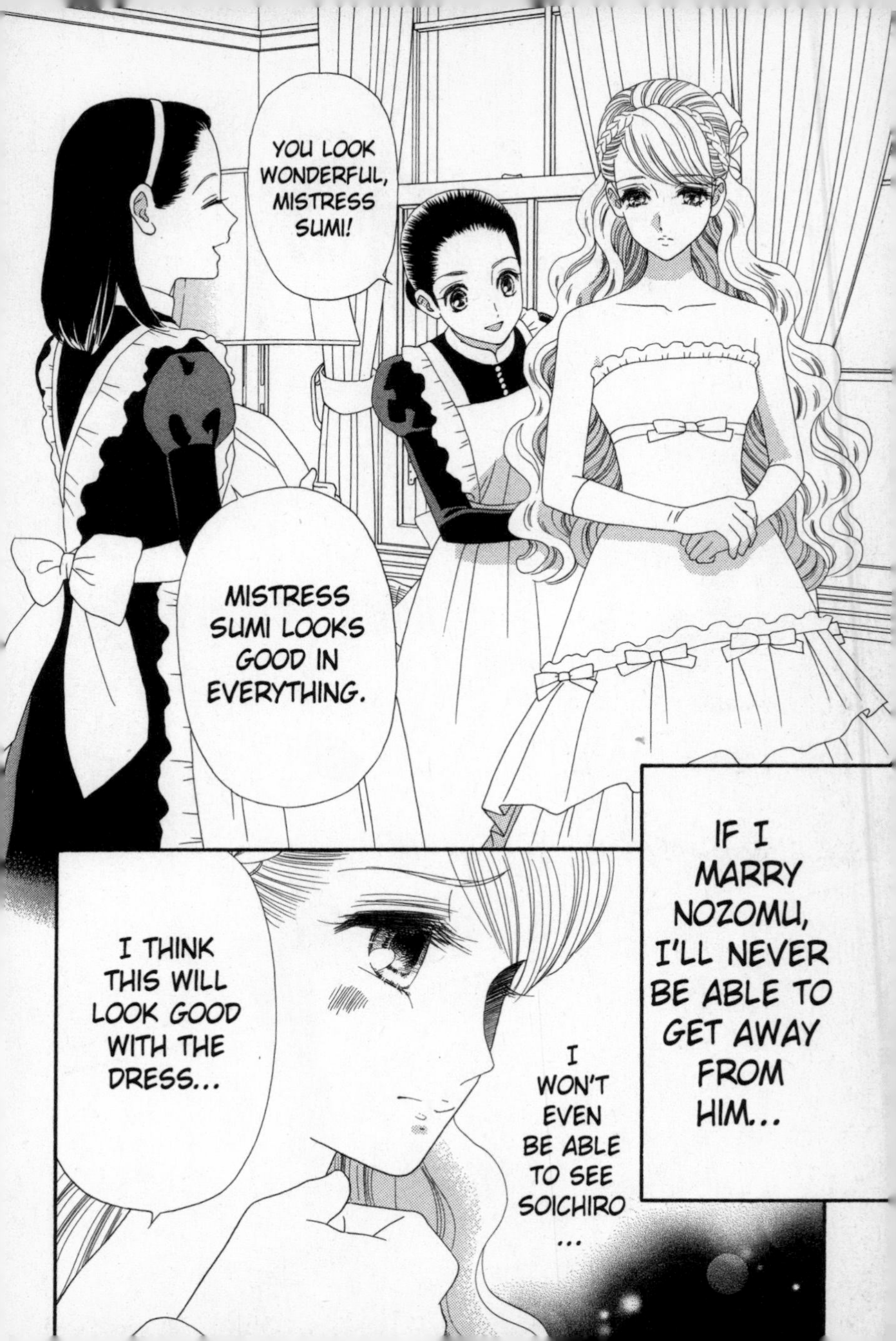
YOU LOOK WONDERFUL, MISTRESS SUMI!
MISTRESS SUMI LOOKS GOOD IN EVERYTHING.
IF I MARRY NOZOMU, I'LL NEVER BE ABLE TO GET AWAY FROM HIM...
I WON'T EVEN BE ABLE TO SEE SOICHIRO ...
I THINK THIS WILL LOOK GOOD WITH THE DRESS...

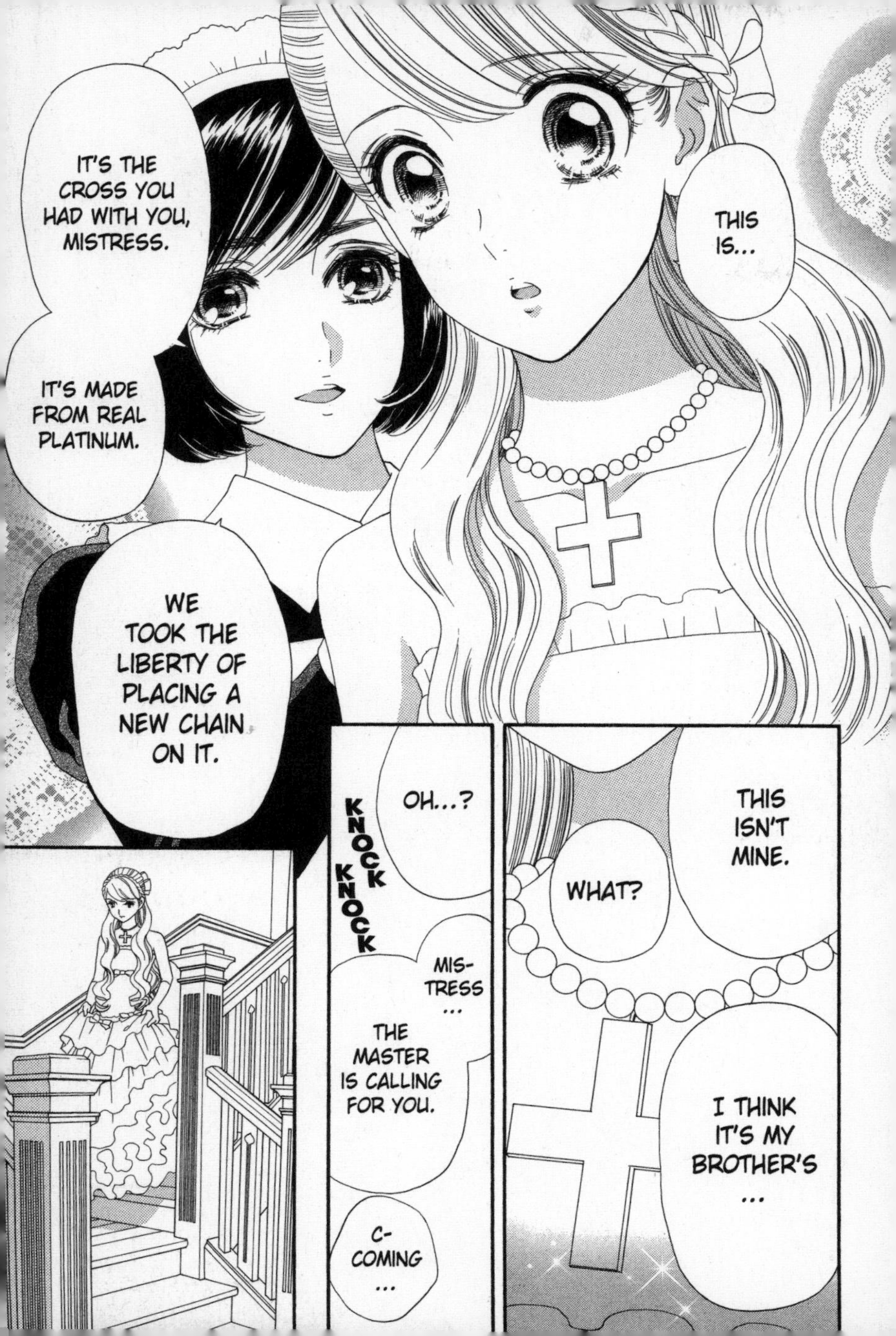

THIS IS...
IT'S THE CROSS YOU HAD WITH YOU, MISTRESS.
IT'S MADE FROM REAL PLATINUM.
WE TOOK THE LIBERTY OF PLACING A NEW CHAIN ON IT.
THIS ISN'T MINE.
WHAT?
I THINK IT'S MY BROTHER'S...
OH...?
KNOCK KNOCK
MISTRESS...
THE MASTER IS CALLING FOR YOU.
C-COMING...

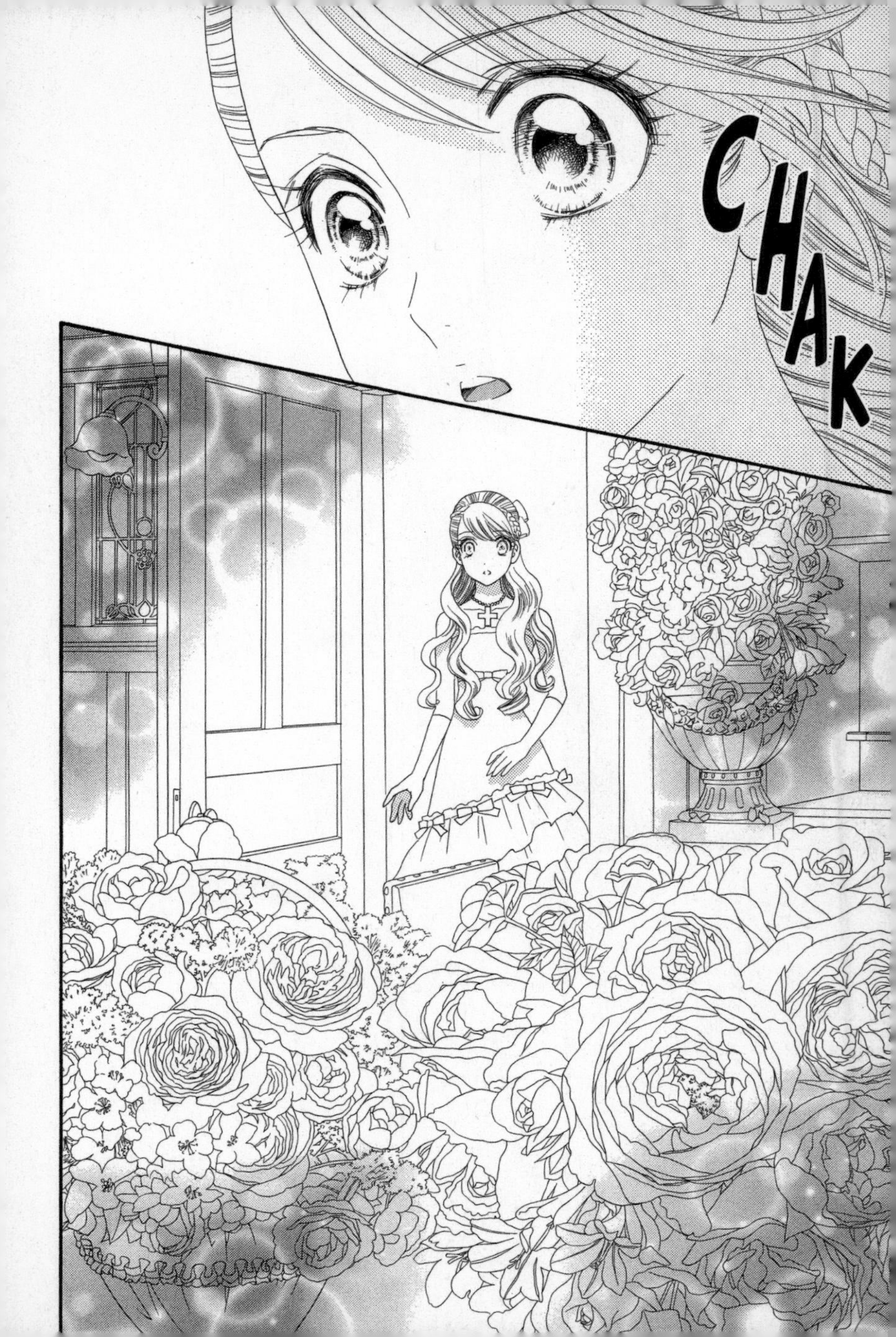
CHAK

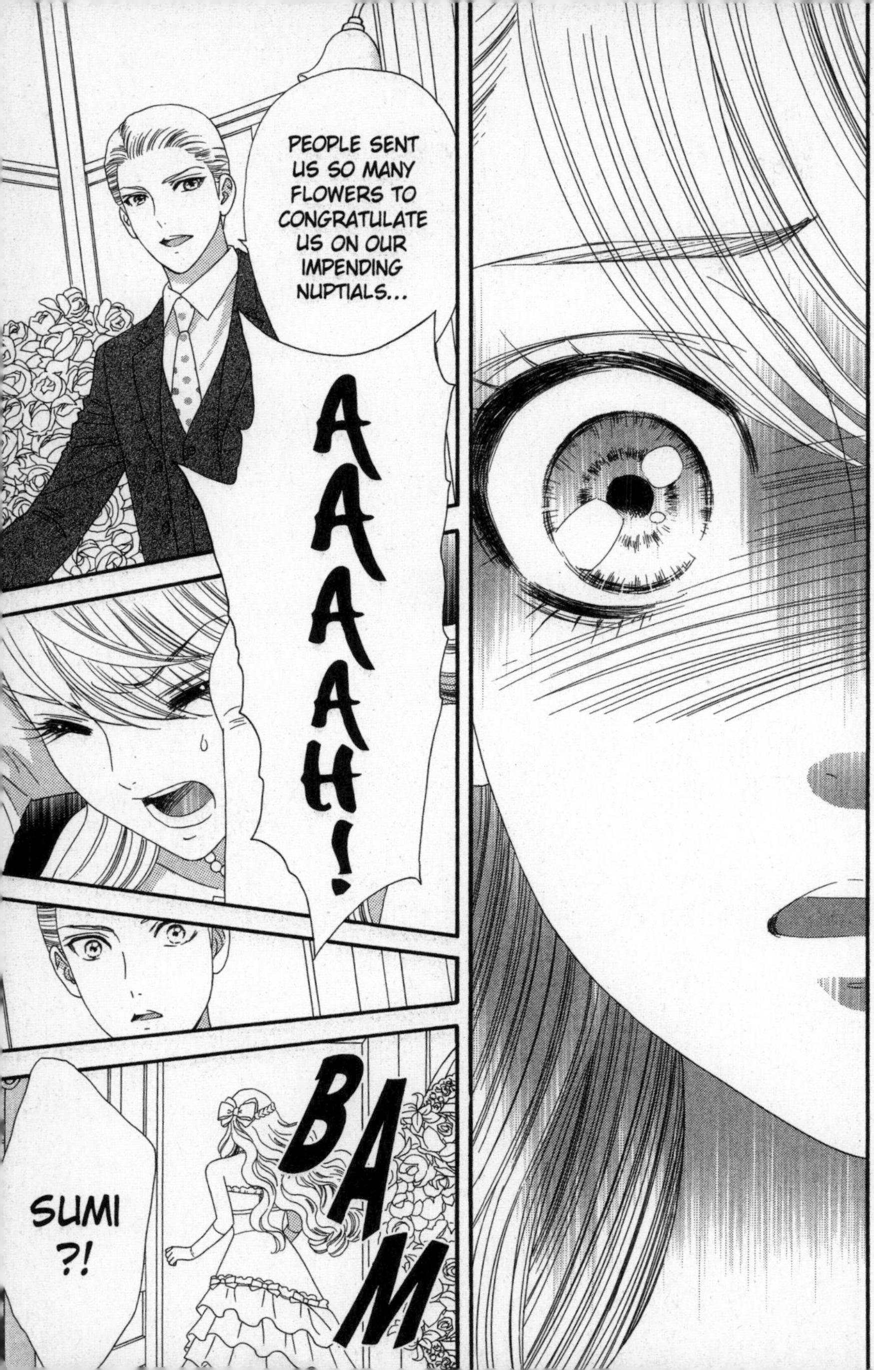
PEOPLE SENT US SO MANY FLOWERS TO CONGRATULATE US ON OUR IMPENDING NUPTIALS...
AAAAAH!
BAM
SUMI ?!

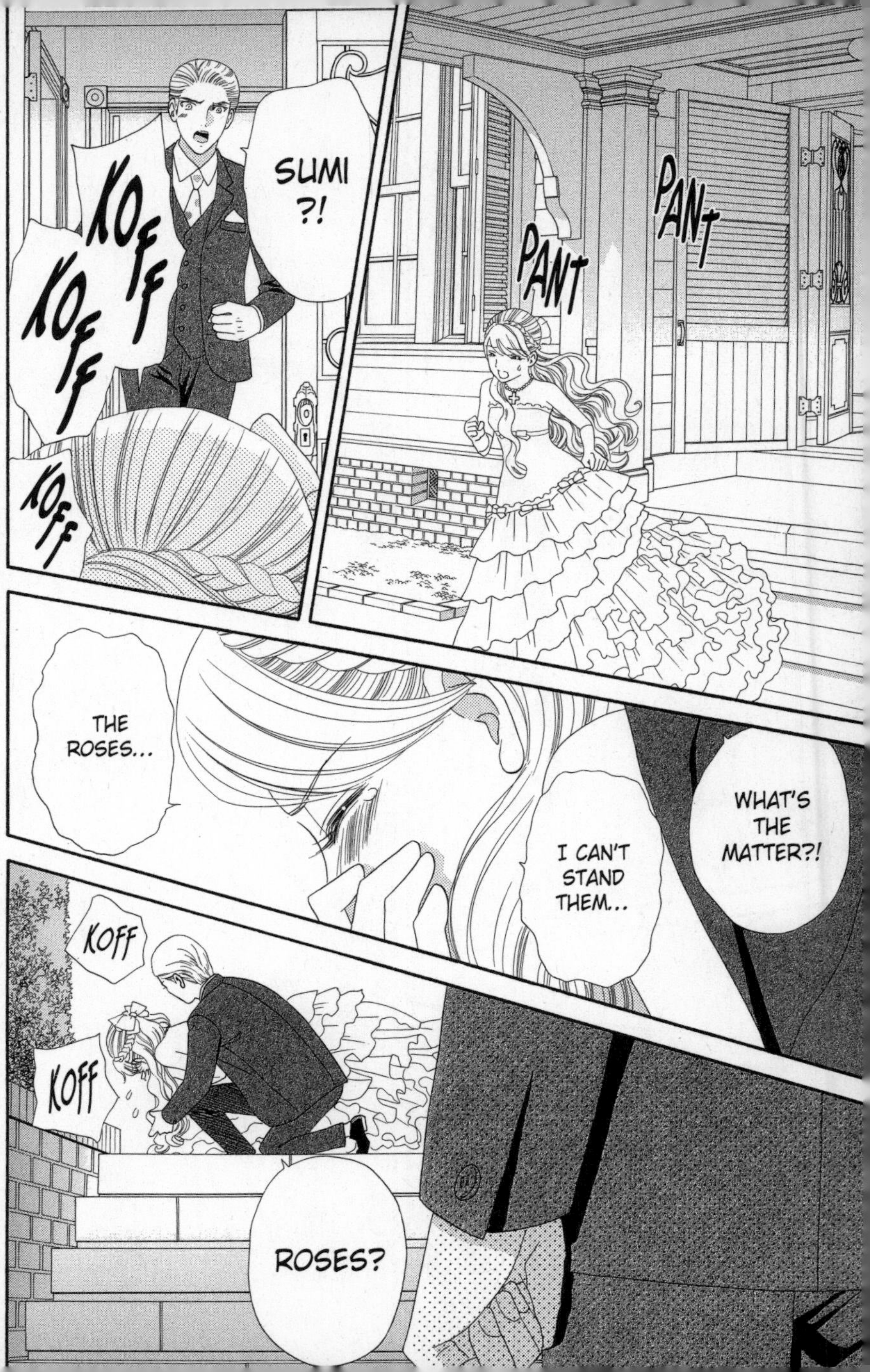
PANT
PANT
SUMI ?!
KOFF
KOFF
KOFF
THE ROSES...
WHAT'S THE MATTER?!
I CAN'T STAND THEM...
KOFF
KOFF
ROSES?

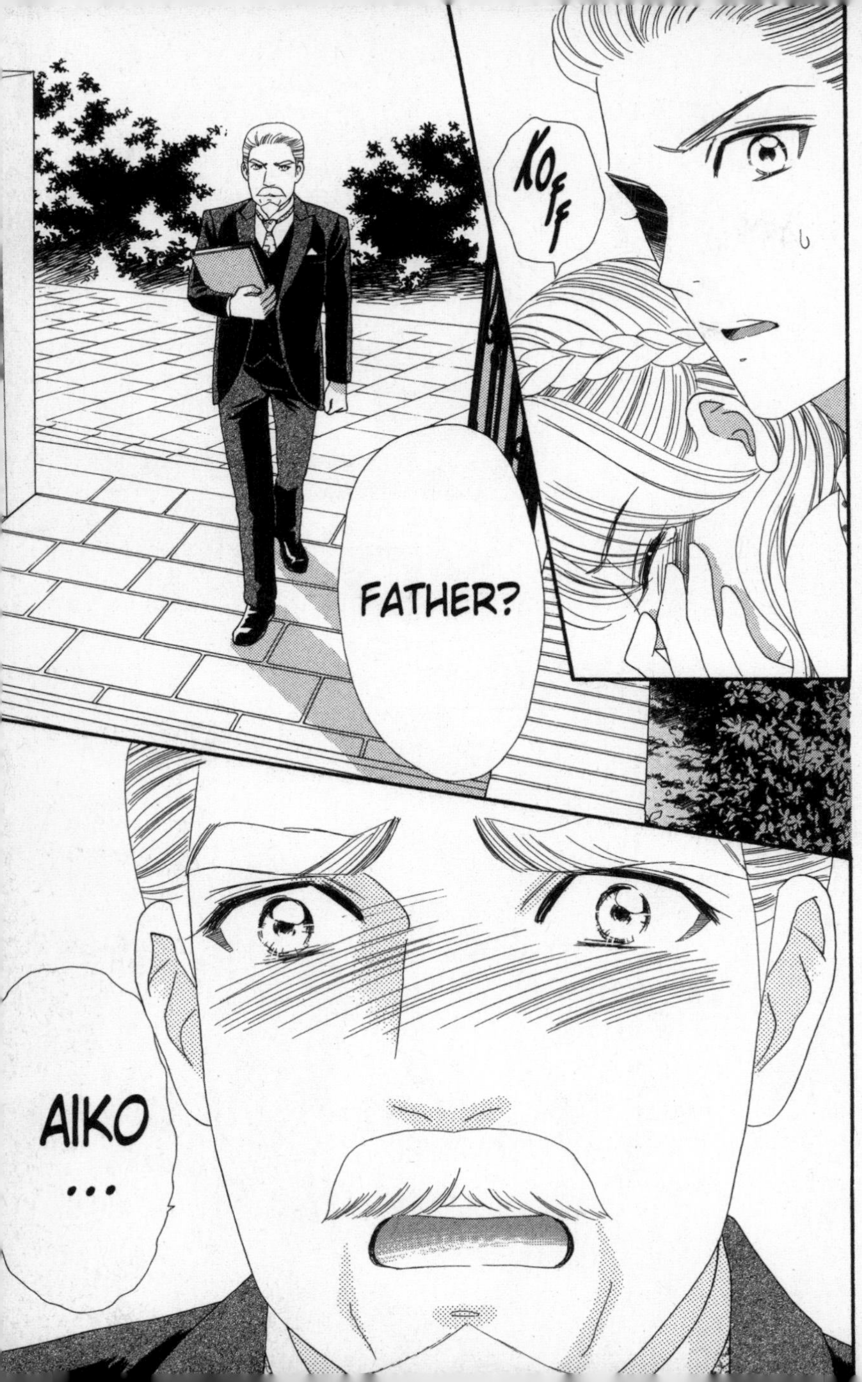
KOFF
FATHER?
AIKO ...

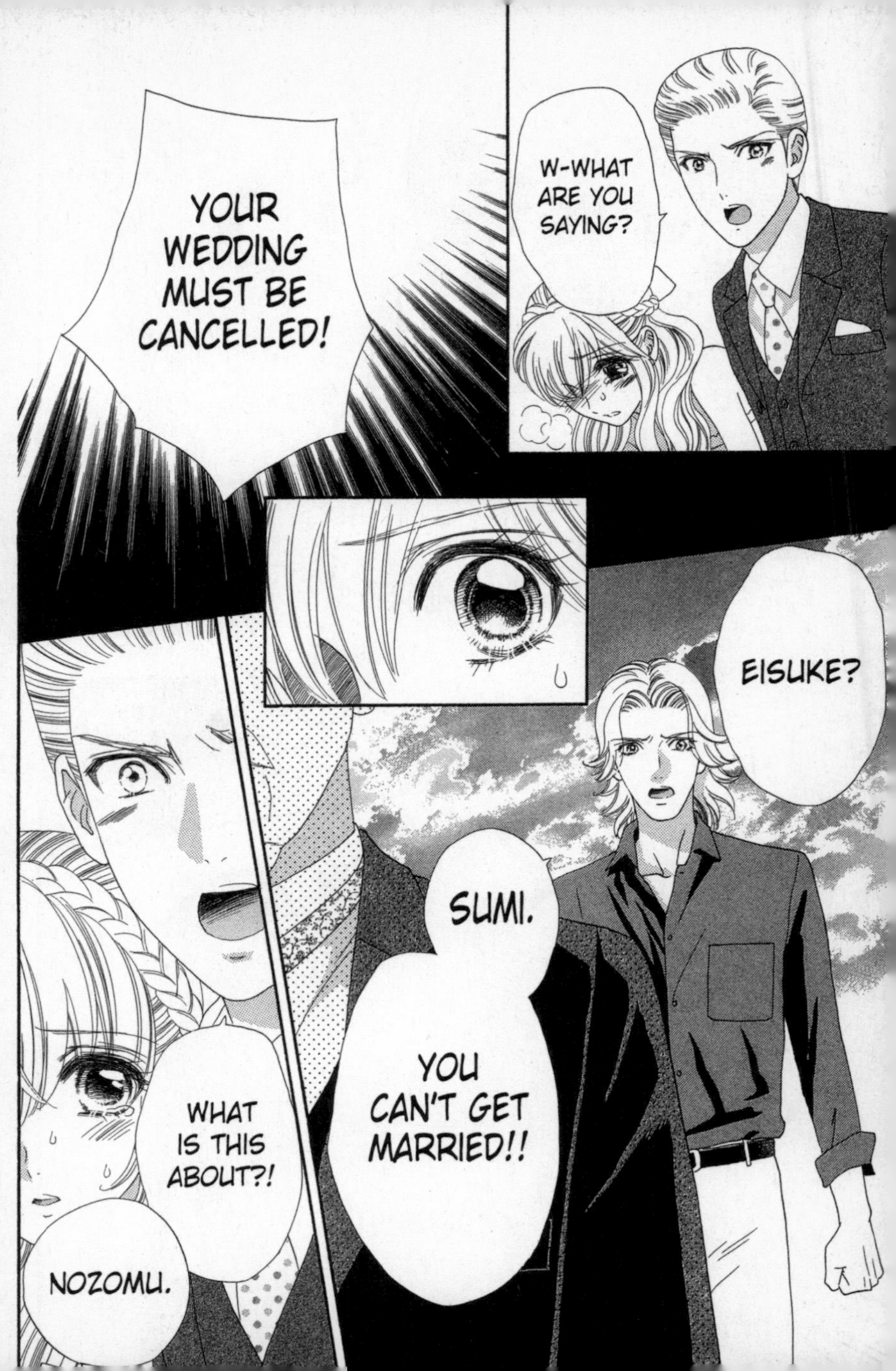
W-WHAT ARE YOU SAYING?
YOUR WEDDING MUST BE CANCELLED!
EISUKE?
SUMI.
YOU CAN'T GET MARRIED!!
WHAT IS THIS ABOUT?!
NOZOMU.

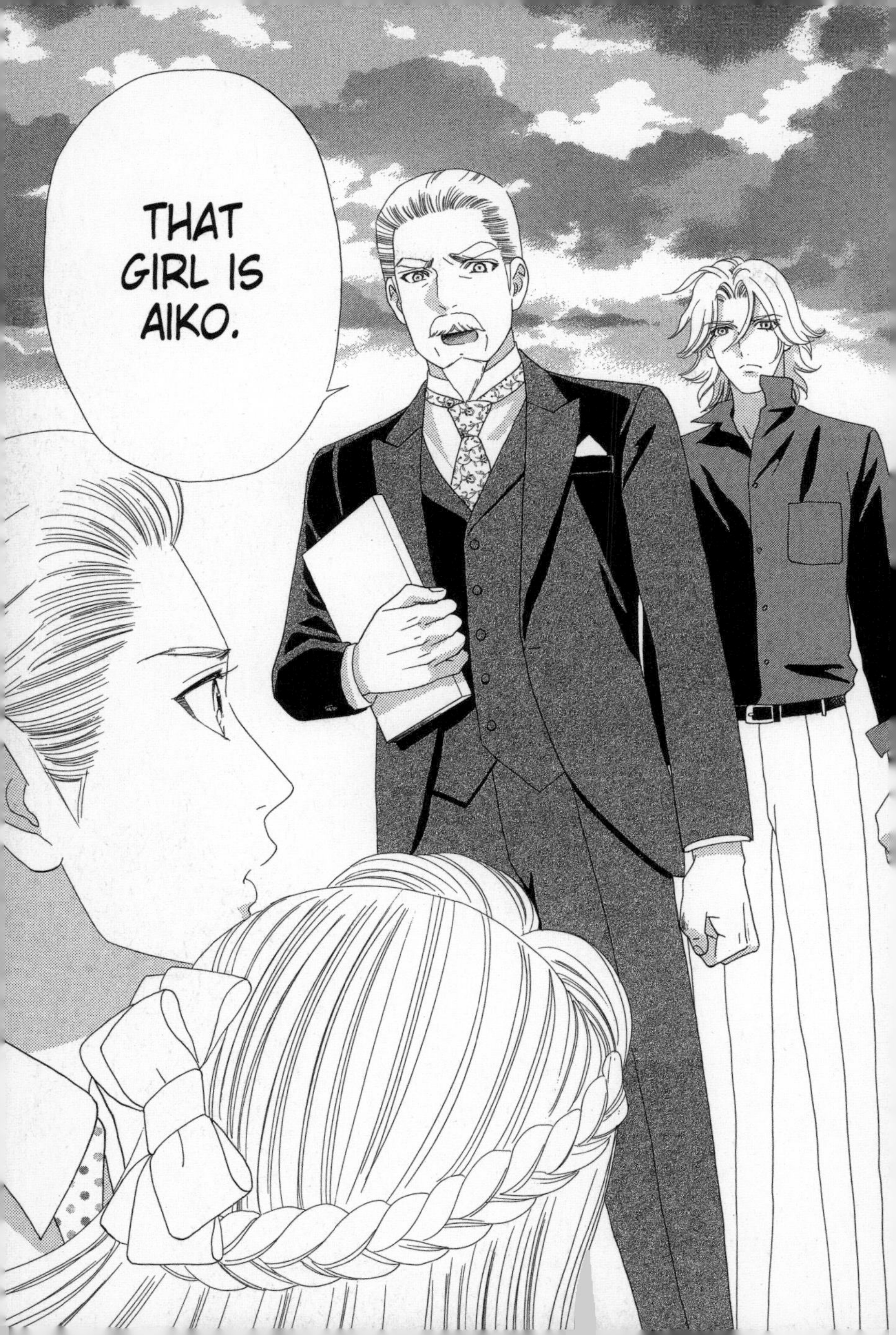
THAT GIRL IS AIKO.

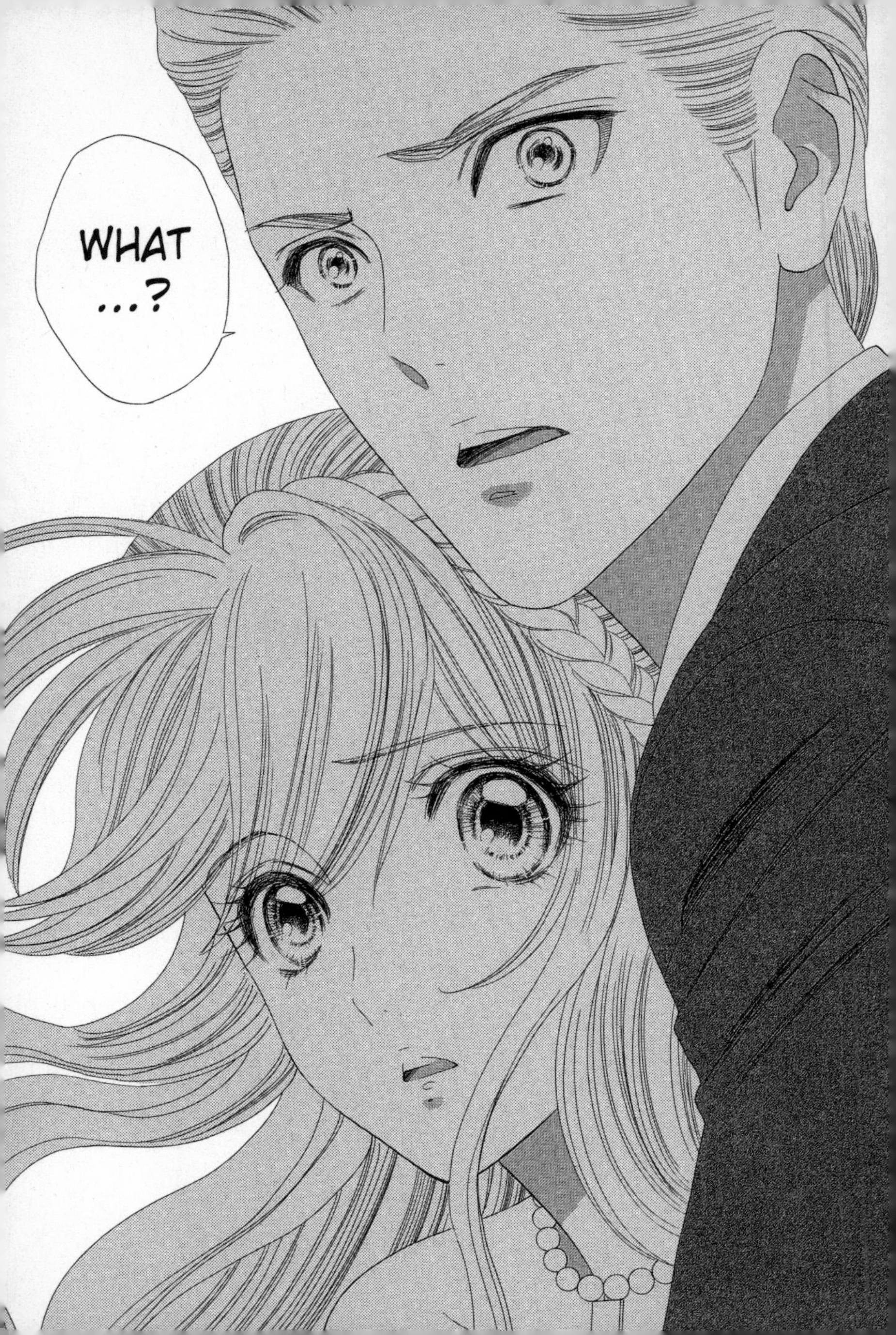
WHAT ...?

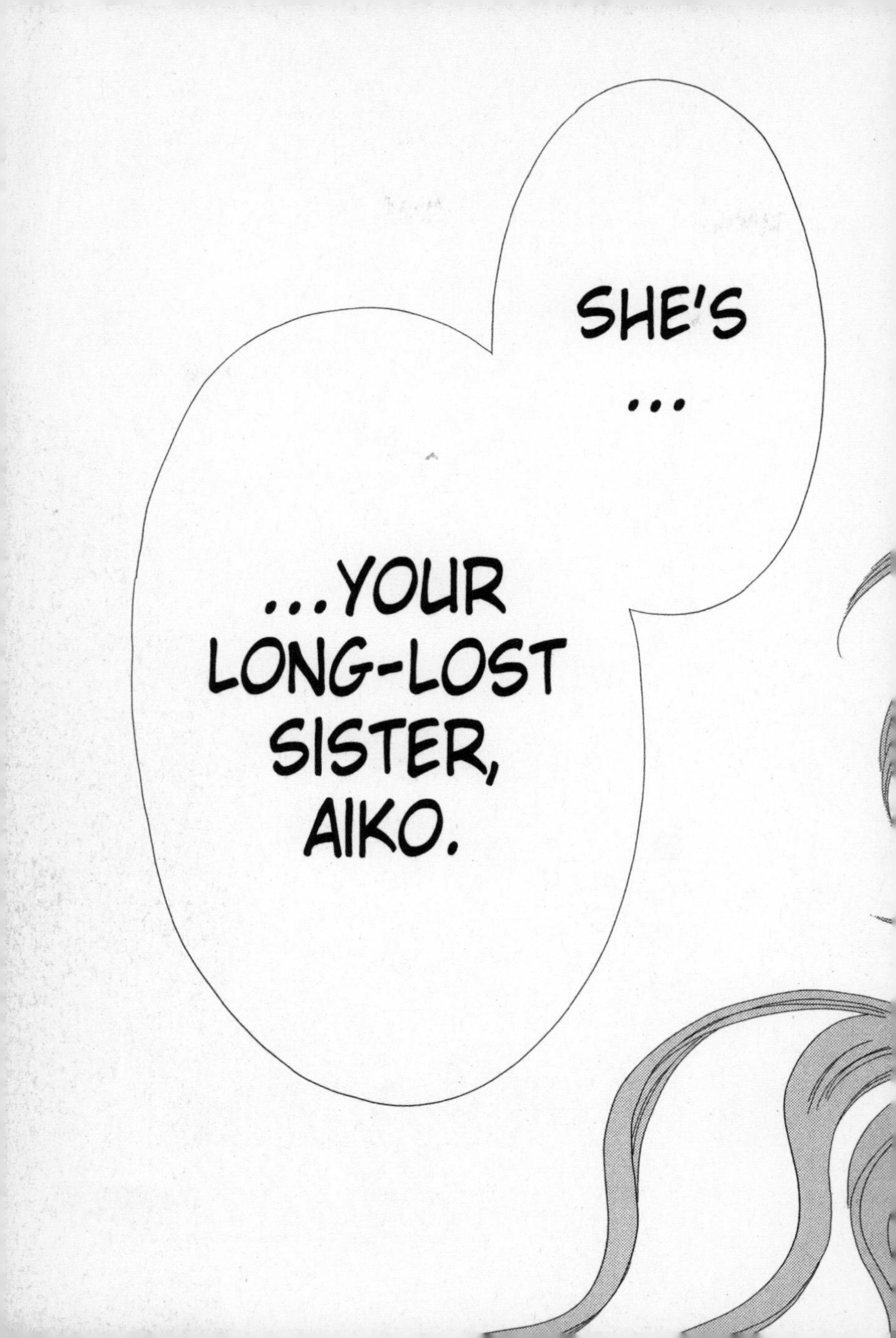
SHE'S
...
...YOUR LONG-LOST SISTER, AIKO.

Stepping on Roses

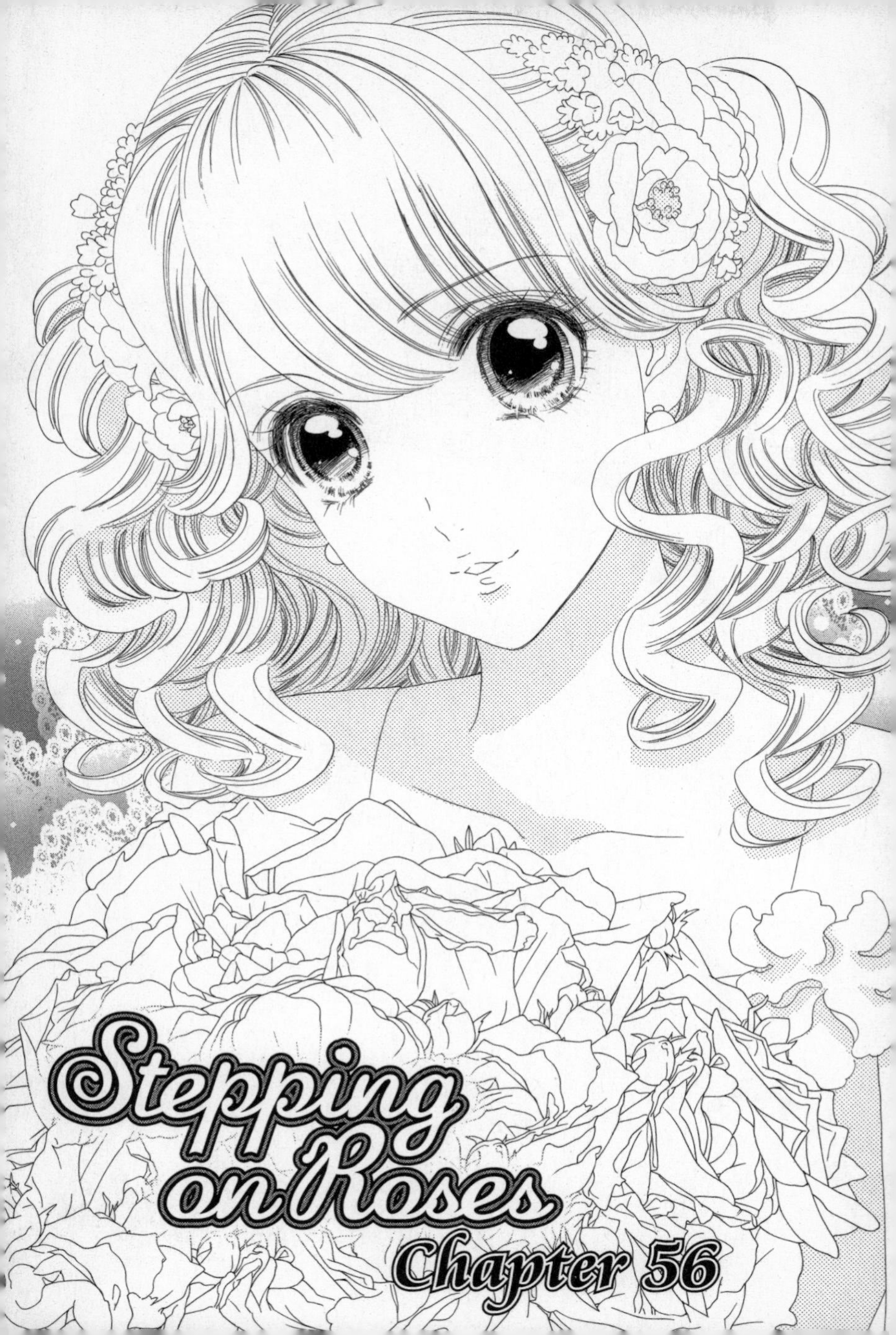
Stepping on Roses
Chapter 56

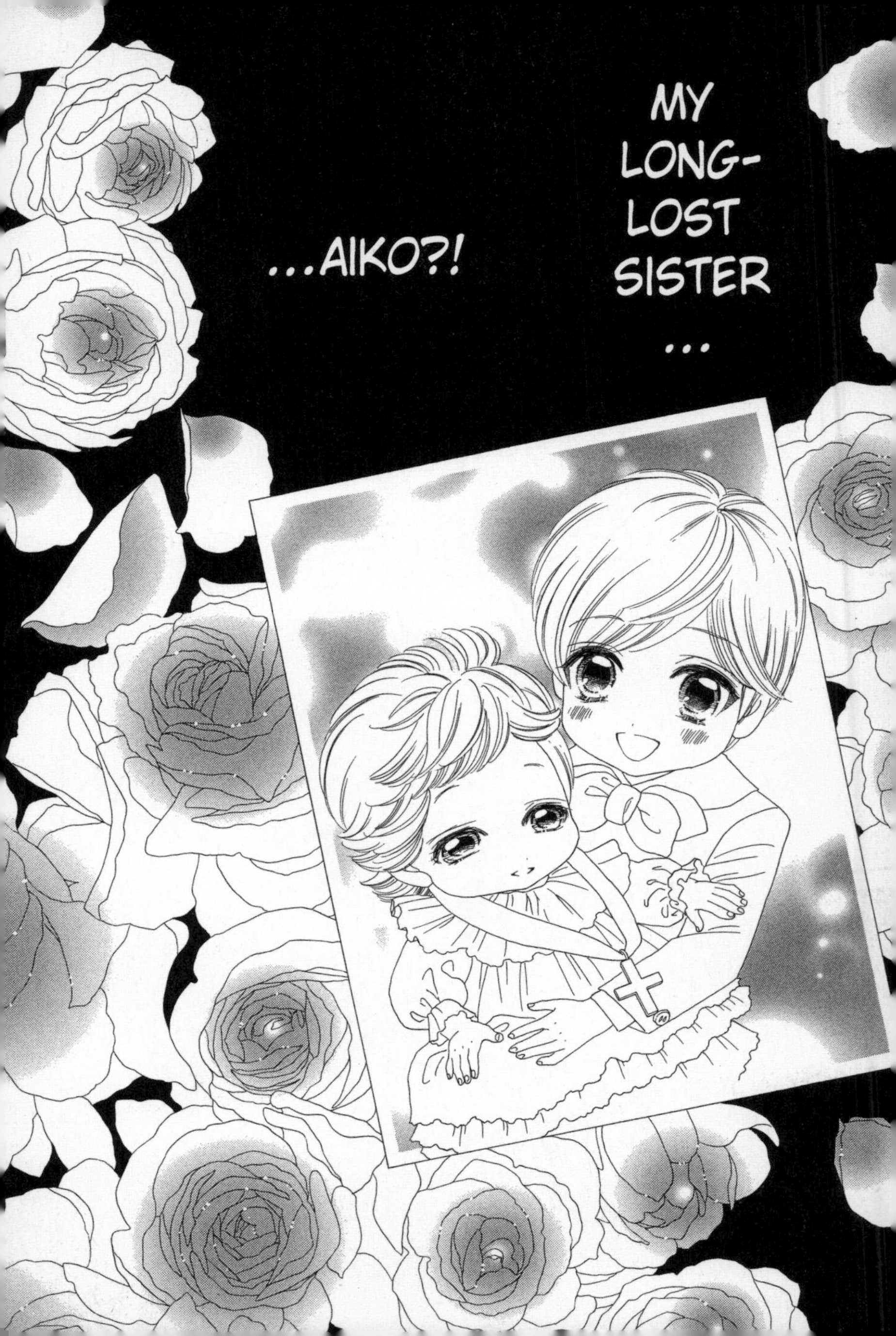
MY LONG-LOST SISTER ...
...AIKO?!

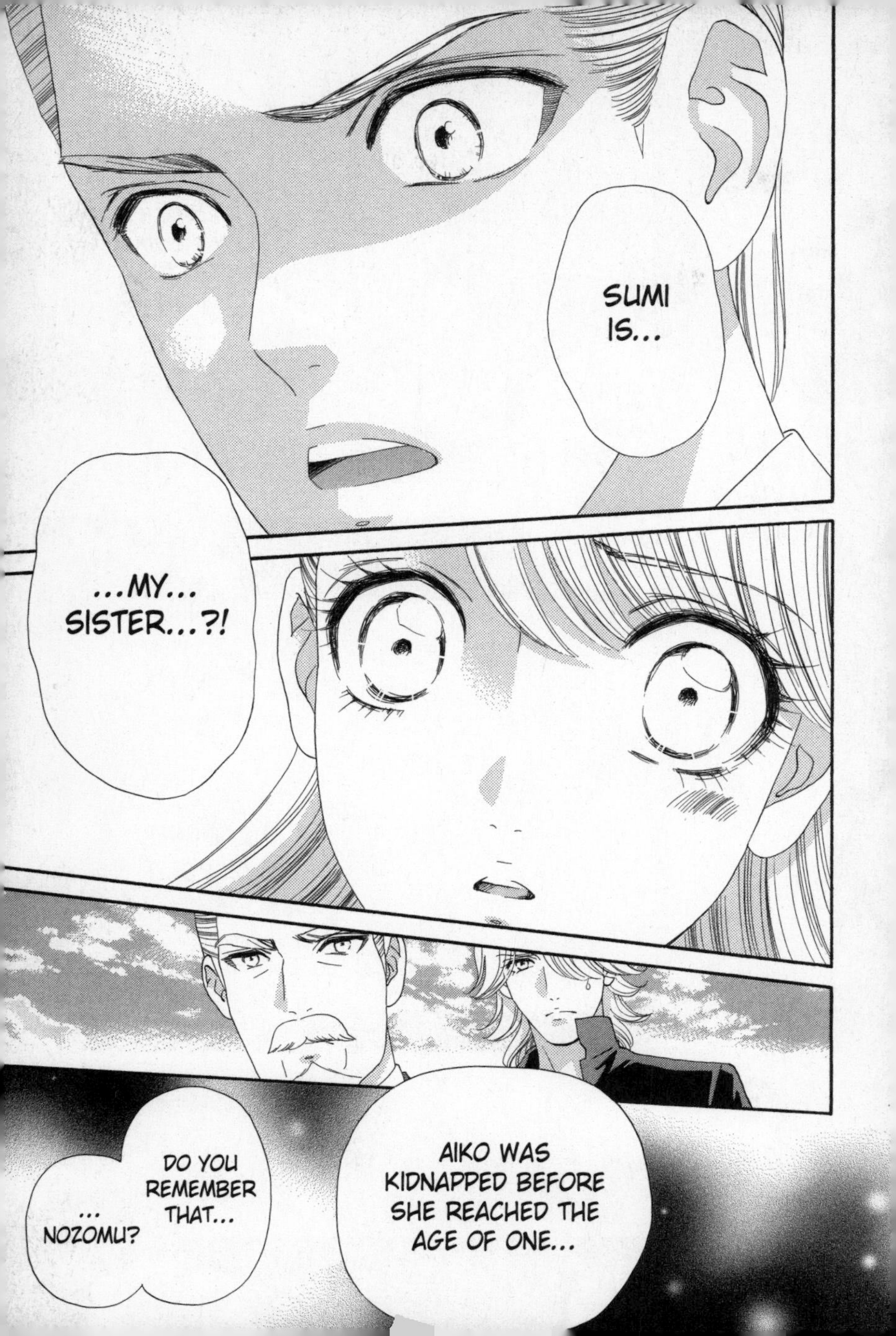
SUMI IS...
...MY... SISTER...?!
AIKO WAS KIDNAPPED BEFORE SHE REACHED THE AGE OF ONE...
DO YOU REMEMBER THAT...
... NOZOMU?

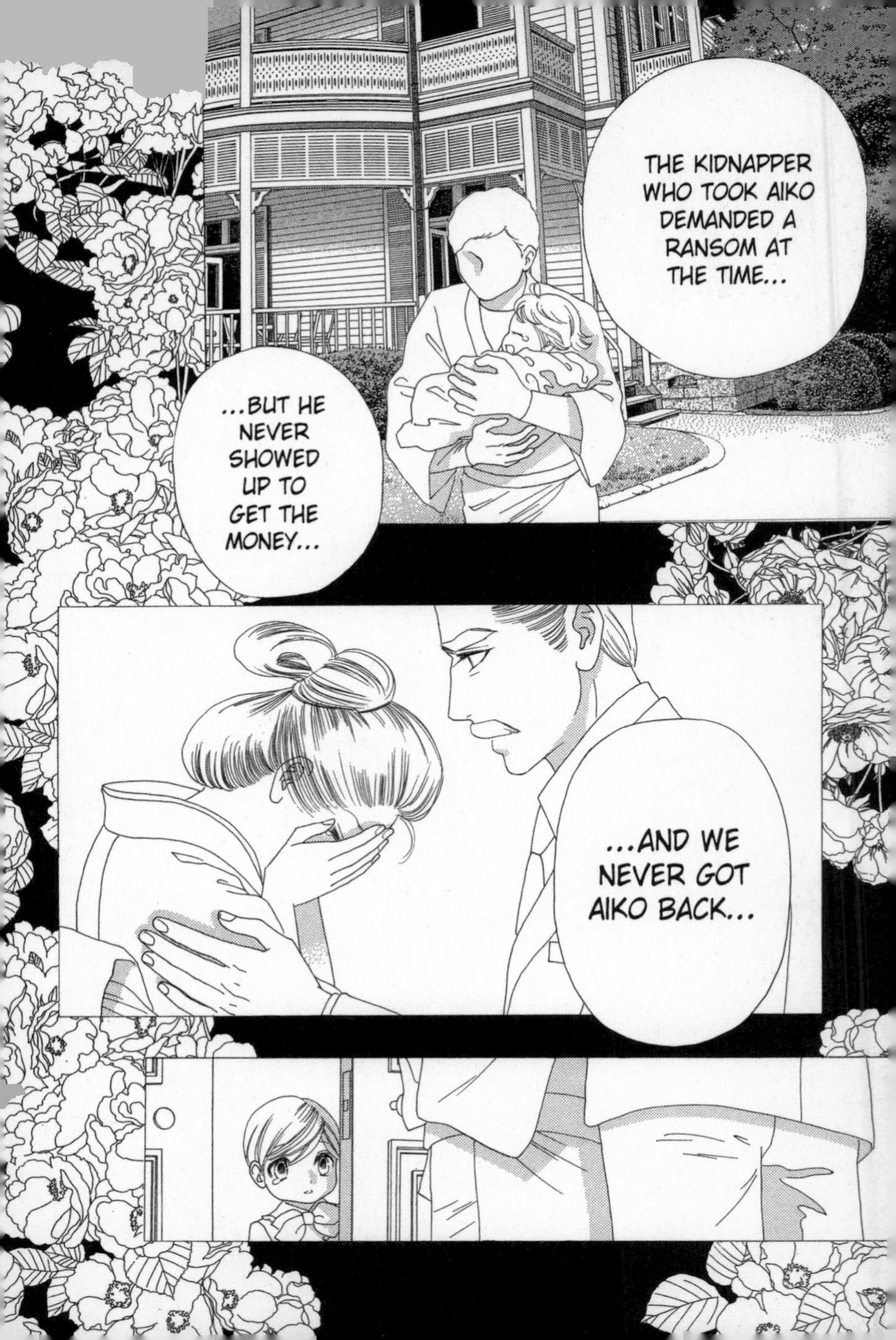
THE KIDNAPPER WHO TOOK AIKO DEMANDED A RANSOM AT THE TIME...
...BUT HE NEVER SHOWED UP TO GET THE MONEY...
...AND WE NEVER GOT AIKO BACK...

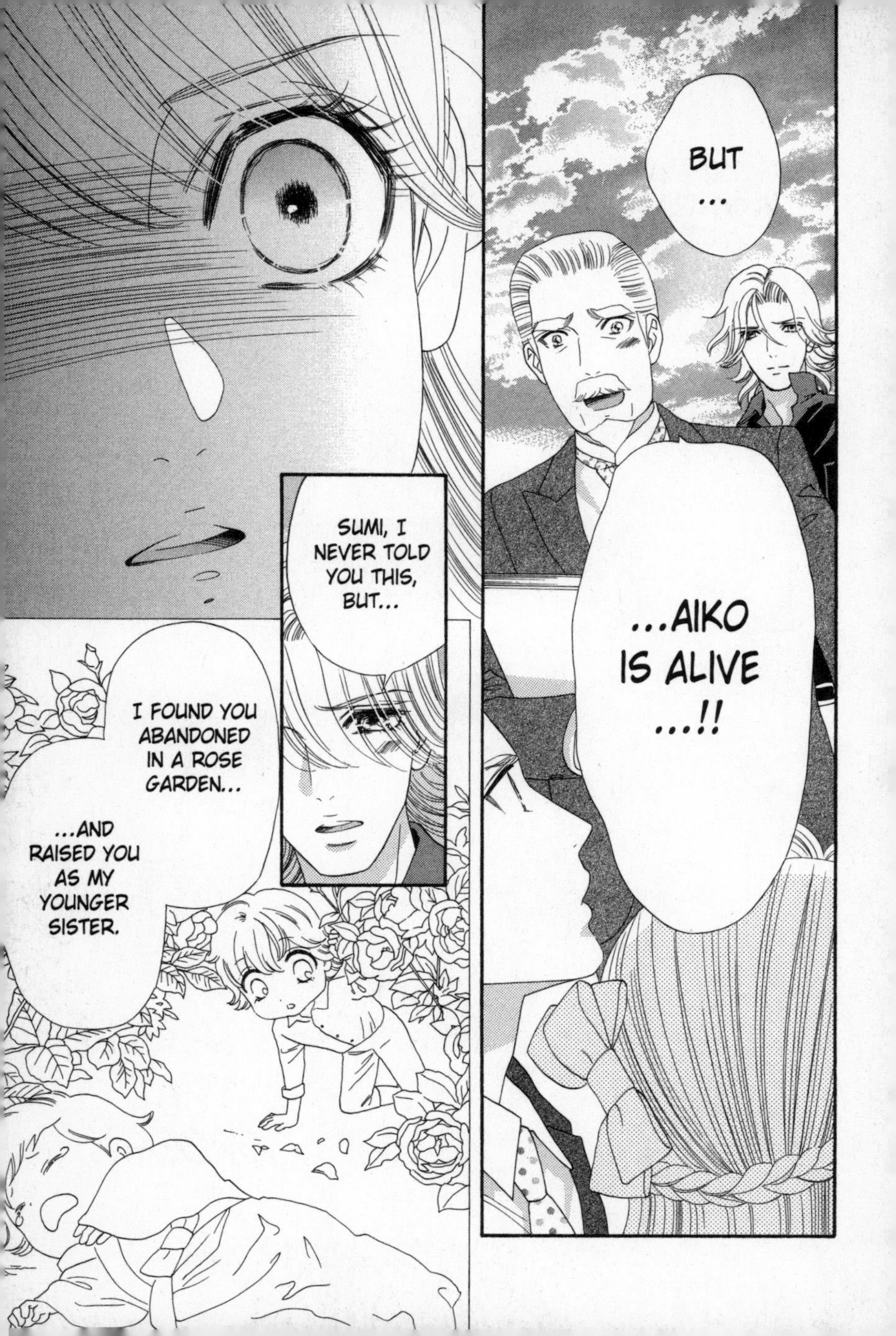
BUT ...
...AIKO IS ALIVE ...!!
SUMI, I NEVER TOLD YOU THIS, BUT...
I FOUND YOU ABANDONED IN A ROSE GARDEN...
...AND RAISED YOU AS MY YOUNGER SISTER.

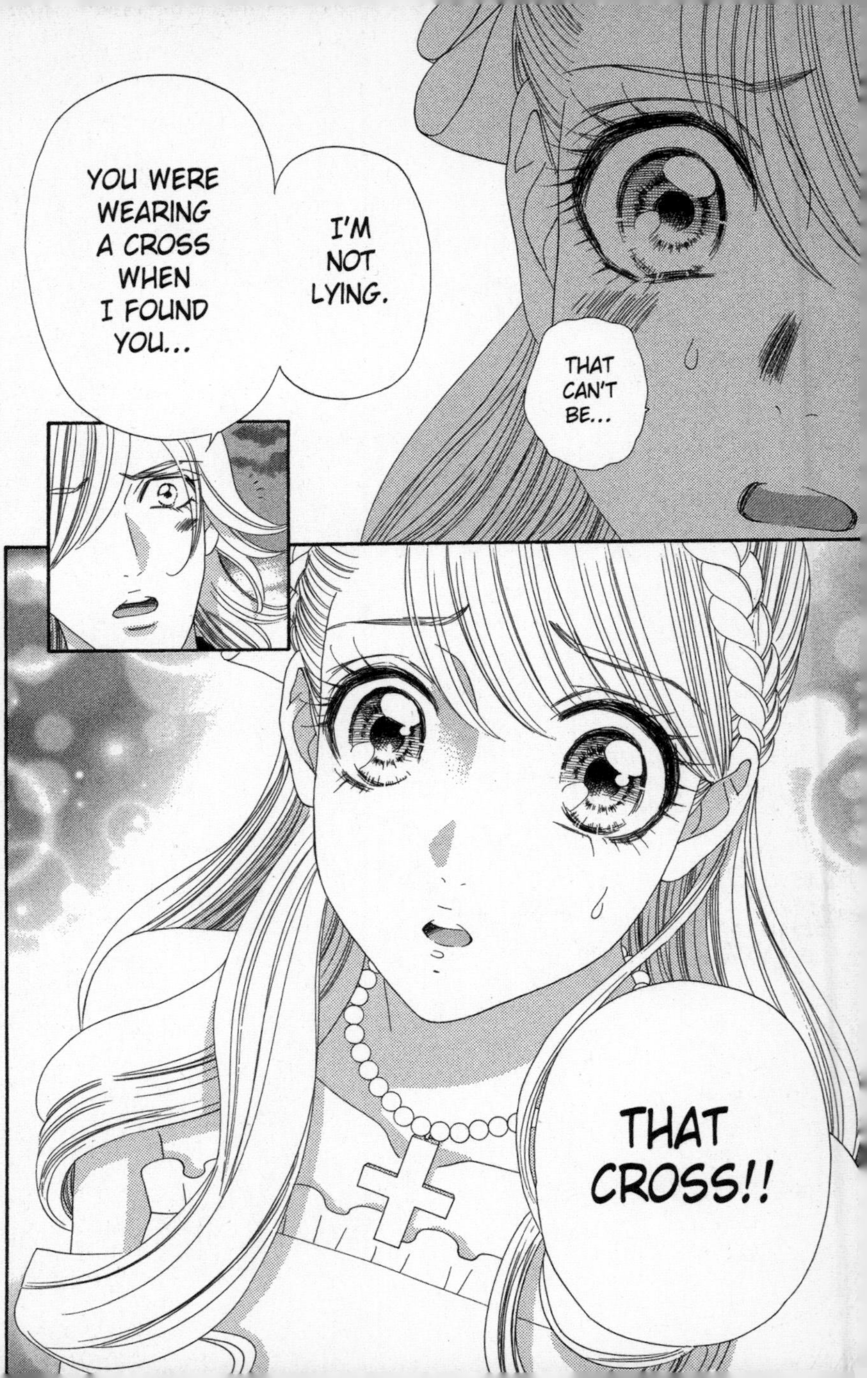
THAT CAN'T BE...
I'M NOT LYING.
YOU WERE WEARING A CROSS WHEN I FOUND YOU...
THAT CROSS!!

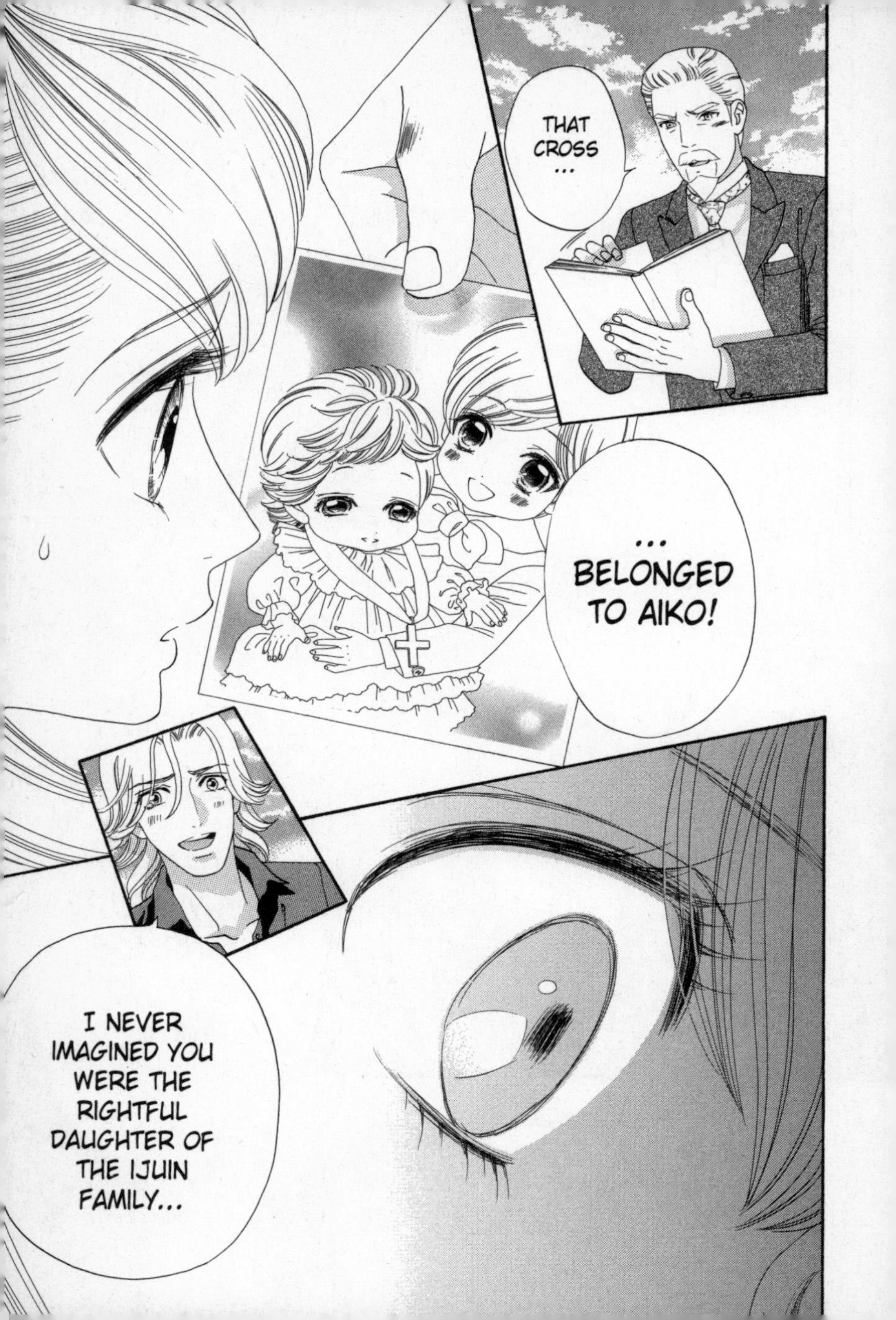
THAT CROSS ...
... BELONGED TO AIKO!
I NEVER IMAGINED YOU WERE THE RIGHTFUL DAUGHTER OF THE IJUIN FAMILY...

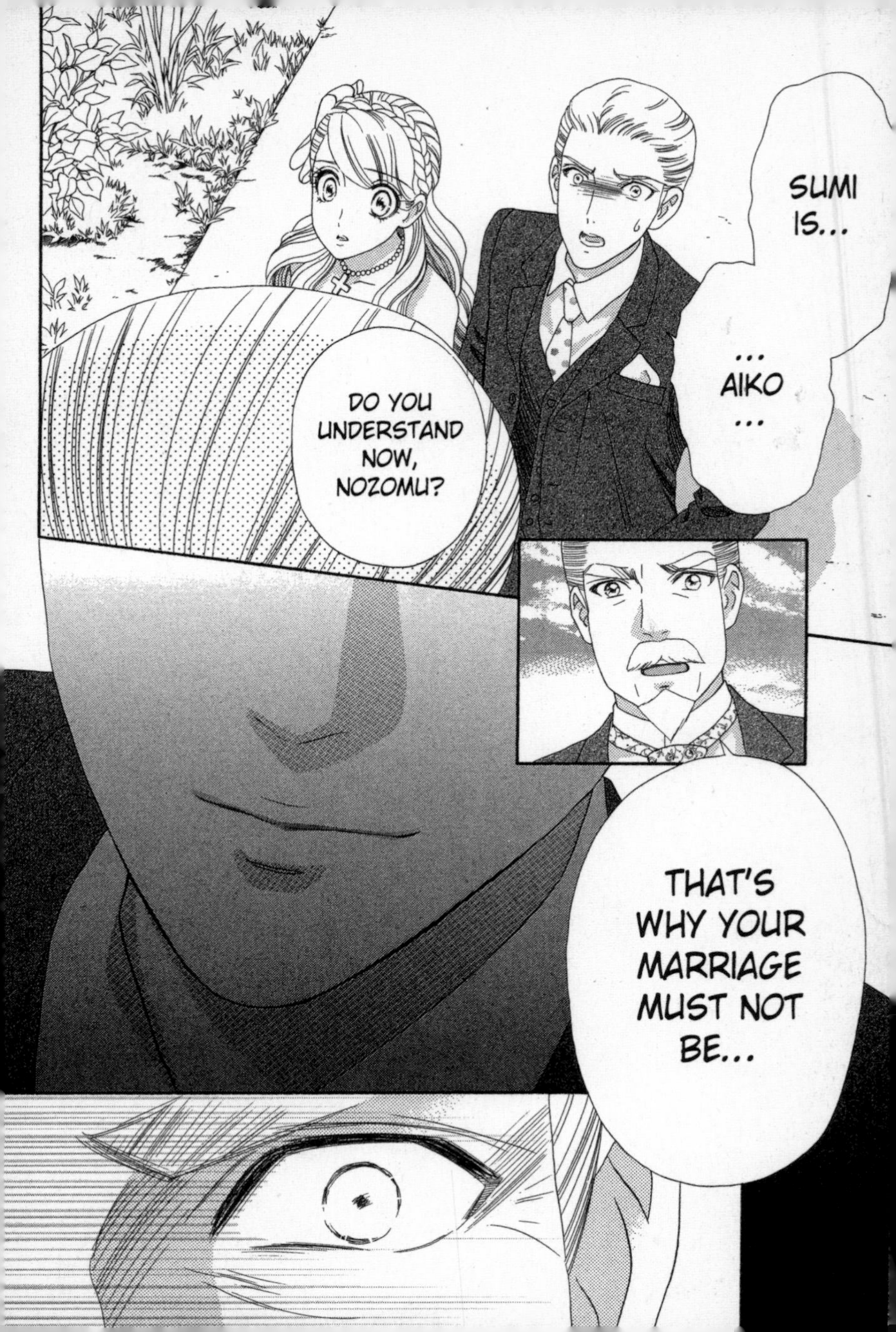

SUMI IS...
...AIKO...
DO YOU UNDERSTAND NOW, NOZOMU?
THAT'S WHY YOUR MARRIAGE MUST NOT BE...

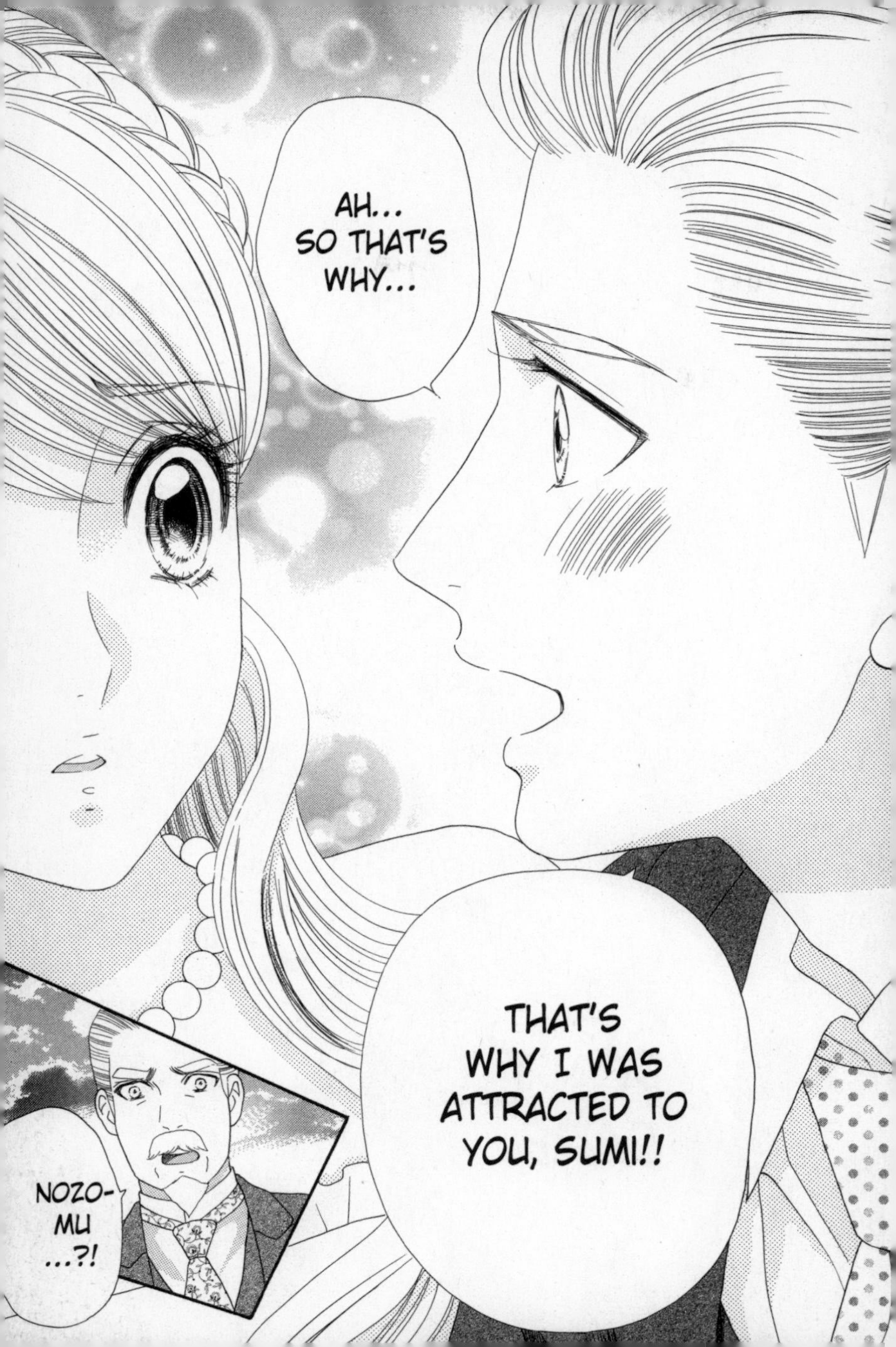
AH... SO THAT'S WHY...
THAT'S WHY I WAS ATTRACTED TO YOU, SUMI!!
NOZO-MU ...?!

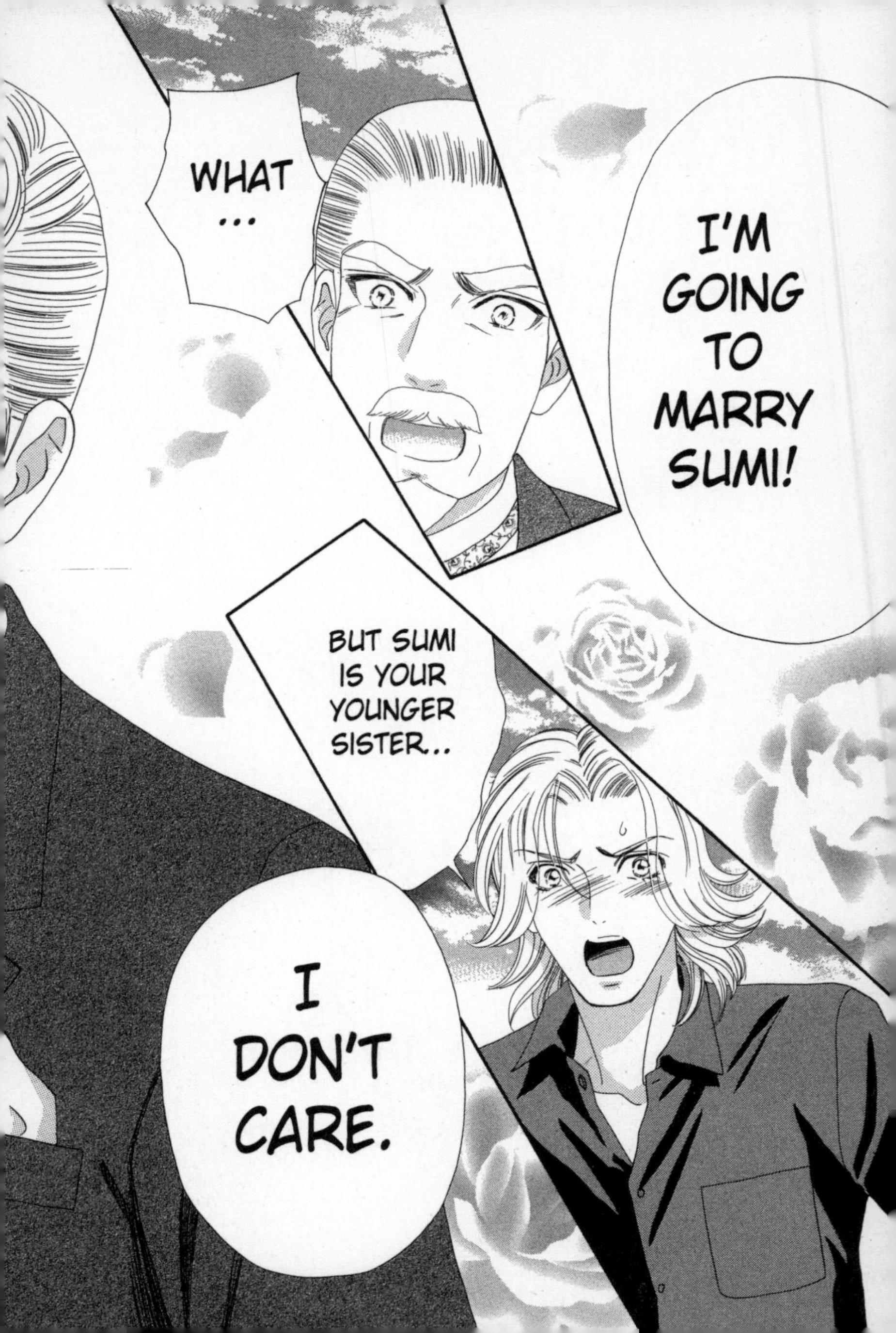
I'M GOING TO MARRY SUMI!
WHAT ...
BUT SUMI IS YOUR YOUNGER SISTER..
I DON'T CARE.

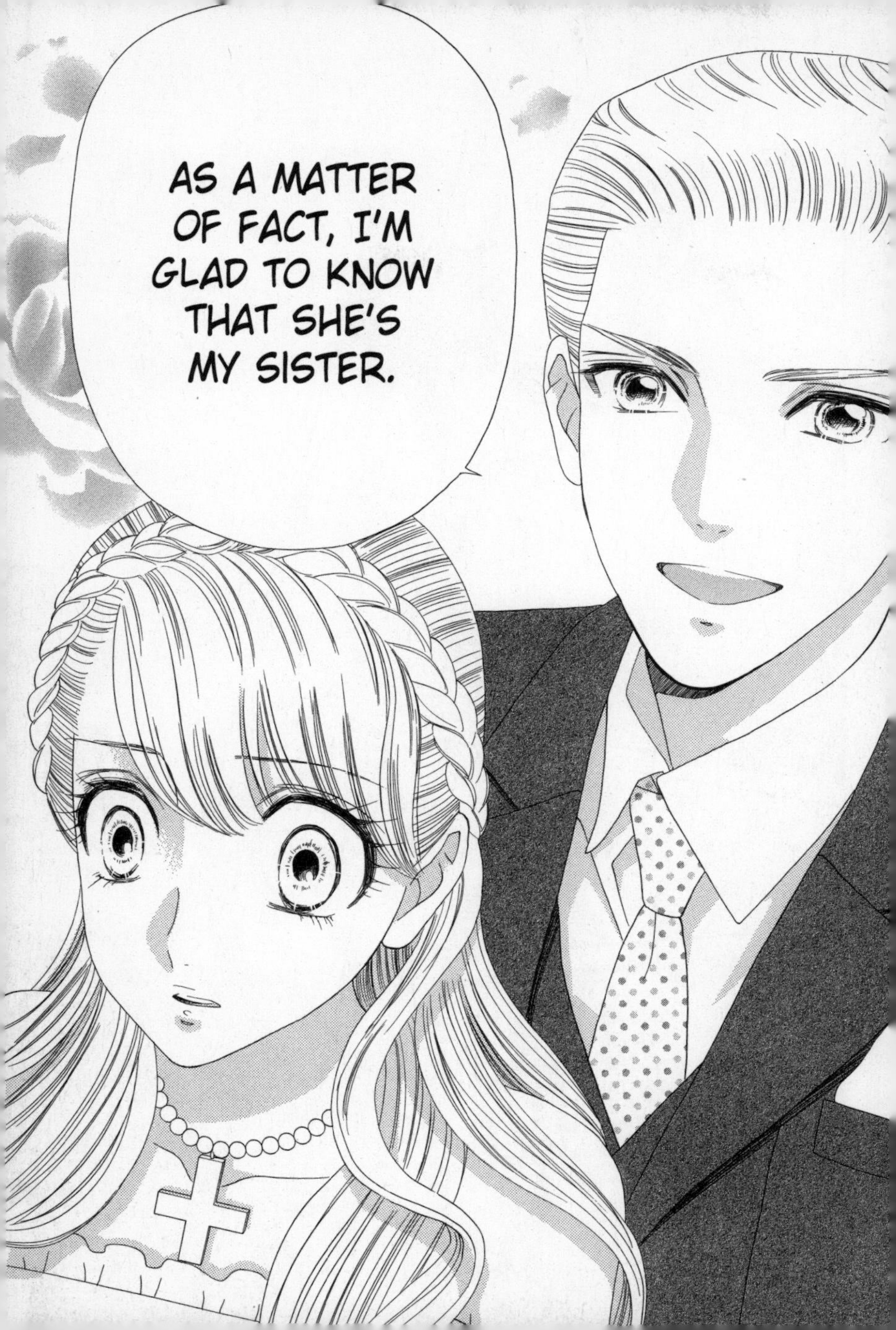
AS A MATTER OF FACT, I'M GLAD TO KNOW THAT SHE'S MY SISTER.

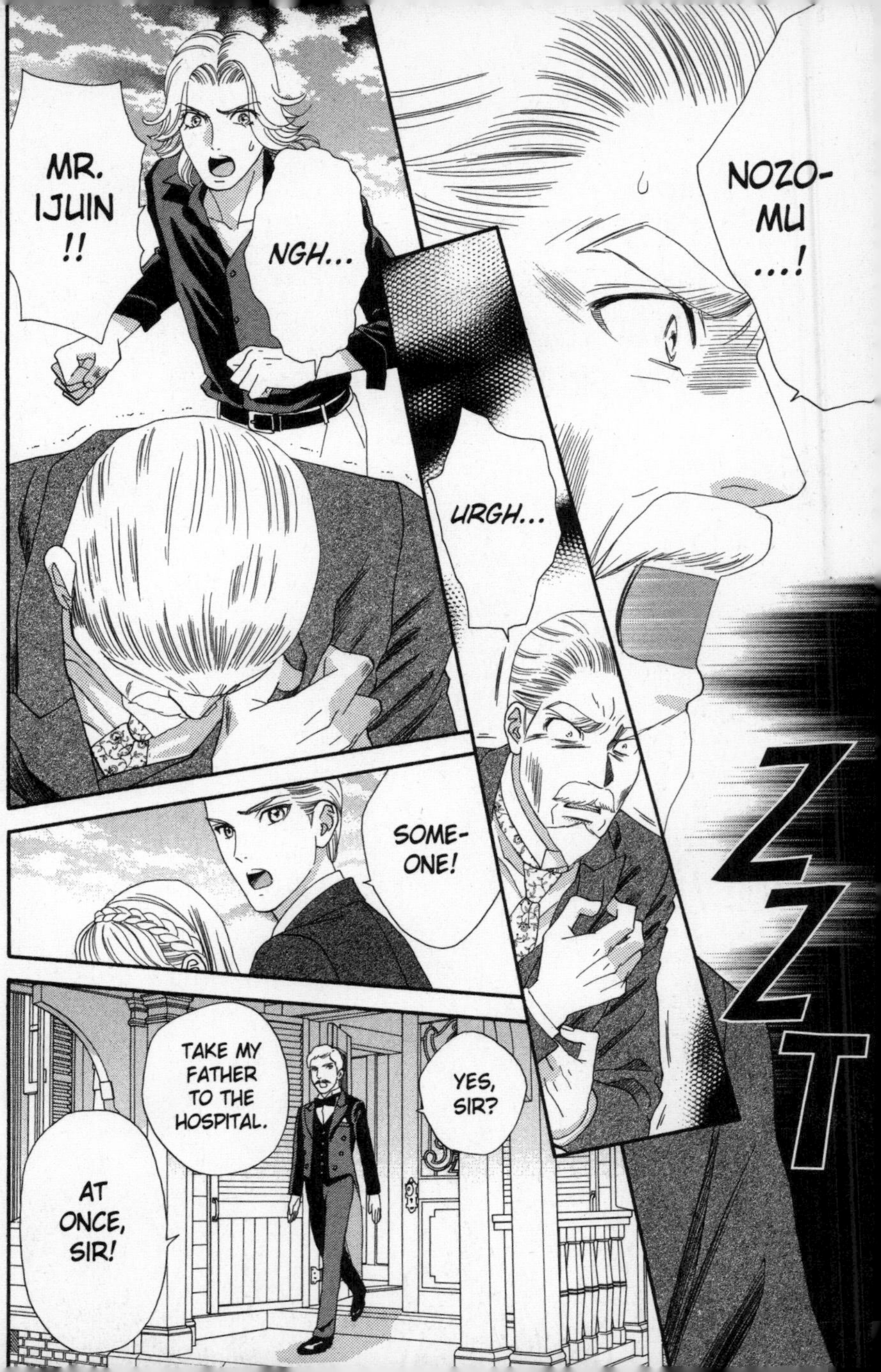
NOZO-MU ...!
NGH...
MR. IJUIN !!
URGH...
ZZZT
SOME-ONE!
TAKE MY FATHER TO THE HOSPITAL.
YES, SIR?
AT ONCE, SIR!

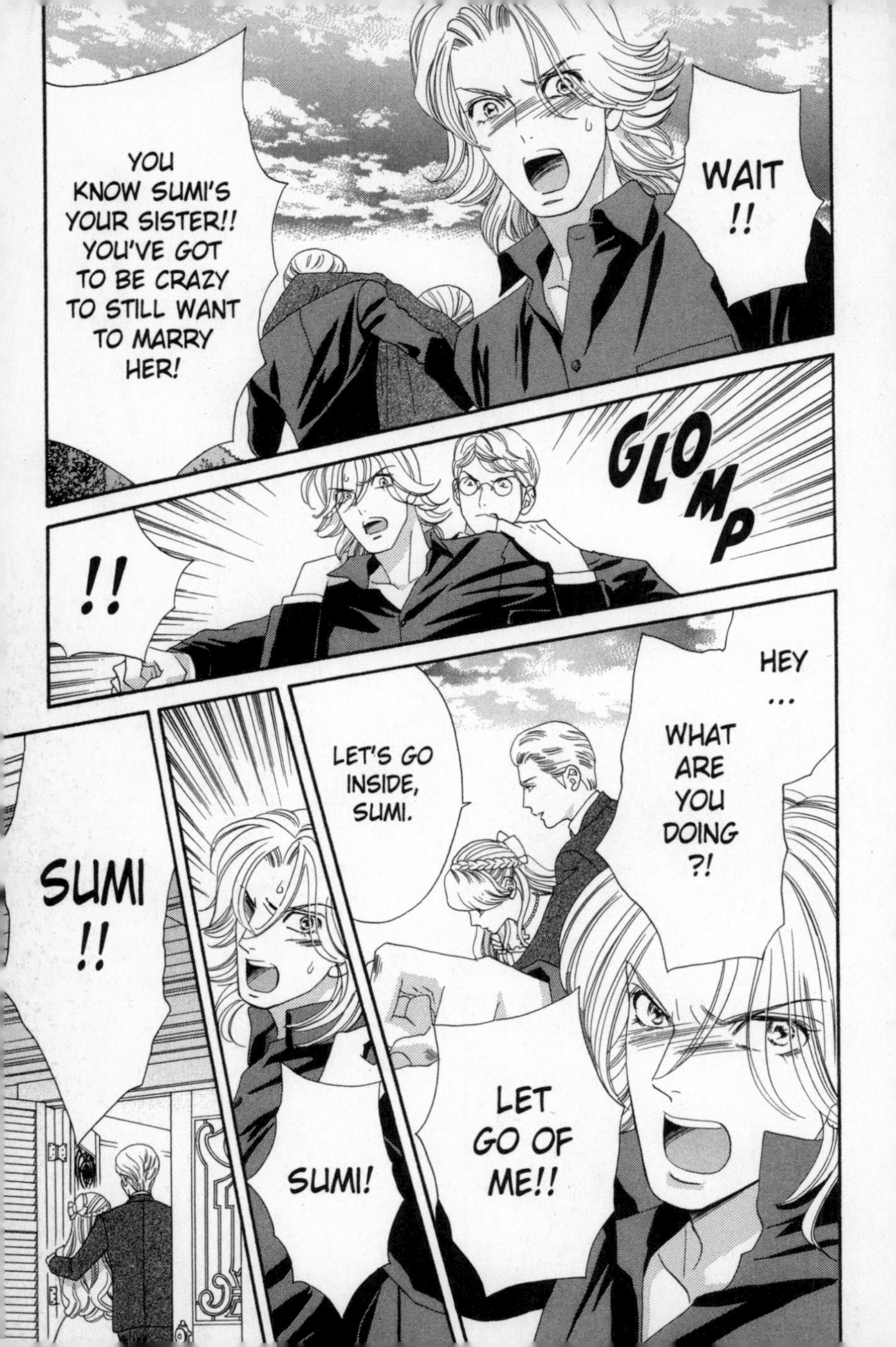
WAIT !!
YOU KNOW SUMI'S YOUR SISTER!! YOU'VE GOT TO BE CRAZY TO STILL WANT TO MARRY HER!
GLOMP
!!
HEY ... WHAT ARE YOU DOING ?!
LET'S GO INSIDE, SUMI.
LET GO OF ME!!
SUMI!
SUMI !!

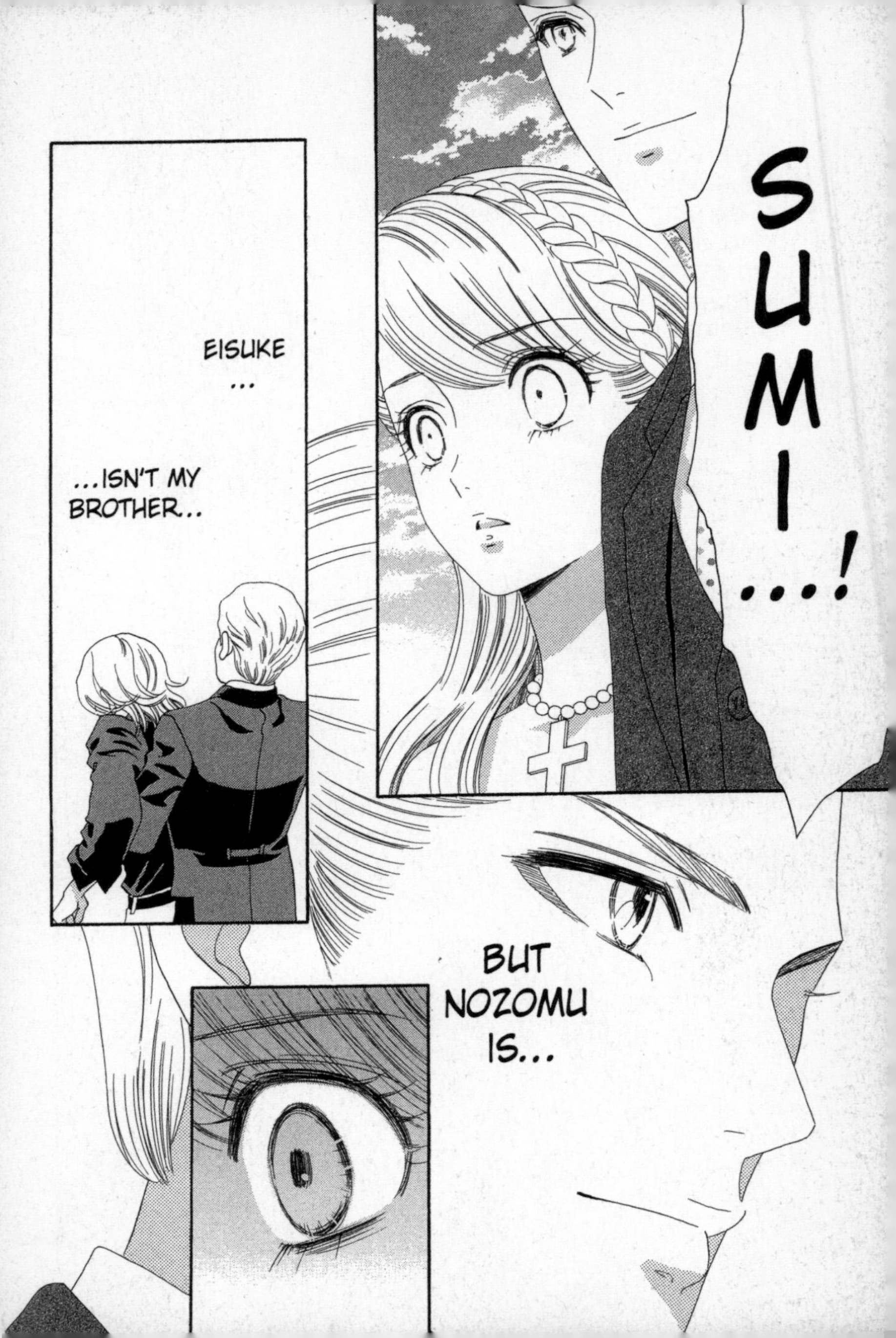
SUMI...!
EISUKE ...
...ISN'T MY BROTHER..
BUT NOZOMU IS...

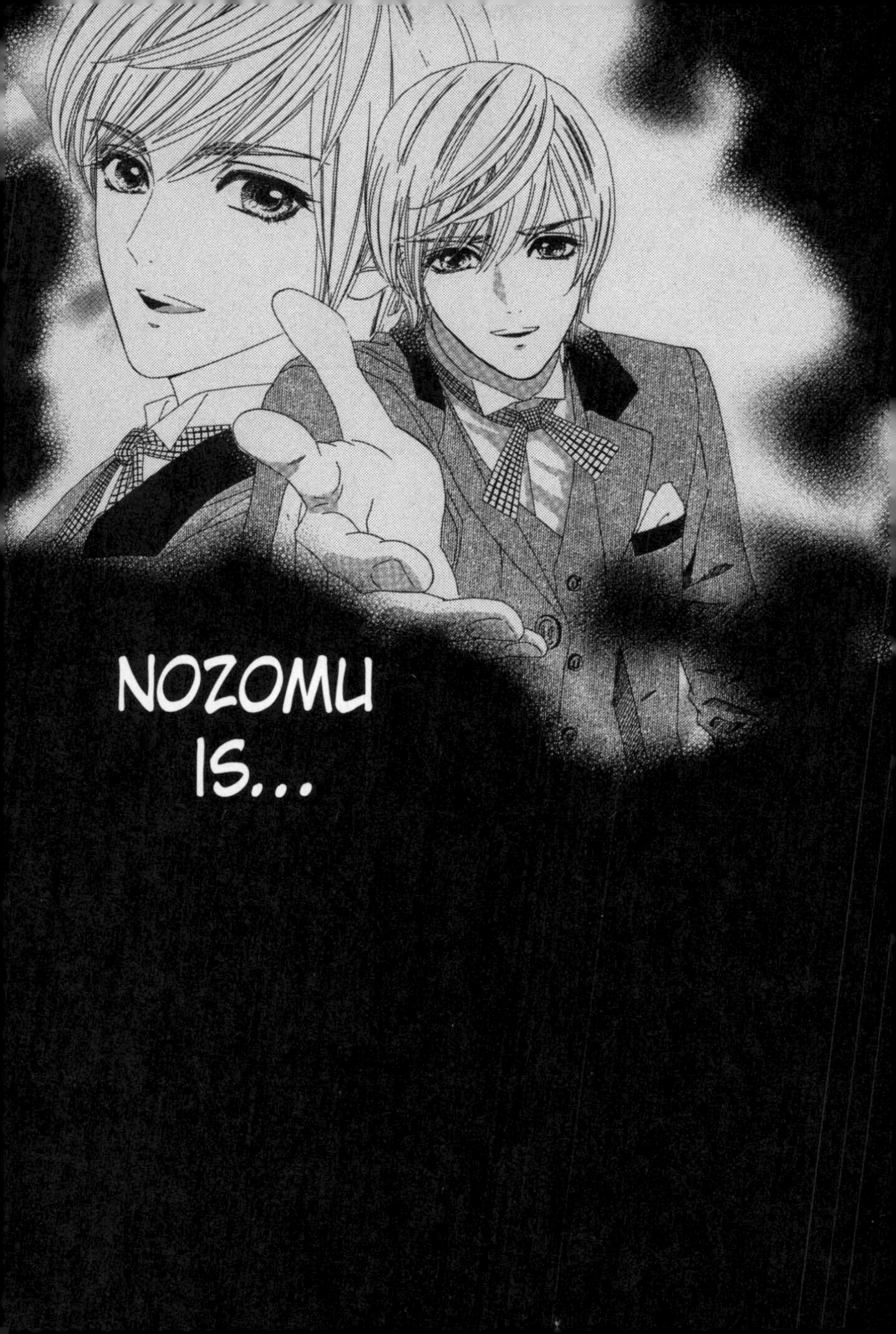
NOZOMU IS...

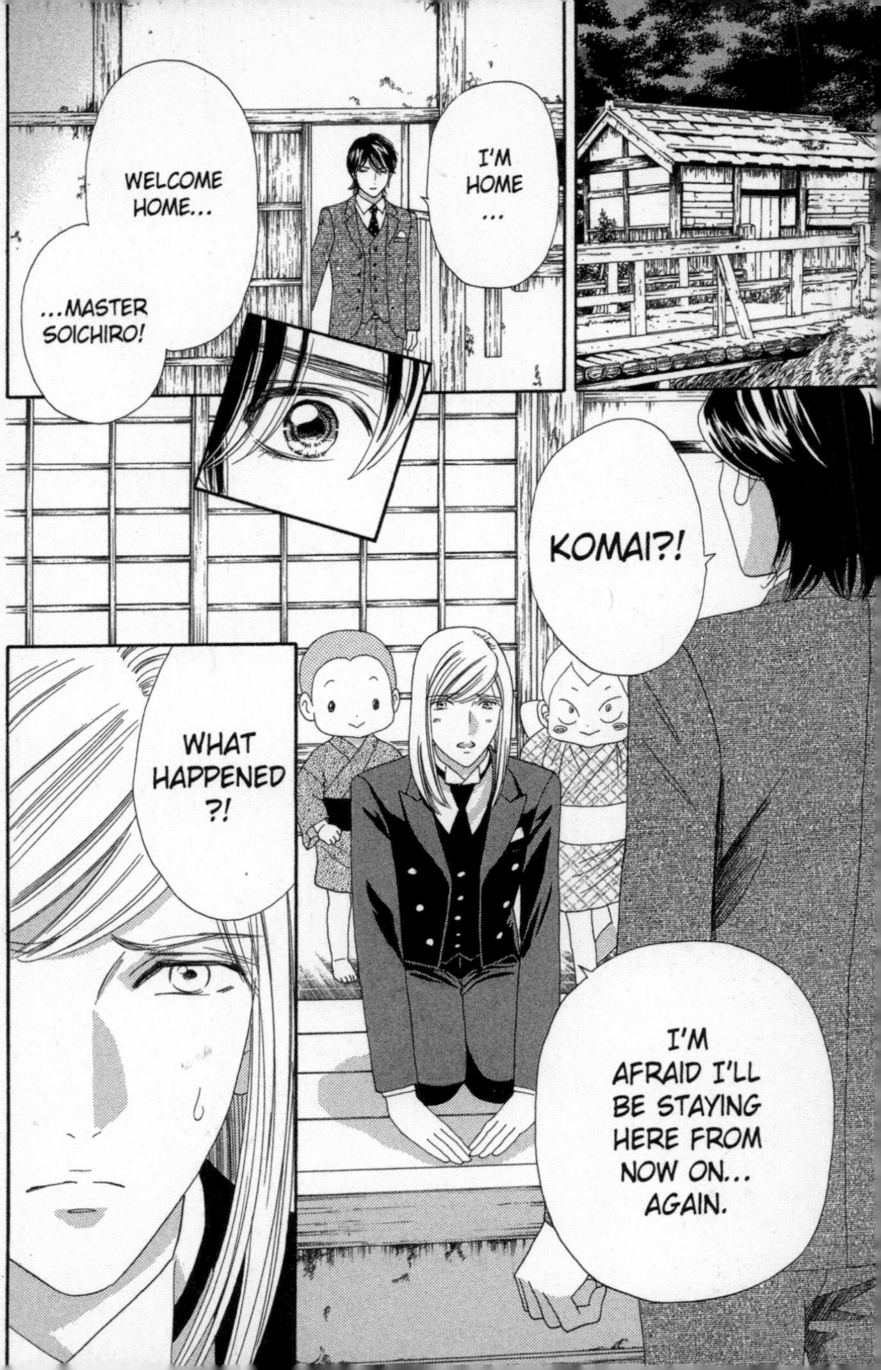
I'M HOME ...
WELCOME HOME...
...MASTER SOICHIRO!
KOMAI?!
WHAT HAPPENED ?!
I'M AFRAID I'LL BE STAYING HERE FROM NOW ON... AGAIN.

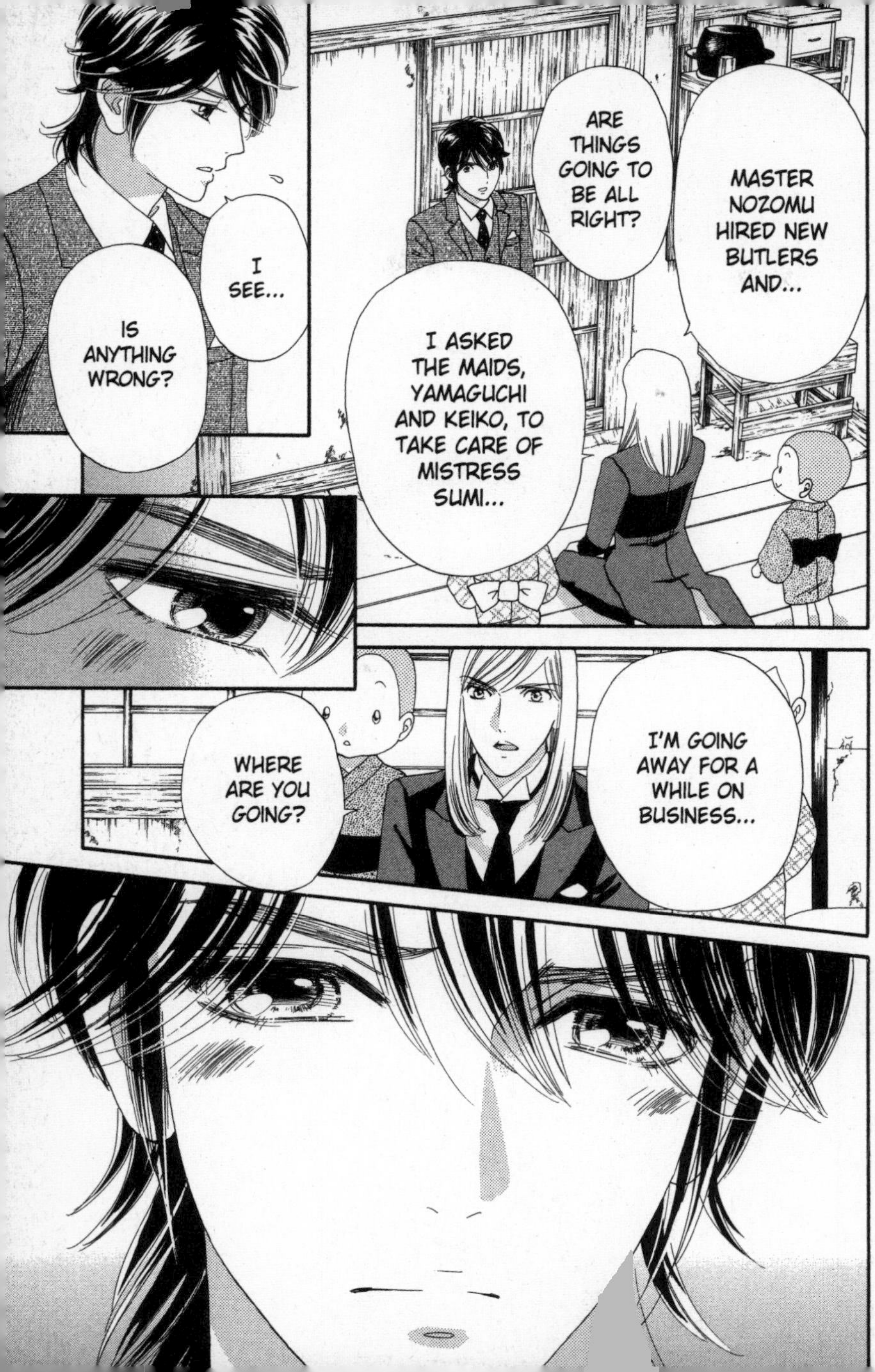
MASTER NOZOMU HIRED NEW BUTLERS AND...
ARE THINGS GOING TO BE ALL RIGHT?
I ASKED THE MAIDS, YAMAGUCHI AND KEIKO, TO TAKE CARE OF MISTRESS SUMI...
I SEE...
IS ANYTHING WRONG?
I'M GOING AWAY FOR A WHILE ON BUSINESS...
WHERE ARE YOU GOING?

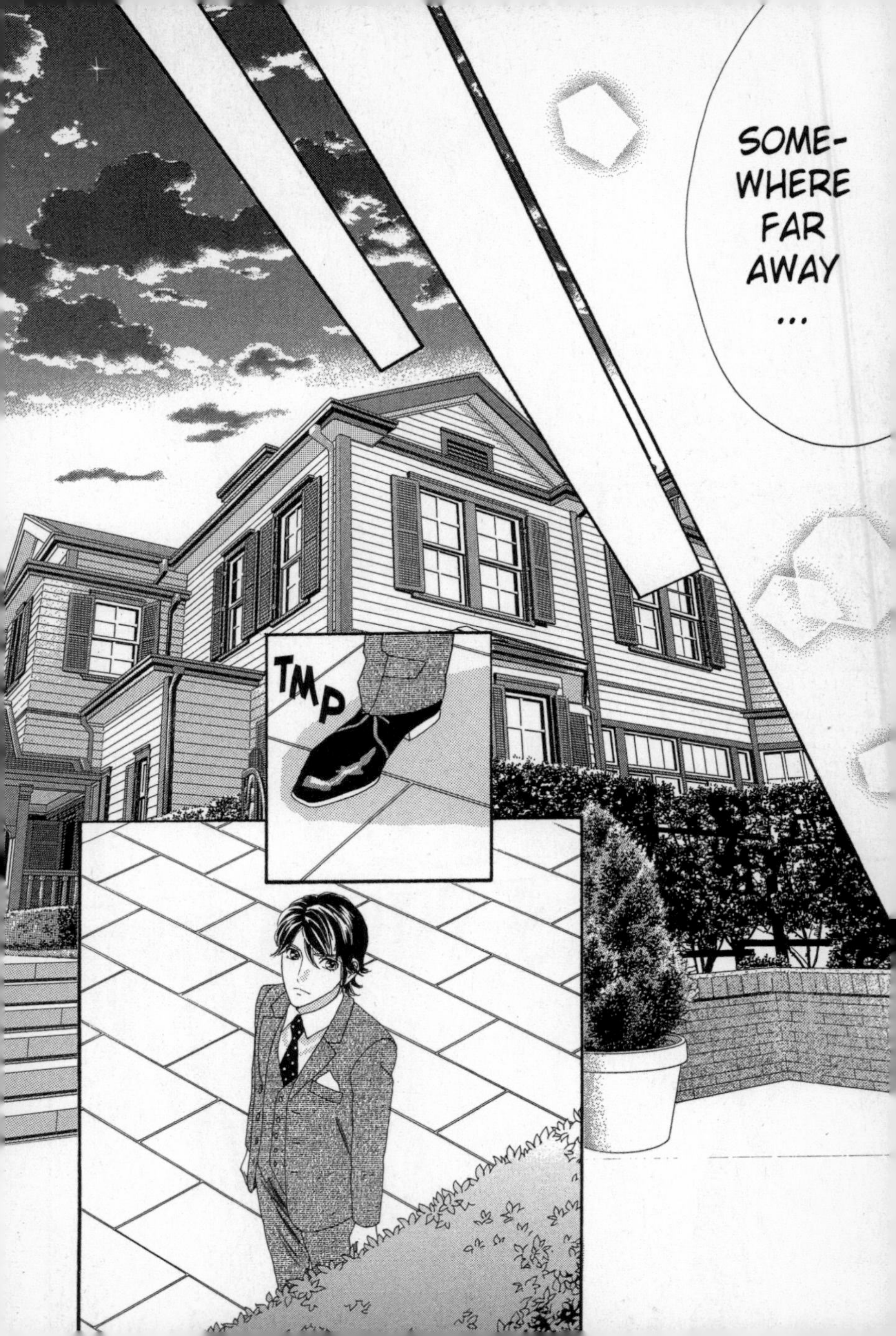
SOME-WHERE FAR AWAY ...
TMP

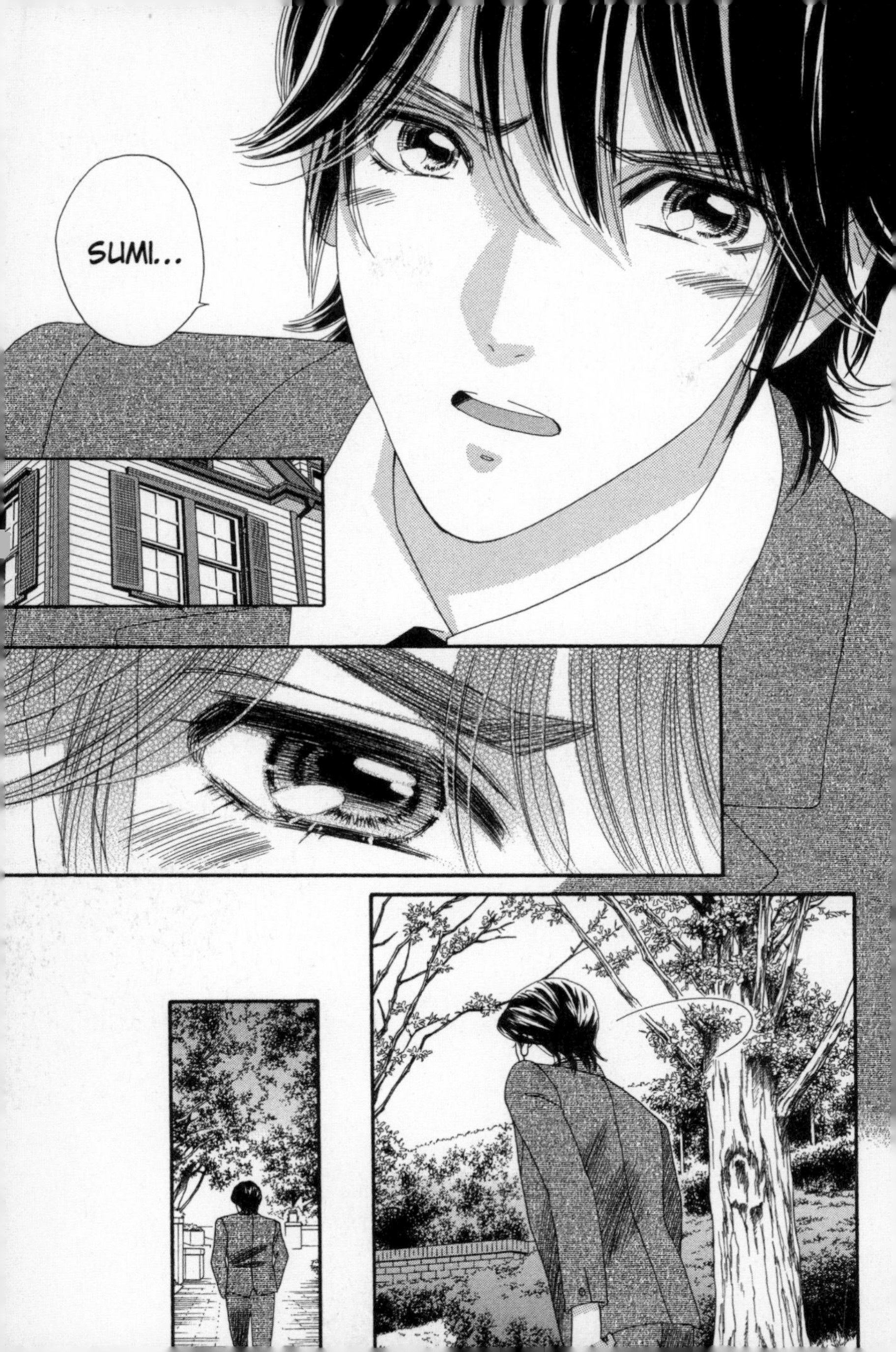
SUMI...

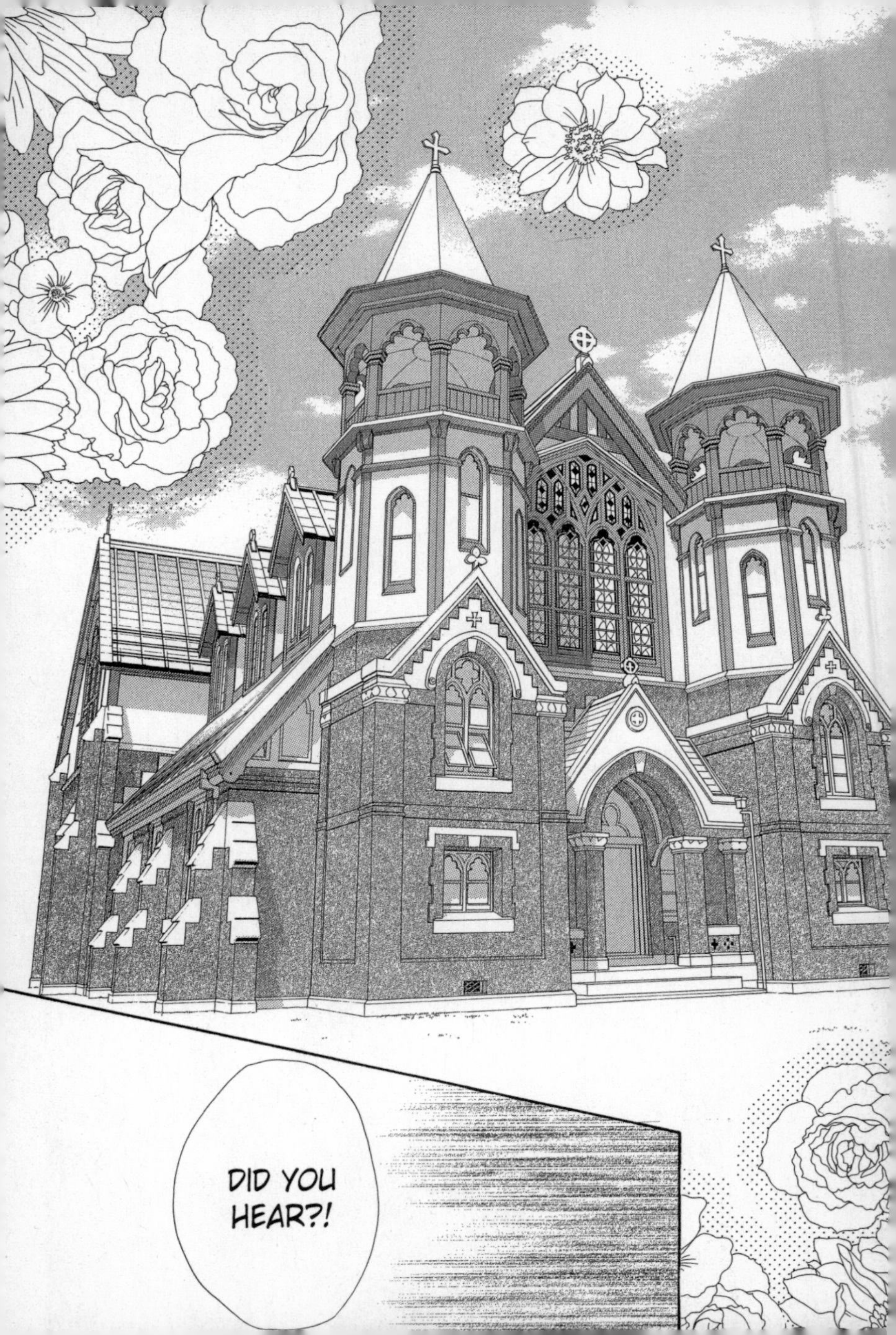
DID YOU HEAR?!

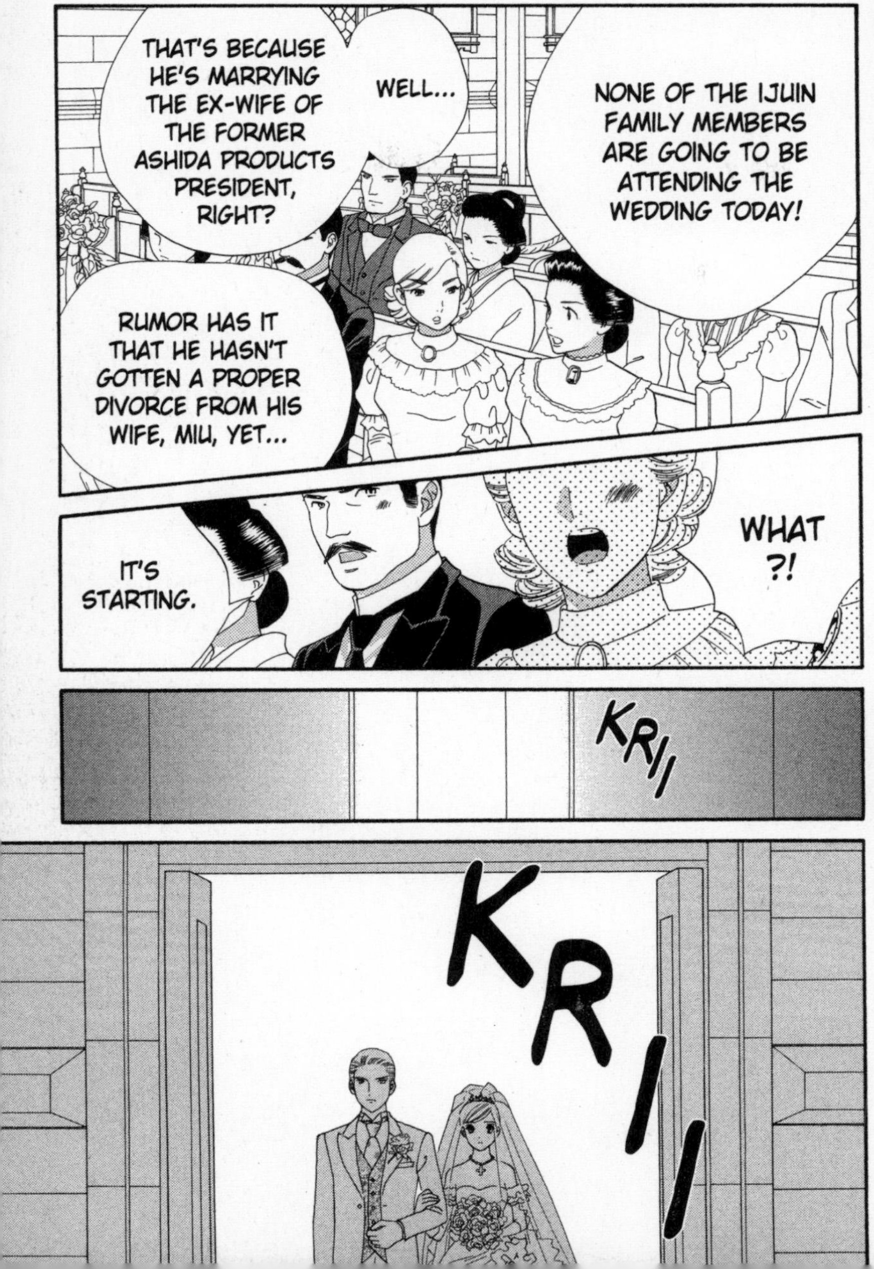
NONE OF THE IJUIN FAMILY MEMBERS ARE GOING TO BE ATTENDING THE WEDDING TODAY!
WELL...
THAT'S BECAUSE HE'S MARRYING THE EX-WIFE OF THE FORMER ASHIDA PRODUCTS PRESIDENT, RIGHT?
RUMOR HAS IT THAT HE HASN'T GOTTEN A PROPER DIVORCE FROM HIS WIFE, MIU, YET...
WHAT?!
IT'S STARTING.
KRII
KRII

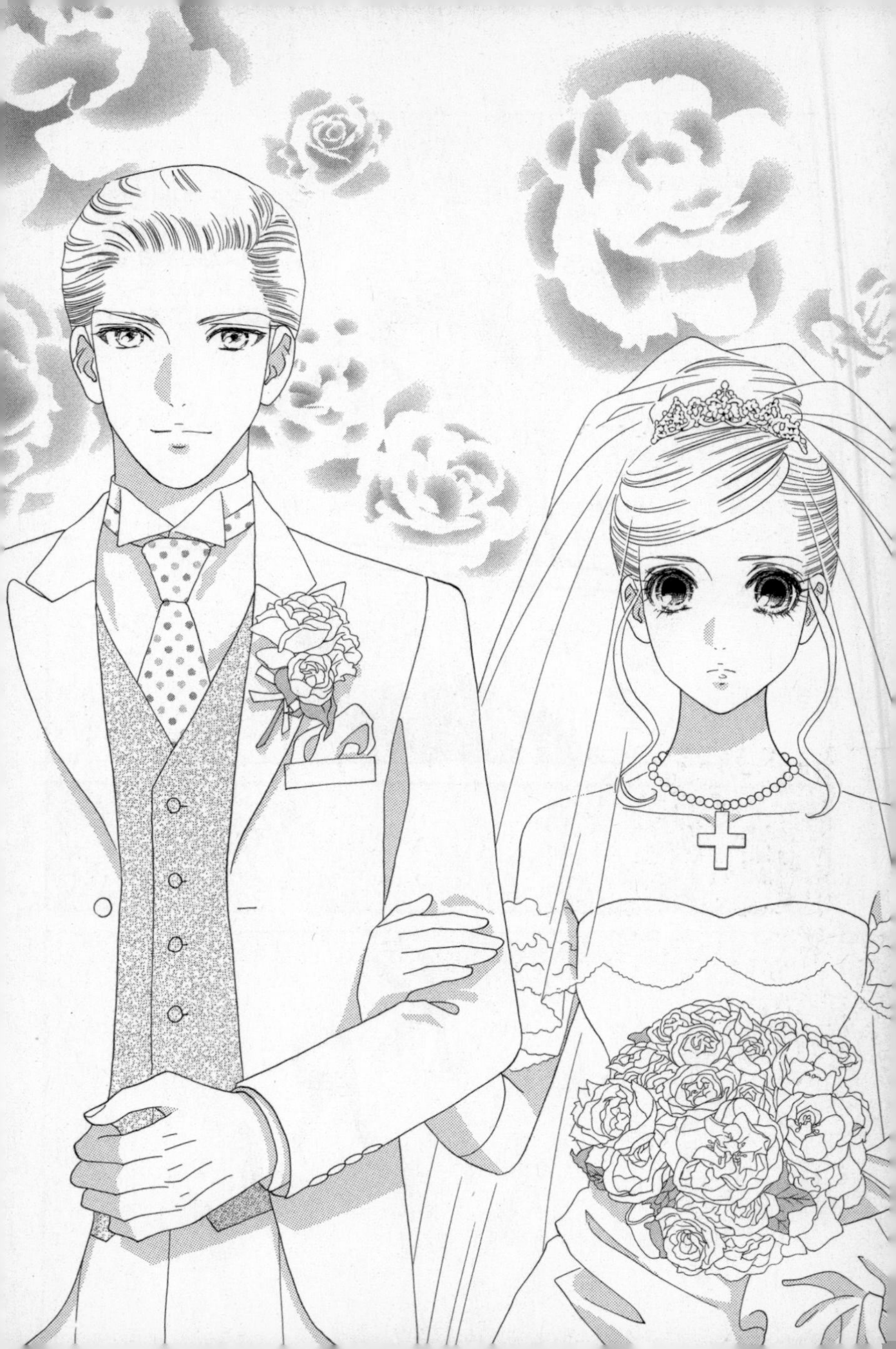

I CAN'T...

...THINK OF ANY-THING.

CLAP

CLAP

CLAP

...WHEN I TRY TO THINK...

MY HEAD HURTS...

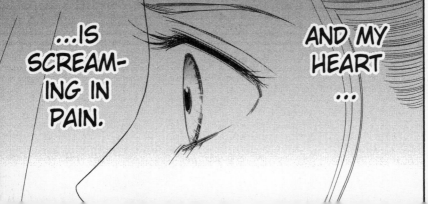

...IS SCREAM-ING IN PAIN.

AND MY HEART ...

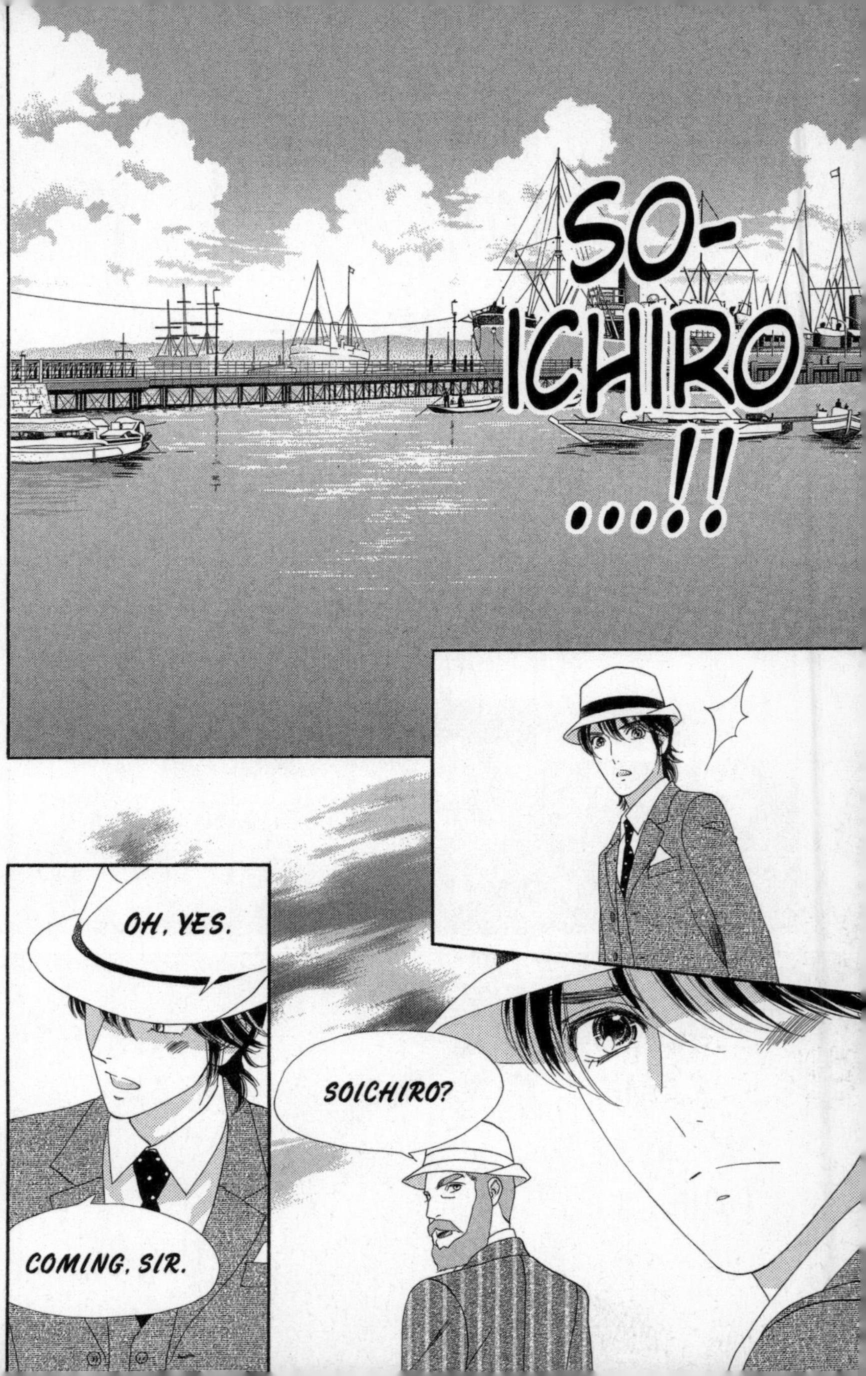
SO-ICHIRO ...!!
SOICHIRO?
OH, YES.
COMING, SIR.

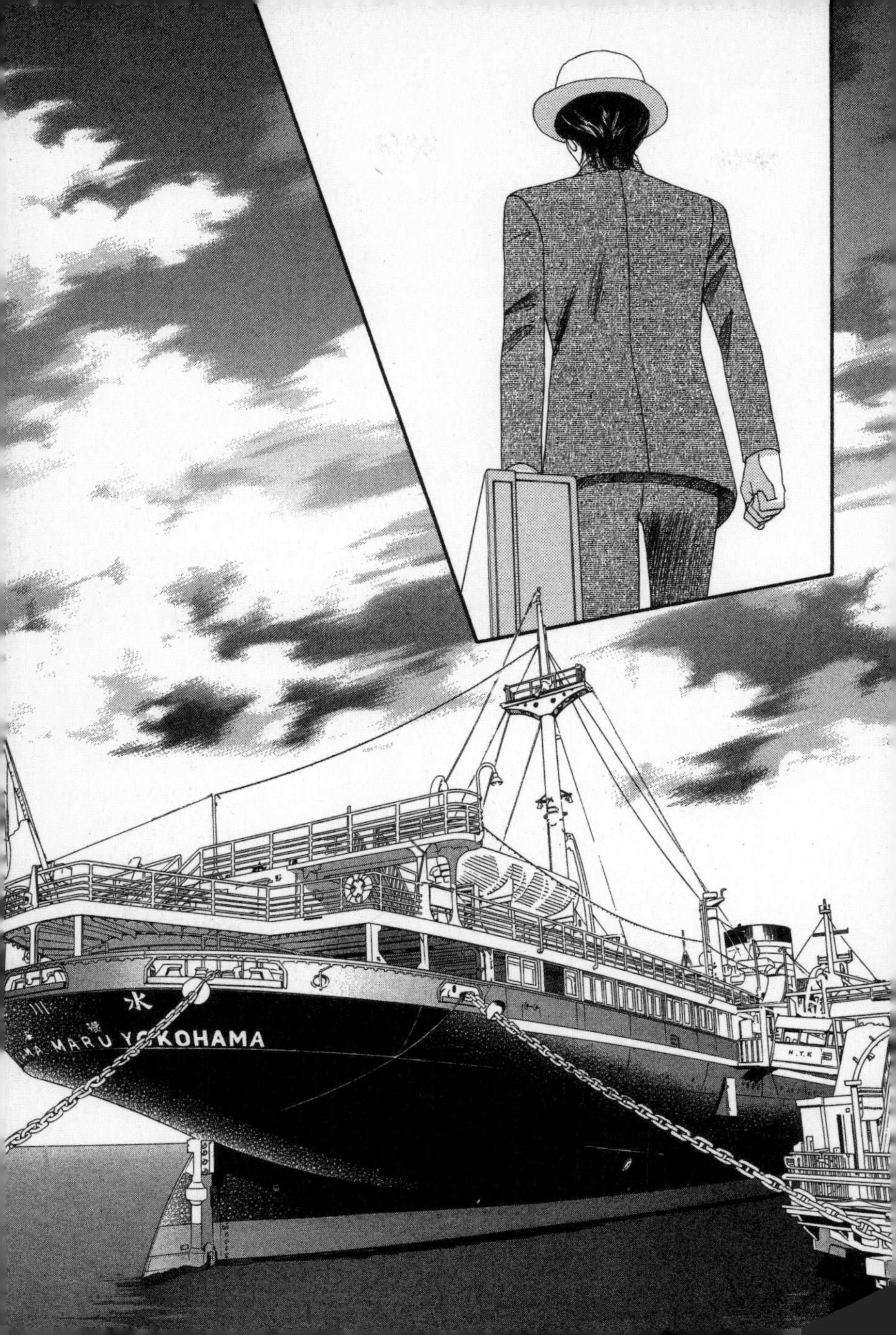
MARU YOKOHAMA
N.Y.K

INTRODUCING A ONE-SHOT!!

A TWO-PART ONE-SHOT CALLED "*HOIKU-MEN!*" (CHILDCARE MAN) WILL BE RUNNING IN MONTHLY *YOU*—IN THE MAY ISSUE (WHICH COMES OUT ON APRIL 14) AND THE JUNE ISSUE (WHICH COMES OUT ON MAY 15). IT'S A SLAPSTICK COMEDY ABOUT A SUPER BUSINESSMAN CALLED SHIRO WHO ENDS UP BECOMING THE TEMPORARY DIRECTOR AT THE NURSERY HIS GRANDMOTHER TAKES CARE OF. THIS IS THE FIRST TIME I'VE CREATED A MANGA WHERE THE MAIN CHARACTER IS MALE (AND NEAR HIS THIRTIES, TO BOOT). THERE'S A POSSIBILITY THAT ONE-SHOTS OUTSIDE *MARGARET* WILL NOT MAKE IT TO GRAPHIC NOVEL FORM, SO PLEASE GET A COPY OF *YOU* AND READ THIS IF YOU HAVE THE CHANCE!

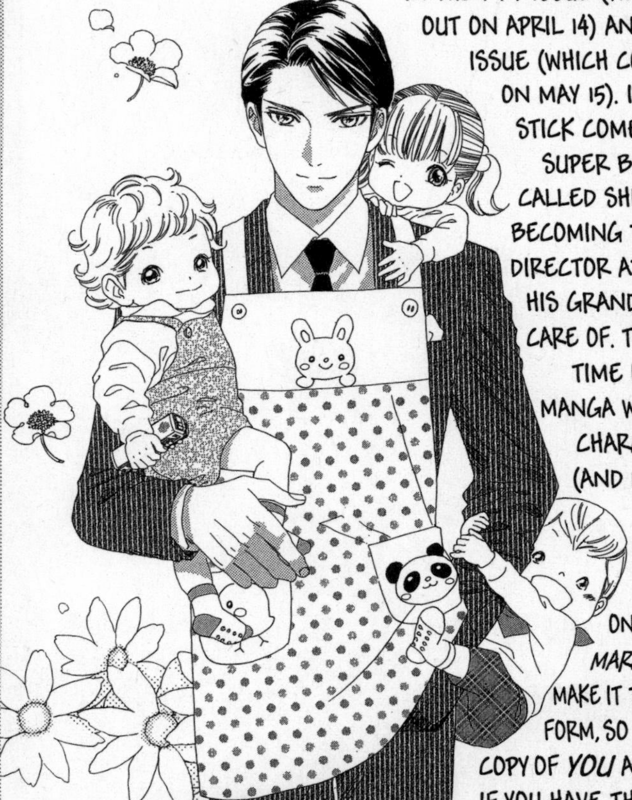

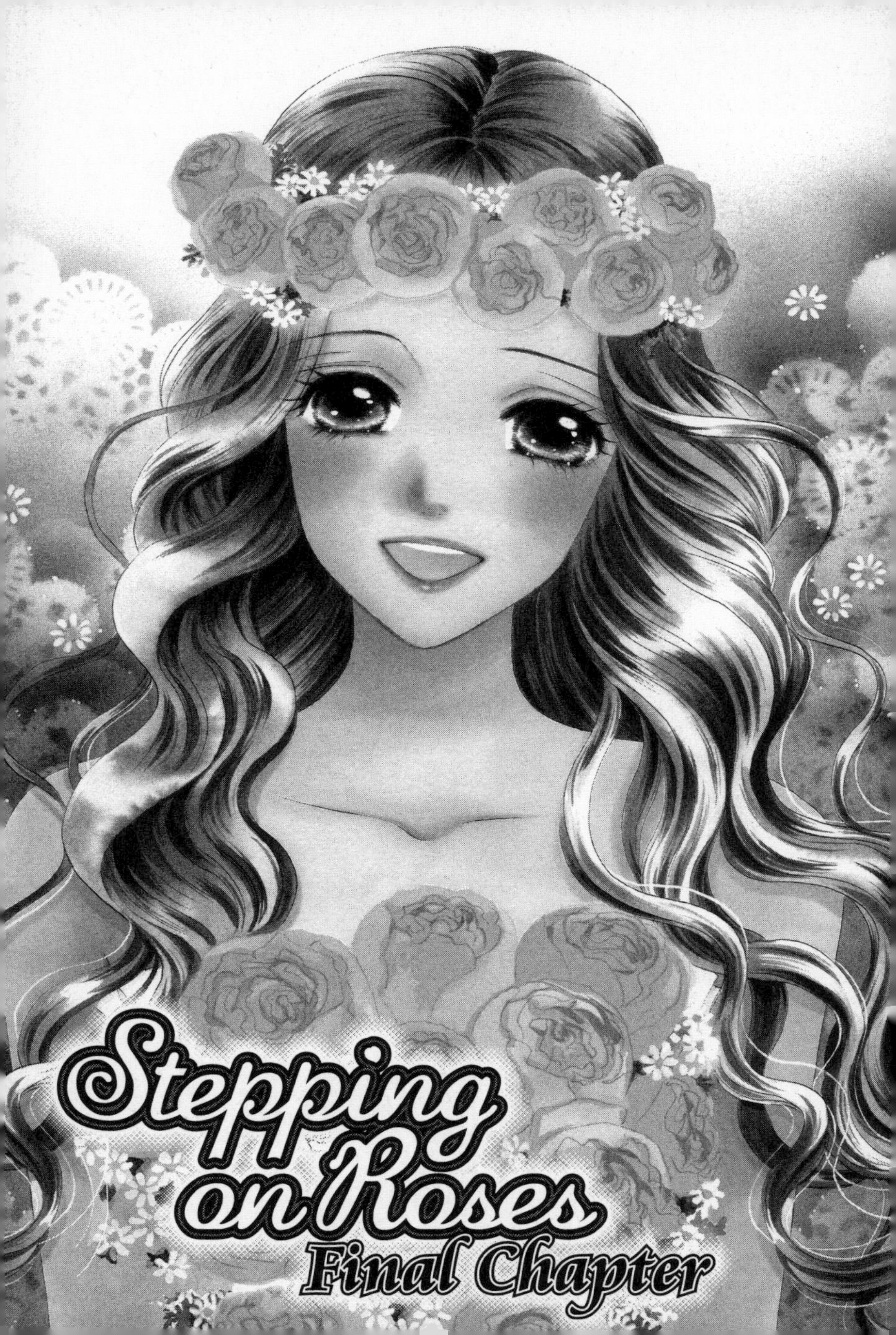
Stepping
on Roses
Final Chapter

Stepping on Roses

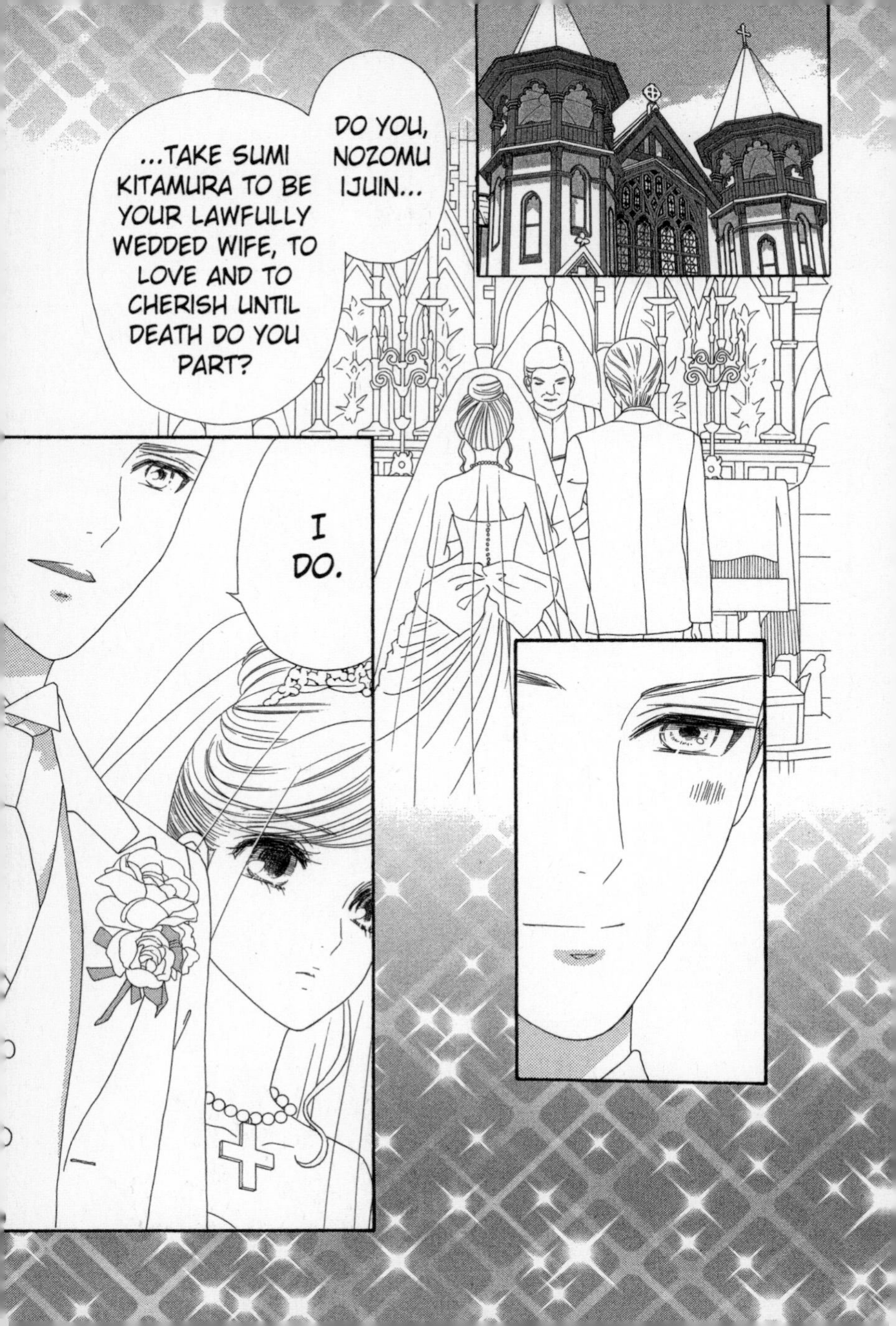
DO YOU, NOZOMU IJUIN...
...TAKE SUMI KITAMURA TO BE YOUR LAWFULLY WEDDED WIFE, TO LOVE AND TO CHERISH UNTIL DEATH DO YOU PART?
I DO.

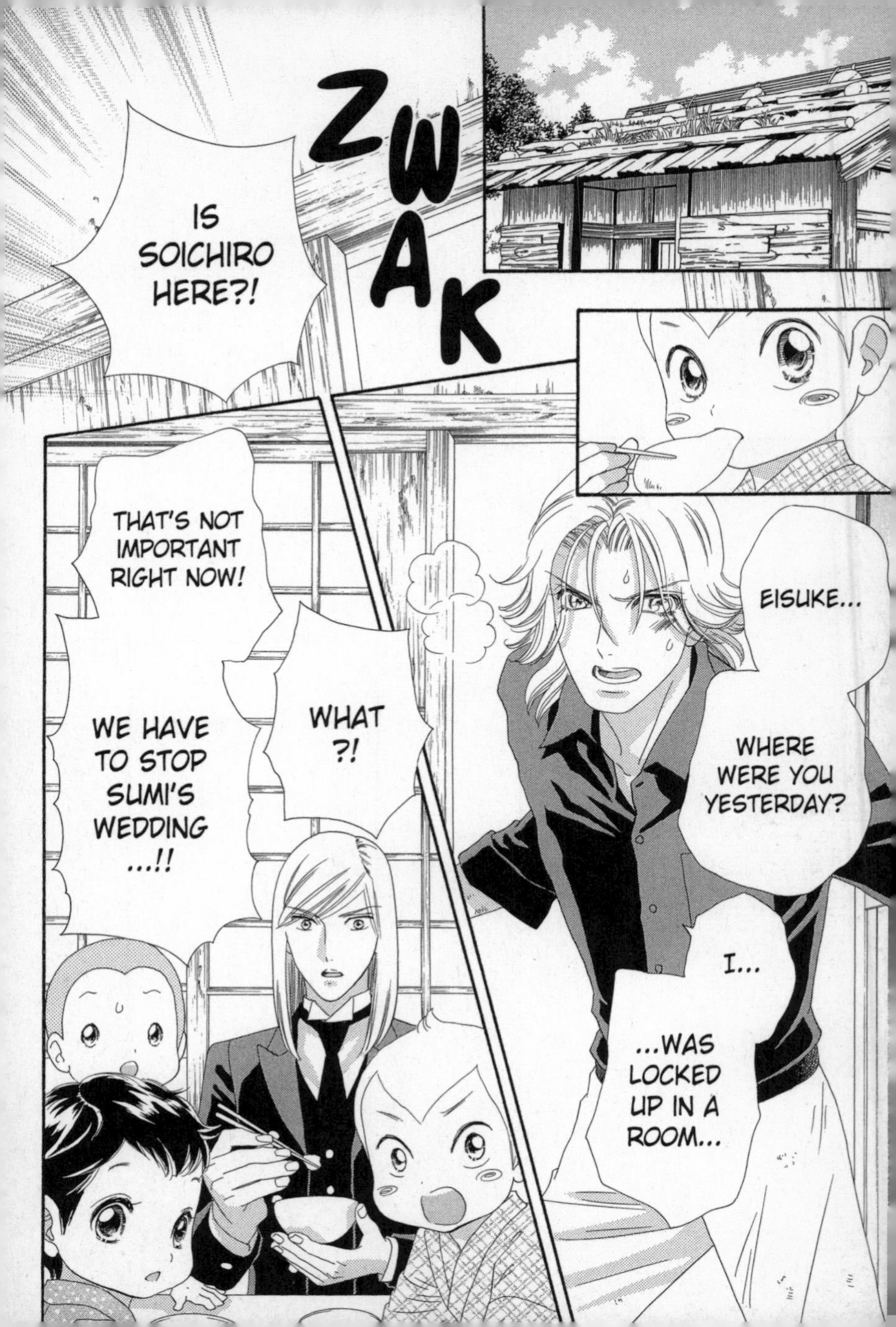
ZWAK
IS SOICHIRO HERE?!
EISUKE...
WHERE WERE YOU YESTERDAY?
I...
...WAS LOCKED UP IN A ROOM...
THAT'S NOT IMPORTANT RIGHT NOW!
WE HAVE TO STOP SUMI'S WEDDING ...!!
WHAT ?!

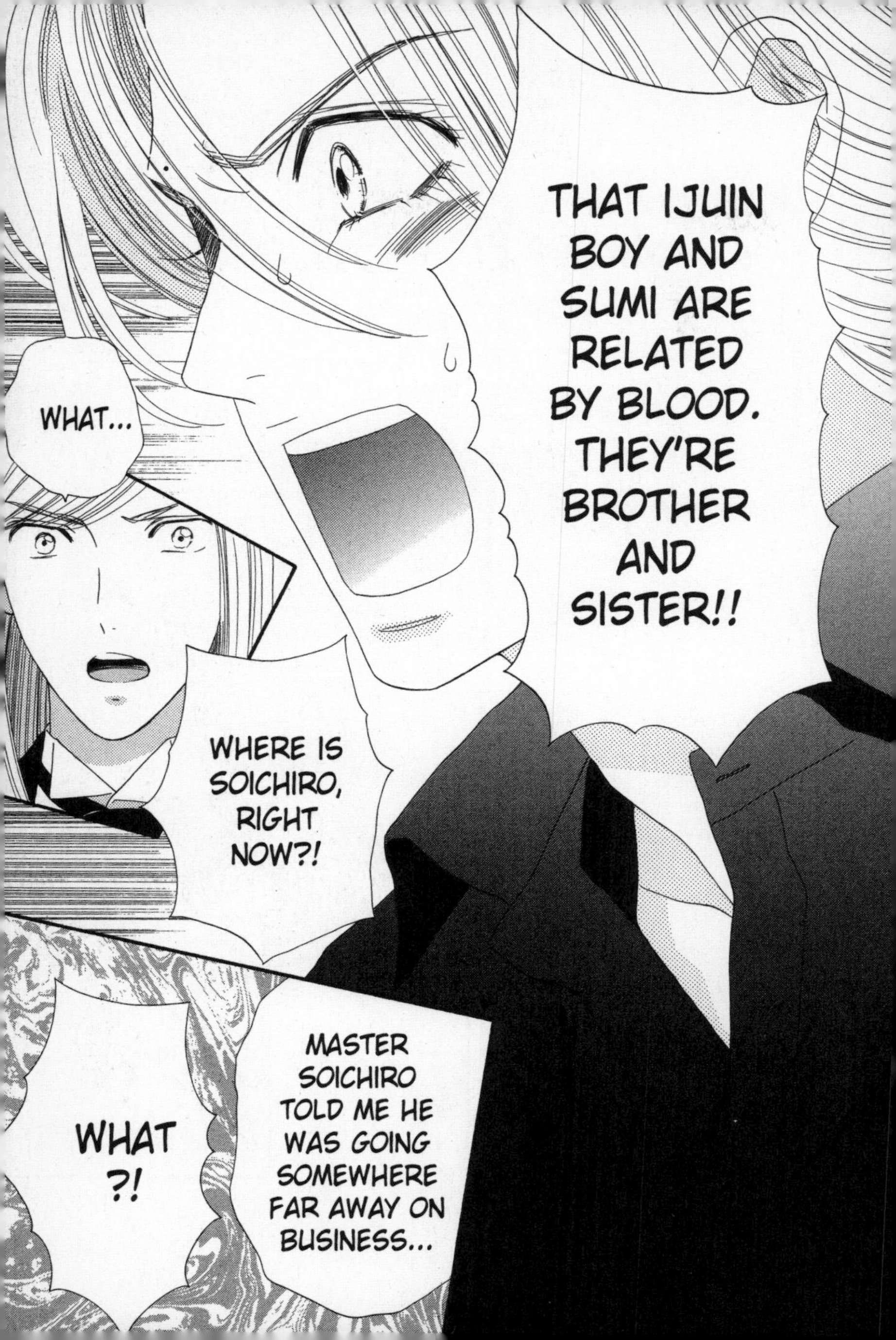
THAT IJUIN BOY AND SUMI ARE RELATED BY BLOOD. THEY'RE BROTHER AND SISTER!!
WHAT...
WHERE IS SOICHIRO, RIGHT NOW?!
MASTER SOICHIRO TOLD ME HE WAS GOING SOMEWHERE FAR AWAY ON BUSINESS...
WHAT ?!

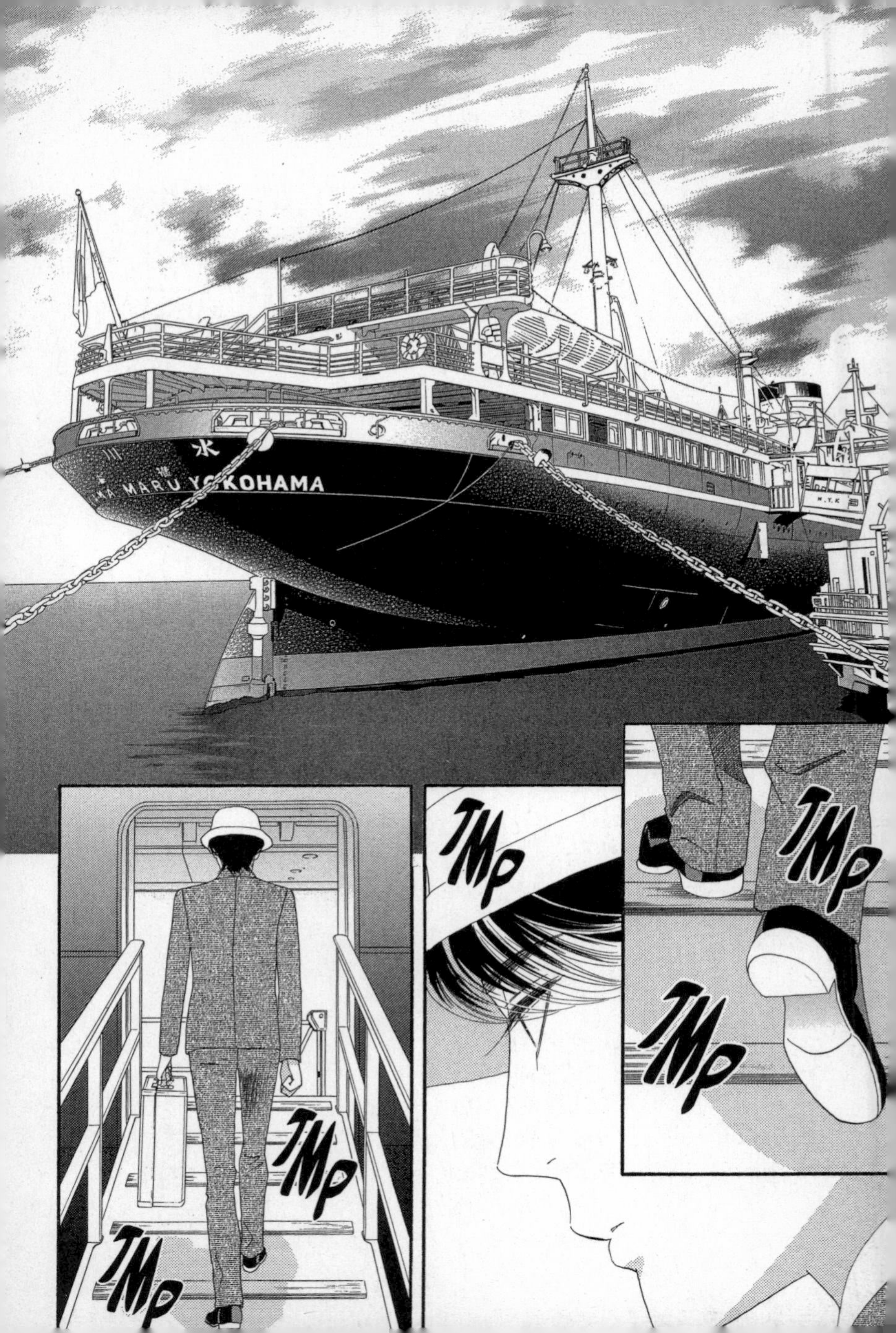
氷
MA MARU YOKOHAMA
TMP
TMP
TMP
TMP
TMP

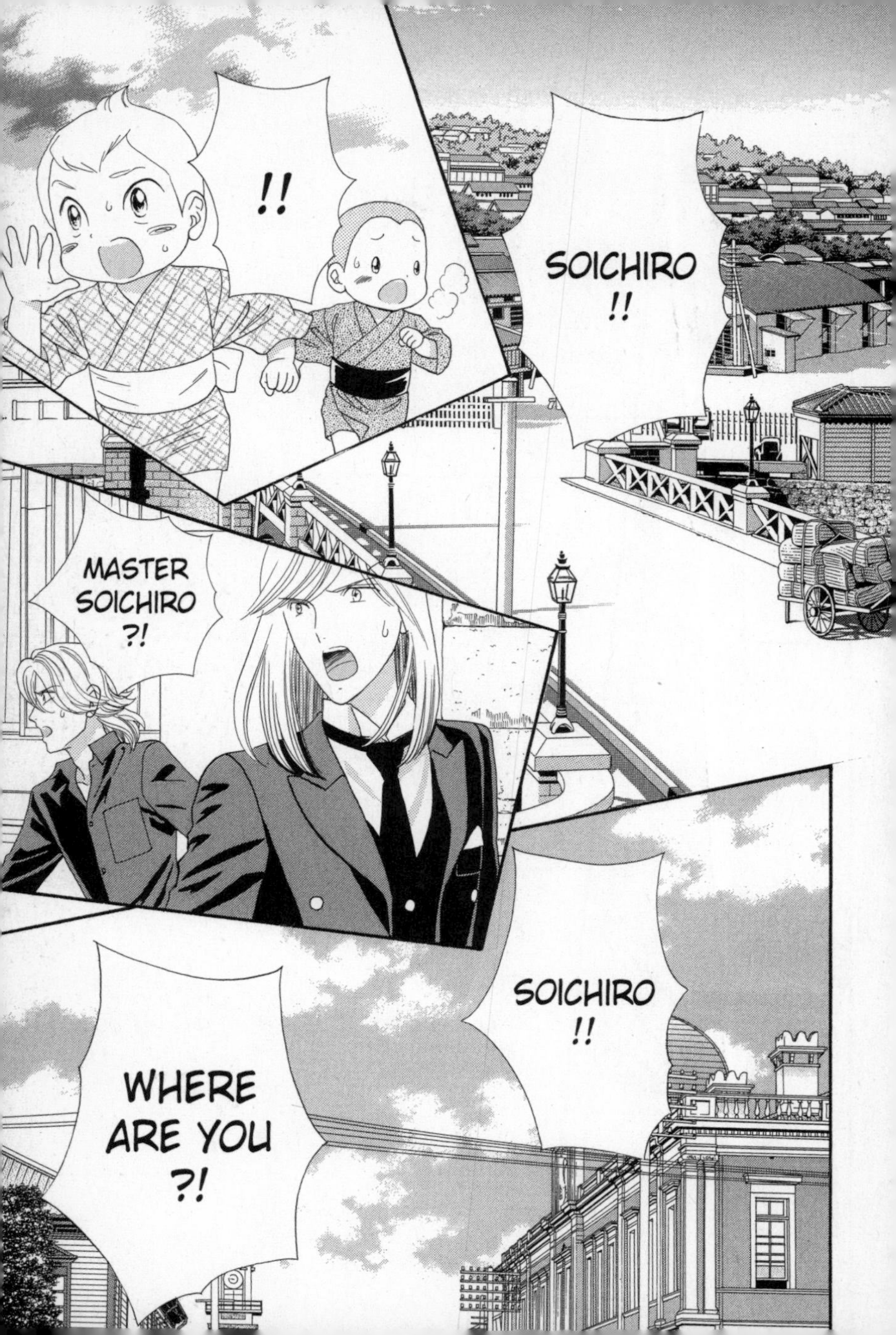
SOICHIRO !!
!!
MASTER SOICHIRO ?!
SOICHIRO !!
WHERE ARE YOU ?!

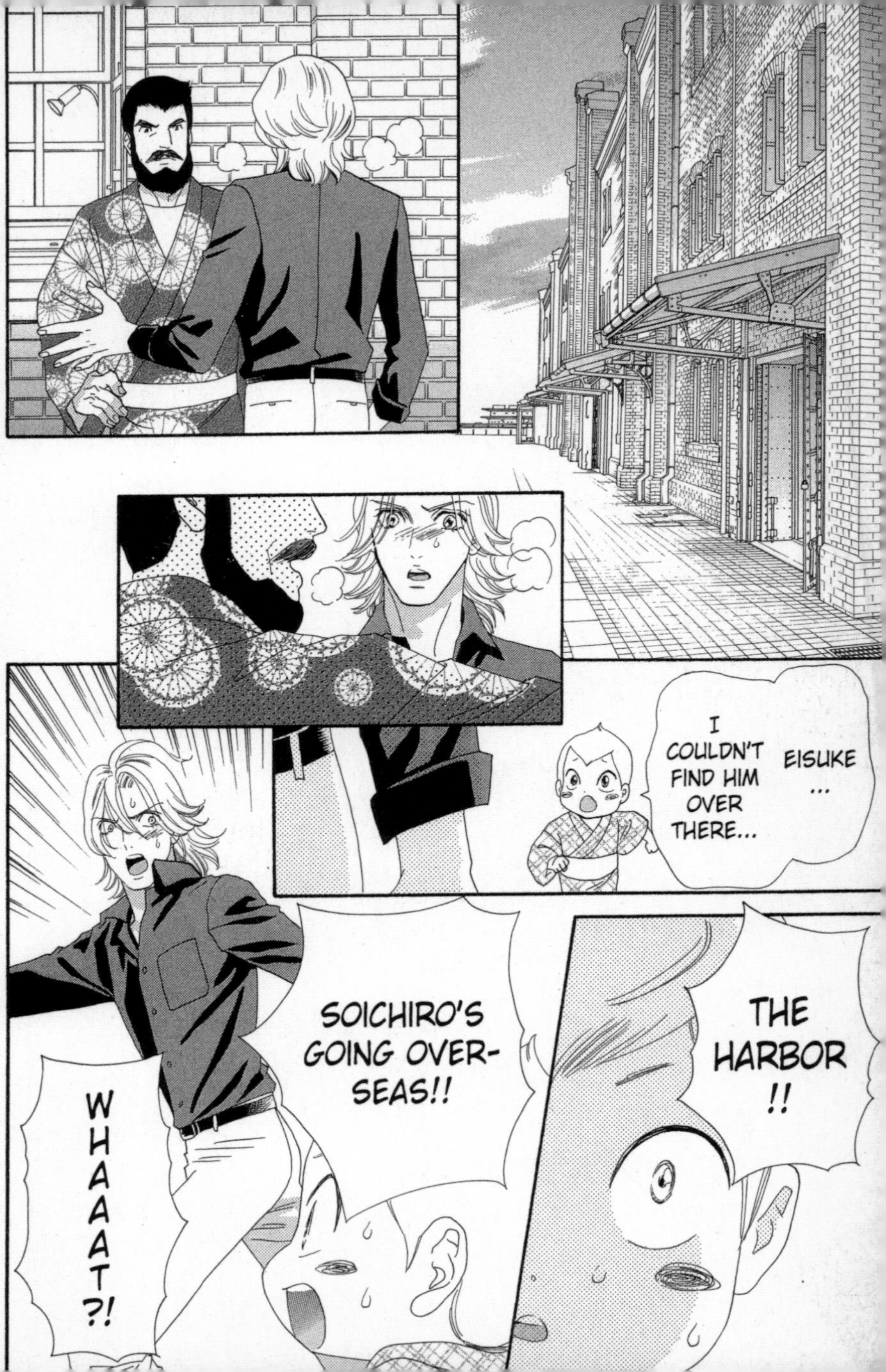

EISUKE ...
I COULDN'T FIND HIM OVER THERE...
THE HARBOR !!
SOICHIRO'S GOING OVER-SEAS!!
WHAAAAT?!

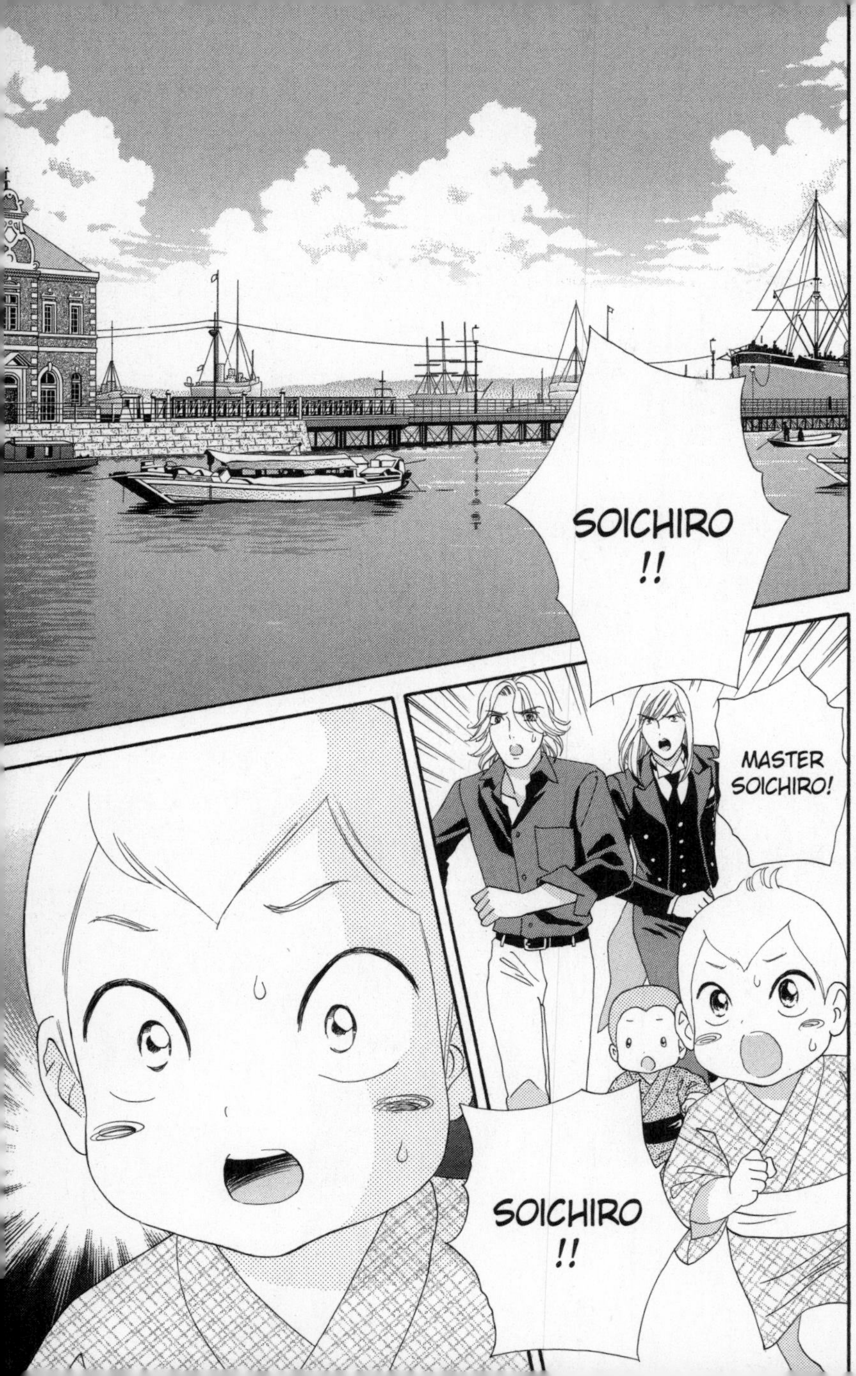
SOICHIRO !!
MASTER SOICHIRO!
SOICHIRO !!

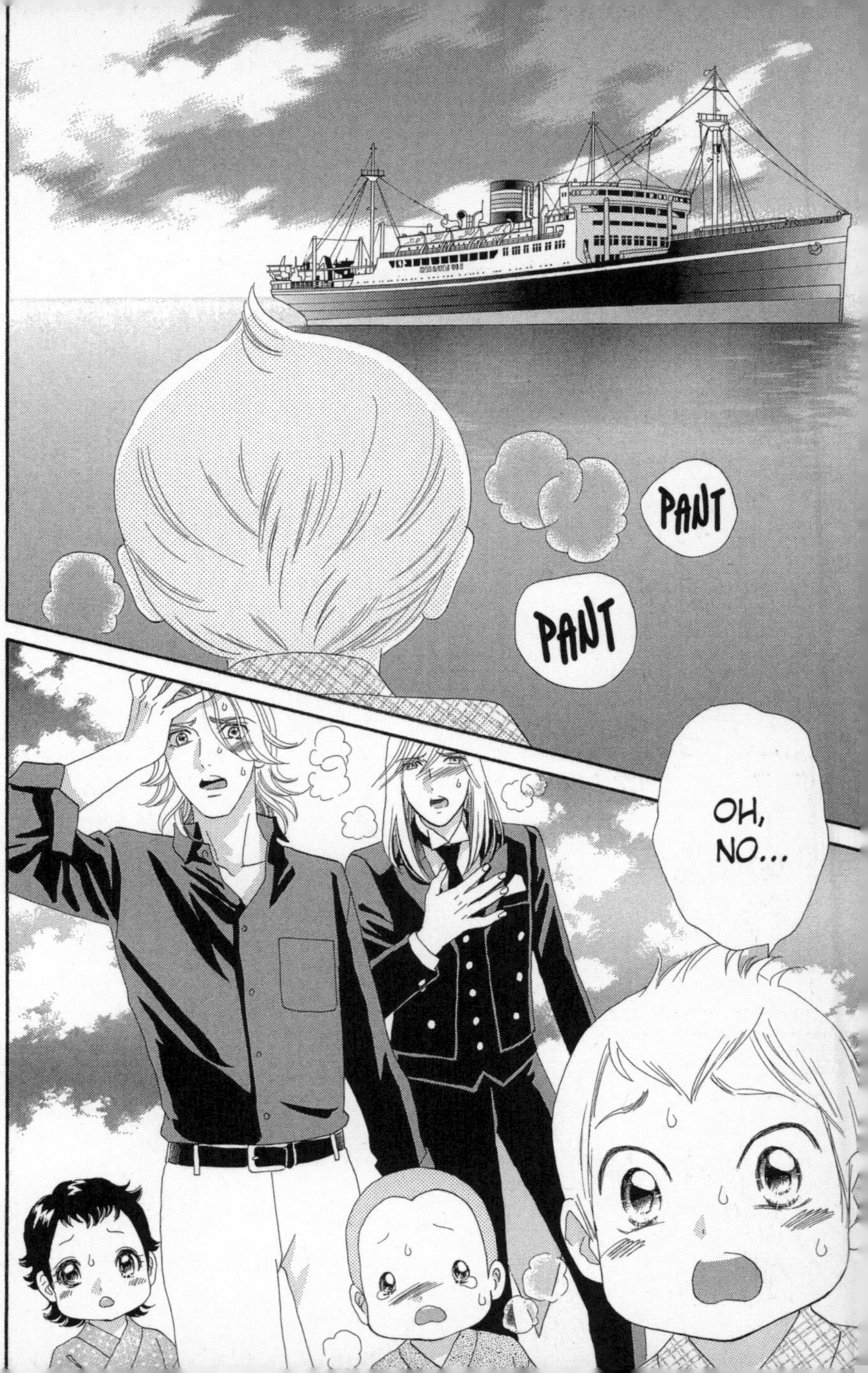
PANT
PANT
OH, NO...

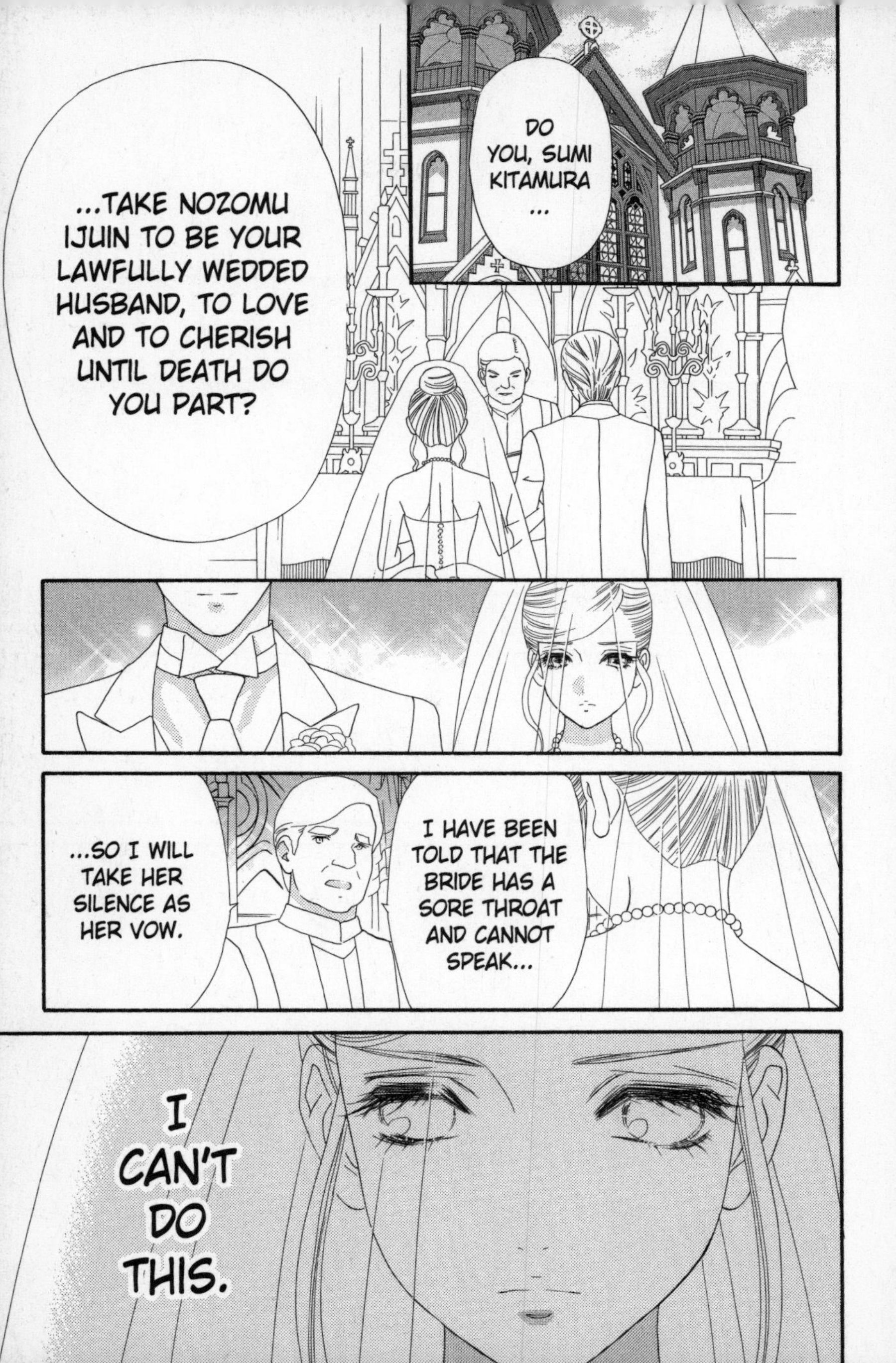
DO YOU, SUMI KITAMURA ...
...TAKE NOZOMU IJUIN TO BE YOUR LAWFULLY WEDDED HUSBAND, TO LOVE AND TO CHERISH UNTIL DEATH DO YOU PART?
I HAVE BEEN TOLD THAT THE BRIDE HAS A SORE THROAT AND CANNOT SPEAK...
...SO I WILL TAKE HER SILENCE AS HER VOW.
I CAN'T DO THIS.

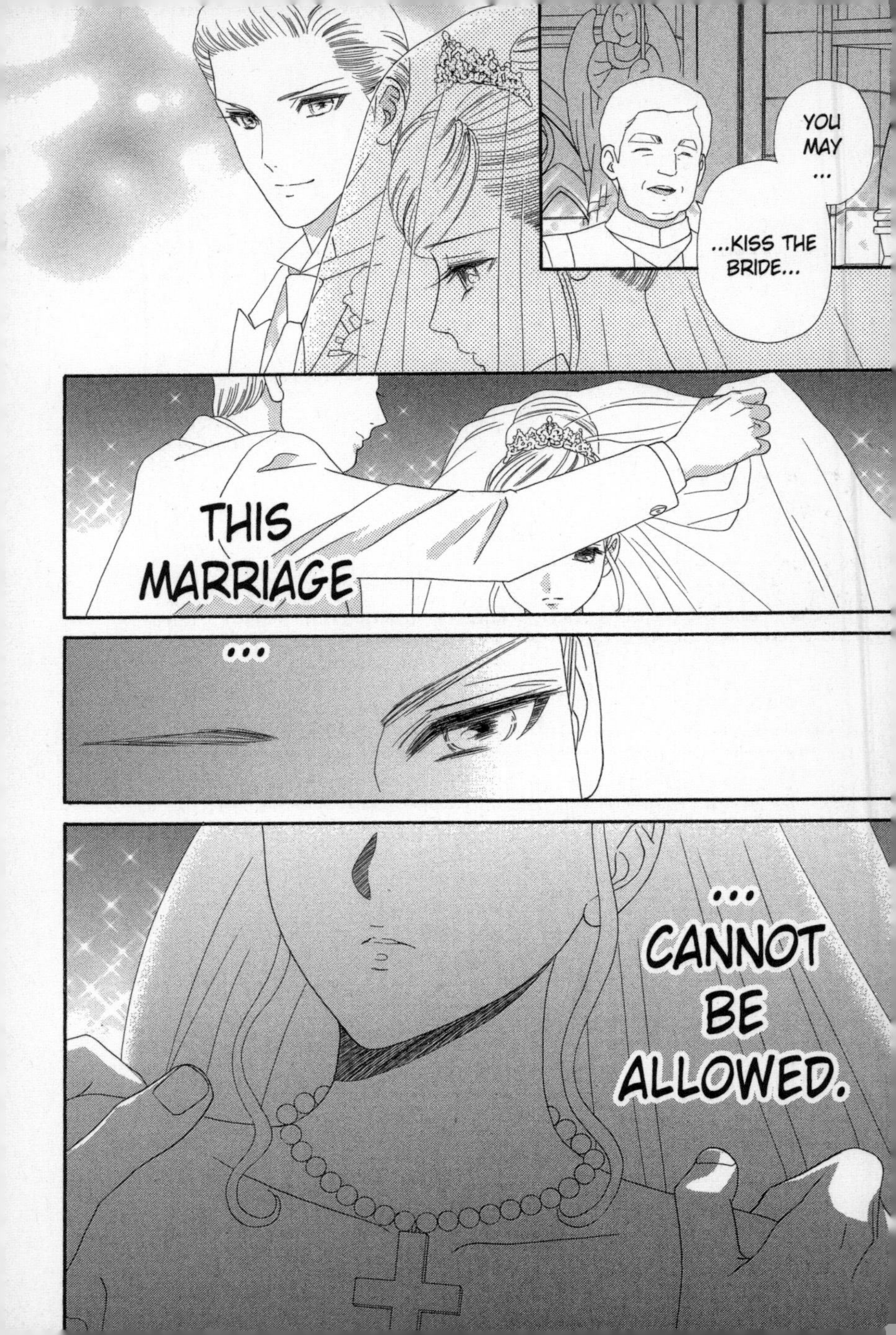
YOU MAY ...
...KISS THE BRIDE...
THIS MARRIAGE
...
...
CANNOT BE ALLOWED.

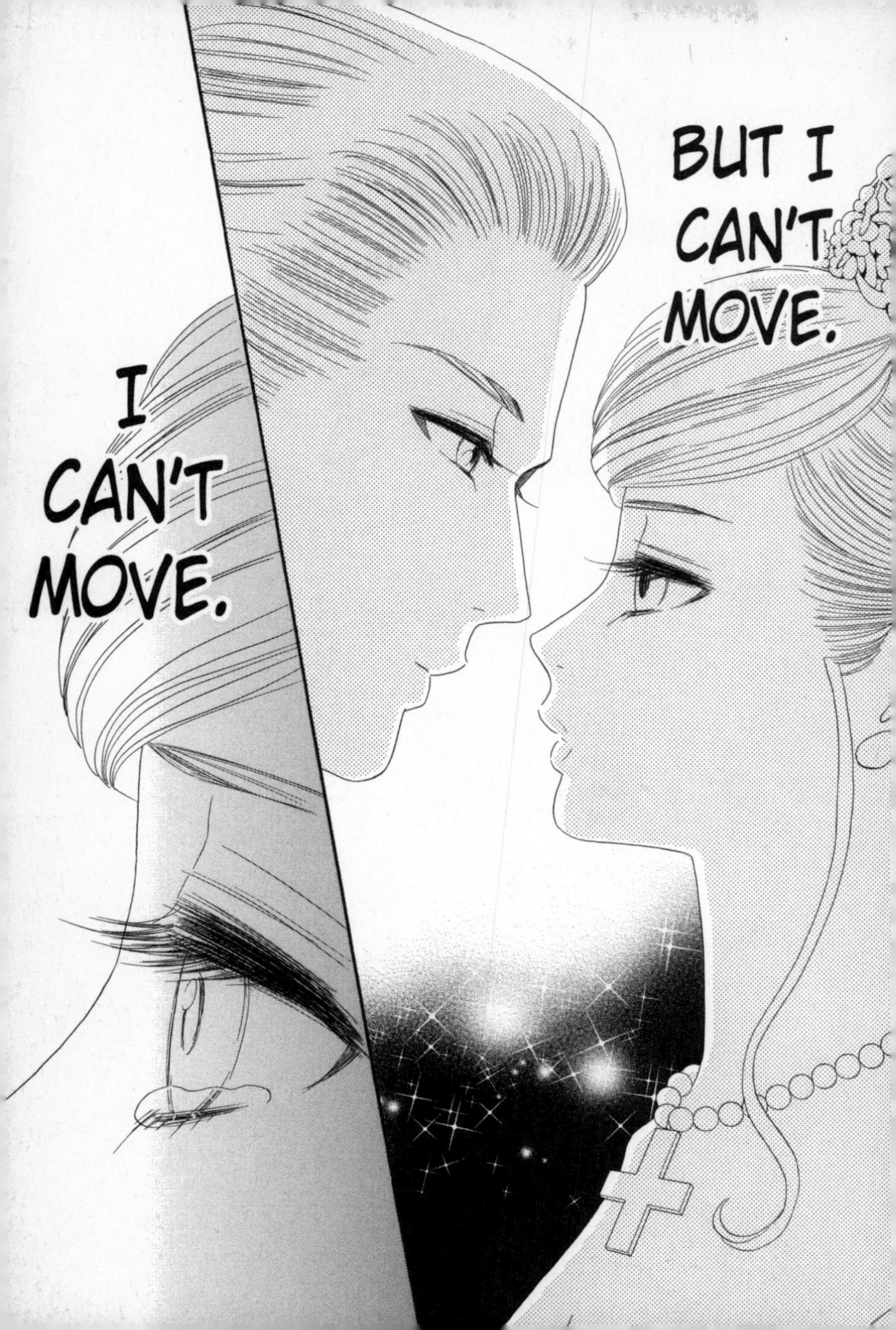
BUT I CAN'T MOVE.
I CAN'T MOVE.

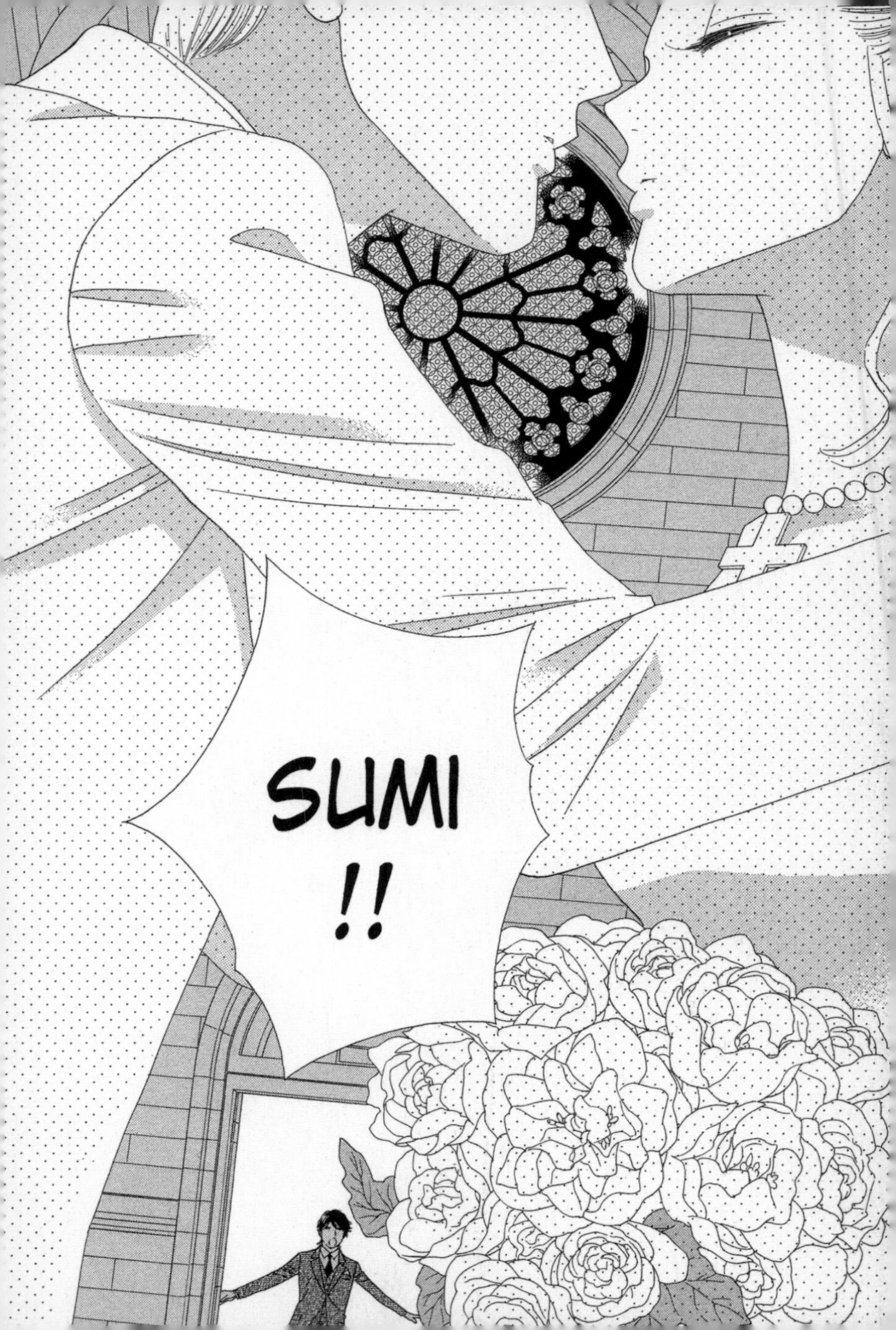
SUMI !!

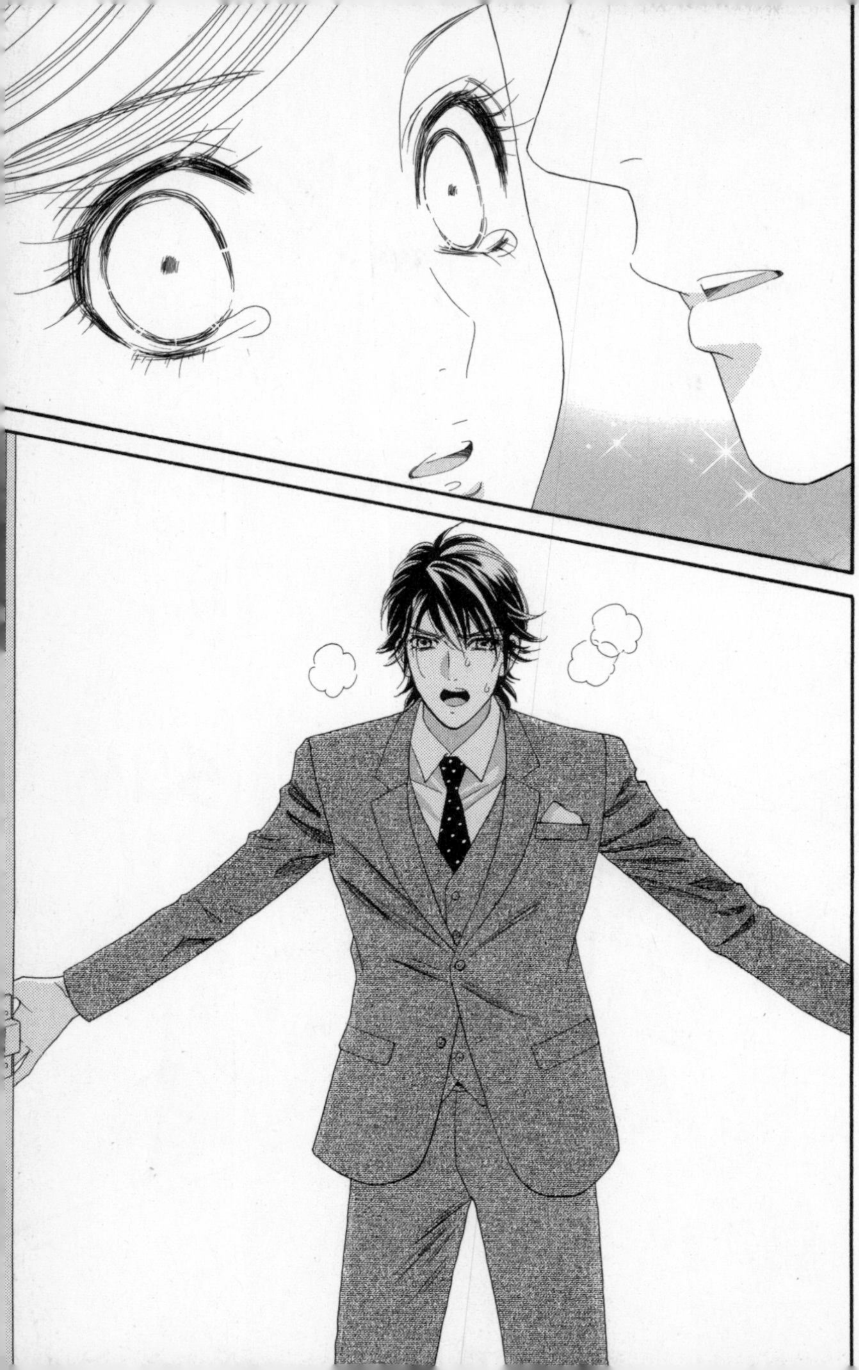

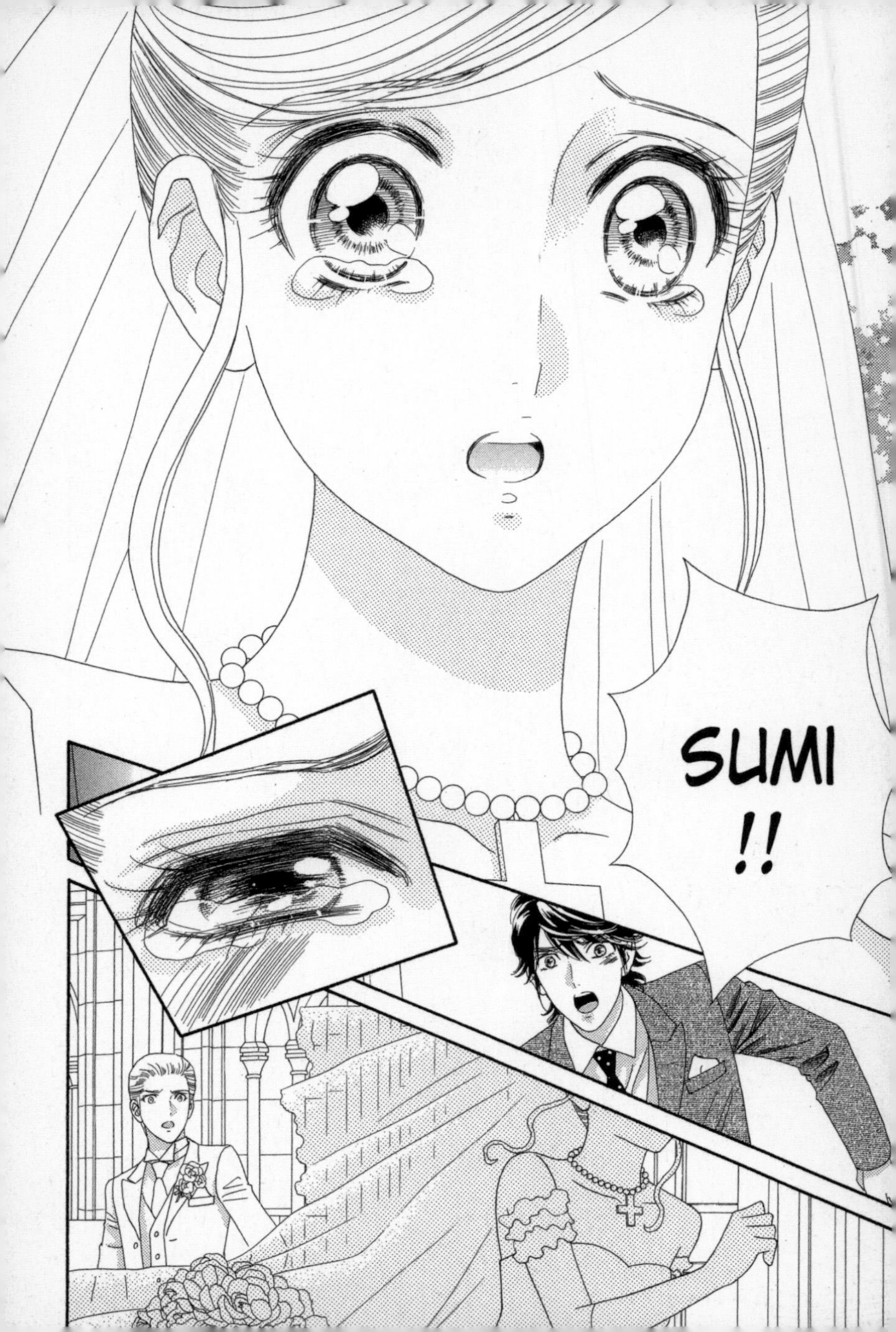
SUMI
!!

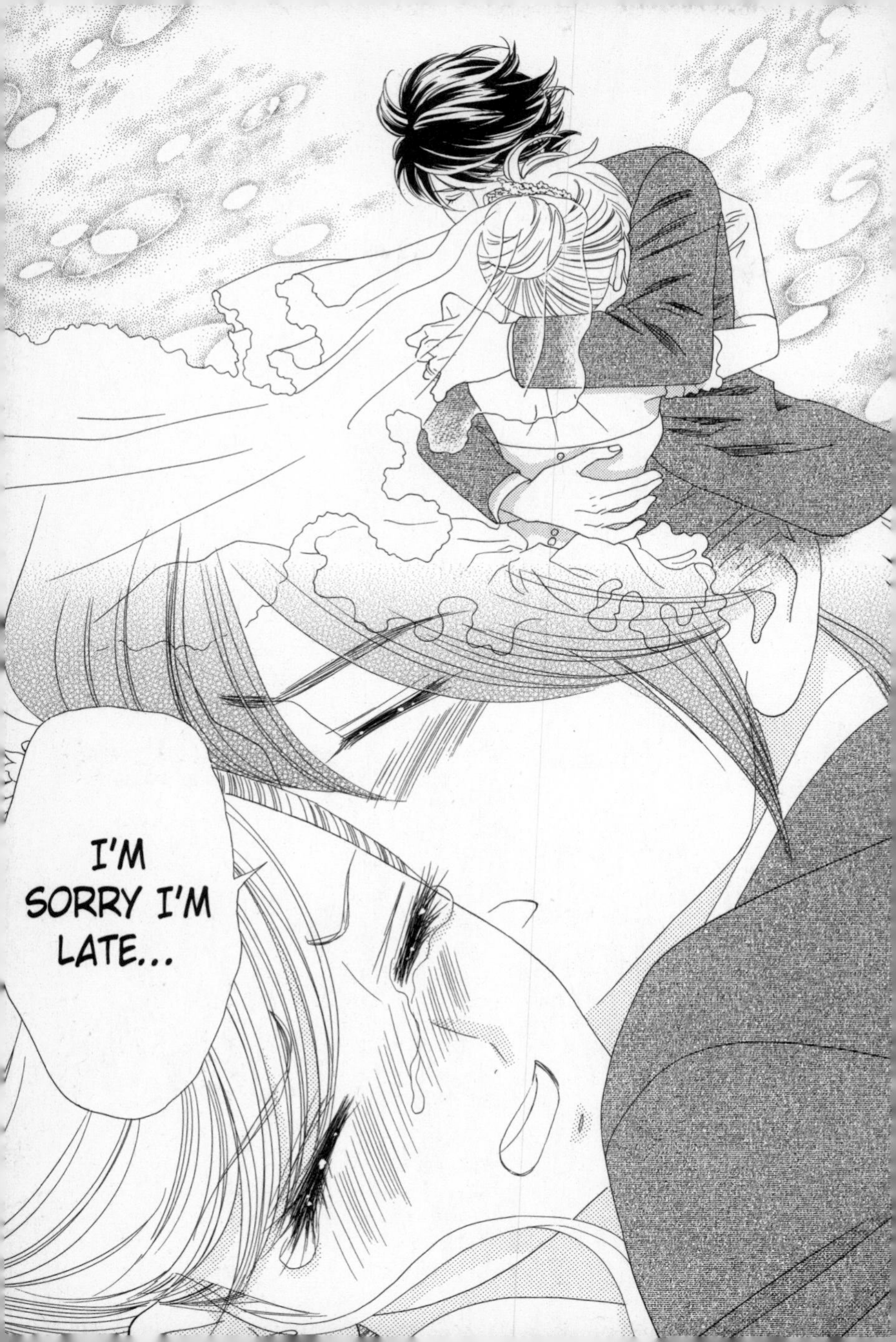
I'M SORRY I'M LATE...

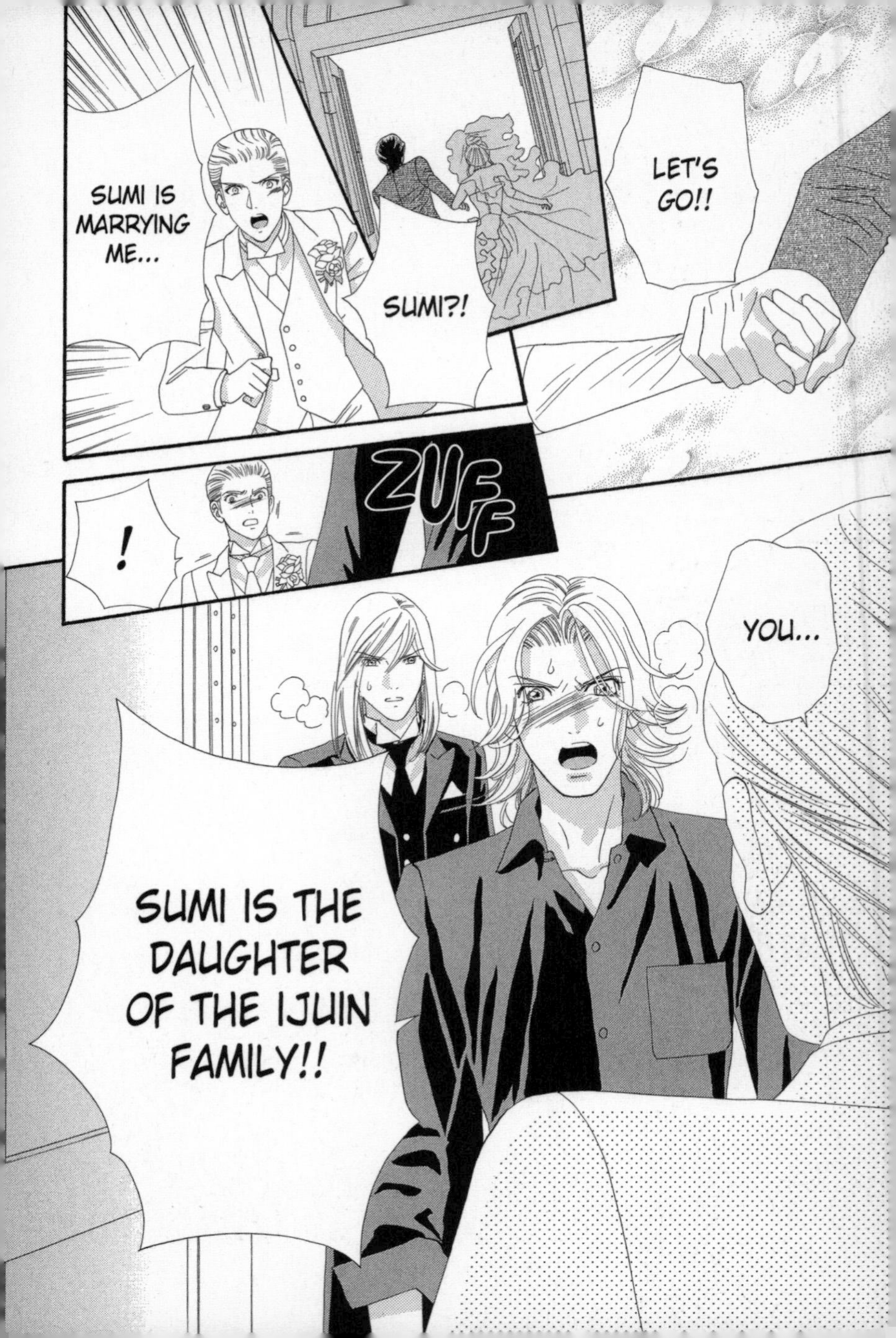
LET'S GO!!
SUMI?!
SUMI IS MARRYING ME...
ZUFF
!
YOU...
SUMI IS THE DAUGHTER OF THE IJUIN FAMILY!!

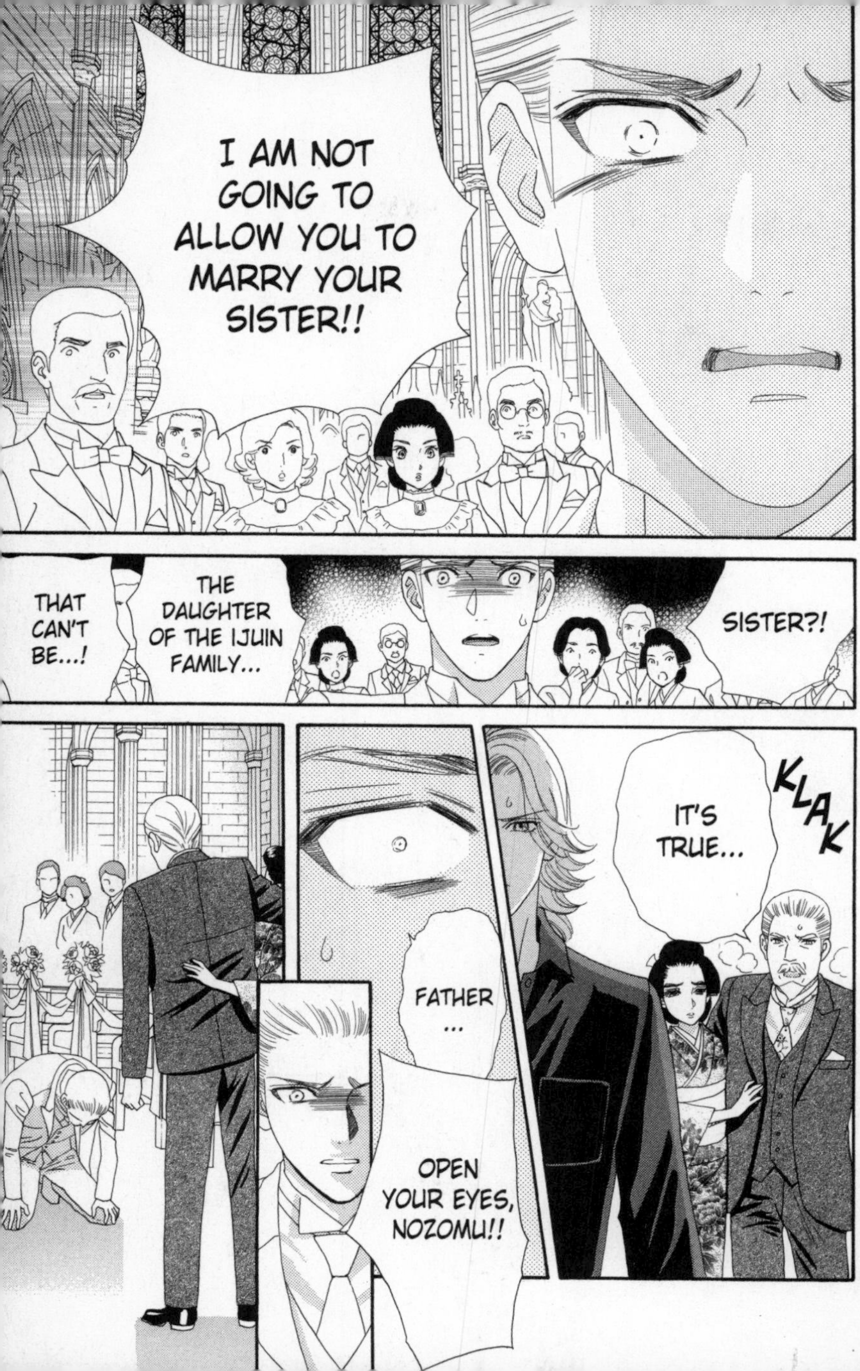
I AM NOT GOING TO ALLOW YOU TO MARRY YOUR SISTER!!
SISTER?!
THE DAUGHTER OF THE IJUIN FAMILY...
THAT CAN'T BE...!
KLAK
IT'S TRUE...
FATHER ...
OPEN YOUR EYES, NOZOMU!!

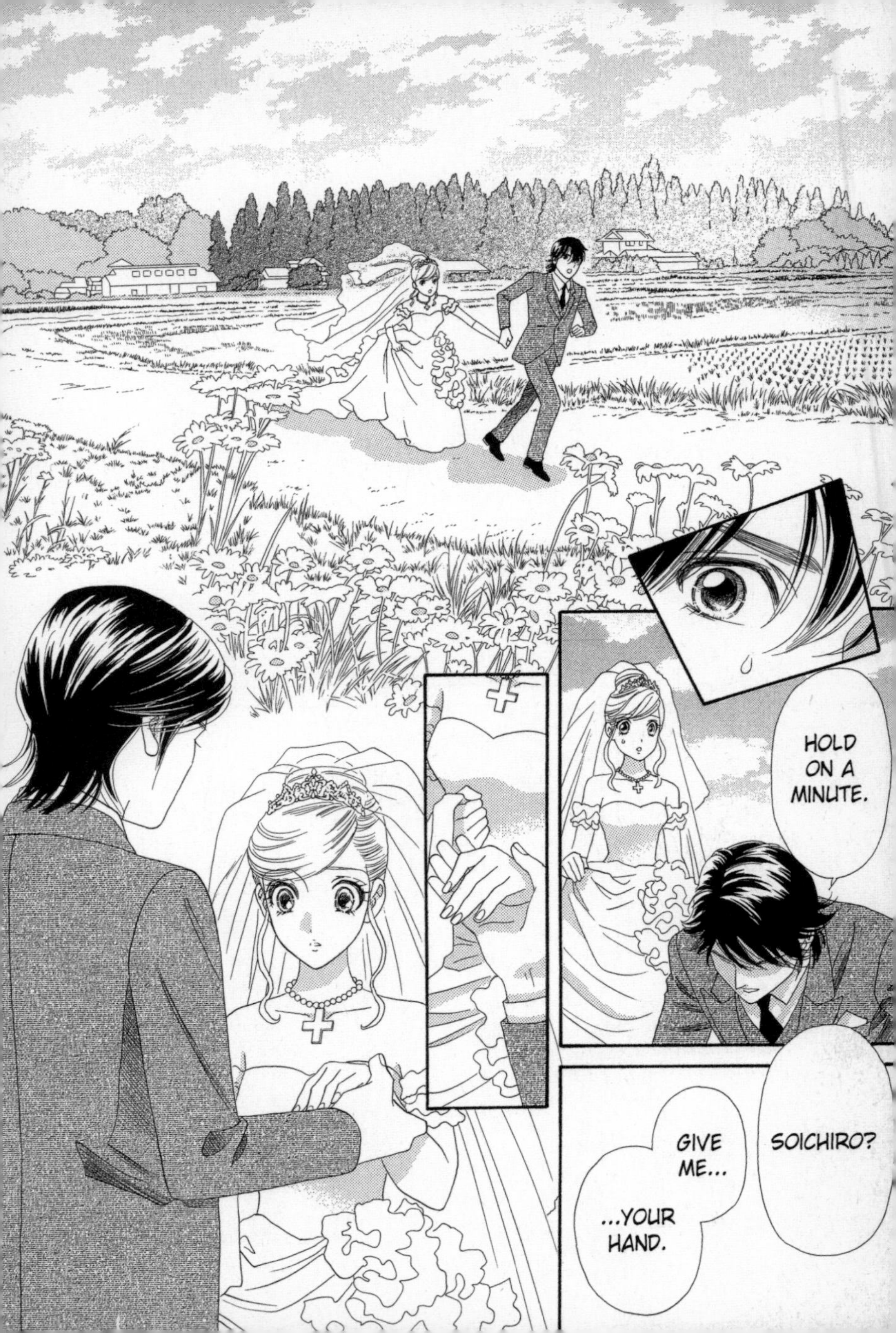
HOLD ON A MINUTE.
SOICHIRO?
GIVE ME...
...YOUR HAND.

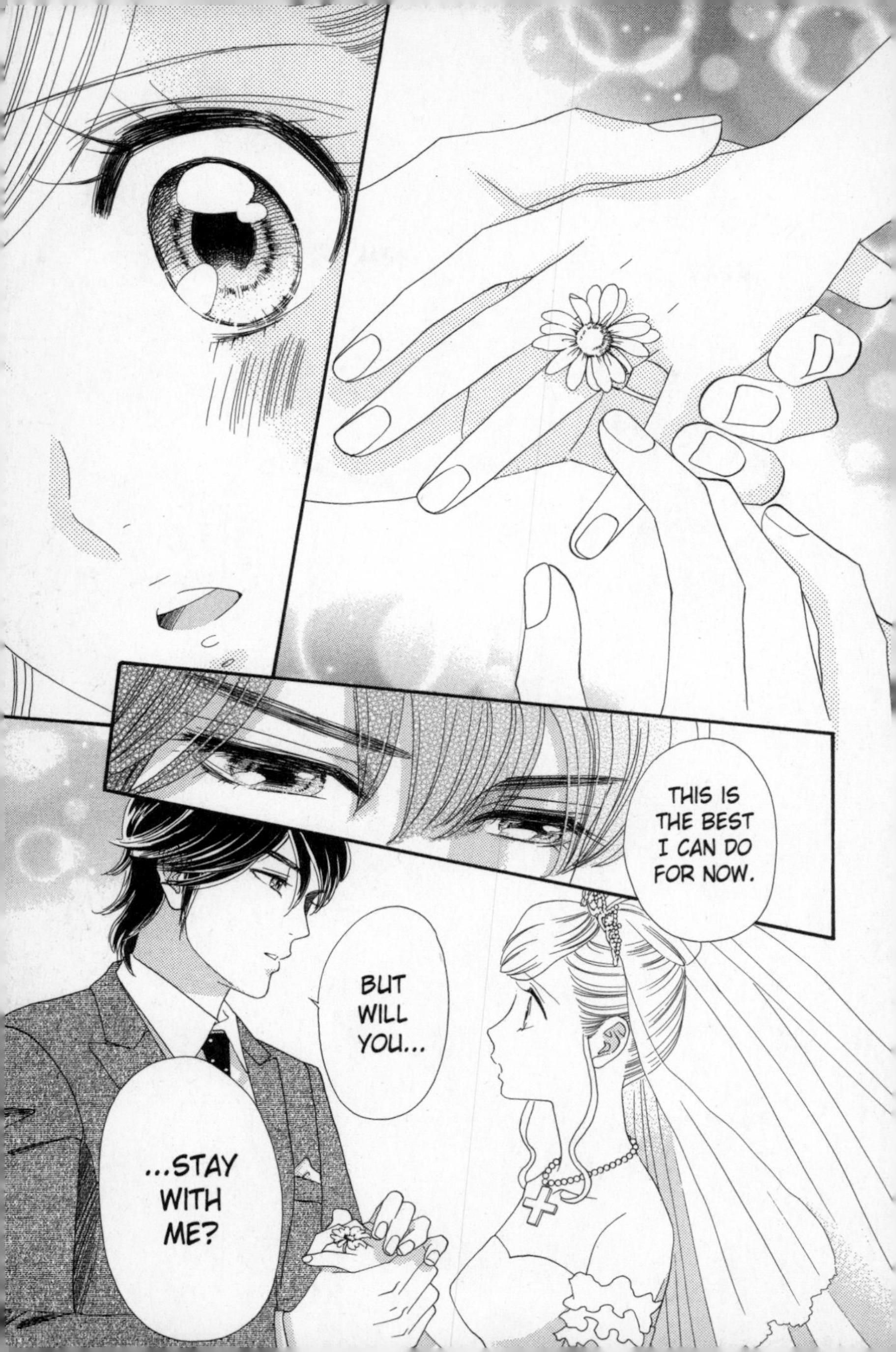
THIS IS THE BEST I CAN DO FOR NOW.
BUT WILL YOU...
...STAY WITH ME?

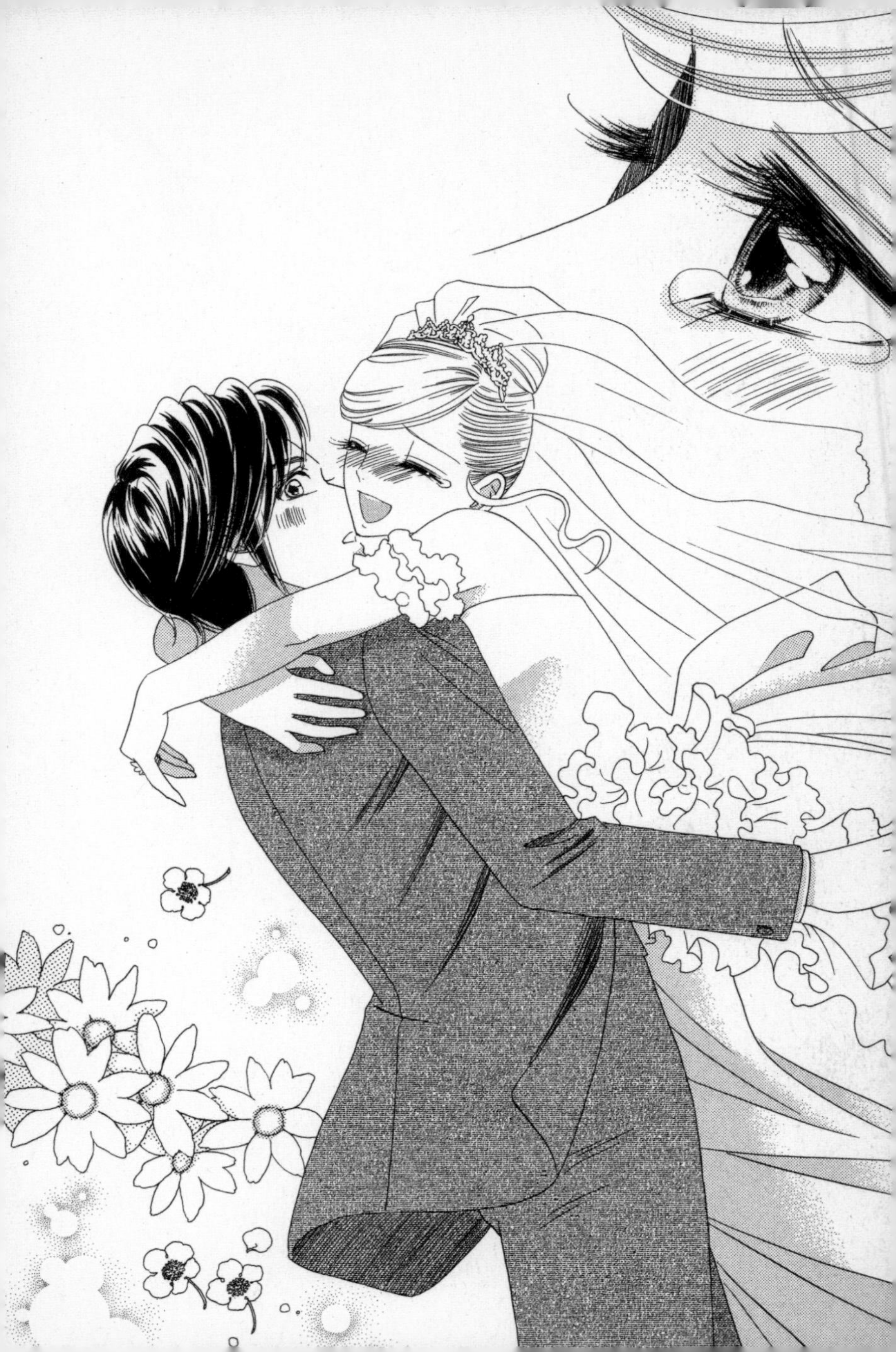

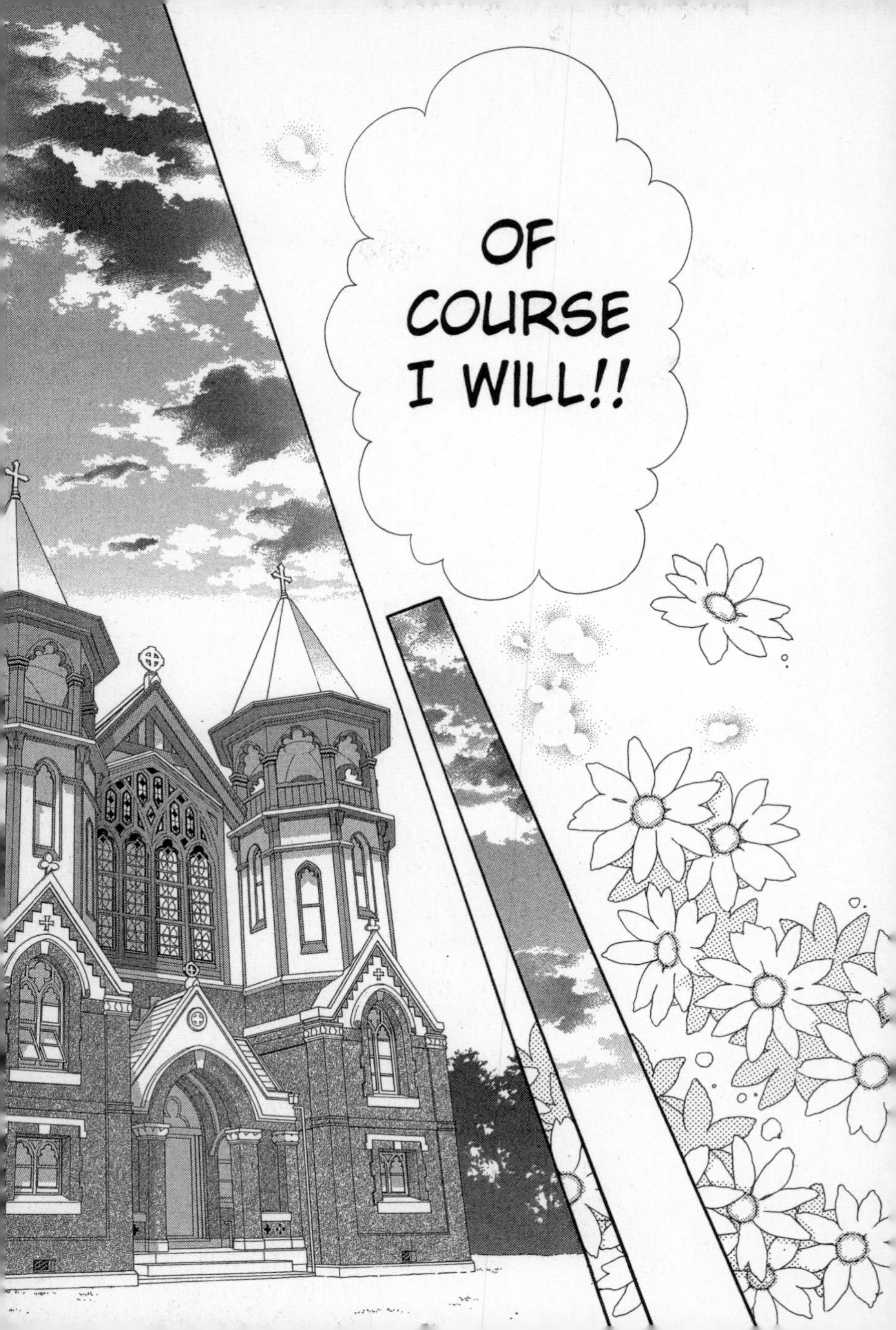
OF COURSE I WILL!!

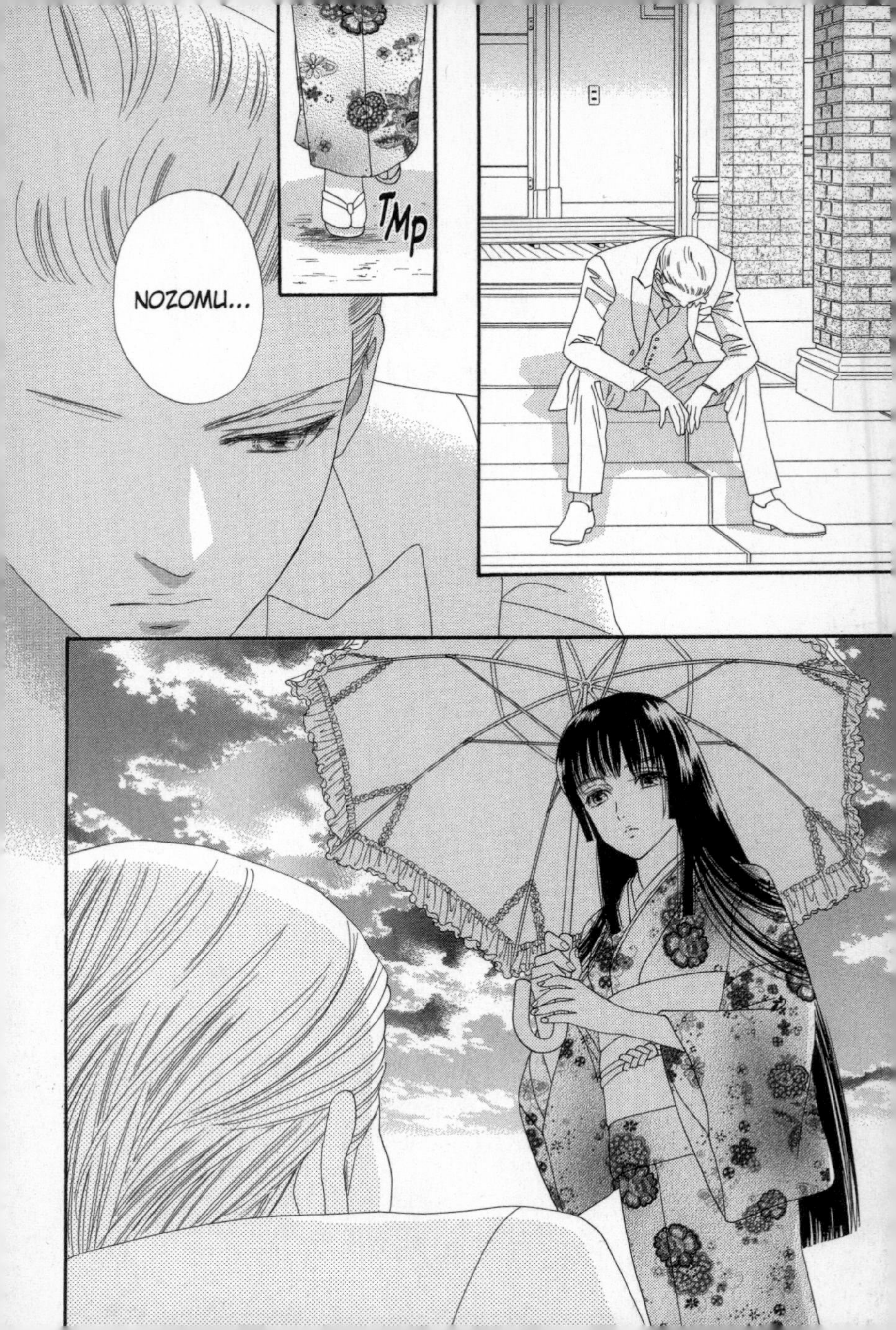
NOZOMU...
TMP

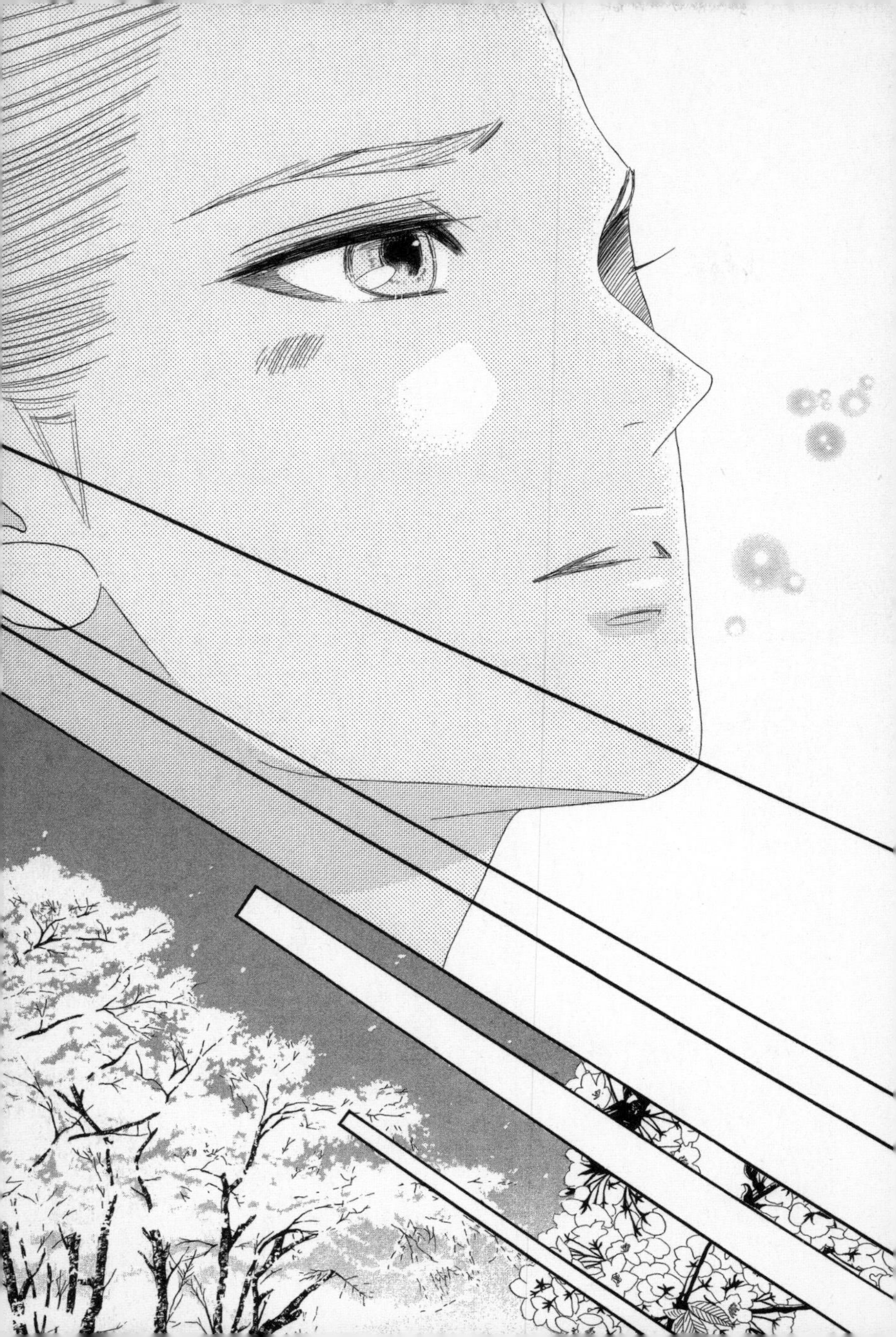

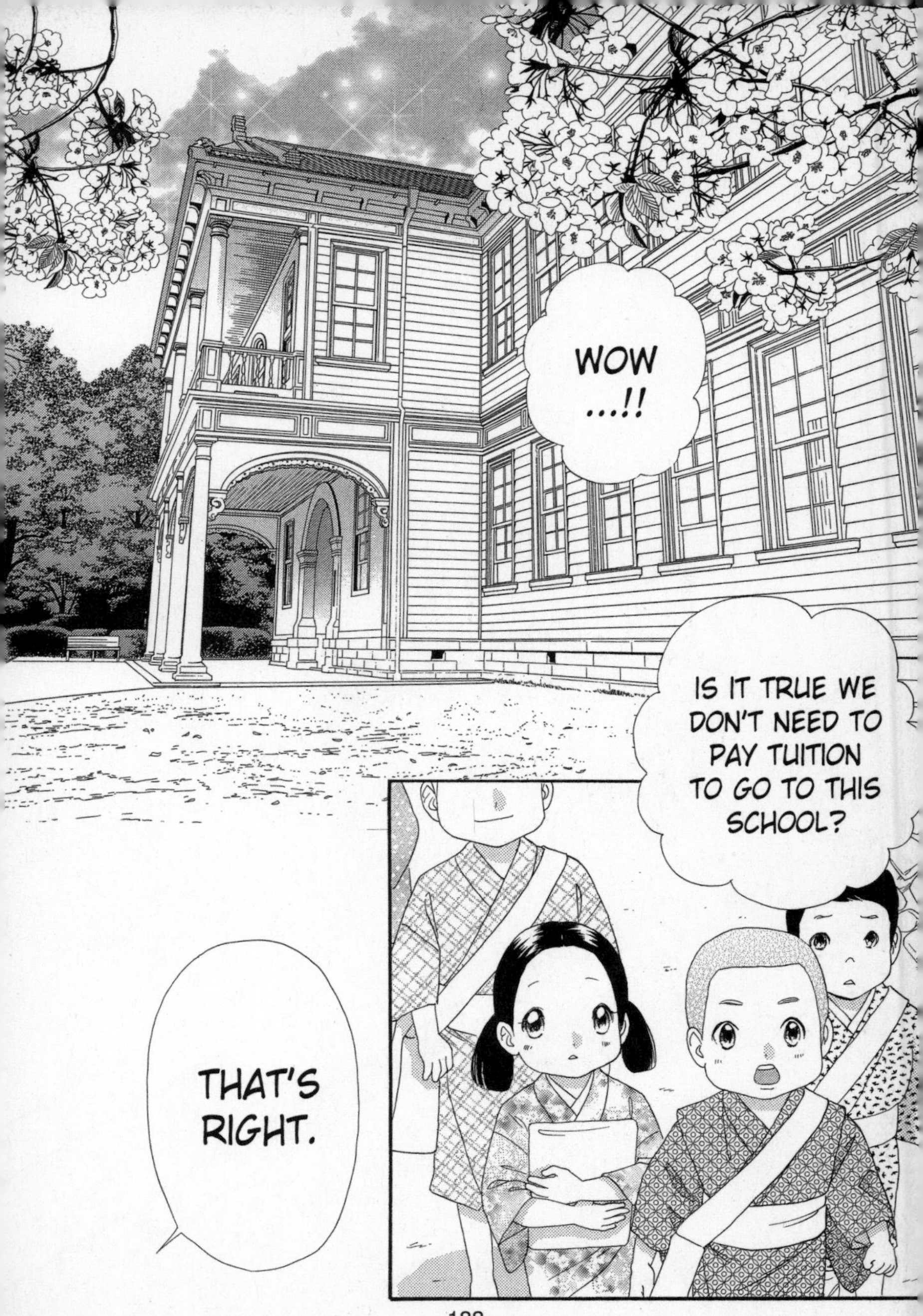
WOW ...!!
IS IT TRUE WE DON'T NEED TO PAY TUITION TO GO TO THIS SCHOOL?
THAT'S RIGHT.

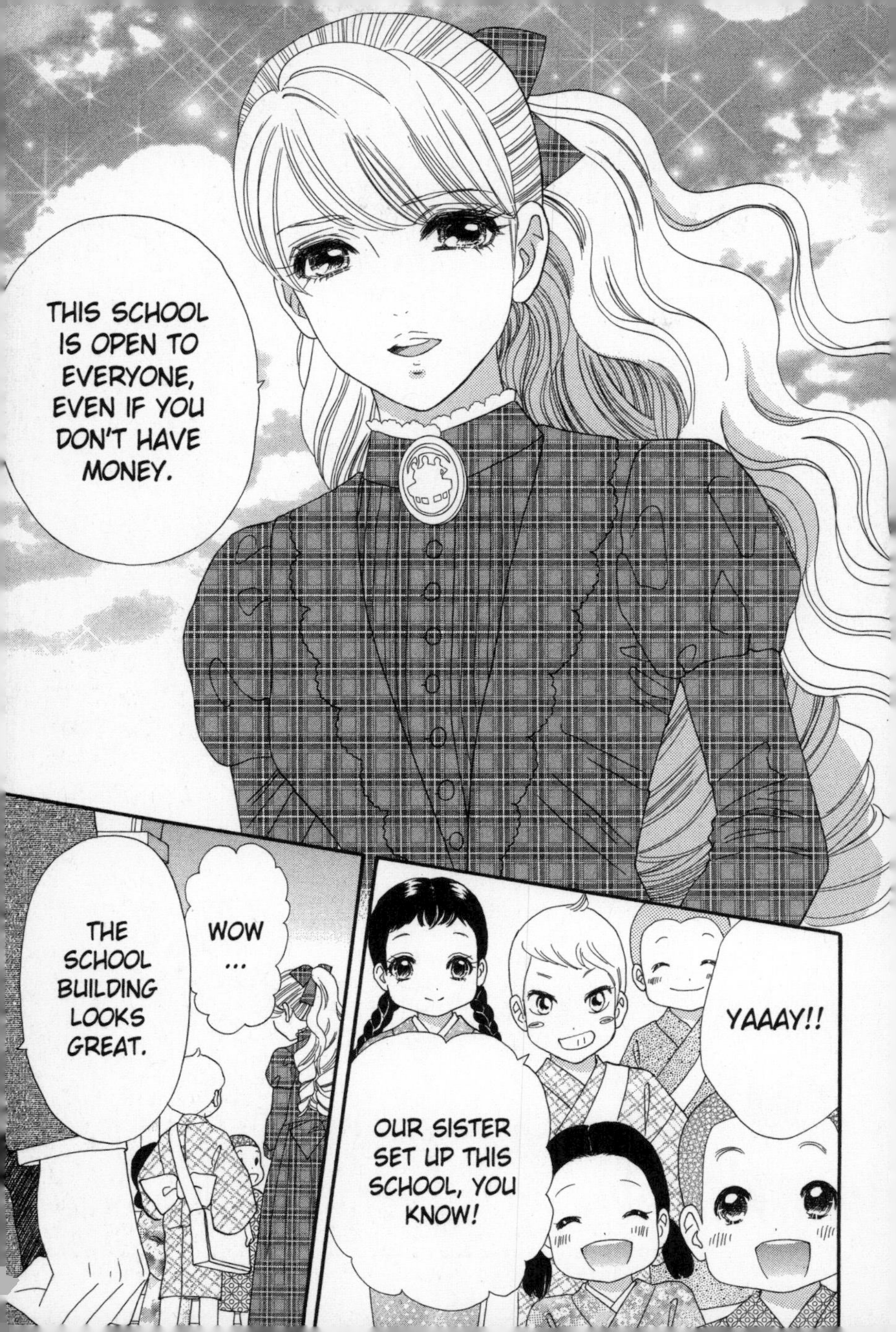
THIS SCHOOL IS OPEN TO EVERYONE, EVEN IF YOU DON'T HAVE MONEY.
YAAAY!!
OUR SISTER SET UP THIS SCHOOL, YOU KNOW!
WOW ...
THE SCHOOL BUILDING LOOKS GREAT.

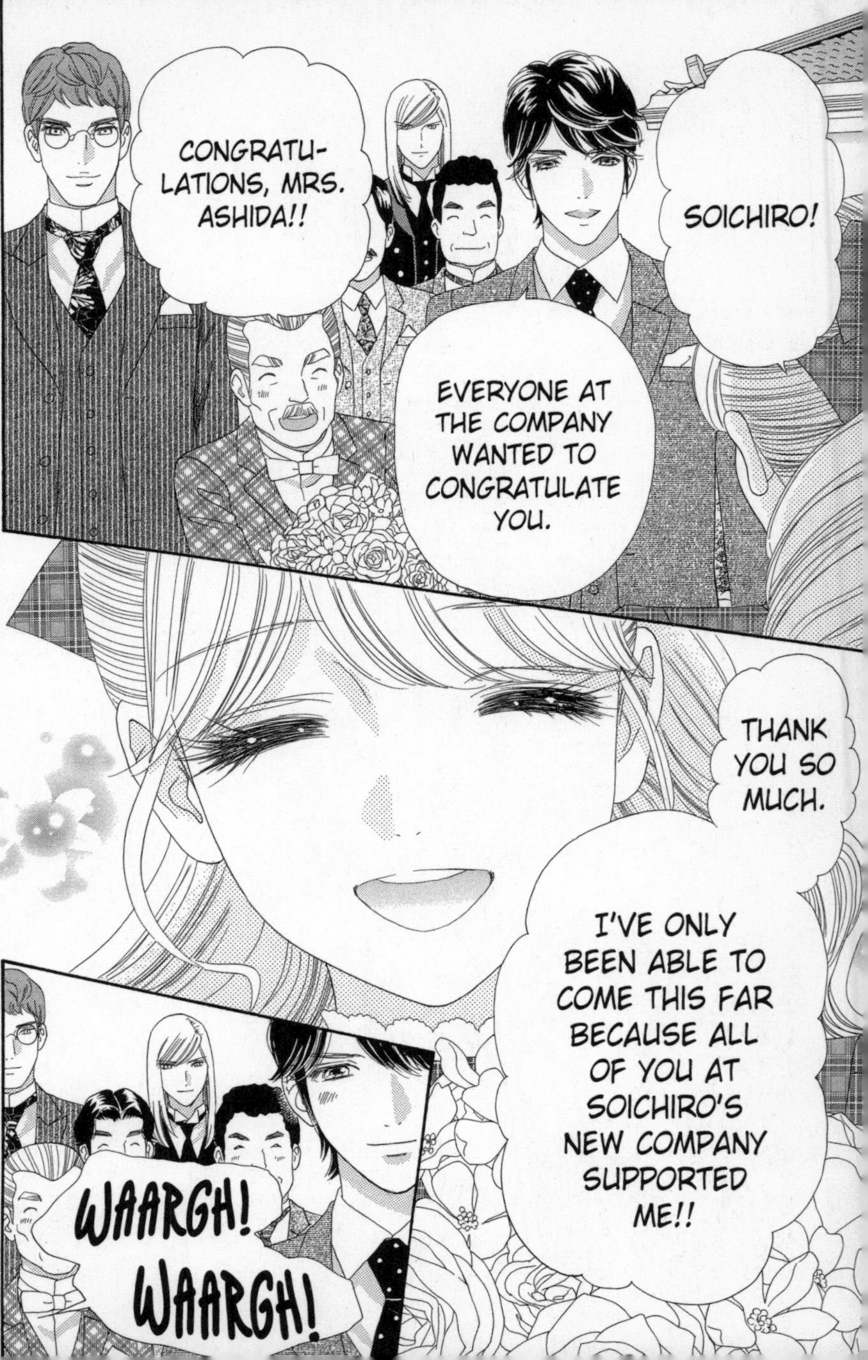
SOICHIRO!
CONGRATULATIONS, MRS. ASHIDA!!
EVERYONE AT THE COMPANY WANTED TO CONGRATULATE YOU.
THANK YOU SO MUCH.
I'VE ONLY BEEN ABLE TO COME THIS FAR BECAUSE ALL OF YOU AT SOICHIRO'S NEW COMPANY SUPPORTED ME!!
WAARGH! WAARGH!

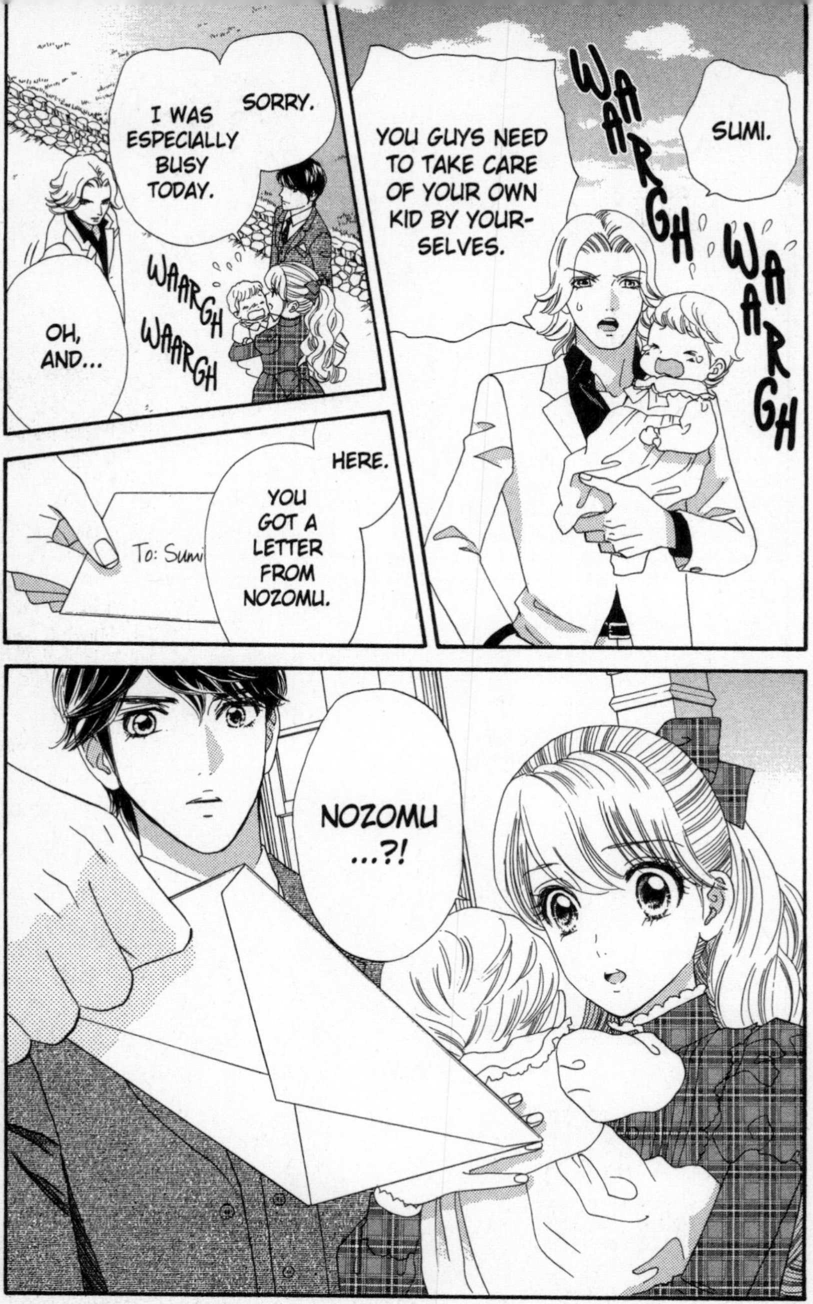
SUMI.
WAARGH
WAARGH
YOU GUYS NEED TO TAKE CARE OF YOUR OWN KID BY YOUR-SELVES.
SORRY.
I WAS ESPECIALLY BUSY TODAY.
WAARGH
WAARGH
OH, AND...
HERE.
YOU GOT A LETTER FROM NOZOMU.
To: Sumi
NOZOMU ...?!

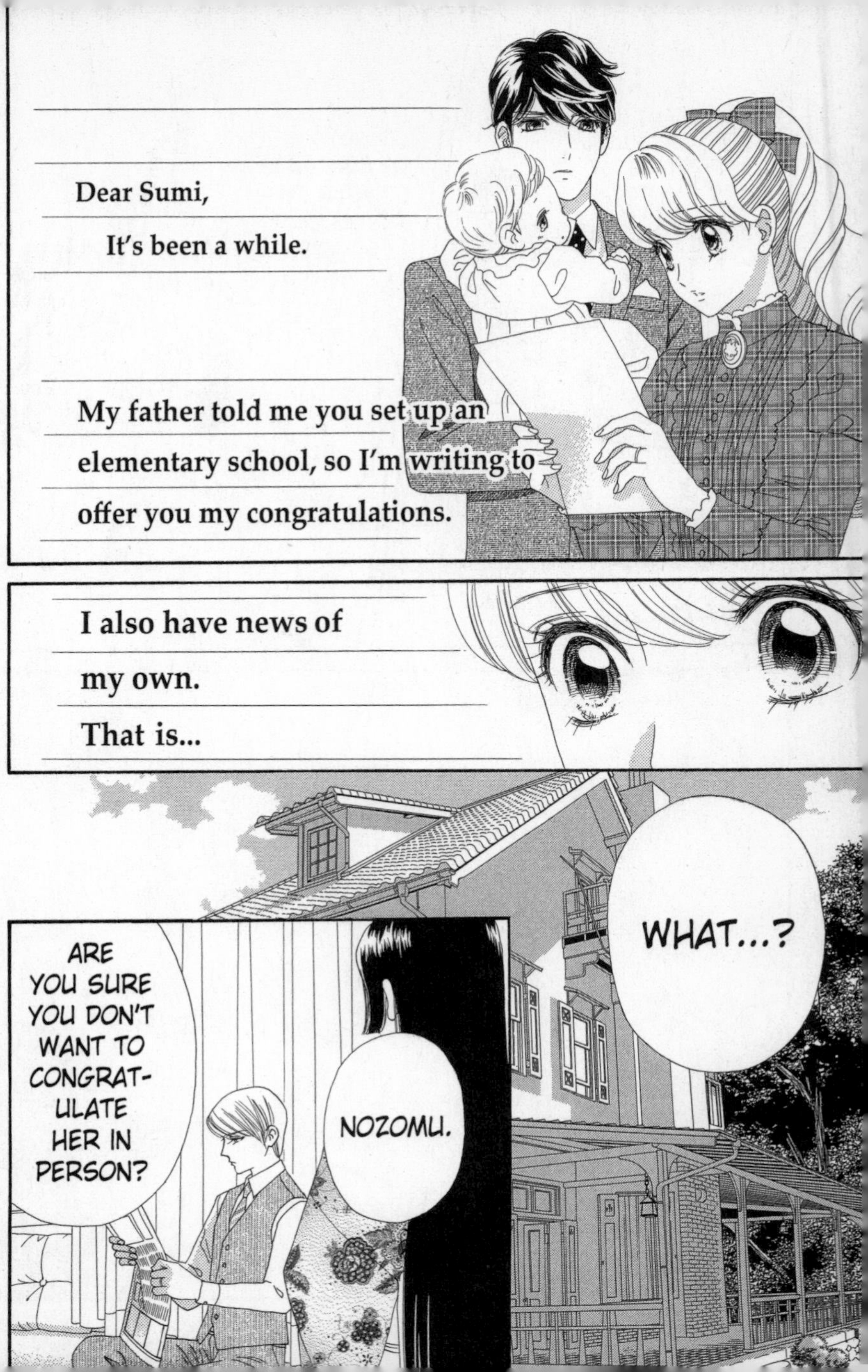
Dear Sumi,
It's been a while.
My father told me you set up an elementary school, so I'm writing to offer you my congratulations.
I also have news of my own.
That is...
WHAT...?
NOZOMU.
ARE YOU SURE YOU DON'T WANT TO CONGRAT-ULATE HER IN PERSON?

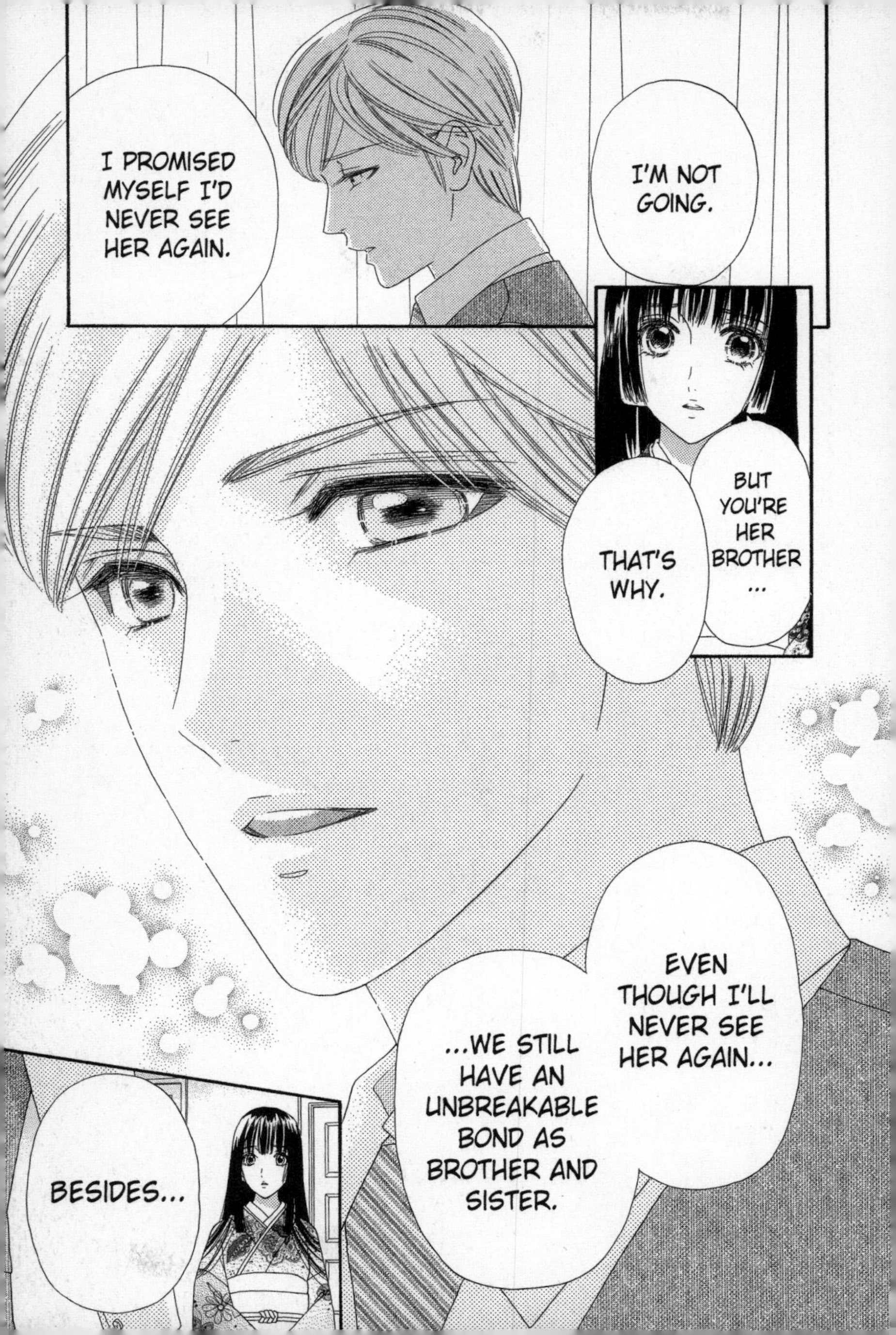
I'M NOT GOING.
I PROMISED MYSELF I'D NEVER SEE HER AGAIN.
BUT YOU'RE HER BROTHER...
THAT'S WHY.
EVEN THOUGH I'LL NEVER SEE HER AGAIN...
...WE STILL HAVE AN UNBREAKABLE BOND AS BROTHER AND SISTER.
BESIDES...

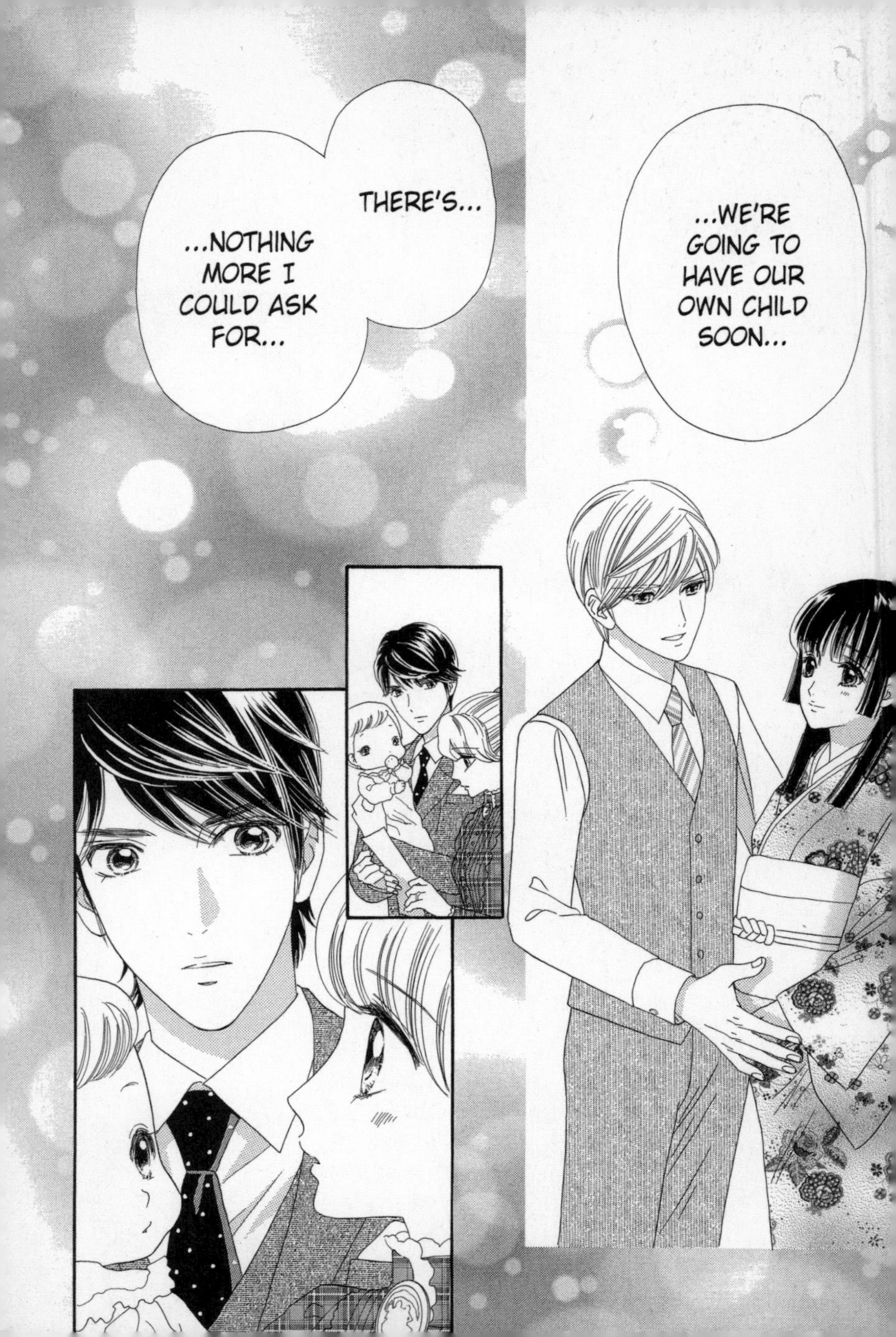
...WE'RE GOING TO HAVE OUR OWN CHILD SOON...
THERE'S...
...NOTHING MORE I COULD ASK FOR...

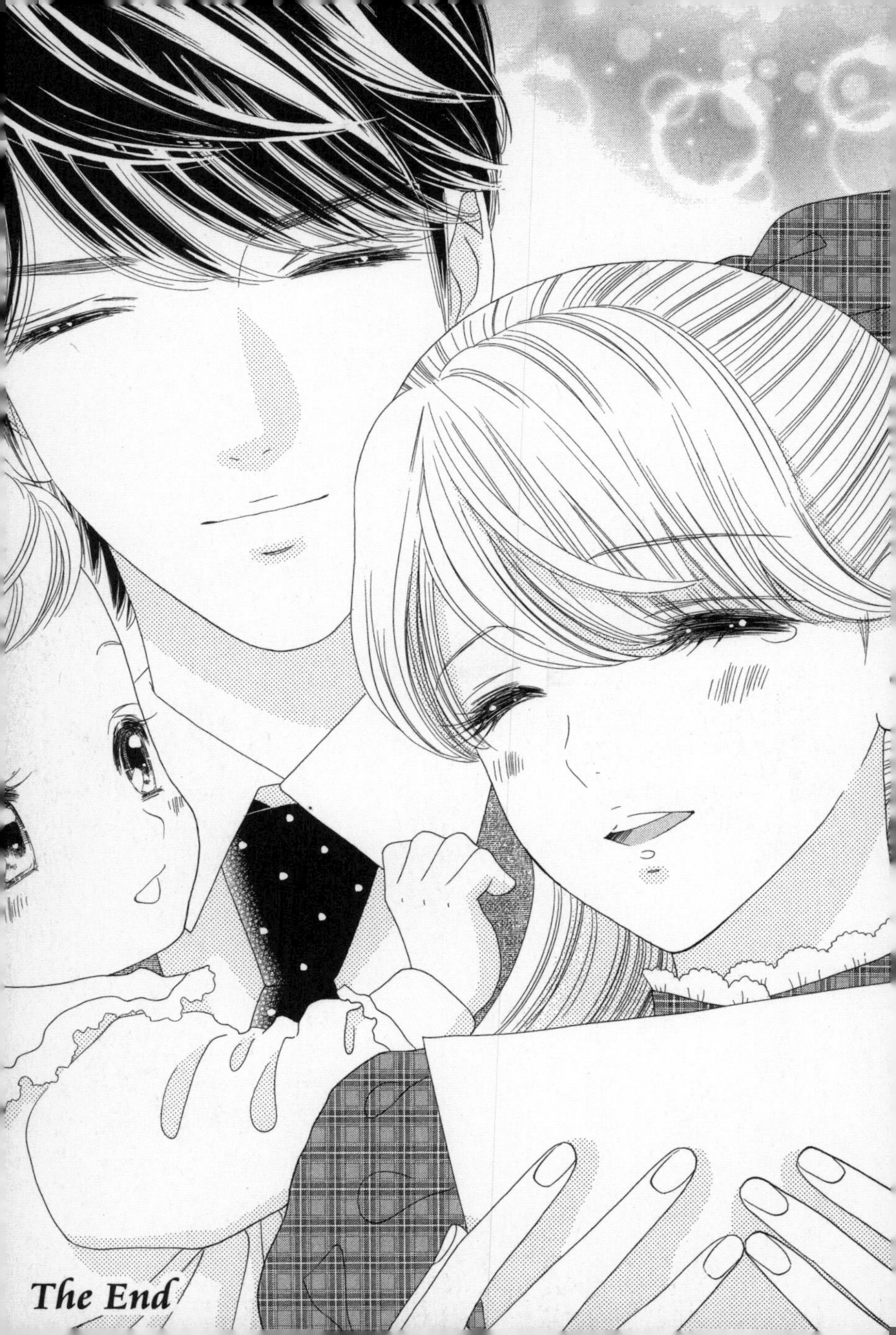
The End

AFTERWORD ～♪

STEPPING ON ROSES HAS FINALLY COME TO AN END. NOW
WHEN I READ THE WHOLE SERIES, I FEEL THAT SUMI, NOZOMU
AND SOICHIRO ALL GREW BECAUSE OF DESIRE AND PAIN.
I THINK IT'S IMPORTANT TO LOOK TOWARD THE FUTURE IN
ORDER TO MAKE THAT EFFORT TO GROW AS A PERSON, DAY BY
DAY. PERSONALLY, I THOUGHT, "THIS MANGA IS GREAT!!" FOR
THE FIRST TIME IN MY LIFE AS A MANGA ARTIST, WHEN I WAS
WORKING ON THE STORYBOARD FOR CHAPTER 52. I WOULD LOVE
TO HEAR WHAT YOUR FAVORITE CHAPTER WAS.

SEND YOUR THOUGHTS TO:

RINKO UEDA
C/O STEPPING ON ROSES EDITOR
VIZ MEDIA
P.O. BOX 77010
SAN FRANCISCO, CA 94107

SEE YOU ALL IN MY NEXT SERIES! ～ ♡

Rinko Ueda

This series turned out to be
a story where two rich young
men named Soichiro and
Nozomu meet a girl called
Sumi and how their lives as
well as their very beings change
dramatically because of it. I
think it's fun and exciting to
think that an encounter with
just one person might change
your life for good.

-Rinko Ueda

Rinko Ueda is from Nara
Prefecture. She enjoys listening
to the radio, drama CDs and
Rakugo comedy performances.
Her works include *Ryo*, a series
based on the legend of Gojo
Bridge; *Home*, a story about love
crossing national boundaries; and
Tail of the Moon (*Tsuki no Shippo*),
a romantic ninja comedy.

STEPPING ON ROSES
Vol. 9
Shojo Beat Edition

STORY AND ART BY
RINKO UEDA

Translation & Adaptation/Tetsuichiro Miyaki
Touch-up Art & Lettering/Mark McMurray
Design/Yukiko Whitley
Editor/Amy Yu

HADASHI DE BARA WO FUME © 2007 by Rinko Ueda
All rights reserved. First published in Japan in 2007 by SHUEISHA Inc., Tokyo.
English translation rights arranged by SHUEISHA Inc.

The rights of the author(s) of the work(s) in this publication to be so identified
have been asserted in accordance with the Copyright, Designs and Patents Act
1988. A CIP catalogue record for this book is available from the British Library.

The stories, characters and incidents mentioned in this publication are
entirely fictional.

No portion of this book may be reproduced or transmitted in any form or
by any means without written permission from the copyright holders.

Printed in the U.S.A.

Published by VIZ Media, LLC
P.O. Box 77010
San Francisco, CA 94107

10 9 8 7 6 5 4 3 2 1
First printing, February 2013

www.viz.com   www.shojobeat.com

PARENTAL ADVISORY
STEPPING ON ROSES is rated T+ for Older Teen
and is recommended for ages 16 and up. This
volume contains brief nudity and sexual themes.
ratings.viz.com

Surprise!

You may be reading the wrong way!

It's true: In keeping with the original Japanese comic format, this book reads from right to left—so action, sound effects, and word balloons are completely reversed. This preserves the orientation of the original artwork—plus, it's fun! Check out the diagram shown here to get the hang of things, and then turn to the other side of the book to get started!